"Hunbatz Men, as a modern Maya *hau-k-in* (teacher), has the courage to remind us about the peace, power, happiness, and harmony found in the life of indigenous cultures of the American continent. His message is of a universal nature, and encompasses art, religion, science, and philosophy that can be used by our contemporary society.

"His contribution fosters the awakening of ancient indigenous ways of life, in which love and respect for Mother Nature is intimately related to the cultivation of the individual as an integral part of the community.

"May the precious seeds that Hunbatz Men is sowing in this book germinate and allow us to create a 'new face' and a 'new heart' full of dignity, love, and respect for the ancient wisdom to be found right here in our American continent: Amerrikua — 'Land of The Wind.' "

—Ana Maria Montero, Aztec dancer

"As far as our Hopi knowledge is concerned, we remember as far back as Palenque—and beyond that. We remember to South America. Hunbatz Men's symbolism in *Secrets of Mayan Science/Religion* is the same as what the Hopi remember. The Hopi still perform ceremonies with these symbols.

"The Maya and the Hopi are connected through their symbols. Those with spiritual understanding will find important information about the nature of the universe through this symbology. This book will open a new channel of the mind."

—White Bear, Hopi artist; illustrator for *The Book of the Hopi* by Frank Waters

"Hunbatz Men unlocks the secret mysteries of Mayan thought in a way never attempted before. As in a safe in which jewels are kept, the hermeticism of Mayan teachings is revealed to the believer in this powerful book. The fact that Mayan philosophy could have influenced Greek thought processes and language is a daring suggestion, the uniqueness of which puts *Secrets of Mayan Science/Religion* in a category all of its own. This book contains revelations that are most needed in today's anxious world. *Secrets of Mayan Science/Religion* is a great contribution to the quest for the ultimate truth."

—Robert Boissiere, author of *Meditations with the Hopi*

"Now is the time during which the knowledge and wisdom of Native American culture is newly emerging in its true value, revealing a scientific and spiritual understanding different from occidental European cultures. It is very important that this knowledge be imparted by someone who has this knowledge ingrained in mind and soul, by one whose roots are indigenus by birth.

"Enlightened in the wisdom of indigenous culture, and in many ways a trailblazer, Hunbatz Men can bring this information to us from his own experience. This Mayan sage from the Mexican Yucatan brings the teachings of his Mayan people to us for our benefit.

"Frequently, we find that aspects of our indigenous culture have been lost, especially in the areas of religion and social structure. This is because they were written by someone who did not understand our languages and customs. In addition, some of the concepts in our indigenous body of knowledge have no equivalents in other cultures. Hunbatz Men, however, has enabled the reader to understand indigenous science through the traditions of the archaic Mayan language.

"*Secrets of Mayan Science/Religion*, inspired by observation, was based on the science of understanding the laws of the cosmos. You, the reader, will gain such profound knowledge through this "new" science. Know that Hunbatz Men, a Mayan teacher, has been entrusted with indigenous traditions, and that in a new cycle we are being given the opportunity to enter step by step into the work of the Great Mayan Spirit!"

—Stephanie L. Betancourt, Seneca

"In the unfolding and fascinating saga of the Mayan Indian civilization, it is refreshing to finally see a deep dissertation through the eyes of a Mayan himself. Hunbatz Men, in the course of many meetings, has never failed to impress me with his profound insight. From the holistic integrity of the ancient Vedic sciences, to the paradigms of modern scientific investigation, *Secrets of Mayan Science/Religion* portrays a point of view which links all of humanity in a continuum of knowledge. To the thoughtful, creative eye, this text will open a whole new vista of understanding about a civilization, past and present, which deserves much greater recognition for advancing the realm of human enlightenment."

—William C. Newell, inventor; Vedic scholar; board member of American Affairs Education Foundation

"Through his explanation of Mayan culture and symbols, Hunbatz Men stimulates an ancient memory circuit to our deep interconnectedness with all life on earth and the whole of the cosmos.

"His book shifts us from the myth of Armageddon and separation to the new myth—one of reverence and sacredness for all 'kin-doms.'

"Hunbatz Men's deep insights transcend cultural and historical boundaries, enabling us to use this material as a road map for our personal and collective awakening."

—**Howard Roske, co-founder of International Sacred Sites Festival and Circle of the Sun Trust**

"Hunbatz Men presents convincing evidence for a profound sacred science underlying Mayan art and architecture. A valuable contribution to the ongoing study of ancient wisdom."

—**John Anthony West, independent Egyptologist; author of *Serpent and the Sky: The High Wisdom of Ancient Egypt, The Travelers Key to Ancient Egypt,* and *The Case for Astrology***

"Hunbatz Men's book takes one on an exploratory journey through the mind of the ancient Mayan. The book is an insightful overview into a shaman's reality."

—**Cynthia MacAdams, author and photographer**

"An impressive, inspiring synthesis of ideas. Shifts the quest for truth from the Old to the 'New' World; to the universal, eternal wisdom of the Maya."

—**Don Papson, editor of *AMERRIKUA!***

SECRETS OF
MAYAN SCIENCE/RELIGION

Secrets of

MAYAN

Science/Religion

HUNBATZ MEN

*Translated by Diana Gubiseh Ayala
& James Jennings Dunlap II*

Bear & Company
Rochester, Vermont

Bear & Company
One Park Street
Rochester, Vermont 05767
www.InnerTraditions.com

Bear & Company is a division of Inner Traditions International

Library of Congress Cataloging-in-Publication Data

Hunbatz Men, 1941-
    Secrets of Mayan science/religion / by Hunbatz Men : translated by Diana
Gubiseh Ayala and James Jennings Dunlap II.
        p.   cm.
    Bibliography: p.
    Includes index.
    ISBN 978-0-939680-63-4
    1. Mayas—Religion and mythology. 2. Indians of Mexico—Mexico—
Religion and mythology. 3. Indians of Central America—Guatemala—Religion
and mythology. 4. Occultism. I. Title.
F1435.3.R3H78   1989
299'.792—dc20   89-6637
                                                                          CIP

Printed and bound in the United States

15 14 13 12

Translation: Diana Gubiseh Ayala & James Jennings Dunlap II
Text review: Darlene Bruns
Cover & interior design: Angela C. Werneke
Typography: Casa Sin Nombre, Ltd.

This book has been selected as material for consultation by the following institutions:

United States of America

NAEP—Native American Education Program

NIYC—National Indian Youth Council

ICIS—International Center for Integrative Studies

Mexico

AGEAC—Gnostic Association for Anthropological and Cultural Studies

ANPIBAC—National Alliance of Indigenous Bilingual Professionals

EAAA—Open School of Applied Anthropology, "Calmecac El Aquila y El Cóndor"

MAIS—Movement for the American Indian Solar Cultures

TENA—Julian Carrillo Center for New Arts, Centro Histórico de México

CONTENTS

We are living in an epoch characterized by fragmentation, specialization, partiality, and consequently by the estrangement of the individual and the fragmentation of the life of society. Religion, science, art, philosophy, and other areas of human activity have separated into small isolated parcels with little effective communication.

There are also signs of a movement which has surfaced, characterized by the search for integration, unification, globalization, and recognition of the interdependency of society, nations, and other large human groupings. In the midst of this search appears the work of Hunbatz Men, revealing to us the work of indigenous Mayan culture whose basic characteristic was, and continues to be, life as an integral, holistic, and complete dynamic. Science and religion for the Maya are not separate disciplines; both constitute a unity, and these principles serve as the fundamental task of the Mayan culture. This task is to practice the culture of the spirit and its transcendence within the cosmic continuum which includes all nature, human beings, and the cosmos.

The author, an authentic Mayan, is an extraordinary interpreter of this great Mesoamerican area; but there is more. He uncovers for us what has been misinterpreted and, up to now, only partially known to contemporary cultures. Hunbatz Men demonstrates how the integral thought and mode of Mayan life was much more universal/spiritual than our culture today. Subsequently, the ancient Maya had a culture equal to other great cultures of the past such as those of the Egyptians, Incas, and Chinese. From this we derive the importance of the Mayan culture as a fundamental human civilization.

Hunbatz Men is an erudite Mayan who not only has penetrated the Mayan world of the past, but who also recognizes in his personal life the great universal task of humans today. In his book, *Secrets of Mayan Science/Religion*, Hunbatz states that all mankind can become Quetzalcoatl or Kukulcan. He also enables us to see that Mayan science/religion offers

13

extraordinary teachings leading to the next step toward a humanity that is more mature, more spiritual, and truly more unified to its cosmic source.

Janis A. Roze, associate professor of biology, City College of the City University of New York

Hunbatz Men was born, raised, and educated in a small Mayan village in the Yucatan. His native tongue is Peninsular Mayan, therefore Spanish, the language in which he wrote the original version of this book, *Religión Ciencia Maya*, is his second language. Hunbatz Men wrote in Spanish in order to offer the Mayan teachings to the indigenous people of Mesoamerica.

The process of translating the Spanish text into English and then editing the translated version was a collaboration of Diana Ayala, James Dunlap, Darlene Bruns, Donald Papson, Barbara Clow, and Gail Vivino. During this process, difficulties were encountered with the language which were a natural result of working with a text written by an author in his second language. Hunbatz Men is a holy man, a spiritual teacher, whose thoughts and understandings are primal and simple. His first priority in writing this book was to teach the indigenous people of the world, who may never have been to school or may never have left their native villages, but who have an understanding of the esoteric secrets of Earth's religion and science. His use of language reflects this priority.

The English-language version of this simple but profound book will also be of immense value to anthropologists, archeologists, linguists, and Mayanists, as well as to spiritual seekers. These are an audience that the book was not originally written for. All efforts by the translators and editors have focused on maintaining the simplicity and clarity of Hunbatz Men's thoughts, without placing a heavy revisionary emphasis on traditional analytic Western literary style.

LIST OF ILLUSTRATIONS

1. All of these drawings are from the Mayan codices: Dresden, Tro-Cortesian, and Madrid.

2. At the end of the seventeenth century, the scientist Herschel defined the form of our Milky Way.

3. Page 71 of the Dresden Codex shows various zeros and several glyphs.

4. Here we can appreciate a mask from Teotihuacan, Mexico State, and other pieces.

5. Detail of the "Temple of the Columns" in Mitla, Oaxaca, Mexico.

6. The Aztec deity Xochipilli; stone sculpture found in the National Museum of Anthropology.

7. Temple of the Sun at Palenque, Chiapas, Mexico. Here we see how the Maya venerated universal values.

8. A classic "smiling face" from the Totonac culture featuring a sacred "G."

9. A terra cotta figure from Zapotal, Veracruz, Mexico, where the ancient inhabitants worshipped the "G."

10. These drawings were copied from the book, *American Indian Design and Decoration*. Mixtecs as well as the natives of Chile and Panama venerated the "G."

11. Page 2 of the Selden Codex shows the mythological birth of a man as he emerges from a sacred tree.

12. Fejérváry-Mayer Codex: In this manuscript we see trees, each of which is oriented toward one of the cardinal points.

13. The Maya of Palenque, Chiapas, Mexico held rituals in honor of the sacred "T" as a symbol of the tree in the temple known as The Palace.

14. (A) denotes Xochipilli, the goddess of flowers, from a fresco. The goddess is shown with a "T" adorning her nose.

15. A Zapotec funerary urn found in Monte Alban, Oaxaca, Mexico. The arrow indicates various "T" forms.

16. An Aztec seal (A) in the form of the sacred "T" depicts a number of birds.

17. This photo of a mask shows the sacred "T" around the nose, a symbol of the divine breath.

18. The so-called sepulchral stone, beautifully inscribed with many Mayan symbols.

19. A detail of Stela 26 from Yaxchilan, Chiapas, Mexico. In the upper part, indicated by an arrow, we see the sacred "T."

20. The ancient people of the great Tenochtitlan venerated the "T" long before the arrival of the Mexicas.

21. A clay statuette found on the island of Jaina, Campeche, Mexico. In Mayan, this personage is called Halach Ol.

22. A clay figure from the Mixtec culture which displays the symbol of *ol* consciousness.

23. A Mayan priest whose knowledge of consciousness is manifested by the mask on his head and by the symbol of the planet Venus.

24. 24-1 shows a seal of the Nahuatlacos. They knew how to use the "O" of consciousness.

25. In this drawing, we see the so-called "Hand of God," as interpreted in Teotihuacan, Mexico State.

26. These illustrate the three sacred symbols as follows: Figure 26-1: "O"; Figure 26-2: "T"; and Figure 26-3: "G."

27. A clay sculpture from the culture of western Guerrero state.

28. A stone slab that adorned the stairway of Temple XXI, Palenque, and an idol from Tiwanaku, Bolivia.

29. Temple of the Sanctuary of Chichen Itza. A priest in the lotus position and other forms of meditation practiced by the Didiques of Costa Rica.

30. The Old One symbolizing fire (1). All of these figures are from the Mexica culture.

31. Seated female figure of bichrome ceramic from Nicoya, Guanacaste, Costa Rica.

32. Stone slab of Aparicio, Veracruz, Mexico shows a personage with seven serpent heads.

33. The descent of Kukulcan in Chichen Itza, Mexico, seen on March 22 and September 23.

34. From the book *The Chakras*, a monograph by C.W. Leadbeater. This diagram shows the seven energy centers of the human body.

35. Clay figure from Etznah, Campeche, Mexico. This piece shows how the Maya used the *chacla*.

36. The Unknown Porrúa Codex. Here we see a Mayan priest officiating.

37. Clay figure from the Chimu culture of Peru. Here we see an individual working in a sexual context.

38. Pictorial Manuscript of the Mayan Culture—Porrúa Codex. The "Cosmic Man" employs sexual energy.

Secrets of
MAYAN
Science/Religion

INTRODUCTION

The Cosmos perturbs us. It inspires fear and causes physical and spiritual distress. Thus we seek help, elements of hope and consolation in this world and beyond. Our imagination has invented heavens and hells, rewards and punishments according to our earthly conduct. Yet reason, determination, free will, and even logic have failed to provide positive proof of the existence of paradise or hell—at least not as depicted by old, nominal religions created to subjugate and to dictate human conduct.

We must judge the validity of human concepts of personalized deities, which may be good or evil according to the criteria of the conceptualizer. Imagination and cultural context are some of the criteria on which the religious promoter bases a doctrine or school. But above all, the promoter draws on the good faith of followers, whose hope for spiritual salvation is constantly nurtured, for better or for worse, in a context of rigorous discipline. Such followers exist because not all humans are inclined to investigation and the pursuit of knowledge. Many prefer the comfort of belief.

History is full of the phenomena of "enlightened" or "illuminated" individuals who declare themselves recipients of God's word in attempts to convince followers that they will be shown the true path—the way to supreme joy and happiness in the hereafter—especially if death is caused by divine order.

History also describes numerous religious wars waged under the auspices of protective gods—gods whose battlefield interventions, at times, led victorious armies in the imposition of one person's faith over

21

another's. Vanquished gods were sometimes assimilated by the victors, but more often they disappeared, to be replaced by the conquering deities. In either case the gods prevailed in one form or another. The loser had no recourse but to recognize the gods of the victors. With the conquest of Mexico, the Catholic saints took on the roles of the lords of air, fire, rain, etc. A metamorphosis of values followed, a syncretism, as it were, that persists to this day.

Human history has also been plagued with religious struggles and warfare motivated by a passion to impose guidelines for salvation on those whose rites and ceremonies were deemed false. Such conflicts confirm disparate interpretations of religious sentiment. Yet, despite this diversity of sentiment, we actually all take the same path, sharing certain ideals. Which path? That which seeks God. However, we each travel our own way, according to our personal theological interpretations.

There are many religions, and each seeks a better interpretation of God or the devil according to human determination and free will. A review of the history of religions confirms this. In every region, territory, and country, religious groups exist—followers of God or the devil. Even within a single religion, as in the case of the Judeo-Christian Roman religion, we find a proliferation of sects with different interpretations of the Bible itself, which is the foundation of Christianity. Yet they all claim to pursue the norms established by Jesus. We reiterate, however, that each nucleus has its own faithful interpretation of the scriptures. In general terms, it is evident that Jews and Christians, as well as Muhammadans, have different ways of translating and explaining the Old and New Testament.

If we review Hinduism, Buddhism and Shintoism, those great theological trees which gave birth and development to numerous branches of the same trunk, we can see how these religions have divided and subdivided. Division comes from a lack of agreement on orthodox principles, for whatever reasons. The result is conversion to heterodoxy and the imposition of new opinions and viewpoints on traditional ideas whose value and veracity once commanded respect.

Rebellion of humankind against religions has been one of the reasons that churches and sects have proliferated, provoking separations and repudiation of developed methods and systems that seek God. Everyone maintains personal opinions with respect to religious feelings. This entire dilemma, in the final analysis, has brought philosophy and science into conflict with religion because no one is in agreement with anyone else. Everyone attempts to impose their personal criteria on others—criteria usually based on belief, and not on awareness and understanding.

Humanity's blindness has created situations in which people of both good and bad faith develop concepts which they then try to impose on the rest of the population by brute force rather than by rational persuasion. The absurd result is the emergence of groups or factions within the same religion which can agree on nothing. The very human tendency of each faction is to believe that it is the possessor of the *truth*. This creates disharmony, and worse—doubt and perplexity about who is right.

We arrive at the point of asking ourselves, dear reader: Do religious feelings have intellectual significance, or are they mere whims?

If we want to define what religion itself is, we must meditate at great length in order to arrive at conclusions that are essentially ethical in nature. It is also necessary to recognize that humans alone have the capability of formulating ideas and concepts regarding religion that correspond to feelings and sensibilities. The word itself—religion—is derived from the Latin expression *religare*, meaning "to reunite."

Restlessness, doubt, and perplexity have surged in the human mind from the moment it was able to reason. Since that moment, people have been preoccupied with the reasons for their existence on this planet, asking questions such as, "Where do I come from?" "What am I doing here?" "Where am I going?" "What am I?" and "Who am I?" From such doubts came the quest for truth, but without the aid of science. It was the incessant search for the truth about cause and effect that led to philosophy and evolved into what has come to be known as science. From this, there also ensued the struggles between religious thinkers, philosophers, and scientists.

Now we shall depart from the Western or European mode of thought. The solutions that we indigenous people seek for the future do not lie in such an individualistic form of thinking. It is, however, important that Western European people attempt to understand Maya/Nahua thought because we are an ancient people who established a great culture. In this book, we will enter into the profound thought of the Maya who created that culture. Unfortunately, some authoritarian eyes may view these investigations with suspicion. This, however, is of no consequence because the destiny of indigenous America is determined by the Great Grandparent Spirits of the Maya, Nahua, Quechua, Inca, etc.

The indigenous American possesses the virtues or faculties of intuitive reason, free will, and determination which result in a sense of logic. These faculties were used in the observation of nature, which became their guide and master. As the Maya acquired further experience of their environment, they came to recognize that they, too, were part of nature and that everything has a soul. The soul, as defined by our Mayan ancestors, has material form due to the fact that everything has form. Soul was not confused with spirit, which was perceived as energy—solar energy. Spirit was named *k'inan*, derived from the word for the Sun—*k'in*— and the suffix *an*, which is a conditional form of the verb "to be." Thus, *k'inan* is spirit or solar energy, and by inductive reasoning, soul is a manifested form of spirit.

Surprisingly, some Greek philosophers intuited that which was a solemn truth for indigenous Americans. For example, Democritus proposed that the intimate relation between soul and organic life reveals that souls are atoms of fire, composed of the most subtle and flighty material, the grandest energy and movement. It is notable that, despite Democritus' ideas, the notion persisted that the soul could be both corporeal and incorporeal. In contrast, the Maya understanding of the concept of the soul is as a manifestation of spirit, that is, of intelligent energy sublimated in body, form and figure. So the soul was perceived by our Mayan ancestors as the object which is a conduit for spirit, the energy which permits human intellectual manifestations.

These aspects of spirit and soul, discussed and lamentably confused by the Greeks and Latins, are the same ideas that are still heatedly discussed today. Our pre-conquest Mayan ancestors, through deduction and synthesis, came to a monotheistic conclusion, with a mathematical sense. Their concept of Absolute Being was defined as *measure and movement*—measure of the soul and movement of the energy which is spirit. We note with a certain pride that modern research has demonstrated that cells and molecules conform to geometric patterns whose dimensions are maintained by molds of vibrational energy. Atomic research has confirmed that material is essentially energy.

The Maya did not formulate a God with a determined and determining personality, as in other mythologies. Hunab K'u symbolizes form and energy, that is, the soul and the spirit. This unique Giver of Movement and Measure represents the Absolute Being, the architect of the universe. The Sun is one of Hunab K'u's most powerful sources of information. It is for this reason that the spirit-energy was called *k'inan*, the solar factor. The Maya knew that, within the scientific realm, the Sun, the astral king, was the governor of all forms of life, without whom nothing was possible.

Despite their marvelous knowledge, the Maya did not repudiate their sense of spirituality and fall into materialism. On the contrary, their ethics and aesthetics were highly spiritual, establishing a binding truth based on the conviction that each individual was one with every other being—the very same entity. Hence, "you" was declared nonexistent, leaving the notion that "you are me" and "I am you." This conjugation of human with human is the *human being*. Thus, ethics were based on the law of mutual respect elevated to the category of religion, but religion in the highest scientific sense—mathematical, rather than merely metaphysical.

The Maya did not have a mythical concept of deities, but instead maintained that lords represented the forces of nature, with a sense of symmetry, a redundancy of plurality in unity and unity in plurality. Thus, the Mayan thinker maintained that lords, humans, and numbers were one and the same. And all, without exception, were dependent on the Absolute Being, Hunab K'u, whose symbolic representation is found on the pyramids as the Giver of Movement and Measure, in the geometric form of a square within a circle.

While people of other lands were locked in philosophical discussion, on this continent, conclusions were made with certainty about what it is to be human, what nature is, and what the cyclical laws are that unite them in the eternal movement with its measure.

The answers to those questions were found in the understanding of the intimate bond among God, humans, and numbers. For indigenous Americans, religion is more than a simple belief to be fanatically adhered to. Their religious understanding explains clearly and simply the truths of human existence as a living reflection of cosmic consciousness, wherein energy—the spirit—conveys to all beings life, material existence. This conviction came from simple observation of our surroundings, the great environment wherein vibrates the essence of the Absolute

Being, Hunab K'u, the One Giver of Movement and Measure that has empowered the human being. Such perception was based on a sense of reason, free will, and volition.

The thinker knew the natural consequences of actions, good or bad, but education provided a sense of responsibility and freedom. All debts—whether large or small—would necessarily be repaid sooner or later. These circumstances permitted, in turn, the maintenance of ethical standards based on mutual respect. The Maya seeks not the destruction of humankind, but instead its exaltation, since love for one's own kind is love for one's self and, by extension, love for the Absolute Being— Hunab K'u.

Thus, the lives of the lords and human beings were intimately linked by the cosmic fraternity represented by the Law of Compensation. This law was based on human values in firm connection with the rest of creation, although not in the sense of a coordinating element emanating from synergism, since, as we stated earlier, for the Maya, humans are an integral part of nature, and hence, part of God. Their conception of the world, based on education, is neither abstract, unknowable, mysterious, nor enigmatic. They attained a perfect understanding of life and their oneness with the Earth. The Maya developed human values but knew that they remained to be perfected, just as a precious stone requires polishing and refinement to enhance its value. So it is with human beings: their innate qualities and virtues need the teacher's guidance to reach perfection. It can be said that the Maya were not ones to ignore their value and worth as human beings.

We initiate this work, *Secrets of Mayan Science/Religion*, with a declaration which, in all its Mayan simplicity, has made a great impression from the perspective of philosophy and science: "The gods need human beings and human beings need the gods." This statement, a fundamental precept of Mayan theology, refers to gods, humans, and numbers as a single entity. The human being is simultaneously an addition, a subtraction, a multiplication, a division, and a common denominator. We are the total result of the Law of Compensation based on these mathematical values, results obtained in accordance with our conduct. Reciprocity with God and the lords basically explains our presence on this planet. We are a projection and a reflection of that cosmic consciousness which is Hunab K'u, the Absolute Being upon which all of life depends. Here we have an acceptable resolution of the disturbing mystery of the hereafter, of destiny beyond death.

Our indigenous American ancestors arrived at the conclusion that, upon death, our soul or physical form remains on Earth, tenuous material that it is; our spirit, however, as igneous energy, reintegrates with the great cosmic focus which is the Sun. Thus, if the departed has earned a reward, it is here on Earth that it will be enjoyed. Likewise, if punishment is merited, Earth will be the scene of the suffering. While this may seem a simple solution to the question of eternal reincarnation, the thought warrants profound meditation. Our Mayan ancestors achieved a scientific definition of the formidable fact that only here on Earth, and in no other place, can the human being be what it is, and as it is, possessing the qualities and value of being human.

We note that, at this very moment, exploration of celestial bodies in our solar system is providing scientific evidence that life as we here enjoy it is not possible anywhere else. The combination of elements on other planets precludes the development of life-forms such as ours. We evolved in a unique environment of materials and gases, combined with solar energy. Thus it is on Earth that we reap our fortunes or suffer our consequences, and nowhere else.

Consider the gallows pronouncement of the indigenous American hero, Jacinto Canek, who refused to accept an unknown god imposed by force of arms and the Spanish Inquisition. The defiant Canek declared that with his death, his god would also die. By extension—if humans die, so die their gods.

When we confront the fact that we are nothing more than a product of nature, believers and nonbelievers alike, born of Earth and Sun, we cannot exclude ourselves from reality. As passengers aboard this boat, this plane, this vehicle, we share the fatal consequences of any mishap. We are all sidereal travelers on this ship of Earth.

Some of us may be Christians or Taoists, or even atheists, but the undeniable, transcendental act is that we all enjoy the fruits of nature, wild or cultivated. In this natural bounty we have made marvelous advances such as the discovery and the awesome exploitation of the atom, its energy and nuclear radiation. How was it done? Through the investigation by scientists who have researched materials extracted from cosmic nature (such as uranium, hydrogen, etc.).

We must bear in mind that the brains of these very scientists are nourished by the produce of Mother Earth. Nature, as we know, provides us with cereals, fruits, meats, as well as the combinations of elements which produce stimulants chemically synthesized in laboratories by scientific brains. Finally, it is inconceivable that humans under any known circumstances can isolate themselves from the vital laws of the elements (oxygen, hydrogen, nitrogen, calcium, and carbon, to name a few). These components, under the rule of natural law, and without the need of special laboratories, are combined by their own miraculous formulas in the human organism. They form a long series of products such as sugars, fat, proteins, etc., which constitute everything: skin, bones, marrow, blood, the nervous system, the brain—in short, the entire human being.

What we are as humans, with all our capacity for intelligence, reason, logic, imagination, and creativity, we owe to the air we breathe, the oxygen and hydrogen we consume as water, the foods we ingest as nourishment, and even the medicines derived from minerals and organic matter. Is it not now evident that the Maya have made a series of discoveries that help substantiate how cosmic energy miraculously combines natural elements to create human life?

This introduction was intended to outline how the Maya created a religion based on secrets gleaned over many centuries from nature— from our earthly planet in union with cosmic laws. With this knowledge, these ancestral savants formulated Mayan science/religion.

CHAPTER ONE

The Form, Sound & Use of the Letter "G" is of Mayan Origin

 A meticulous investigation of the letter "G," its pronunciation and configuration, has led us to convincing linguistic and philological evidence that demonstrates close relationships among many nations. Such proof is found in the occurrence of many Mayan words in the languages of Europe, as well as those of Asia. As in the case of the use of the letter "G," it is interesting to note that several aspects of Mayan syntax are evidenced even in Spanish. We will demonstrate in axiomatic form, through the Mayan language, the early existence of these relationships in all parts of the world—relationships which continue to this day.

The explanations derived from language are not a product of simple hypothesis, nor are they based on whim. They are based on linguistic studies and research which palpably demonstrate the motivations and the sources from which this admirable and virtuous language emerged. Early Mayan sages defined language as *yak*, which when inverted (as is a characteristic dynamic of the Zuyua Mayan language) reads *k'ay*, meaning "song." Linguists have concluded that the human being learns to speak by singing. Therefore, the Mayan philosopher was absolutely correct in equating language and song. This was plainly proven by investigations into the development of speech, which reveal, in effect, that an infant learns to speak by singing, a splendid confirmation of the value of the Mayan intellect, which long ago revealed that speech can be learned through song.

This synopsis reveals that the Mayan sage was in reality practicing *panche be*, "seeking the root of truth" in order to know and understand; that is, knowing in order to understand. Investigation and study are based on induction and deduction and comparisons leading to precise conclusions based on discernible truth, rather than on simple theories — products of the imagination — or hypotheses based on debatable suppositions. With the latter process, today's truths become tomorrow's lies. Promoting a theory is easy; proving it is the difficult part. The Mayan sage uses great discipline in seeking the root of truth. What is most extraordinary is that, after diligent analysis, Mayan culture becomes nothing less than pure science.

Our linguistic investigation has led to surprising revelations and conclusions. The Tower of Babel mentioned in the Bible was at a center where there existed a confusion of languages which preceded the dispersion of humanity. The Mayan word *babal* or *babel* means "confusion," and moreover, the Mayan expression meaning "to speak in confusion" is *babel than*. What would the apparent inclusion of Mayan words in the languages of Asia and Europe (as previously stated) indicate? Is it possible to conclude that within the Mayan context there existed, in effect, a primitive language from which other world languages are derived?

Meticulous, step by step, linguistic and philological analysis uncovered other surprising "coincidences." Especially notable are certain similarities in Saxon and Mayan syntax. An example of this is the English or French phonetic value of *sh*, which is best written *ch* for Mayan, though the sound is the same. Examples in Mayan are *ooch* or *oosh*, which mean "nourishment," or *nooch* and *noosh* — "chin."

With an understanding of authentic Mayan cultural values, one can discuss religion, science, or philosophy, all within the context of things Mayan. Where most modern philosophy, religion, and science have deviated from the original perceptions of truth, the Maya have remained consistent with the original findings of their philosophy, religion, and science. However, we do not base our deductions on the Mayan context exclusively, but also in what modern science is corroborating, as with the phenomena of wave energy. The use of mathematics is essential, and quintessential is the value of the zero (0), in Mayan named *ge*, and symbolized by the egg, creator of the universe. Is it not fascinating, dear reader, that among peoples of other continents, this *ge* or "G" is also a symbolic root of sacredness?

Well then, let us proceed with the study of the letter "G" in drawings taken from Mayan codices. In Figure 1, we observe how the Maya used the "G" in different aspects of their daily lives. Drawings numbered 3, 7, 8, 9, and 10 illustrate how they worked with energy. The presence of dots around a hieroglyph indicates activity. In this case the active energy is that symbolized by the glyph "G."

One will ask then, "What does this symbol represent in Mayan?" "What is it used for?" The "G" is symbolic of the beginning, the germination, the Egg-Creator, the essence, the seed from which all life—human or otherwise—springs. It is the word used when Moses was asked who Jehovah (Geoba) was, to which he responded by saying it was the name of the molder of the most primitive things; God; that which is sacred. For the Maya, the "G" symbolically represents The Beginning.

A deeper reflection will take us to levels of investigation and analysis of every aspect of the much discussed Mayan culture. Because of its scientific achievements and admirable art, modern technicians and scientists seek its roots and its fruits. Mayan writings are among the most researched; but, lamentably the road taken by supposedly authoritative investigators is the wrong one. Despite all their efforts, the hieroglyphs have not revealed their great knowledge. Moreover, we have noted a lot of false information in philological and linguist works. None of this eases the task of elucidating the secrets and enigmas of Mayan culture. For this reason, we were compelled to discard 99 percent of the material produced and used by official researchers, and resort to sources closer to our indigenous American culture. We have employed linguistics in a careful analysis based on phonetics and pronunciation. And, we have conducted field research throughout the continent, visiting pyramids and participating in indigenous rituals in areas where people live the culture of their ancestors. The deductions we will put forth here are largely based on these direct experiences.

The Honduran researcher, Medardo Mejia, has stated that in order to understand Mayan culture, it is necessary to begin with the religion that generates the rituals. Using this concept and the example of other great teachers, I reached the conclusion that the Mayan "G" is the omnipresent germ, the essence, the seed. Observing the form in codices and on pyramids, I eventually concluded that the symbolic form of "G" also exists in you, dear reader, in the form of the cosmic essence which you are.

The Maya took the symbolic "G" from our universal memory, from

FIGURE 1

All these drawings are from the Mayan Codices: Dresden, Tro-Cortesiano, and Madrid.

Drawing 1: Page 36, Dresden Codex
We see a lord standing in water looking upward and receiving the falling water. This all happens in relation to the sacred "G" of the Milky Way.

Drawing 2: Page 41, Dresden Codex
We see a lord sitting upon a T-shaped structure. In the middle is a spiral symbol of time; in his hand we see the "O" of consciousness in dynamic action.

Drawing 3: Page 24, Tro-Cortésiano Codex
A dog carries two flaming torches, and to the right is a man with closed eyes. Here we see the "G" in full function.

Drawing 4: Page 26, Madrid Codex
Man seated in front of an altar in which we see the sign of the sacred "G" or Milky Way in front of him.

Drawing 5: Page 82, Tro-Cortesiano Codex
Lord carrying the symbol "G" or Milky Way; here we see the energy moving upwards.

Drawing 6: Page 30, Madrid Codex
Man carrying a functional spiral in his hands; activated energy spirals up and down.

Drawing 7: Page 25, Madrid Codex
A divinity moving his hand to accelerate the process of energy symbolized in the altar. The energy is depicted in full movement.

Drawing 8: Page 8, Madrid Codex
A bee flies over an altar where the "G" is fully active—moving the energy of the Milky Way.

Drawing 9: Page 7, Madrid Codex
A lord sitting before an altar containing what is apparently a flaming spiral. The lord attempts to touch the energy in motion.

Drawing 10: Page 5, Madrid Codex
The bee lord suctions what it holds in its hand. In Mayan culture, this personage is known as Lord of the World. Here he is making contact with the energy of the Milky Way.

FIGURE 1.

the place where we came as seeds, which Moses called the mold of most ancient things. But Mayan sages made this symbol, as religion and science, part of their consciousness. Their people still live this consciousness. The ancient grandparents knew the Logos was there, and as such, the Maya observed its form as they saw it. It is this form which is imprinted in the codices and sculpted on the pyramids. The Maya lived integrally worshipping that which is *represented* by the "G." I will reveal to you, dear reader, with all due respect for the sacred Hunab K'u, from whom came my illumination and who enabled me to see it, the place of origin of this form. It is nothing less than our galaxy. Yes, the Milky Way! (See Figure 2.) So, dear reader, when you see this symbol in the codices or on pyramids, remember that you are looking at the beginning—the symbol of your essence!

The ancient Maya were always searching for a more accurate description of observed reality. The symbology of the Milky Way included another graphic form besides the spiral representation.

From persistent observation of the cosmos, the Maya knew precisely and scientifically the positions and movements of the planets and other astral bodies. Astronomy and astrology were the foundations of their philosophy. For this reason, they also understood that our galaxy had another graphic configuration, which they adopted and began to use as the mathematical symbol for the Milky Way. This new symbol was that of the egg, visible in the Mayan hieroglyphs. They called it "G." In Figure 3, you can see the juxtaposing of zeros with the figure representing the Milky Way as used by our Mayan forefathers. This demonstrates how similar they are in form. These ancestors were the first people on Earth whose reasoning assigned to the zero a real value in mathematics. It has been said that a "zero on the left has no value." Could it be that the culture which teaches this way of reasoning has no value?

For the Maya, wherever the symbol of zero is marked, its value is known, for it represents the essence of the beginning, the Logos. It is the form of the seed. Thus it is said that in order to understand the sacred Hunab K'u, the Only Giver of Movement and Measure, one must venerate the origin of the zero, the Milky Way, because it is there that the mold for the most ancient things was located. As mathematics helped define their religion and philosophy, the zero assumed value. It was represented, as can be seen in Figure 2, in different forms. As at the bottom

FIGURE 2.

FIGURE 2.

At the end of the eighteenth century, the scientist Herschel attributed a definite form to the Milky Way. Years later, other scientists calculated that the Milky Way is composed of approximately 100 million stars, and that the obscure part of the galaxy might possibly contain hundreds or thousands of solar systems. They tell us that to cross the Milky Way one must travel 100,000 light years. There is no doubt that the Maya knew this information. Their recognition of this source as the generator of life led them to call it *ge* in the Mayan language. They related it to the beginning of all existence. Thus it was depicted on their pyramids, sculptures, and codices; and its form was copied and worshipped in sacred rites. In this way, Mayan religion approaches science. Note the photograph of the Milky Way in this figure. Below it are various stepped-fret symbols of the sacred "G."

FIGURE 3.

On page 71 of the Dresden Codex, we see various zeros and some hieroglyphics. Here we observe how the Maya related mathematics to the symbol representative of the beginning. The Maya closely relate the zero and the Milky Way; in Mayan language, the zero is called *ge*. The proof can be seen in this figure, where it is demonstrated how the Mayan teachers copy the graphic form of the Milky Way and use it to represent the zero in their mathematics. For this reason, they were the first people on Earth to give real value to the zero. But their reasoning did not end there. They also related it to the cosmic seed from which springs all human life.

FIGURE 4.

Here we can appreciate a mask from Teotihuacan, in the National Museum of Anthropology, Mexico. Observe that near the nose appear two sacred "G" forms.

FIGURE 4A.

This drawing shows the sacred "G" of the Milky Way stylized in an artistic form. Remember that in Mayan culture, art, religion, and science are as one. This stepped-fret design is from Uxmal, Yucatan, Mexico.

FIGURE 4B.

The Zapotecs, of the same heritage as the Maya, also worshipped the symbol "G" for its high scientific value, and they represented this in artistic forms such as can be seen in Mitla, Oaxaca, Mexico.

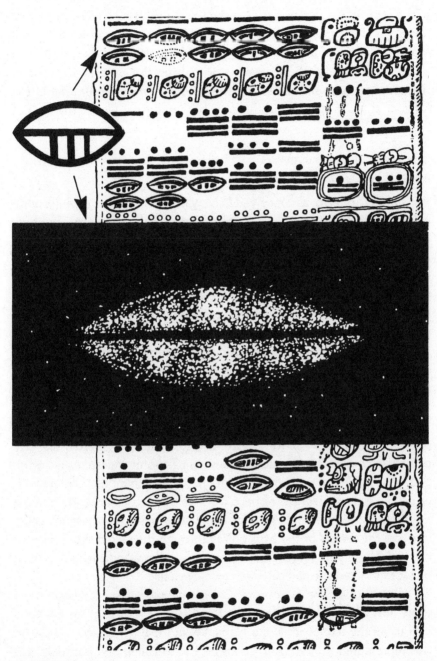

FIGURE 3.

of the page, it was sometimes a sea shell or conch. It is depicted in vegetal forms on the terrestrial plane. In other instances, because of its oval shape, it takes the form of animal eggs, or the male testicles or the female ovaries. Ultimately, those persons who have the capacity to discern human auras have indicated that they see the whole-body aura in the form of an auric egg. Could this possibly imply that we are the aura of the Milky Way?

The Teotihuacans & Zapotecs
Revered the Ge with Great Rituals

The "G," or zero, as conceived in Mayan and Teotihuacan philosophical thought (see Figure 4), was highly revered. This mask from Teotihuacan in the National Museum of Anthropology in Mexico depicts the highly sacred symbol of the "G" on either side of the subject's nose. Unfortunately, it is not properly described to those who come to see it. Guides are apt to tell visitors that the geometric forms are merely decorative. Figures 4A and 4B represent two other stylized versions on the pyramids of Uxmal, Yucatan, Mexico, representing the spiral form of the Milky Way. The second is a stylized spiral adorning Mitla's pyramids in Oaxaca, Mexico. In this majestic representation, the Zapotecs capture the essence of the Milky Way throughout their structure in Mitla (see Figure 5).

As can be seen in the illustration (Figure 5), the sacred "G" appears in different geometric variations. According to researchers, these walls were painted in colors. This is logical because our Zapotec ancestors, like other people of indigenous America, maintained their ceremonial centers with impeccable cleanliness and respect. It was in this particular center that the Zapotecs consecrated their new initiates in the mysteries of science, religion, and the secrets of the Milky Way through the sacred symbolism of the "G." Allow your imagination to expand on the wondrous rites carried out at this sacred site dedicated to cosmic essence.

In my book, *The Astronomical Calendars of the Maya and Hunab K'u,* I show how the Nahua or Mexicas adored Hunab K'u. They worshipped him using the names In Tloke Nahuake and Ipalnemohuani. This god was represented in the Aztec calendar, the so-called Sun Stone. In this present book, I will attempt to demonstrate that the Mexicas, as well

FIGURE 4.

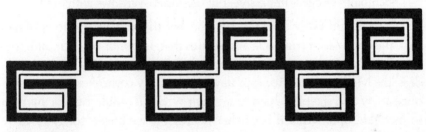

FIGURE 4A.

FIGURE 4B.

as the Maya, worshipped the Milky Way, as represented by the symbolic "G."

In Figure 6, we see a sculpture of Xochipilli. In his book, *Aztec Christic Magic*, the teacher Samael Aun Weor writes of this Mexica deity:

> In the Museum of Anthropology and History of the city of Mexico, D.F., one can find Xochipilli seated upon a beautifully sculpted block of basalt. With raised knees and legs crossed like St. Andrew, thumb and forefinger touching, she gazes at infinity. She wears huge jade earplugs and a large pendant fringed with tiger claws and viper fangs. On her breast, two Suns are emblazoned with two half Moons. Bracelets and knee guards are finished in floral patterns of six petals each. Small rings with talons grasp her ankles and shin coverings display two bell flowers. The hanging corolla of one emits six seeds and the other fire and cacti. The legging straps are graciously knotted over her feet.
>
> Xochipilli: Xochitl—flower; pilli—principal. Goddess of agriculture, the flowers, music, song, poetry and the dance. "Flower and song are the highest things on Earth that can penetrate the confines of truth," taught the Tlamatenene in the Calmecac. Because of this, all of their philosophy is bathed in the purest essence of poetry. Xochipilli's visage is impassive, but her heart overflows with joy.

Samael Aun Weor cites the key concept that flower and song penetrate the confines of truth. He also relates that, in honor of Xochipilli, the people sang, made poetry, and danced. Before these rites for the goddess, the Mexicas fasted for four days, eating only corncakes without salt once a day and sleeping apart from their wives. It would be worthwhile to meditate upon what this teacher relates. As we know, today's Mexicans have lost this traditional discipline. This is one reason we suffer disorientation, particularly in the spiritual sense.

There is little to add to the narrative of Samael Aun Weor. But what is important to point out is that these rituals were performed in honor of the "G." This can be concluded by studying the symbols carved on the pedestal upon which Xochipilli sits. The Mexicas adored Xochipilli, as she represented the Milky Way, where energy is in perpetual movement, giving life and bodily and spiritual energy to all living beings.

FIGURE 5.

UNDERSTANDING MAYAN HIEROGLYPHICS
& SACRED TEACHINGS

"On October 12, 1992, the so-called European world will celebrate the quincentennial of Columbus landing on an island in the Caribbean. Columbus met with the aborigines, and finally proved once and for all that the earth was round, and not flat as thought.

"For thousands of years the Mayan teachings taught of the galaxy and of the earth belonging to the solar system, but these teachings were nearly destroyed and lost by the Europeans. Today we are finally beginning to realize the seriousness of these atrocities. We have totally ignored the sacred Mayan centers of knowledge, viewing them as relics of a forgotten culture and a tourist attraction.

"Hunbatz Men's *Secrets of Mayan Science/Religion* is one of the first books written by a Mayan of such highly advanced knowledge. It is fortunate that a man with such unique qualifications has undertaken this task. He reveals the fulfillment of the prophecy, analyzing the great cyclic changes and how we are directly or indirectly interrelated with the elements. Strange astonishing events that were prophesied centuries ago by the Mayans will be happening in the years to come.

"Reading this book is a must for those who realize that the world as we know it is close to self-destruction, and for those who are seeking the ultimate in our co-existence and harmony with the world.

"The sacred Mayan centers (receivers of energies and knowledge) like Chichen Itza will once again become centers of learning. It will be very beneficial in expediting the deciphering of this important knowledge to print the book in the English language."

—Alfredo Acosta Figueroa, chairman of the board of directors,
Escuela de la Raza Unida

"Through symbolic and linguistic analysis, Hunbatz Men's *Secrets of Mayan Science/Religion* provides a necessary link connecting indigenous Mayan thought to the present moment. In so doing, he has constructed a bridge that leads us from our own limiting and separatist perceptions to a unifying experience of galactic selfhood. In demonstrating the actual livingness of Mayan religion, Hunbatz Men has performed an indispensable service for this time of global transformation."

—José Argüelles, Ph.D., author of *The Mayan Factor*,
***Surfers of the Zuvuya, Earth Ascending,* and *Transformative Vision*;**
preside

FIGURE 5.

Details of the interior patio of the so-called "Temple of Columns" in Mitla, Oaxaca, Mexico. Here we see the sacred "G" within the temple, in different forms of both high and low relief, in innumerable artistic manifestations of stone. Some archeologists affirm that this temple was painted in colors. It is known that new initiates were consecrated in the science/religion at these locations and given the secrets and knowledge of the Milky Way through the forms and symbols of the "G." It was a place of teachers and students.

FIGURE 6.

Here we see Xochipilli of the Mexicas, a sculpture found today at the National Museum of Anthropology. Samael Aun Weor says of this sculpture: "Flower and song are the highest things on Earth that can penetrate the confines of truth." This is logical, since we know that the Maya worshipped the Milky Way with song, dance, and flowers. In this figure, an arrow indicates a circle, the symbol of *ol*—"knowledge" (in Mayan language, it means "consciousness"). It is the symbol for spiritual management as conducted by the Mexicas. In the lower portion, two arrows point to the "G," symbol of the Milky Way. Flowers and song are necessary to reach the point of purification, according to their teaching.

FIGURE 7.

Temple of the Sun in Palenque, Chiapas, Mexico. In this figure we can appreciate how the Maya revered universal knowledge. We see two priests in meditation, offering gifts to the Milky Way. Arrow 1 indicates the eyes of the solar symbol with "G" symbols inscribed. Arrow 2 points to the symbol of a celestial band with the spiral of life, the sacred "G." The third arrow points to two bearers of the celestial slab whose eyes also have the spiral of the Milky Way. For the Maya, the Sun or suns are the eyes of Hunab K'u.

FIGURE 6.

Mayan Priests of Palenque, Chiapas, Mexico Venerated the Sacred "G"

In Palenque, Chiapas, Mexico is the Temple of the Sun, situated at the foot of the hills. Palenque has numerous structures, including some pyramids that have never been fully explored. The Temple of the Sun occupies the west side of the plaza. It features the typical Palenque architecture known as Nah Chan in Mayan. The portal pillars, as in other pyramids, bear hieroglyphic inscriptions and human figures modeled in stucco. One of the didactic elements of this religious center, a stone mural in the Temple of the Sun, represents a scene of worship of the universal teachings. Precisely in the center, carved in low relief, is the lord Sun, symbolized by a round shield with two crossed spears resting on a ceremonial slab held up by two human figures. On either side is a solar priest, or *hau k'in*, each making an offering. Glyph-covered columns complement the central scene.

Figure 7 shows details of this sculptural masterpiece. Arrows indicate spirals inscribed in the eyes of the central subjects. These spirals represent the "G," the form of the Milky Way. Arrow 1 points to the Sun. Clearly, the Sun (or suns) symbolize the eyes of the Milky Way represented by the Mayan "G." The second arrow indicates the spirals which convey to us energy from the Milky Way upon which we are inevitably dependent. Beneath this, arrows point to the eyes of two figures, labeled slaves by most self-appointed authorities, but whom we more correctly call "the lords who bear the material weight of the world."

These lords imply by their position that they are responsible for the material world. Since we have deduced that material is projected energy, we conclude that their attitude is symbolic. This conclusion is affirmed by the spiral representing the Mayan "G," the Milky Way.

The Ge Was Part of the Religion of the Totonac People

On the coast of the Gulf of Mexico, between the southern Olmec Zone and the northern Huasteca, lies the Totonac homeland. The people of this region created wonderful clay figures, standing as much as 130 centimeters (4 feet) high. In addition to their technical refinement, these figures are notable for their form and expression—particularly their smiling faces. The Totonacs generally used the color red to paint these

FIGURE 7.

figures—red, the color associated with the creator Sun. According to Alfonso Medellin Zenil, the Totonacs were "content and peaceful. They exalted nature, fecundity, and feminine beauty." The Totonac smiling figures seem to celebrate the Sun and nature. One could continue praising the qualities of these figures; but it is most important to illustrate that the Totonacs possessed knowledge of the universe, as did the Maya.

Figure 8 (top) illustrates a smiling face of the Totonac culture. The Totonacs also venerated the "G" form because they understood that their people emanated from intergalactic material. They used the spiral form to likewise represent the energy of the Milky Way, from which their essence derived. Could it be that the smiling expression of contentment came from knowing their origin and purpose for being on Earth?

In the lower portion of Figure 8, we see another figure which appears to be a woman carrying a child on her back. This terra-cotta figure, from El Zapotal, Veracruz, pertains to the Tajin culture. It is presently on display in the Southwestern Museum of Los Angeles, California, USA. This little sculpture features a prominent "G." As in Figure 9, from the same archeological site, it is evident that the subject assumes a position of adoration. Most probably, the meditation is related to the symbol worn on the chest.

Nelly Gutierrez Solana and Susan K. Hamilton offer interesting insights in their book, *Terra-Cotta Sculptures from Zapotal, Veracruz*, published by the National Autonomous University of Mexico. They refer to the site where they made important discoveries in 1971 and 1972. They write:

> Next to this offering, which must have been buried during a great collective ceremony, appeared the Ossuary I of section A. There were veritable columns of human bones composed of skulls, femurs, ribs and vertebrae that varied in height from 1.36 meters to 4.76 meters. In total, 82 skulls were counted.
>
> Four secondary graves were excavated which contained related pieces of high artistic value, such as smiling figures, zoomorphic sculptures, clay whistles of Mayan figures, rattles elaborated with cream-colored clay and urns. Among the smiling figures were two with articulated legs and movable neck and arms. Torres Guzman notes that "there are scarcely any ceramic diagnostic types of the

Totonac culture in the semiarid central zone." In total, only four hundred objects have been classified.

Torres Guzman has surmised that the mound marked #2 functioned "as a funeral center where cult service was rendered to the world of the dead...as is evidenced by the ossuary."

The altar and mound suffered a series of transformations over time, including architectural superimpositions.

Clearly, Zapotal, Veracruz, Mexico was visited by the Maya. This was, undoubtedly, an area where collective ceremonies were held, and it is also clear that, as the above researchers indicate, it was a burial site. If we observe Figure 9, we will see the subject in a meditative position, with crossed arms. In its mouth is a figure terminating in spirals and, once more, the symbol "G." Ms. Solana and Ms. Hamilton inform us that the objects found in the tombs confirm that the Maya were in this area. This new phase of the use of the symbolic "G" by the people of El Zapotal and the Maya is of great interest. It begs a brief explanation from Mayan thought on the relationship between corporeal essence and the Milky Way.

The first element, for the Maya, is the visible element, the physical body. We all know that it is made of visible material which is tangible and palpable. Any normal human being can detect this with the five senses.

The second element consists of more tenuous or ethereal material. It is invisible under ordinary circumstances. It is comparable at times to body heat.

Third, the element of spirit or personality is mental and is nourished by psychological energies. It can be compared with the ego. As we all know, ego is the source of our planet's present woes.

Fourth, vital essence is pure essence. The Mayan *ge* represents the essence of energy. It can be said that everything is made of energy.

It seems that the people of Zapotal carried out their ceremonies bearing in mind the four basic principles described above and, in particular, the last principle referring to the universal essence as depicted in Figure 9. They and the Maya shared knowledge of the essence of the human being and symbolized it with the "G," the Milky Way of which we are a product.

FIGURE 8.
A classic Totonac smiling face (top) features the sacred "G". In the photo below, an arrow indicates another "G". This piece, found in Tajin, Veracruz, Mexico, is now in the Southwest Museum of Los Angeles, California, USA. We can see that it is a figure of a woman in a meditative attitude with a child peering over her left shoulder. This little clay figure gives us another insight into indigenous culture. Our indigenous American ancestors knew how to worship and meditate in the proximity of their children. Perhaps this was how they began spiritual discipline for their infants.

FIGURE 9.
This terra cotta figure was found in Zapotal, Veracruz, Mexico. As was previously stated, the ancient people of this location worshipped the sacred "G," in this case in relation to death and transmutation. Nelly Gutierrez Solana and Susan K. Hamilton have determined that offerings like this were deposited in the graves of approximately four hundred persons during a great collective sacred ceremony at Zapotal. They added that many figures had Mayan characteristics. Undoubtedly the most significant discovery was the altar of a deity associated with death. It was concluded that the sacred "G" bore great importance at this site, where the Milky Way was venerated as the energy of reincarnation.

FIGURE 8.

FIGURE 9.

Surely these ancient indigenous people understood the secrets of death and its relation to the Milky Way. It is clear that everything that has been discussed relative to the "G" and its importance in Mayan, as well as other cultures, points to this symbol's sacred and scientific characteristics.

A Brief Glossary:

1. Mayan Words Which Refer to Manifested Essence on Earth & Beyond

MAYAN WORD	MEANING
ge	zero, egg, essence, aura, Milky Way
geo/gea	terrestrial globe, egg-shape, world
gelmen	creative essence, egg creator, creative vibration
gelman	past essence, egg that passed, past vibration
geoba	this cosmic egg or this form of cosmic egg
gene	egg with a tail, name of the seed
gente	egg, seed or essence from here

2. Mayan Words Which Refer to the Human Being

The following conjugation is for the first, second, and third persons, in both singular and plural forms. The idiomatic relation in reference to the human serves to recall galactic origins.

MAYAN WORD	MEANING
gelenah	here I am
gelecha	here you are
geletia	here he/she is
gelona	here we are
gelexa	here you (plural) are
geletioba	here they are

3. Mayan Words Referring to the Human Material Presence in Direct Relation to Cosmic Essence

MAYAN WORD	MEANING
gele	yes

gelabin	Are you going?
galaan	changed or different
gel	change
gelel	to detain oneself
gedzal	detained

As you can clearly see, the first examples of *ge* words refer to the essence from which we emanate. The second set of examples refers more directly to the human being. In all cases, one can clearly see the reference to the Milky Way—the Mayan *ge*.

In Espita, Yucatan, Mexico, it has been a custom to celebrate the Day of the Dead. At one time I heard some of these words used in reference to the dead; that is, by the use of these words, the essence of the departed spirits was invoked as part of the Milky Way. All of the appearances of the "G" in the previous figures confirm for us the intimate relationship between this symbolic "G" and the dead; between their union with the cosmic laws and the understanding by the Maya that we are all products of the Great Spirit found in the essence of the Milky Way. In one way or another, beginning with Moses, ancient peoples in all parts of the world worshipped and respected this essence.

Mayan language plainly confirms the reverence that was held for the Milky Way by the ancient Maya. There exists other evidence found in the pyramids, in the codices, murals, vases, and other objects of our indigenous culture. The *ge* was in all senses an integral part of our heritage.

The cultural core of Mayan existence was *panche be*—the search for the root of truth. Using logic, they found the true nature of things and understood the Milky Way, naming it *ge* in Mayan. The form of the "G" was not developed as a whim, but was based on the original form of the Milky Way and its primordial configuration—the spiral. With this knowledge, the Maya emblazoned their sacred sites with graphic celebration of the symbol and revered its essence. They lived in harmony with the natural laws which govern us and which emanate from the cosmic "G."

Most of the official history of the Maya was written by foreign "experts" such as Brinton, Seler, Goodman, Bowditch, Morley, and Ales

Hrdlicka, as well as some friars given to writing history, who undertook the task of providing accounts of the indigenous peoples of the Americas. Disgracefully for us Mexicans, what we are taught is based on what they have written about our sovereign culture. As most indigenous Americans know, these incorrect teachings only serve to cause harm to the indigenous peoples of Mexico.

Indigenous American people know that the Western European culture has yet to comprehend much of our knowledge, including a true understanding of the Mayan *ge*. In actuality, there is much contemporary talk of the need to incorporate native Americans into technological, mechanized civilization. I believe that this would be disastrous, considering the spiritual decadence of European or Western culture. If governments and their officials could only see that the so-called progress of machine technology is simply a mirage. I implore Hunab K'u that these managers of power be mentally awakened and that they respect their Indian relatives. In Mexico, our Indian roots offer the only hope for enlightenment and awareness of the essence of the "G" symbol, the vital energy that we, the cosmic indigenous people, still possess.

To conclude this brief analysis of the use and pronunciation and graphic form of the sacred "G," it is very important to repeat that this symbol is not unique to Mesoamerica. In my travels to ten countries of Central and South America, I encountered numerous vestiges of the "G" symbol. Indigenous peoples of the entire New World used the symbol in the same way as the Maya. Clearly, they called it by a different name, but the form used was identical to the form used by the Mesoamerican grandparents of the Maya, Nahua, etc.

The Indigenous People of Tierradentro, Columbia, South America & Their Use of the Sacred Ge

The Indian inhabitants of Tierradentro, Columbia, South America used the "G" symbol for sacred communications in ceremonial rites conducted in the secret passageways of funerary temples. The elaborate tombs here are unique in all of South America.

The "G" adorns these subterranean temples, carved from the living white rock. The temples each contain a great variety of tombs, numbering from ten to seventy. They range in depth from very shallow to over seven meters. Spacious chambers have five to seven surrounding niches.

In many instances, to enter these vaults, one must descend spiral stairs hewn from the same rock. The entire construction is detailed with geometric design, predominately the "G" form in white, red, and black. Colombian anthropologists unearthed funeral urns of fine ceramic. Little is known of these ancient people and their cultural leaders who designed and built these magnificent tombs. The only date ascribed to the site thus far is 1100 A.D.

According to Duque Gomes, the tombs were apparently built for secondary burials. That is, they served as a final resting place for ashes after cremation. How extraordinary that even in their funerary temples, the ancient people of Tierradentro, Columbia, revered, like the Maya, the cosmic symbol "G."

The Chavin of Huantar, Peru, South America Also Revered the "G," Sacred Symbol of the Milky Way

Continuing my travels throughout South America, I observed that the Chavin People of Huantar, Peru had an ancient tradition of reverence for this sacred symbol. Confirmation was found in the subterranean galleries of Chavin. Forming a network throughout the entire archeological zone, their architectural design links diverse pyramidal constructions. The rooms and corridors are a veritable beehive: the walls of passageways are dressed with carved stone. Vestiges of paint on the walls imply that this must have been a ceremonial center of almost incalculable grandness. The subterranean galleries are on several levels, with flights of ascending and descending stairs of stone. In the interior, one of the galleries takes the form of a cross. In the immediate center of the cross is a carved stone which is called *lanzon*, "the great image." This tall, slender block is a triangular prism five meters high. The prism surfaces are incised with designs of the "G," a form venerated by the cultured people of Chavin.

It is difficult to establish all the uses of these subterranean caverns of Chavin except that they were intimately linked to the spiritual world of the people. The Zapotal, Veracruz piece of Figure 9 comes to mind in association with the chambers of Chavin, and the ritual worship of the sacred symbol of the "G." In ceremonial centers throughout our dubiously named America, this symbol has been revered for thousands of years by the Nahua, Maya, Inca, Aymara, etc.

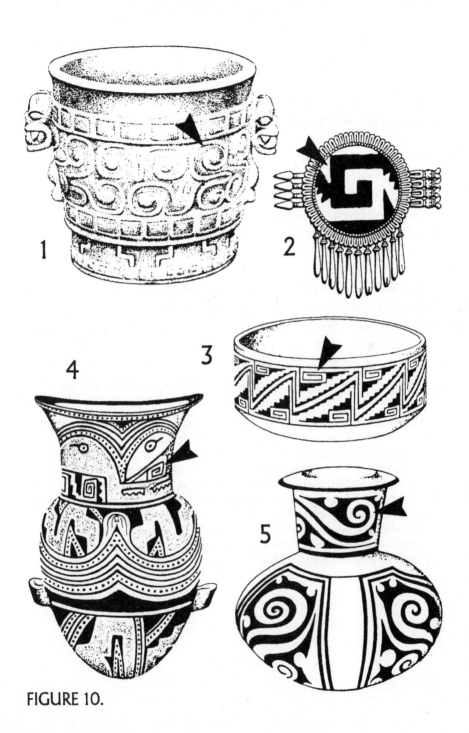

1

2

3

4

5

FIGURE 10.

Well then, dear reader, if doubt remains about the universality of the "G" symbol of the cosmic Milky Way in the New World, here are further examples. Figure 10 shows artifacts of: the indigenous people of Honduras (1), the Mixtecs of Mexico (2), the indigenous people of Chile (3), Argentina (4), and Panama (5). All clearly feature the sacred symbol. We can conclude that the entire continent, originally referred to as Tamuanchan, Hanahuac, Tauantinsuyo, or by some other traditional Indian name, venerated the symbol of the Milky Way, the source, the cosmic essence.

We have revealed the use of the "G" in its symbolic, ideographic, and iconometric forms so that you, our continental brothers and sisters, will recognize it at sacred sites and respect and revere it. By doing so, you will be opening the door through which the cosmic essence of the Milky Way will enter your being and stimulate your spirit as a vibration. You will newly awaken to the feeling of Hunab K'u—the Only Giver of Movement and Measure, the God of our ancient indigenous American grandparents.

FIGURE 10.

These drawings were taken from the book, *American Indian Design and Decoration*, by LeRoy H. Appleton, USA. The creators of these pieces were master artisans. Their significance lies in the fact that original people of the continent, as well as their descendants, were and continue to be united in their worship of religion and science, as are the peninsular Maya.

Honduran, Mixtec, Chilean, Argentinian, and Panamanian indigenous Americans venerated the sacred "G" as the symbolic representation of the Milky Way. They shared an awareness of energy which produces cyclical terrestrial changes, changes which we need to become more conscious of in order to truly become the children of Hunab K'u.

CHAPTER TWO

The Letter "T":
Its Use, Form & Sound is of Ancient Mayan Origin

 When we stop to observe cultural aspects of the Mayan world, we are astonished by the level of wisdom attained by the Maya. The ancestors termed their philosophy *panche be*, "seeking the root of truth." In their tenacious commitment to investigating their surroundings, the ancestors became convinced of their oneness with the natural environment and adopted it as their guide and teacher. Thus thought the Mayan philosophers, and clearly, their religion arises from nature itself. In their minds, nature nourishes the body, mind, and spirit. The Maya identify with their brother, the Sacred Tree, *yaxche*, which is to say, "first the tree." *Yaxche* is the stately and sacred Ceiba tree. All religions have a Sacred Tree. For the Maya, the Ceiba is this symbol.

First there was the tree, then the animal. If the last tree should perish, animals and humans alike would cease to be. In the word *baalche*, human and tree are related. The expression is *baal*, "thing of"; and *che*, "tree."

Regarding the Tree, Christianity states that "beneath the shade of the Tree, human development began when Eve gave Adam the fruit of science, of good and evil." Here the Sacred Tree is the Tree of Life, a surprising parallel between the Maya and Christian concepts. Unfortunately, as we shall see, the tree became associated with evil within the Roman Catholic religion. Among the Maya, the tree was never associated with evil, since it is a symbol of that which is sacred, and a cultural axis of religion, science, and philosophy.

Mayan culture, controversial and much discussed for its great achievements in the sciences and arts, remains a topic for research by scientists and academicians seeking its roots and fruits (see Figure 11).

The now-common Mayan word for tree is *che*, but in ancient Mayan there was another word, *te*. And so we begin our study of the letter "T." It is interesting to note that if we join the past and present words for tree, *te* and *che*, we get *teche*, meaning "you"; that is, *teche* forms the second person pronoun in the Mayan language. Moreover, *te* is the root of the first, second, and third-person pronouns. All are linguistically tied to the Sacred Tree.

Examples:

MAYAN WORD	MEANING
ten	I
teche	you
leti	she, he, it

(*Leti* is composed of *le*—"tree leaf", and *ti*—"there on it," together meaning "leaf on the tree.")

A functional analysis of the letter "T" and the word *te* corroborates the Mayan concept of the tree embodied in the word *yaxche*—"first the tree," the Ceiba, the Sacred Tree of the Maya. It also explains the Mayan reference to human and animal forms, and helps elucidate the concept of life, *baal che*, "thing of the tree." The axiom prevails: "without the tree (vegetation), the animal would not exist."

In order to give you, dear reader, an idea of the antiquity of this use of the letter "T," I refer you to a great writer and researcher who lived in India 300 years before the birth of Christ. This writer, Valmiki, compiled the two most sacred books of India, the *Ramayana* and the *Mahabharata*, foundations of Hindu ideology and cosmology. In his work, Valmiki states that around 2700 B.C. the Naga Maya brought their culture to India. It is my belief that the Naga Maya introduced as part of their knowledge the use of "T" to the Asian people.

Ancient Mayan culture ratifies biblical references to the apple tree in the Garden of Eden, where the human progenitors committed the so-called original sin. When Eve plucked the apple from the tree of good and evil and offered it to Adam, a conjunction between them resulted that was not simply a sexual union. A new entity came to be, called *religare*, the foundation of true religion.

FIGURE 11.
Page 2 of the Selden Codex: The mythological birth of humanity shows a person emerging from a sacred tree. This image has historical content. Those of us with knowledge of Mayan/Aztec culture recognize the sacred "T" as the symbol of the tree that produced the human being. This knowledge was ours long before the arrival of the Catholic priests, who brought their Christian concept of Adam, Eve, the tree, and the serpent. We worked with this knowledge in the remote days of Hanahuac, Tamuanchan, Ixachitlan, Tauantinsuyo, or America.

The name "Eva" ("Eve" in Spanish), assigned to the first feminine being to acquire physical presence, is derived from the substitution of the labiodental "V" of Latin for the original "U," in the same way that *civdad* was used instead of *ciudad* in old Spanish. This linguistic curiosity can be attributed to a Roman Vatican pope who decreed such a change in Europe based on the religious prejudice that the "U" was common in pagan countries. "Eva" in Mayan is *eua* and signifies "isolation, separation"—exactly what transpired with Adam and Eve. Adam might aptly have exclaimed, "Eua!" when he became aware of the feminine entity emerging from his androgynous body!

Interestingly, the substitution of the "T" in "Adan" ("Adam" in Spanish) results in *atan*—the word for "wife" in Mayan. Through the science of the Mayan language and the philosophy of *panche be*, "seeking the root of the truth," a clear and simple understanding of *religare* is possible. It refers to the concept of reuniting two beings or things that have been separated. In this case, it is the separation of two sexes that were once a single body.

The Bible also tells us that Jehovah, troubled by the solitude of Adam, caused him to sleep and took from him a rib which became woman. For what reason would evolution have commenced in this way? If Adam had been created from earth and a breath of air—if the male were so formed—could not Eve have been created in the same way, rather than from the body of Adam? Certainly this legend serves to disguise sexual evolution. Evidence for this comes from the fact that nature often produces beings that are bisexual at birth. Similar conditions exist when hormones interact magnetically with certain mental frequencies. There is an indication that if a male being has more female hormones than male hormones, he may become homosexual, as might a woman who has a predominance of male hormones. This must be considered in the light of the androgynous nature of the first beings. The Bible maintains that woman emerged from the masculine body of Adam. The same Bible proposes, in axiomatic form, the existence of the phenomenon of organic evolution.

Obviously, the creation of human beings, the tree, and all sacred things have been linked since the beginning of time. A transcendental synthesis of human religious experience is inherent in the word *te*, Sacred Tree, which emerged from the words *teol* and *teotl*, the names of God the

Creator in Mayan and Nahuatl. These most revered and sacred words of the ancient people, symbolized by the Sacred Tree, were represented in Mayan hieroglyphs as the symbol "T." Additionally, this symbol represented the air, the wind, the divine breath of God. The relationship which the Maya made between the tree and the wind is notable because it was based on their own experiences and scientific observations. They understood that the tree is the best regenerator of the air we breathe, as modern science has proven. But despite this corroboration, science has failed to recognize applications of wind and the divine breath known to the ancient Maya. For instance, did you know that the Maya used wind to communicate over long distances? Did you also know that the wind was used in spiritual rituals? These are just two of many examples that illustrate how the Maya applied the wind to practical and spiritual use, while recognizing its sacredness as symbolized by the "T."

Contemporary science is discovering more qualities of the tree. A book by Piero Bainuccio, *From the Atoms to the Cosmos* (Daimon Press), discusses variations in the rotation of the Earth. Bainuccio asserts that:

> Gauged by atomic clocks, our planet has been shown to be inconsistent or to falter. The Earth has the tendency to "lose spins"; that is, it progressively decelerates in its rotation.
>
> This phenomenon has been attributed to friction produced by the ocean tides due to the gravitational attraction of the Sun and Moon. At times, however, the earth begins to speed up almost as if it were experiencing a "seasonal frenzy." Generally, it slows its rotation each spring, and accelerates in autumn and winter. Various hypotheses have been proposed to explain these variations. One proposes that the spring decelerations are due to the flow of sap in the highest branches of plants and trees. The Earth slows down to maintain "periods of rotation" imposed by the laws of physics. This implies a balance in the distribution of rotations in much the same way a skater spinning in place on ice is slowed by raising the arms.

As previously stated, the Mayan word for tree is pronounced *te*, and its symbol, which adorns pyramids, codices, and pottery is the "T." All the circumstances related to religious aspects of the tree offer evidence of the relationship between the name of the Creator—*teol*, the tree, and human existence. These are the fundamental links between humans and the supreme architect. This was well understood by the Mayan philosopher who associated the tree with the Great Spirit through the word *teol* (*te* meaning "tree," and *ol* meaning "consciousness" or "spirit"). It remains an amazing manifestation of transcendental proportions that the Maya recognized the tree as possessing life sensibilities! Modern science has proven this by conducting experiments and analyses of plant life and plants' reactions to the treatment to which they are subjected.

All of this demonstrates that the consideration and respect which the Maya had for the tree was not only because they used its fruits for nourishment, but also because they were convinced that trees are life-forms with reactions similar to those of humans. Once again, the Mayan language confirms this fact. *Wuinic* is the Mayan word meaning "to be human." This word combines *wui*, "tuber," and *nic*, "immensity," or "cosmos." Thus, *wuinic* is another way of saying that the human being is a cosmic entity. To complement the philosophical and scientific concept of *wuinic*, we add the particle *lil*, meaning "vibration," to describe the human body as a mass of energy, since all things and beings that exist on Earth are a product of the projection of energy in the form of vibration.

In analyzing the material previously described, we realize that our Mayan ancestors understood that plants and trees were sentient life-forms capable of producing the paranormal phenomenon which parapsychology strives to explain. In Figure 12, dear reader, you see part of a codex entitled Fejérváry-Mayer, but which should have been named *uahomche*, the name said to have been used by the Maya to denote the Cross of the Tree. What reasons were there for such a definition? Why was this expression used? The definition is fascinating: *uahomche* in Mayan clearly means "the tree which awakens us" or "we awaken in the tree." We wonder about this Mayan expression since it means many things; but above all because of its mystical relationship to paranormal phenomenon in human experience. *Uahomche*, the indigenous name for the cross, has truly transcendental ramifications depending on our perspective or point of reference, be it historical, religious, philosophical, or even political or social.

It is significant that *uahomche* was the Mayan name for the cross (made of wood) before the arrival of the Conquistadors. This is especially significant in the context of world religion, for several foreign writers have suggested that the Spanish were preceded by earlier travelers who came to

NORTH

SOUTH

FIGURE 12.

The Fejérváry-Mayer Codex: In this manuscript we find four trees oriented toward the cardinal points. In the center, a figure controls energy. Also present are birds and other symbols used in this codex, which should be named *uahom che*, the word used by the Maya to designate "the cross of the tree." To what do we attribute this designation? It is interesting to discover the clear meaning: "The tree that awakens us" or "within the tree that awakens conciousness."

exchange and study culture. These travelers could have come from Asia, Babylon, Egypt, etc.

A singular aspect of this case occurs in the ancient expression relating the cross to the specific form of the tree—that "redeeming wood" which awakens us. This concept of *uahomche* is truly impressive. In addition, when we notice that all crosses, including the famous Maltese Cross (see Figure 12), appear in our codices, and among the fret designs, etchings, and paintings, we recall the investigations of those foreigners who describe remote relations between our pre-Columbian ancestors and the nations of the Middle East, Asia, and Africa. This codex, which we shall henceforth call *uahomche*, requires new study. Only one percent of the results of previous study has value. The rest we shall dispose of, and investigate the document afresh to discover a new horizon in our indigenous American culture.

In our study of the Sacred Tree, it is important to note further examples of Mayan knowledge of its sentient qualities. The Tree is conceived of as a projection of intelligent energy, and as such, we deem it natural that it possess psychological qualities similar to those of humans; *teol*—spirit of the tree. Mayan teachers and sages aware of the sensory and extrasensory characteristics of trees accepted that plants and trees had such capabilities as a logical result of the energy they possessed. Contemporary scientists are just now recognizing the sensibilities of plants and the truly phenomenal reactions that the Maya have long recognized and understood. This was a rational extension of their premise that intelligent energy exists in *all* things. Evidence of this ancient awareness is found in Palenque, Chiapas, Mexico, where one can appreciate the use of the graphic form "T" on the walls of the temple designated *El Palacio* ("the palace") (see Figure 13).

In the southern part of this structure, subterranean galleries connect the sacred temples to the palace via interior stairways below the southern facade. The galleries were used for rituals and it is quite probable that here the Mayan initiates venerated the symbol "T" as a physical representation of the Sacred Tree. Inside some of the passageways, tablelike rocks were found which probably served as altars. The enclosed chambers may have served as meditation rooms for the priests. The palace was profusely decorated with figures and hieroglyphs, even on the stair risers.

Interior walls were pierced by small windows in the shape of the "T." Columns at the end of the galleries and around the patio were adorned with stucco reliefs of the chronological calendars. It is evident, from vestiges that remain on the walls and ceilings, that this structure was elaborately painted. There is much to be learned here about our relationship with the tree. This sacred site was misnamed Palenque by the Spaniards. The Mayan name, *Nah Chan*, more aptly describes this place of worship for the Sacred Tree, and the scientific study of the qualities of *te* and *che*. We have only outlined some properties of this sacred place, *Nah Chan*, where for many hundreds of years the Mayan savants lived with the integral knowledge imparted by our relative, the tree.

Another field of knowledge explored by the Maya dealt with energy, *k'inan*, in the form of suggestion, telepathy, and hypnotism. They understood that when a person was hypnotized or under suggestion, it was because energy was received that made the person subject to the suggestion and will of the hypnotist. They also knew that the tree possesses psychic faculties (the *ol*—"spirit") similar to those of a human being. Does it seem strange that a tree can produce, via its energy, echoes, visions, screams, cries, and moans, or even evoke apparitions such as *x'tabay*, the trickster, who always appears near a tree and tempts the solitary off-road traveler? All of this leads to a Mayan phrase which states, "We live in an environment surrounded by echoes and images which can be materialized by our mental force."

The use of the sacred symbol "T" was not limited to the Maya. The Nahua also revered it for its great spiritual energy and value (see Figure 14A). In this drawing we see Xochipilli, Goddess of the Flowers (from the Diego Rivera Collection), with a "T" under her nose symbolizing the divine breath. We can also observe in Figure 14B the God of Rain reproduced from a vase found in the sacred city of Teotihuacan. The figure's mouth has the form of the sacred "T." At the bottom of the page (Figure 14C) one can see that our fellow Delaware Indians also knew the great symbolic value of the "T" as a representation of the Sacred Tree. It is probable that the Delaware worshipped the Tree in a similar way to the Maya, Nahua, and other indigenous American peoples.

As a point of observation, the name Teotihuacan begins with the "T" of the tree, and includes the "O" of the spirit of the tree. Please recall that when we speak of the spirit of the tree, we also speak of the human spirit.

FIGURE 13.
The Maya of Palenque, Chiapas, Mexico performed rituals in honor of the sacred "T" as a symbol of the tree. The temple known as The Palace is one of the sacred sites where the Maya worshipped the tree. This knowledge was an integral part of their lives for thousands of years.

FIGURE 14.
(A) designates Xochipilli, goddess of flowers, from a Teotihuacan fresco in the collection of Diego Rivera. The deity displays a prominent "T" below the nose, symbolizing the divine breath. (B) denotes the rain god as shown in a fresco on a Teotihuacan vase from the National Anthropology Museum. Below (C) we see the stepped fret as the "T" of the tree, used by the Delaware Indians in the USA.

FIGURE 13.

A

B

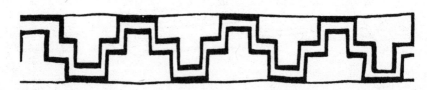

C

FIGURE 14.

Before discussing a series of words which further illustrate how the *te* of the Sacred Tree and the *ol* of the Great Spirit relate to the physical matter of which we are composed, we would like you to recall the "G" as associated with the essence of the universe and its source, the Milky Way. Let us also look briefly again at Zuyua Mayan, the esoteric idiom of the Mayan language. (In my book, *The Astronomical Calendars and Hunab K'u*, I discuss this at greater length.) A significant aspect of Zuyua Mayan lies in the use of word inversion to establish understanding of particular relationships. For instance, if we take the word *te* and invert it, we obtain *et*, which means "companion" or "relative." This describes an implicit relationship between the tree and the person. By describing the tree as a companion or relative, a pact was made with Mother Nature, who was considered their teacher and guide.

With this in mind we shall delve into a few Mayan words and their meanings. First, we shall consider those that refer to the physical human being, then those that refer to human anatomy, and finally, those related to sacred matters.

For the Maya, everything is organized and based on science and religion as a single entity. The following serves to illustrate how the symbolic "T" of the Sacred Tree relates to human beings and also to the divine breath, as distinguished from the "G," symbol of the most ancient essence, as well as from Hunab K'u, the Only Giver of Movement and Measure. Dear reader, take these sacred symbols as they are given, and revere and study them as did the ancient Maya, Nahua, and other peoples who lived by the lessons of these relationships for thousands of years.

1. Personal Pronouns in Singular & Plural Form

MAYAN WORD	MEANING
ten	I
tech	you
leti	he, she, it
toon	we
teex	you (plural)
letioob	they

2. Anatomical Words

MAYAN WORD	MEANING
tuch	umbilical cord, navel
tuncuy	heel
tzen	chest
tzec	skull
tzootz	hair
ton	cheekbone, cheek

3. Words Related to the Spiritual Aspects of the Sacred Tree & the Human Being

MAYAN WORD	MEANING
te	Sacred Tree
et	companion, relative
teol	spirit of the tree
teuz	tree, divine breath
toz'	pertaining to ceremonials
tzin k'in	Day of the Departed Souls
taan	ceremonial ashes
tec ol	instant mover of the spirit, inspiration
tzeec	a sacred speech

As you can see, dear reader, these words show that the Mayan *te* is equivalent to the symbolic "T." For the Maya, the use of *te* in a word implies a relationship of physical, spiritual and psychological union with the tree. We all know that the tree nourishes us with a great variety of types of physical sustenance. However, European or Western culture provides little information concerning aspects of the tree which govern our spiritual development. The Spaniards and their culture had nothing to teach the Maya, Nahua, and other indigenous people of this continent. For this reason, we must reaffirm our true indigenous heritage, the legacy of our grandparents.

The ancient Zapotec and Maya both lived in the zone called Monte Alban, Oaxaca, Mexico, and some of the symbols of Zapotec culture are shared by Yucatan Maya. For instance, the "T" in Figure 15 was venerated

FIGURE 15.
A Zapotec funerary urn from Monte Alban, Oaxaca, Mexico. The arrow
indicates the "T" symbol, or Sacred Tree, in various forms. This piece was
found in the repository of the mortal remains of an ancient Zapotec governor. Like the people of El Zapotal, Veracruz, the Zapotecs also used the
sacred "T" in the transition to the world of the dead governed by Hunab
K'u as the Only Giver of Movement and Measure.

by both the Zapotec and the Maya. Here it is incised on the base of a repository for the remains of some ancient Zapotec governor.

Paul Westheim observes that Monte Alban, although "constructed over several centuries, maintains an astounding unity of design." In this sacred place, one notes the symmetry of pyramidal construction as well as an asymmetry; these combine in a harmonious whole. One is also impressed by the symbology, which meant the same to the Zapotec as it did to the Teotihuacans, Maya, and Nahua, and which adorns lintels, stelae, and commemorative slabs. From an early epoch, they developed a culture of great splendor, which was reflected in surrounding settlements. The Zapotec sages had their own calendrical system for knowledge and management of time. In addition to the symbolic "T," they used glyphs, and a numerical system of bars and dots similar to the magical numerology of the Maya. Westheim adds: "The commemorative stones of the Zapotecs are notably religious. They tend to show events of a mystical-religious nature, divine myths, and feats of the gods." All of Westheim's observations regarding these ceremonial centers are confirmed by the Mayan language and the use of the sacred "T." Moreover, the death of humans is related to the sacred "T" symbols on the tombs at Monte Alban.

Tamuanchan is an ancient word associated with the sacred "T" in our millennial indigenous America. According to oral tradition, Tamuanchan was the home of the human race! (See Figure 16B: Codice Vendobonensis.)

Tamuanchan signifies for the Maya the bringing together of human and vegetable life. It is symbolized by a tree from whose upper branches rises a human figure. This undoubtedly reaffirms the union with the tree, the Mayan premise that human and tree are of similar substance. The Maya say *yaxche*, "first the tree" and then the animal, *baalche*, or "the thing of the tree" in Mayan. This is the Mayan concept of human and tree.

If you, dear reader, review Figure 11, you will see that in addition to the person emerging from the tree, there are two intertwined serpents. Please bear in mind that, according to the conceptual duality of our native language and culture, these two serpents represent positive and negative energy, *can* and *nac*. Figure 11 relates to Figure 16B, where again a human emerges from the Sacred Tree. The latter image is also related to Tamuanchan. Laurette Sejourne, in her book, *Thought and Religion in*

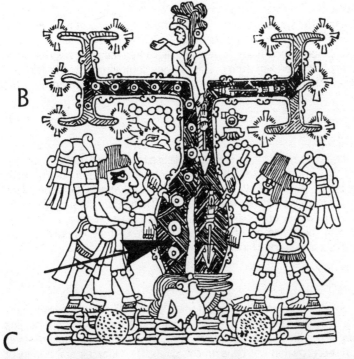

FIGURE 16.

FIGURE 16.

An Aztec seal (A) takes the form of the sacred "T" incised with birds. Below (B) we have the symbol of Tamoanchan, the original land of humankind as described by the researcher Laurette Sejourne: "The Nahua (Aztecs) claimed descendence from the trees and illustrated their origin with a figure emerging from a broken trunk." This drawing comes from the Vindolonesis Codex. At the bottom (C) we see stepped-fret motifs in the form of the sacred "T" from Teotihuacan, Mexico state.

FIGURE 17.

This photo of a mask in the Prehistoric Museum in Rome, Italy, reveals the sacred "T" in proximity to the nose, which recalls the symbolism of the divine breath generated by our tree relative. As we remember, upon taking the first breath we connect with the wind. Then, after the passage of the years when we lose our bodily essence, we take a last breath and break the bond with the divine breath that gave us terrestrial life. Thus, this mask embodies a true lesson of indigenous culture.

FIGURE 18.

The so-called Sepulcral Slab, this stone is beautifully inscribed with many Mayan symbols, the most important being the tree with the emerging human. The official Palenque guide book by Alberto Ruz Lhuillier states (with respect to what was beneath this slab): "The supernatural powers of this personage (surely a deified ruler) continued to grow after burial in this tomb; he still kept an eye on his people and interceded from his proximity to the all-powerful gods to help cast off sickness, hunger, misfortune, and even death."

FIGURE 17.

FIGURE 18.

Ancient Mexico, states: "It is the split tree which symbolizes the garden of Tamuanchan, the house of rest, place of birth, the mystical West where Gods and humans originated." From this image we further understand the Mayan concept that we human beings are sons and daughters of the Sacred Tree, and why all of the peoples of Mesoamerica have glyphs, writings, and symbols containing the "T" which represent the same Sacred Tree. Sejourne adds, "The Nahua called themselves descendants of the trees, and illustrate their origins with a human figure emerging from a broken trunk." Let us recall the Mayan word *teol* and the Nahuatl form, *teotl*, which joined the Sacred Tree and the name of God. Two words sharing idiomatic and iconographic symbolism unite two indigenous peoples of the Americas.

We can see in Figure 16A an Aztec seal in the form of the "T" which is related to Figure 18. Visible in this seal are two birds, symbolic of the spirit, which will be more amply discussed when we speak about Figure 19. In Figure 16B, notice the thirteen circles on the tree. For a deeper study of the magic number thirteen in the Mayan culture, I recommend that you read *The Astronomical Calendars of the Maya and Hunab K'u*. The number thirteen serves to synchronize calendrical time, but also has other uses. Figure 16C reproduces ornamental designs from the Temple of Mitla in Oaxaca. Here the "T" is stylized but still fills a teaching function for those people who were attuned to the laws which the tree dictated to its younger relatives.

That the "T" in hieroglyphic writing also symbolizes *ik'*—"air" or "divine breath"—is axiomatically corroborated in Figure 17, where a mask displays a "T" under the nose. A newborn is lightly spanked so that it will draw its first breath. In this way the divine breath arrives, which gives life to this new being. The infant cries, and from that instant is considered alive. After the passage of years, it dies, gives its last breath, and becomes disconnected from the divine breath which has given it life in this earthly world we are passing through. (This mask, made of various colors of jade, is in the collection of the Prehistoric Museum of Rome, Italy.)

At the Temple of Inscriptions and Origins in Palenque, Chiapas, Mexico, much remains to be learned of the scientific and religious knowledge that was exalted here. Inside this temple, there are stucco figures representing men and women carrying babies. Along the walls of this great scientific sanctuary, carved stone slabs bear hieroglyphic inscriptions. This temple could well be designated the Temple of Our Ancestral Laws (see Figure 18). The "Funerary Crypt," a compartment measuring nine meters long by four meters wide, has a narrow entrance with stairs. The walls display stucco reliefs of nine richly dressed priests carrying a solar shield and the scepter of the rain god. These nine lords symbolize the *bolonti k'u*, lords from beyond the third dimension, from the nine inferior worlds of the night. Also in this chamber are symbols representing the Sun. In the center lies Pacal's Tombstone; the Maya call it "Pacal's Stone." On it is carved a tree emerging from a human navel, upon which sits a bird, symbolic of the spirit. Its meaning could not be clearer: this image reveals the integration of the divine with the human. A similar metaphysical notion cost the Greek philosopher, Socrates, his life when he stated that the human being is the basic point for understanding the divine. Obviously, the Greeks had their doubts about these Socratic statements. Therein lies a vast difference between their community and that of the Maya. Philosophers in the Mayan tradition practiced and applied ethics and aesthetics as a discipline to arrive at the conclusion that God, nature, and humans are one and the same, a unity. One of the principal symbols used to demonstrate this was the integration of the great Sacred Tree and the human being, as in Figure 18. From the human being emerges the Sacred Tree, and the bird, symbol of their spirits, in the cosmic union of past and future time.

As we have seen, the Mayan philosopher knows, understands, and manifests a scientific concept through the systematic search for the root of the truth, *panche be*. With their developed culture and their high level of conceptual understanding, the Maya were able to establish categories for each concept. For this reason, there were no doubts among the Maya, as there were among the Greek community when Socrates was obliged to drink the hemlock. The Maya classify the Supreme as Hunab K'u, the Only Giver of Movement and Measure, and proudly represent the concept with a square superimposed on a circle, a synthesis of universal geometry based on the human body. In this way, the Mayan philosopher attains oneness with God, Hunab K'u, knowing that God is energy and energy is God. For this reason, the Giver of Movement is also the Giver of Measure, because in reality there can be no movement that does not have measure.

As an example of this, we say life is movement and death is measure. Thus, existence is called *canil curtal*, the serpent of life, implying that death is an act of transition into the other life: evolution or involution in accordance with one's conduct in the physical dimension. This is quite distinct from the total finality which death signifies for the Western European. The Maya also reached the conclusion that "death is a great dream from which one always awakens." In our earthly existence, do we not "disconnect" each night and "reconnect" the next day? This is comparable to dying in the night to be born again the next day.

In the language of the Itzaes Maya, there are words like *tulacal*, meaning "all." Why is this so? Let us observe the words *teol*, *ten*, and *teus*, to see what the Maya are joining. *Teol* means "God"; *ten* means "I" (personal pronoun, first person singular); and *teus* means *te*, "the tree," and *us*, "to blow." It has been established that the Maya represented the air, wind, and oxygen with the symbol "T" in hieroglyphic writings. Therefore, the relationship of which we write here is the symbiotic one between nature, humans, and God. Science has proven that trees help to purify the air. Can it be said then that plants help humans to breath pure air?

The symbol "T" appears with great frequency in architectural work, codices, etchings, ceramics, sculpture, stelae, monoliths, and murals. Why is this so? Because of the transcendental importance which the Maya attributed to the "T" and its significance as the root for first, second, and third-person pronouns which symbolize the integration of the human and the divine by means of the *te*—"tree." The *teol*, too, is transcendental, with the tree and the bird, symbol of *ol*, "spirit," emerging from the *tuch*, the navel of the human being incised on Pacal's Stone. The human lies below the tree; from this we get *wuinic*, "being." This word is made up of *wui*, "tuber," and *nic*, "cosmos," an ingenious Mayan concept about how the tuber evolves from the root of the plant that produces it. The human being, according to ancient Mayan philosophy, is a tuber of the cosmic root, of *teol*, the cosmic consciousness, the intelligent energy, God. The human is also a mass of energy, *wuin-clil*, and by deduction the Mayan philosopher concludes that the human is nothing less than a faithful reflection of cosmic energy.

The history of our pre-conquest ancestors has been judged and criticized primarily from the perspective and criteria of the Conquistadors. For this reason, the true history of the original inhabitants, especially the

Nahua and Maya, has not been written in a positive or elective manner based on truth.

In addition, the historian-friars, committed to Christianizing us, dedicated themselves to recording and "improving" the Mayan language. It is no wonder that their manuals, treatises, and dictionaries of the Mayan language are full of errors and falsehoods to the point that, instead of aiding in teaching the language, they make it more obscure. We must correct these errors in order that they are not perpetuated. Even more appalling are the works of contemporary writers like Erich von Daniken, who further distort our indigenous history. After the conquest, it was the friars and priests of the church; now it is the likes of Mr. von Daniken who come to tell us that "Pacal's Stone" is extraterrestrial. Fortunately, we Maya know well the true origin and meaning of "Pacal's Stone."

In the study of spoken Mayan, the original phonetic values are prevalent, but the influence of Spanish is pernicious. It creates many obstacles for the dedicated investigator in determining what certain Mayan words, poorly transposed in the Spanish alphabet, signify. Also, in many cases the early Mayan writers withheld or disguised much of their knowledge because of persecution by the Conquistadors.

On the phonetic plane, however, there is little need for dispute, as the original pronunciation of ancient Mayan words is still applicable. An example is the simple "T" and "T' " (with the use of an apostrophe). The latter is articulated in linguistic-palate pronunciation by opening the teeth and lips slightly, placing the tip of the tongue upon the palate in back of the two front teeth and rapidly expelling air. Some words spoken by using this palatal tongue placement are *than* or *t'an* meaning "to speak"; *t'el* meaning "crest"; *t'in* meaning "to tighten"; etc. The pronunciation of the *te* with the apostrophe is explosive. Without the apostrophe, it is pronounced the same way as the Spanish T. Notice the difference in meaning in the following example: *tan* means "opposite" or "in front of," while *t'an* means "to speak." We also have the instance where the "T" supplants the "C"; in the possessive one would say *t'otoch*, meaning "in our house," instead of *c'otoch*, which means simply "our house." For emphasis, the "T" is used with implied prepositions indicating place, as in *tela*, meaning "here," and *telo*, "there."

Many circumstances serve to demonstrate the antiquity of the Mayan tongue. In the case of the use of "T," we find countries outside the continent using it along with its attributed symbolism. An example of this is the Mayan word *teol*, which is also the root of the Spanish word meaning "science of God," *teo*logia (theology). In Mayan we find that the translation of those words contains the same basic concept as in Latin or Greek; this was true with the "G," as well as the "T," especially in the sciences and arts where they are still found. This symbolically relates to the conjugation of *tulacal*, "the all"; the integration of God, nature, and human beings. These concepts were never isolated by the Mayan sages with their knowledge and understanding derived from *panche be*, the search for the root of the truth; once a concept is codified axiomatically it becomes and continues to be a truth.

The cross, symbolized by the "T," and upon which the Christian Roman apostles preached that the savior was crucified, is also conceptually associated with the Mayan language. Jesus Christ taught generosity, affection, and love of one's neighbor. When asked, "How do I love God?," Jesus responded, "Love me and you will love God." The questioner asked why this was so, and Christ replied, "By loving your neighbor, you also love God." This parallels the ancient Mayan phrase and teaching, *in lak'ech*, meaning "You are me and I am you." The Maya also conceived that God was in us and we are in God.

The Bible maintains that God created us in the divine image and likeness. This is analogous to the idea that God is energy, and that we are a reflection of that intelligent cosmic energy, that cosmic consciousness. The Mayan sage codifies this by naming the body *wuinclil*, from *wuinic*, "to be," and *lil*, "vibration." This logical and rational concept clarifies the matter of God's image and likeness. This is the clearly and simply defined truth of Mayan philosophy.

Philosophy is science. For the Maya, this is so because the root of truth is sought in reality, in the process of *panche be*. Mayan culture serves as the foundation for human efforts to discover causes and principles, as well as effects and consequences, in a detailed and meticulous analysis of all that exists. The Mayan sages, focusing first on their own origins, reached the scientific understanding that everything is born of energy, which gives life as well as form. The form is the body: elements, cells, and molecules combined by natural biochemistry with carbon and calcium to constitute matter (in which energy vibrates). This matter is infused with the quality of *anima*, and consequently becomes the rational and irrational animal. It is surprising that science has only recently clarified this process. As a result, we have confirmation that vegetable life-forms possess sensibilities similar to those of humans. The only thing left is for trees to walk and talk. But otherwise they can be considered animal because they possess energy so efficacious that our ancestors used that energy to communicate over short and long distances.

If we analyze the word *tele* in Mayan, we find some interesting correspondence with Greek. The Mayan word *tele*, formed by *te*, "tree," and *le*, "tree leaf," symbolized "the word which travels like a leaf," and means the same in Mayan as it does in Greek: distant, distance, far, remote. An extension of this apparent coincidence can be found in the German word *telefunken*. (We need to bear in mind that old Spanish used the "F" in place of the "H" currently used. Thus, ancient Spanish would spell the word for "child," *fijo*, instead of the current spelling, *hijo*.) We can now proceed to analyze this word: *te*, "tree"; *le*, "tree leaf"; *fun*, "sound" (the Mayan word *hum* was *fum* and it means the same thing—"sound," "noise"); and *ken*, "I am" or "it is I" (the Maya use *cen*). Thus, the extraordinary result is that the German word transposed into Mayan means "I am the one who speaks from a distance."

These phonetic circumstances suggest the existence of one language, thousands of years ago, which fell into linguistic confusion with the separation of the continents. Subsequently, human nuclei inhabiting different regions and continents eventually developed numerous linguistic variations. Examples can be found in the many dialects of Western Europe, and in various forms of Spanish spoken throughout the world. For reasons detailed in the *Astronomical Calendars of the Maya and Hunab K'u*, Issa del Campo, in her book, *Our Race Confronts Its Ancestors* (Mexico: Orion, 1965) states that "Castillian is not an adequate linguistic vehicle for understanding the subtleties of the esoteric Zuyua Mayan because it lacks the precise words necessary for that objective and it has never acquired the complex symbolic connotations which after ten millennia characterize the Mayan language." The Spanish language simply lacks the resources for such a task.

The singular fact that the Asian and European languages reveal Mayan roots is undeniable proof that the language of the Itzaes and Chanes Maya dates from antiquity. What greater proof can one ask for than the palpable linguistic evidence which is compounded from moment to moment? And the "T" is a transcendental corroboration, both for its phonetic as well as its intimate and truly universal graphic relation ship in the religious and mystical fields. In this case, no people have revealed spiritual and human values like the Maya, nor have they demonstrated how humanity and nature are linked. And this is done not in a fanciful way, but in response to the cosmobiological laws to which we, like it or not, are subject. Circumstances which modern science now confirms have been known by the Maya for thousands upon thousands of years.

When our Mayan ancestors defined this link between the human and the tree, it was not based on simple speculation, but from a root of the truth. For, if animals are vibrant with energy, so, too, are plants. If animals subsist on vegetal elements and if plants serve to cure our physical and psychic maladies, they are certainly our protectors. In fact, they are veritable companions and valiant protectors! Because through the sacred Hunab K'u, the Only Giver of Movement and Measure, plants help the human being defend life, its very existence. Moreover, in moments of anxiety or desperation, the human can turn to the tree for help and, being a relative, it will provide help.

In this way, the Maya recognized the sensory and extrasensory faculties of the tree, now similarly recognized by modern science. A result: the Mayan use of *te* in the formation of pronouns showing the bond between human and vegetable matter. In this ingenious and admirable way, the Maya symbolize *teol*, the sacred, by way of the tree.

In this form, the Maya declared this human condition to be a manifestation of energy and the tree to be a symbol of the supreme architect. There is no religion which does not use this symbol in conjunction with the cosmobiological laws to which we are subject. Whenever we use these symbols in our rituals and ceremonies, we are reuniting ourselves with our true origins and Hunab K'u. Our ancestors recognized this communion and illustrated their understanding symbolically with the circle superimposed on the square, the synthesis of universal geometry, as well as with the sound and symbol of the sacred "T." Thus our Mayan grandparents felt in union with the laws of nature, mathematics, and God.

Figure 19 shows a detail of Stela 26 found in Yaxchilan, Chiapas, Mexico. In the upper portion, we can see the sacred "T." Unlike any other

"T," this one is adorned with nine hieroglyphs. We will not enter into a discussion here of the meaning of each of these glyphs, but we will indicate that the number nine in Mayan means "to stop, to limit." It appears that with this symbol the ancestors are saying that the tree is the boundary of some type of teaching. This is confirmed by the appearance of the *balam* (jaguar head) carried by the woman facing the priest. In Mayan culture, the *balam* signifies observation. We can then infer that the teaching of the tree forms a kind of limit.

Continuing our observation of this stela, we see the sacred "T" projected directly over the priest's forehead. Scalloped marks on either side of this projection give a total of five. In Mayan, the number five means "to go out of, to leave." The woman bears the symbol of the sacred "T" in her hair, and from it emanates the *ol*, the spirit of the tree.

The Maya associate the symbol "T" with the mystical number nine, which reinforces the traditional teaching: "With the death of the last tree, comes death to the last human." Further analysis of the tablet of the cross of Palenque verifies this relationship between the "T" and the number nine. As we noted, the crypt discovered in the Temple of the Inscriptions measures nine meters long by four meters wide, and the chamber walls bear stucco reliefs depicting nine priests. These nine persons represent the *bolonti k'u*, the roots of Hunab K'u, the Only Giver of Movement and Measure. This symbology can be paraphrased as "the place which marks the sacred cycles of human beings in union with the tree." There is additional confirmation in the jade mask of the illustrious personage interred in that temple. In its mouth, we can see once again the symbol "T" of the Sacred Tree.

To conclude our study of this symbol which the Maya have conceptualized as a part of their cosmology, we offer one additional piece of data. Figure 20 depicts part of a wall found in the excavation of the Templo Mayor in Tenochtitlan, now the center of Mexico City. Clearly, the people of this great center knew of the meaning and value of the "T" as a symbol for the Sacred Tree. Unfortunately, the official archeologist, Eduardo Matos Moctezuma, offers no profound explanation of the symbol on the excavated stone. He calls it merely a glyph containing the sign "3 calli" (three house) whose calendrical equivalent is 1469 A.D., and says that it was from the wall of a stage IVb platform.

FIGURE 19.

FIGURE 19.

A detail of Stela 26 at Yachilan, Chiapas, Mexico. An arrow indicates the symbol of the sacred "T" at the top of this photo. Unlike other "T"s, this one has a series of glyphs; to be exact, nine blocks of glyphs. We will not attempt here to decipher these glyphs, but it should be remembered that the number nine for the Maya signifies "to detain" or "a limit."

FIGURE 20.

The inhabitants of the great Tenochtitlan, long before the arrival of the Aztecs, or Mexicas, venerated the "T" as a symbol of the tree. It is known that this stone was discovered by Eduardo Matos Moctezuma in the Main Temple near the Zócalo or Constitutional Plaza of Mexico City. Unfortunately, the archeologist does not enlighten us about the sacred "T" symbol and its relationship with the tree.

FIGURE 20.

The destiny of this city is ordained, and all of the colonial structures, houses, and churches in the center of Mexico City will succumb to the design of time impelled by the autochthonous symbols deposited at this sacred site by our Indian grandparents. This will fulfill the mandates of Hunab K'u and Intloque Nahuake, ending centuries of nightmare with the resurgence of Teol, Huitzilopochtli, Chac Mool, Tlaloc, Nictlan-tecuhtli, Coyolxauhqui, etc.

As we all know, the time has arrived. For this reason, the sacred symbols of the true Mexican people are complying with their destiny. From this time forward, we will live as one with our roots in science and religion.

CHAPTER THREE

Ol Consciousness: The Use & Sound of "O" Is of Mayan Origin

 The Tree is a religious symbol for many peoples of the world, but the most profound and esoteric explanation of its significance is found in the culture of our earliest ancestors: the Maya, Nahua, Inca, and Aymaras.

As we saw in Chapter 2, the "T" is a universal symbol of the Sacred Tree relative. Many ancient people used it in religious iconography, and even today it remains a sacred symbol. Let us turn now to the testimony of the priests of antiquity like Berossus, the Chaldean, who told how the Maya arrived at his homeland. According to this great priest/historian, the Maya descended in the form of fish, bringing their culture. Manetho, the famous Egyptian priest, mathematician, and historian, maintained that the Maya lived in Atlantis for 13,900 years. We could name many other great historians, priests, and philosophers of antiquity who methodically described the Mayan role in bringing culture to the world.

I think it is important to note that Euclid, the Greek philosopher, played a part in the influence of the Maya in Greek culture. In the year 403 B.C., this philosopher helped reform the language then in use by introducing Mayan elements. The Greeks took this knowledge from the ancient culture of the Cara Maya.

For this reason, the "G," "T," and "O" became common to many ancient tongues. The "T" in Greek and other languages was considered sacred. In this way the people of Europe, Asia and Africa were influenced by native American culture. Fortunately, some of us who truly know the Mayan language can comprehend the basics of the languages spoken on those continents.

Moreover, those of us who truly understand Mayan could teach philosophy, mathematics, religion, science, etc. to the enthusiasts of Greek philosophy. We could also teach the roots of true religion, drawing from the glorious wealth of knowledge to be found within our 21,000 ceremonial centers called pyramids. Additionally, we can further benefit humanity by reimparting knowledge to the Europeans who have misused or neglected the teachings, the sacred knowledge, of our Grandparents. These ancestors were known by various names depending on where and when they visited. In Africa they were called Mayax. In Hindustan, they were called Naga Maya; others, like the Greeks, called them Cara Maya.

In this chapter, we will discuss the symbol *ol* in its ideological, iconographic, and visual aspects as represented by the Maya. These two letters were used separately as "O" and "L." The first was used as a symbol of "awakened consciousness," and the second represented "vibration." Together these two symbols meant "awakened consciousness in the form of vibration." We will analyze both forms and see how the Nahua and Maya, as well as all indigenous people, used the graphic form of *ol* on pyramids, stelae, codices, etc.

In the first illustration (Figure 21), we see the clay effigy of a priest from Jaina Island, Campeche, Mexico, now in the Museum of Anthropology in Mexico City. This is Halach Ol, the grand lord who knows the cosmic awakened consciousness, whose name is derived from *halach*, "great lord," and *ol*, "awakened consciousness." Upon his head rests a great bird symbolic of the spirit, implying that the spirit, *k'inan*, must reside in the conscious mind in order to attain *ol*, "awakened consciousness."

For this reason, when a Maya says *teol*, or a Nahua says *teotl*, each is speaking of the Sacred Tree and the consciousness that unites cosmic laws and transforms the essence of the "G" for the benefit of humankind. As we all know, we depend on *teol* for all aspects of Life, including the air we breathe. Clearly, this epitomizes Maya/Nahua thinking and reveals the path followed in the formulation of the philosophy which became science/religion. The sacred values of other peoples can likewise be seen in the linked symbols of the "G" and "O," as in the aforementioned Hebrew word *Geova* (Jehovah). To reiterate, the Maya have much to teach regarding the use of these symbols in their multiple aspects.

The Greeks, unfortunately, can teach us little about the religious sense of *geo* since they related it mostly to the Earth and terrestrial laws. As we saw in Chapter 1, the Maya also relate the "G" to the Milky Way, both in its tangible physical form and in essence. The Maya not only related *geo* to measurement, but they knew that this combination of "G" and "O" formed the essence upon which we all depend, like it or not. For this reason the "G" is sacred to initiates. Future initiates can attain lasting knowledge of the three sacred symbols by reviewing Chapter 1 on the "G," Chapter 2 on the sacred "T," and Chapter 3 on awareness of awakened consciousness of the "O."

Figure 22 depicts a Mixtec clay figurine. As you can see, dear reader, the subject's neck is marked with the Mayan "O." We will attempt to substantiate our explanation of this symbol with scientific data.

Photographic documentation has shown that when a person dies, subtle energy, like smoke from a cigarette, rises from the breast. It is after this discharge process that the person is considered dead. It has been proven that when this happens the deceased loses 20 grams of weight. Ancient people such as the Maya knew this and much more. Priests like those in Figures 21 and 23 knew of the "O" and its relationship with sublimated spirit. The circular symbol "O" on the Mixtec figurine indicates the place through which the "G" essence will leave. It is our human obligation to know and understand this essence in order to transform it into consciousness. That is, we need to become conscious of the universe which governs us.

Our investigations have shown us how the Mayan philosophical concept of life and death is distinct from the European perspective. Looking further, we can similarly analyze the conjunction of the symbolic "T" of the Sacred Tree, and the "O" of the spirit, as codified in *teol*, "the essence of the conscious tree." This signifies that you, dear reader, and I, reason with a measure of consciousness because our tree relative gives us its fruit with the already digested essence which is consciousness. Thus we receive not only material nourishment, but the divine breath in the form of spirit which we first inhale upon arriving on the planet Earth. The tree's fluids, which slow the Earth's rotation each spring, as expostulated in Chapter 2, are referred to in Mayan as *k'ik*, or "the blood of the tree." The Mayan word for human blood is the same, further codifying the concept of tree and human as a single entity.

Using this reasoning, the contention by Erich von Daniken that the occupant of the famous tomb of Palenque was "an astronaut" is repudiated (see Figure 18). Obviously, this writer has not studied this major cer-

FIGURE 21.

This clay statue was found on the island of Jaina, Campeche, Mexico. Currently, it can be viewed at the National Museum of Anthropology, Mexico. In Mayan, this figure is named Halach Ol, meaning "the Grand Lord who understands awakened consciousness." For greater insight, observe the headpiece of this Mayan priest, where you can see a bird symbolizing the spirit. Adorning his attire are various circles symbolizing the *ol*— consciousness of the Maya.

FIGURE 22.

Clay figure from the culture of the Mixtecs, exhibited at the National Museum of Anthropology in Mexico. Undoubtedly, the ancient peoples of Mesoamerica knew the laws of consciousness. In this Mixtec figure, we can see the symbol of *ol*, here enlarged for better recognition. This form of "O" symbolizes consciousness. It is located in the place where the energy of spirit-consciousness is centered.

FIGURE 23.

This Mayan priest (A) is a knower of consciousness, as can be confirmed by the headpiece he wears. In addition, the hieroglyph representing the planet Venus is shown in this piece. We can also see Chac, deity of rain, in the form of "O"s on his headpiece. On top of the frontal area is the symbol for "heaven." We also see a series of symbols which refer to the cosmic laws, where the beginnings of consciousness can be sought in order to understand our existence on Earth. This piece is originally from Tikal, Guatemala, Central America.

In section (B), we see a Mexican-Greek fret in the configuration of a series of "O"s.

FIGURE 21.

FIGURE 22.

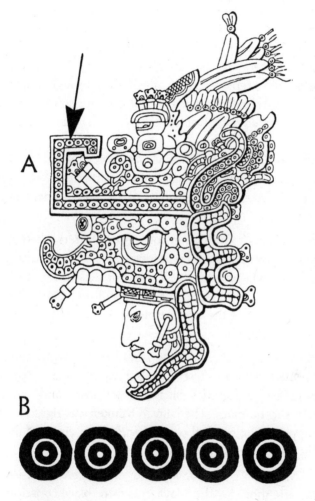

A

B

FIGURE 23.

emonial center in depth, resulting in fallacious deductions. On the side of the inappropriately named sarcophagus are sculpted ten priests emerging from the Earth together with the sacred plant which they venerated in every respect. Palenque is a sacred site. Here the ancestors exalted the "T" symbol, as indicated by Figure 13. This respect and knowledge is still alive among the Mexican people, but modern consumer society has distracted us from our true cultural essence. The greatest disgrace was when a religion arrived with us which related the Sacred Tree of our Maya/Nahua ancestors to the serpent of evil. By association, the Tree was converted into a representation of evil. But, through renewed love of *teol* or *teotl*, we can vindicate our true culture, our science/religion, and return to the proper path walked by our indigenous American progenitors.

We will now explain a series of Mayan words related to *ol* consciousness so that you, dear reader, may see the difference between the so-called European/Spanish culture and the father and mother culture of the Greeks and Latins.

Ol—"Consciousness": The Mayan concept of *ol* refers inherently to conscious recall or awareness of consciousness. "To recall the past is to awaken" is a key Mayan saying. *Ol* consciousness offers an interesting approach to the understanding of Mayan culture. Only through consciousness can we attain the sacred state of sensing within ourselves the divine laws of Hunab K'u.

Cimaac ol—"Happiness": The very sound of the word announces its concept. Formed from *ci*—"tasty" or "agreeable"; *maac*—"person"; and *ol*—consciousness; it signifies pleasant, delicious, and "good being" (when it refers to humans). The Mayan thinker was right to imply that only the happy person can feel content with the divinity of the universe and thereby comprehend Hunab K'u.

Dzah ol—"Attention": From *dzah*—"fix" or "place" and *ol*—consciousness. To pay attention, for the Maya, means to place consciousness in a state of total alertness. When we deal with important matters, it is essential to direct all consciousness to what one is observing, hearing, and feeling, using all eight of our senses. The conscious state or condition should be on ready alert to achieve sublimation before Hunab K'u.

H'uayak' ol—"Dreamer": The aspirant "H'" preceding the qualifier gives masculine gender to *uayak*—"to dream," and *ol*—"consciousness." This expression applies to the person who lives life in a dream, or with illusions. Those who abide with their illusions are not centered in their consciousness. They are outside the divine reality of Hunab K'u.

Chak'ab ol—"Free will": It is important to observe how the Mayan thinker defines the concept of freedom of volition in accordance with the governing laws. Free will in Mayan comes from *cha*—"let go"; and *k'ab*—"hand"; in combination with *ol*. This implies that free will simultaneously holds on and lets go. But free will can only be complete in conjunction with universal consciousness, and in this sense is converted to the consciousness of Hunab K'u.

Tem olal—"Satisfaction": From *tem*—"to pacify," "to make content" (*tem* also signifies "temple"); *ol*—"consciousness"; and *al*—"child." Thus, satisfaction for the Maya means to relieve, to leave the consciousness content. Is this not an apparent truth? Satisfaction results from freeing the consciousness from nervous tension. This lesson shows that to find satisfaction, one must know how to utilize consciousness as a child of Hunab K'u.

Nac olal—"Sensibility": From *nac*—"to run into"; *ol*—"consciousness"; and *al*—"child." This expresses the faculty of perceiving an impression of material and immaterial things that affect us for good or bad. The Maya correctly evaluated this state of psychosomatic sensibility, equating it with an abrupt encounter or impact on the most profound part of the being. As we know, to truly influence another person, whether for good or evil purposes, we seek to affect the innermost recesses of the person and in so doing we affect the consciousness of the child of Hunab K'u.

Yah olal—"Melancholy": From *yah*—"pain"; *ol*—"consciousness"; and *al*—"child." An emotional state. Melancholy is a state of disgust, an affliction provoked by emotional causes that influences the consciousness of a person. A sense of great disappointment leads to an involuted demeanor. The sufferer refuses to face contrary situations, which leads to increasing emotional pain and a belief that everybody is against him or her. Melancholy is not centered in consciousness. Deception and resentment are companions of melancholy. A single incident creates the internal affliction which can damage consciousness. The state of melancholy precludes the perception of the sacred aspects of Hunab K'u.

Dzamal olal—"Despair": From *dzamal*—"to crumble" or "gradually decay"; *ol*—"consciousness"; and *al*—"child." This condition, for the Mayan thinker, is analogous to a collapsing building. With the crumbling of consciousness comes the collapse of the temple (the human body) given to us by Hunab K'u for the living celebration of the sacred.

Ziiz olal—"Serenity": From *ziiz*—"cold"; *ol*—"consciousness"; and *al*—"child." This word implies that the serene being remains cold or cool. Serenity displays a consciousness that does not flare up when provoked by people or things. In the face of difficulty, the serene person's sentiments remain cool and detached. Serenity is an ideal, but within the context of the consciousness of Hunab K'u.

K'az olal—"Antipathy": From *k'az*—"ugly" or "disagreeable"; *ol*—"consciousness"; and *al*—"child." At times, the mere presence or the attitude of someone causes a sense of disgust or antipathy. But a little reason tells us that such conscious negativity parts us from the divine laws and creates an ugly consciousness. This result is alien to the beauty of Hunab K'u.

Tup olal—"To Discourage": From *tup*—"turn off"; *ol*—"consciousness"; and *al*—"child." The Mayan concept of discouraging or disheartening is like putting out the fire of consciousness that ignites our "spirit," or *k'inan*. A dampened consciousness no longer believes in the divine laws that govern us. This spiritless state presents an extinguished consciousness before Hunab K'u.

Lep' olal—"Anger": From *lep*—"violent"; *ol*—"consciousness"; and *al*—"child." In the manner of the Mayan philosopher, we need to see the way anger and violence are associated with consciousness. Anger and violence are bad counselors that lead us to forget consciousness. Intimately related, anger and violence can cause us to harm fellow human beings and thereby damage the sacred attributes of Hunab K'u.

Pedz olal—"Dominion": From *pedz*—"to grasp" or "subject"; *ol*—"consciousness"; and *al*—"child." In effect, the action of dominating a person or thing connotes subjecting its consciousness. This explains the use of *pedz*, which implies pressing one thing beneath another. In this instance the pressure may come from our own consciousness. Of similar derivation, the word *pedzan* means usurp, appropriate, take for one's own, with either good or bad intentions. The Mayan phrase *pedzan ol tech* can be translated as "take your being unto yourself." This implies that you must make your own being a part of your consciousness in order to deliver yourself to Hunab K'u.

Nib olal—"Devotion": There can be little doubt that the Mayan thinker firmly believed in religious fervor. This philosopher arrived at the conclusion that it must come from the heart and the will of the believer. Thus he or she combined *nib*—"to recommend," "to make a commitment"; with *ol*—"consciousness"; and *al*—"child." When human beings commit their consciousness to the sacred Hunab K'u, they are practicing religion.

K'ub olal—"To Deliver": This word might better be translated as "to devote oneself." From *k'ub*—"to deliver"; *ol*—"consciousness"; and *al*—"child." To deliver oneself to consciousness as a child. For the Mayan philosopher, devotion to consciousness creates consciousness, and by extension this form of thought process creates great culture. These ways led to delivery of self to consciousness and the encounter with Hunab K'u.

Yahal olal—"Repentance," "Awaking of Consciousness": From *yahal*—"to awaken"; *ol*—"consciousness"; and *al*—"child." To repent is to wake up or to awaken in the consciousness the act of repentance. The Maya equated this action with emergence from a dream state to return as a child of the sacred to the world of Hunab K'u.

K'ex olal—"Discord": From *k'ex*—"change" or "to change"; *ol*—"consciousness"; and *al*—"child." Discord for the Maya is changed consciousness, which translates into opposition, divisiveness, and war. What yesterday was love becomes hate and disgust today. The Mayan thinker explains that consciousness suffers change in an unperceived way which affects the child of Hunab K'u.

Ik'ilik' olal—"Restlessness": This is the Mayan expression for want of tranquility, uneasiness, turbulence, anguish, and anxiety. It evokes the image of a leaf borne on a violent burst of wind, flipped from side to side. From *ik'ilik'*—"agitated winds"; *ol*—"consciousness"; and *al*—"child." Thus we get "agitated consciousness"—like a windblown leaf.

At this point we have reviewed a series of examples of the use of *ol* in the Mayan language, but the lessons of *ol* do not end here. This representation of the spirit is to be used in its three geometric dimensions. You will see how the Maya perceived that every human being is within *ol* as both the essence and the consciousness of the universe. And each human being has the capacity to use the *ol* after the necessary development.

To achieve this development, it is important to understand that the *ol* can be used in linear, square, and cubic measures, i.e. in the three geometric forms. Figure 24 shows three representations of the "O" used by Nahua sages. In Figure 24-1, we see a Nahua stylization of *ol* as a flower. In its center is the "O" form, while the outer part can be viewed as petals. According to Nahua and Mayan traditions, this image also represents the Sun and its rays. From the Sun comes the essence of our consciousness. When we speak of the flower, we are also speaking of the Sun. This graphically illustrates the intimate relationship of that which is above with that which is below.

Another way to analyze the *ol* depicted in the flower image is through the study of the Mayan language. To say flower, we use the word *lol*. The etymological roots of this word are:

L = vibration ("L" is a contraction of *lil*, "vibration")
O = consciousness
L = vibration

This phonetic combination will always be associated with cosmic consciousness.

The study of Suyua Mayan provides more insight into the symbology of the flower. The Maya also associate *lol* with the Day of the Dead and the dimension in which the dead exist, for they have reverted back to essence of consciousness. *Lol* confirms that consciousness—yours, mine, and that of the universe—consists of vibrations in this third dimension where we mortals reside. But *lol* also exists beyond this dimension on the plane which the Maya share with the departed.

As an indication of what the ancient Maya did in this other dimension, I quote from anthropologist Alberto Ruz Lhuillier's work, *El Templo de Las Inscripciones*, (*The Temple of the Inscriptions*)—Palenque, Chiapas, Mexico (the magic conduit):

There is no reference to any Mayan site other than Palenque, where a tomb has been discovered equipped with a conduit that in some magical form established communications between the crypt and the temple as in the Pyramid of the Inscriptions.

As we can deduce from this citation, our Mayan ancestors achieved an awareness through *lol* that makes European growth in such knowledge seem infantile.

The Mayan *ol* was used to represent the microcosm of the atom and the macrocosm of both the world and the infinite. Let us embrace the teachings of our Mayan sages, dear readers, and consciously make *ol* part of our consciousness.

In frescoes unearthed at Teotihuacan, near Mexico City, we find the image of a hand that is considered symbolic of the hand of Hunab K'u, the sacred or God (Figure 25-1). In this illustration, we see the "O" at the bottom in proximity to God's hand. Also, the "G" and "T" symbols, previously studied in this book, are shown in union with the "O."

Figures 25-2 and 25-3 also depict forms of *ol*. The centers of the "O" symbols in Figure 25-3 contain the figure known as the Cross of Quetzal-coatl, which again links the concept of the tree and the spirit with *ol*, or consciousness in the totality of *teol/teotl*.

We have considered three sacred symbols of the Maya which were known and used throughout this continent. In ancient times, these symbols were taken to the people of Asia, Africa, and Europe. With the passage of time, these symbols returned to us with the Spanish conquest, but most of them carried a distortion of their sacred content, as in the case of the "cross of Jesus," a symbol of the suffering of humankind. Our Mayan people cried like children when, during colonial times, the friars exhibited the cross bearing a crucified and bloody Christ. Clearly, they could not understand why anyone would be subjected to such torture. The Spaniards in turn could not understand what was disturbing the Maya. Here we have a classic example of the misuse of symbols—in this case, the cross.

The European use of the cross is both good and bad—a great difference from the Mayan concept of its unique goodness. An analysis of other symbols "brought" to us by Western European cultures reveals that these symbols lack profound significance and are far removed from the cosmic laws of Hunab K'u.

This book, *Secrets of Mayan Science/Religion*, should be read and used in the way the great Mayan priests used their codices, because herein are revealed some of the mysteries which our initiatic culture developed to benefit humanity. It was inspired by all that is sacred to the Maya, by that sacred god, the Only Giver of Movement and Measure—adored by the name of Hunab K'u from the earliest of Mayan times, many millennia ago, when we lived in harmony on this continent.

The Mayan priests urge us to again practice our science/religion by mandate of the Great Spirit. Thus we should take and use this divine book as the Mayan priests used the codices which contained the history of the laws of the universe.

To illustrate an aspect of the life of a Mayan priest, the sacred way of reading codices and the ritualistic form of public prophecy, we cite *Codices Mayas (Mayan Codices)* by J. Antonio Villacorta C. and Carlos Antonio Villacorta:

> The Mayan priests took special care of these books. They were the principal objects taken on pilgrimages and on the final journey to the grave, where they were buried with the priests. These codices were unfolded before the public only during the most solemn ceremonies and when divination was necessary.
>
> In the month of Uo, which begins on August 5th, a religious ceremony was celebrated in which the books played the principal role. "They brought out the books," says Landa, "and spread them in a freshly prepared place. . . meanwhile they would dissolve a bit of verdigris (copper sulfate) from the books in a vessel of virgin water from the mountains where no women go. The priests smeared the wooden covers of the books with this preparation. Then, the most erudite of all priests opened a book and read the prophesies for the coming year, and proclaimed them to all those present."

This gives you an idea, dear reader, of the ritual involved with reading the codices.

Now let us look at Figure 26 from the Dresden Codex, which features the sacred symbols "O" (1), "T" (2), and "G" (3). Once you have looked at the whole Mayan codex and learned the lessons of this book, you will be prepared to fully understand the initiatic path dramatized in

FIGURE 24.

FIGURE 24.

This figure (24-1) of a seal of the Nahuatl-speaking people shows their knowledge of the use of *ol* consciousness. The seal also represents universal consciousness.

Figure 24-2 depicts an Aztec incense urn incised with the symbol "O." It served in rituals for imploring the great spirits to awaken the consciousness of the worshippers.

Figure 24-3 is from an Aztec seal found in Tlatelolco, Mexico, D.F. In it we see four forms of the symbolic "O." Perhaps the creators of this piece are referring to the four elements.

FIGURE 25.

Figure 25-1 shows an interpretation of the "Hand of God," from Teotihuacan, Mexico. This fresco incorporates various symbols, but the most important is the symbol of *ol* consciousness.

Figure 25-2 again shows us the *ol* consciousness in the form of a flower as a decorative geometric design. This seal was found in "El Contador Mexico."

Figure 25-3 shows a seal with crosses similar to the "Cross of Quetzalcoatl." We know that the cross and the "O" of consciousness have been linked since the beginning of civilization.

FIGURE 26.

This illustration from the Dresden Codex features the three sacred symbols: "O" (1), "T" (2), and "G" (3), key elements of science/religion. We hope that these sacred teachings will be used only for good purposes. As you have seen, these symbols were used by the indigenous people of Hanahuac, Tamuachan, Ixachitlan, and Tawantinsuyo, and especially by the Mayan people.

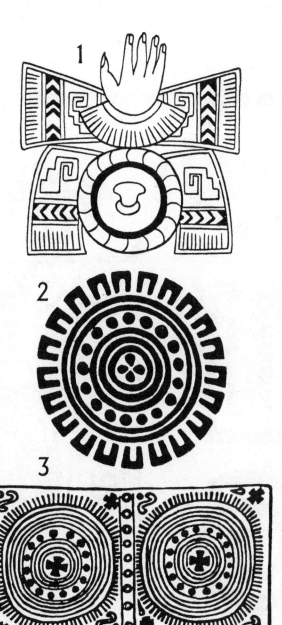

FIGURE 25.

FIGURE 26.

this illustration. But don't forget to make the lessons learned so far a part of your life, because the consciously assimilated knowledge of science/religion will help you understand the remaining content of this sacred book. All of this knowledge, we must also remember, is a gift from Hunab K'u to help you as well as others in the salvation of spirit and soul in this time of greatest need—a moment of danger in our third dimension and the other dimensions in which we consciously or sub-consciously abide.

Looking again at Figure 26-3, we find the Mayan "G" symbol studied in Chapter 1. Here this symbol is confined within the "T." Seated above the two symbols is a representation of Hunab K'u. In his hand we see the "O" symbol, in this case delineated by dots. When a glyph is depicted in this way it means that the object is functioning or that it is activated and ready for use. In this illustration, the Mayan priest is demonstrating that the *ol* of consciousness is functioning together with the "T," Sacred Tree, and the "G" essence of the universe. One of the lessons of the Dresden Codex, codified in this illustration, is that with our own hands we can use *ol* consciousness in direct relationship with "T," our relative the tree, either through the use of the divine breath that we breathe, or through other phenomena, often considered paranormal, which we do not fully understand but that affect us all.

It is also possible that knowledge of the use of the fruits of the tree can transport us to favorable dimensions (as exemplified by Maria Sabina, the famous Mazatec shaman) where we may better use *ol* consciousness in union with the "T." In this way we may achieve the conjugation of "T" and "O" to form the word *teol* (in many places called God) and fully comprehend the symbolic significance. But we will not only share the understanding of the Greeks, but the far deeper comprehension structured by the Maya. Dear reader, I implore Hunab K'u to help you understand what the Maya knew and used so that the sacred symbols may fulfill the purpose for which they were created.

In this same illustration from the Mayan Dresden Codex (Figure 26-2), the "T" contains the figure "G," implying that the tree is an essence of the Milky Way (see Chapter 1), origin of the essential emanation of earthly life. Thus, brothers and sisters, we have seen how the wisdom of the Mayan initiates has been conveyed through the sacred teachings for the benefit of you and me and all of the beings on this planet.

In summary, the "G," essence, within the "T," tree, governs our tree relative, and is available for human use, as is indicated by the priest seated above the two symbols. But we must use these symbols with our consciousness. Thus, empowered with the knowledge of the so-called phenomena of our tree relative, we may travel with our *ol* consciousness to the "G" essence and soar through the universe. We will attain the revelation of *k'uatzal* of the cosmos and we will know the mysteries of the Milky Way. All of this will be done within the consciousness of our essence, aided by the Sacred Tree, just as was done by our Mayan sages and teachers.

CHAPTER FOUR

We Can All Become Quetzalcoatl or Kukulcan

 Much has been said about Quetzalcoatl (the Nahuatl name) or Kukulcan (Mayan). An analysis of Mexican history reveals infinite references to Quetzalcoatl, notably in the surviving Aztec or Nahua chronicles. The Spanish, who learned of this historical/mythological figure upon arriving in Mexico, badly misused this information for their own benefit. We would like to know if these so-called Conquistadors had the least bit of understanding about what they learned.

Self-appointed "official" historians have created the great colonial lie of the "white, bearded, and blue-eyed" Quetzalcoatl—a deception still perpetrated in histories of our beloved Mexican people. The true nature of Quetzalcoatl/Kukulcan remains a mystery that is accessible only through Nahua/Mayan science/religion.

The first thing the Spanish friars did was to order the destruction of the native chronicles. Then they set about writing their "histories." It is no wonder that contemporary historians who use these sources provide little insight. It is safe to say that no deep understanding exists today of Quetzalcoatl and Kukulcan, the cultural symbols of the Nahua and the Maya.

From this moment on, I would like you to realize that we are all Quetzalcoatl or Kukulcan. We need only to develop our faculties of consciousness to fully realize that status. But I emphasize that development of consciousness must be based on profound knowledge of the true indigenous culture in all of its manifestations. Only in this way can we veritably become Quetzalcoatl. No one rooted in Western European culture can hope to become Quetzalcoatl/Kukulcan, simply because Europeans have never achieved the level of spiritual culture attained by the native people of America.

The historical misappropriation of Quetzalcoatl began when conquering Spaniards (in collusion with "official" historians) proposed that a "pale and bearded" figure brought wisdom to the indigenous people. The factual deception is not all: in contemporary times, an individual appropriated the guise of Quetzalcoatl to govern us for a time before returning to his "origins."

In the times of the Nahua and Maya, one attained the status of Quetzalcoatl only through knowledge of religion, mathematics, astronomy, and the other sciences that govern the spirit—knowledge that is inherent in indigenous culture. Now there is a new fraud against our indigenous people: in the midst of the twentieth century, the Western-educated impostor comes to govern with his European system. This way of governing owes nothing to our native culture and flaunts the exalted knowledge represented by Quetzalcoatl or Kukulcan. If such lack of respect for our authentic native culture persists, we will eventually be governed by a supposed father of Quetzalcoatl.

To be Quetzalcoatl or Kukulcan is to know the seven forces that govern our body—not only know them, but also use them and understand their intimate relationship with natural and cosmic laws. We must comprehend the long and short cycles and the solar laws that sustain our lives. We must know how to die, and how to be born. In Mesoamerica, such knowledge exists. In this chapter we will discuss where the teachings of the true nature of Quetzalcoatl/Kukulcan can be found and the event of the appearance, year after year, of the seven isosceles triangles during the March 22 and September 23 equinoxes at Chichen Itza, Yucatan, Mexico.

This event was originated by the Maya and demonstrates knowledge found only in Mexico—an exclusive Mexican knowledge that remains our good fortune. It reveals our profound understanding of mathematics combined with the cosmos—the movement of the Sun and its governing laws. Such knowledge was not attained by the Greeks or other people of the world whose cultures were relatively limited. If the Greeks lacked this fundamental knowledge, it logically follows that their culture could not have given rise to a true Quetzalcoatl.

We know that the Greeks were students of ancient cultures. This is quite evident to the student of Cara Mayan, an obvious source of documentation for Greek culture. Euclid himself affirmed that in 403 B.C. the Greeks incorporated Cara Mayan elements in the restructuring of the still-extant Greek alphabet. But while Cara Mayan words were assimilated, the all-important question remains: did the Greeks comprehend the mysteries and esoterica of these ancient Maya? It would be interesting to hear a response to this question from a scholar of Greek culture. Those of us familiar with the true culture of the Maya of Yucatan know that the Greeks and their European progeny have very little to teach the un-Westernized Indian. On the other hand, with a little knowledge of archaic Mayan we can understand the words mentioned by Euclid that the Greeks adopted from Cara Mayan.

There is currently a lot of talk about new directions in ideological instruction that originates outside of Mexico. It would be a waste of time to embark on a profound analysis of socialism here, but we all know that so-called "scientific socialism" is structurally based on European patterns. Unfortunately, a number of people believe that this "scientific socialism" offers solutions for indigenous America.

I think it is important to mention again the other ancient cultures, like those of India, where we find roots of words similar to peninsular Mayan. Valmiki wrote that the Naga Maya brought their culture to India around 2700 B.C., although we believe it was even earlier. We also maintain that they brought their culture to other parts of Asia and to Africa, where they were called *Mayax* according to Manetho, the Egyptian priest-historian.

There are notable similarities between Indian culture and the cultures of the Maya of Yucatan and other indigenous people of America, especially in esoterica. Figure 27 shows a clay sculpture from western Guerrero state (Marti collection; photo by Luis Quintero). This piece represents a meditating figure seated in the Hindu "lotus" position of yoga. Here is clear evidence, dear reader, that our ancestors practiced this system of meditation in Mexico. Furthermore, the very word *yoga* exists in Mayan. Written *yok' hah*, it combines *yok*, "above" or "on top of," and *hah*, "truth." The sacred book, *Popol Vuh*, mentions the fasts of the Maya while awaiting the rising of the parent Sun. It is probable that the Maya kept this vigil while in the meditative posture shown in Figure 27.

It has been claimed that the Christian Spanish brought to Mexico the practice of kneeling in worship. As is quite evident from Figure 28, the native people, being eminently spiritual, used this posture in adoration of the sacred. This was true for not only Mesoamericans, but all of the original people of America, as shown by Figure 28, which depicts the idol of Tiwanak'u, Bolivia.

The Mayan word *xoltal* means "kneel before the sacred"—that is, before Hunab K'u or some other deity. The Xoltales are religious people who from antiquity have knelt before the sacred—Catholicism had nothing to show them in this respect. The temples of Palenque were begun before the people of Mexico knew Christianity even existed! Figure 28 corresponds to the inappropriately named Tomb of Palenque. It shows a kneeling Mayan priest in meditation. Those of us who have visited this sacred site have observed many figures in meditative poses. We are convinced that forms of worship supposedly introduced by Spanish friars were merely a rehash of the religion which was already practiced here.

Further confirmation is found in Figure 29, where a Mayan priest is shown seated in the lotus position, as the Hindus call it. Observe the placement of the arms and hands. Figures 1, 2, and 3, below, come from the Diquis culture of Costa Rica. Our investigation of such evidence has shown great similarity in forms of worship throughout the so-called continent of America. We could provide examples of this uniformity to the point of exhaustion.

Looking again at the priest in meditation (you can find the original in the principal sanctuary at Chichen Itza) we note that this position is common to the Buddhists except that, in the Mayan position, the hands are placed across the chest, rather than on the knees as in Buddhist meditation. Note that in the place of the navel we find the "T" symbol examined in Chapter 2. Also notice that the priest wears an apron. The Masons use a similar sacred apron in their rituals. Some investigators, Augustus Le Plongeon for one, have suggested that Masonry began with the Mayan culture. The presence of the sacred "T" and the apron in Figure 29 support the contention that the ancient Maya provided the creative genesis of many religions.

Catholic saints are often depicted with an aura around their heads, supposedly implying a state of illumination or enlightenment. Accepting the dogma that only saints can attain this state is a serious error, since this process of enlightenment was well known to Indian people long before

FIGURE 27.

FIGURE 27.

This clay figure is from the culture of western Guerrero State (Marti Collection; photo by Luis Quintero). It can be said that this individual assumes the lotus position of meditation to attain Hunab K'u as a symbol of what is sacred for the native people of America.

FIGURE 28.

A drawing (1) from one of the two stone monoliths that adorn the stairs of Temple XXI at Palenque—from the official guide book. In Mayan, *xoltal* means "kneel before the sacred," before Hunab K'u or another deity. The Xoltales of antiquity were religious people who knelt while praying to the sacred. The second drawing depicts the so-called idol of Tiwanaku, Bolivia, which also reveals the *xoltal* position.

FIGURE 29.

Some researchers such as Augusto Le Plongeon maintain that Masonic rites are derived from Mayan culture—further evidence of the Mayan role in creating religions. Figures 1, 2, and 3 at the bottom of the page are from the Diquis culture of Costa Rica.

FIGURE 30.

Figure 1 is Mayan. Figures 2 and 3 are from Aztec culture. An old man (1), called Huehueteotl, symbolizes fire, and thereby indicates antiquity. Figure 3 represents a personage attired in the typical Arab manner, futher evidence that people from many lands came to Hanahuac seeking culture in early times.

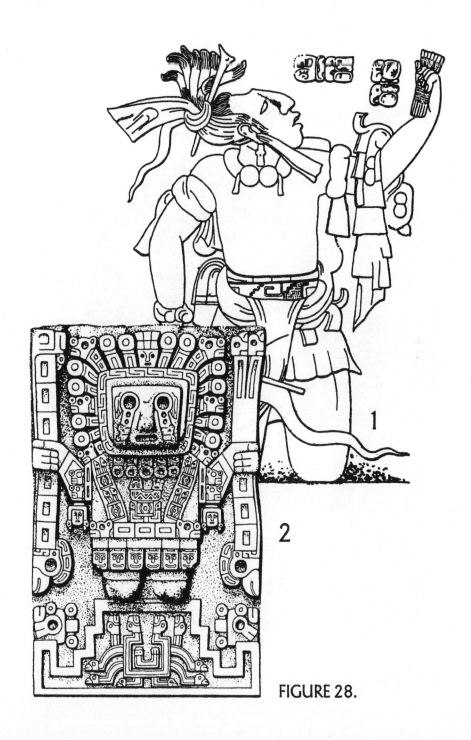

1

2

FIGURE 28.

FIGURE 29.

FIGURE 30.

the arrival of the Spanish. Obviously, this knowledge was not the exclusive property of European saints. The illumination of a Mayan priest is represented in Figure 29 by lines or feathers surrounding the subject's head. It can be inferred that this priest has auric energy throughout the body. However, a clear difference between Catholic saints and Mayan initiates is evident with their use of energy. Knowledge of the planets was obligatory for the Maya while using this energy. The illustration shows the priest seated on a celestial band embellished with planetary symbols. The Maya consciously produced the auric phenomena by using energy—in marked contrast with the Catholic saints, with whom the existence of the phenomena is simplistically considered a miracle.

The Mayan word for illumination or enlightenment is *cizin*. Unfortunately, its significance was distorted by the Spanish friars, such as Landa, as well as by the laws of the Inquisition. *Cizin* means radiating energy. But today, in the Yucatan, the word is associated with the devil because of the friars' distortions. Over time, Mayan spiritual refinement has been brutalized by Catholic ideas.

People with an ancient heritage such as the Maya and Nahua of Mexico are creators of culture, and as such they can impart knowledge to those people who falsely claim to bring us culture. Our cultural antiquity is symbolized by the Nahua deity of fire, Huehueteotl (Figure 30-1). The indigenous person teaches us that fire is very old and should be worshipped as a symbol of the beginnings of human life, as heat. The lessons of fire and the human being will be amply discussed when we deal with the seven bodily forces and the explanation of the Kundalini Maya.

Interestingly, one of the other two figurines illustrated in Figure 30 represents an individual in typical Arab attire. We are convinced that in ancient times many visitors came to Hanahuac (America) seeking the vast knowledge held in the thousands of sacred centers scattered throughout Mesoamerica. Arabs, Babylonians, Egyptians, etc. all came to learn from our indigenous culture. With the passage of time, cataclysmic geological changes occurred—some continents sank beneath the sea, and others emerged. As a result, we were apparently isolated for a time in all respects. Then the slumbering Europeans came to life and presumed to "discover" our Hanahuac or Tawantinsuyo, which they baptized with the names "New World" and "America."

Hunab K'u Gave Us
The Seven Powers to Become
Quetzalcoatl

 Hunab K'u gave us seven powers. They are distributed in our bodies. The ancient peoples of Mesoamerica knew how to use these seven forces. These seven powers, taken into our consciousness, help us become Quetzalcoatl or Kukulcan. Hunab K'u, as the Only Giver of Movement and Measure, taught us to understand those qualities. We came to know that everything in existence has movement and measure; we were aware of our true cosmic faculties as children of Hunab K'u. Thus it was taught by the Hau K'inoob, and they said, "All that exists is only movement and measure in the memory of Hunab K'u."

When we sovereign Mexicans of Hanahuac believed in our true culture, we were a people with our own personality. By abandoning that belief, we have become a weak people and are now called part of the Third World. From now on, if we want to become a strong people with self identity, we must reclaim our true sovereign culture. When indigenous culture is discussed, many neophytes say there is no need to return to the past. I tell these friends that it would have been better for them not to have been born in Hanahuac, or Tawantinsuyo, at all, for neither in life nor in death will they find a spiritual resting place within any of the 21,000 sacred centers of Mesoamerica, or the additional thousands in South America.

As some of us know, European culture only teaches us to live a material existence of consumerism and material servility set in the dense third dimension. This impoverished society knows only how to live within its poor material world, ignorant of the true laws and forces of the spirit. When members of this society, who understand only European culture, are abandoned by their physical bodies, their spirits, their essences wander aimlessly in an unknown dimension. Then our great indigenous spirits can perceive them straying disoriented and involuted beyond the third dimension. Of course, all this would seem unrealistic to those who know only the culture brought to us by the Spaniards. But this is the truth revealed to me in each of the centers where we conducted sacred ceremonies in more than thirteen countries of Hanahuac (America).

Hunab K'u wants us to be saved because the *Chilam Balam-Noob* [sacred scripture] has prophesied that difficult times lie just ahead. Some of us realize that human beings have forgotten the sacred teachings of the ancient Naga Maya, Mayax, Cara Maya, and Maya. The lessons found in this book are explained in many different ways because they were inspired by Hahal K'u, the only true God, for all God's children. Let us not, however, fall into the error of heeding only hollow words, as is done in other cultures. The teachings of the Maya are very different. For example, in the initiation to Mayan culture, the student must learn to use basic solar energy and, in other instances, the forces which come from the Milky Way, from other planets, and even other solar systems.

From infancy, the Mayan initiate knows how to manage energy with both the body and mind, for this knowledge is structured in the teaching process. The Maya refer to the spirit as *k'inan*, meaning "of solar origin." Since the Maya innately defined spirit as originating from this source, they understood the law that governs the essence of the human being.

To be Kukulcan or Quetzalcoatl is to know how to transform that sacred energy in our minds and bodies. The first example we will use for this Maya/Nahua teaching is Figure 31. We can observe four marks in the lower part of this piece. They are called *can*, the word for the number "four" and "the serpent." This word also forms part of *canzah*, meaning "teacher," and *canbah*, meaning "student." Additionally, it is used when referring to the initiates, *luk'uben tunben can*, meaning "those absorbed by the knowledge."

The Maya, who understood the human being, knew of the seven forces and where they are located. These forces were associated with *k'ul*, a root word for the sacred Hunab K'u. The completeness of their knowledge is evident in Figure 31. *Can*, "four" and "serpent," name and numeral, alludes to the highest esoteric knowledge of our Mayan ancestors.

Next, let us study Figure 32, in which we see a person with seven heads in the form of serpents. The ancient peoples of Asia tell us how Buddha, the great teacher, was bitten by the serpent with seven heads while in the river of initiation. This serpent is called *chapat* in India. Curiously, the people of the Yucatan, Mexico have the same word and it, too, refers to the seven-headed serpent, just as in India.

These indigenous teachings will help us learn how to use the seven forces of energy with our minds and bodies. In this way we begin the process of becoming Quetzalcoatl or Kukulcan.

Let us observe anew that these powers are symbolically represented by the serpent. Only here in America was the serpent worshipped as a symbol of movement and measure—a cosmic synthesis. We can find references to the seven energies in any of the pyramidal sacred centers constructed by our ancestors throughout America. Remember, dear brothers and sisters, that to become a Quetzalcoatl or Kukulcan is to recognize and know how to use these seven energies.

The seven serpents that we see in place of the head on the stone tablet of Aparicio, Veracruz, teach us that to learn how to manage these seven powers (or brains) one must consciously use the power of the mind. This intelligent energy must not be used by minds stultified by the uncultured society the Spaniards brought with them, but should be used for the good of humanity and all living beings, because this is the energy of the Giver of Movement and Measure, Hunab K'u.

The sacred seven, reminders of the galactic origins of Mayan culture, are also the seven isosceles triangles we see each year on the 22nd of March and the 23rd of September in Chichen Itza, Yucatan. There, the masters teach us in a living way, and you and I can experience the sacred moment when Kukulcan/Quetzalcoatl arrives to imbue us with cosmic energy. At that moment, we feel the vibration of Hunab K'u as the only giver of life. He comes to remind us that in this precise moment we must reject those dense three-dimensional laws that tell us Mayan culture has expired. On March 22nd, we perceive the presence of Hahal K'u, delineated by our parent Sun. This is the time when the plentiful ripe sap of our tree relative slows the rotation of our earthly orb. It is also the time when our true teachers, called *hau k'in* (solar priests), indicated the moment when desired offspring should be engendered. All of this is inspired by the calendrical laws of Hunab K'u. Every year on the

FIGURE 31.

Seated female figure. This bichrome ceramic piece from Nicoya, Guanacaste, Costa Rica is from the National Museum of Costa Rica. The four marks on the lower part of the figure, called *can* in Mayan, represent the number "four" and "the serpent." We know that in this area is centered the great power that awakens the kundalini.

FIGURE 32.

Monolith from Aparicio, Veracruz, Mexico. Here we observe a personage with seven heads in the form of serpents. The ancient inhabitants of Asia asserted that when Buddha was immersed in the river of initiation, he was bitten by a seven-headed serpent. This serpent is called *Chapat* in India. Curiously, the same word occurs in the peninsular Mayan of Yucatan.

FIGURE 33.

The descent of Kukulcan at the Castillo pyramid at Chichen Itza takes the form of seven triangles which denote the two equinoxes—March 22 and September 23 of every year. For some people, this seven represents religion; for us Maya, it is science. Contemporary culture should understand that science and religion must be recombined.

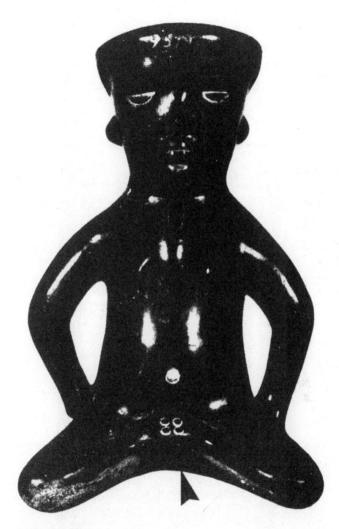

FIGURE 31.

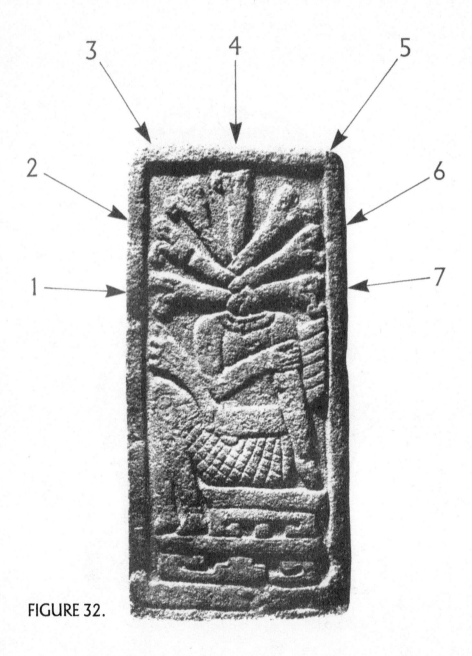

FIGURE 32.

FIGURE 33.

equinoxes of March 22nd and September 23rd, one can witness Kukul-can's descent from the sacred temple of the ill-named "castle" of Chichen Itza (Figure 33).

In this moment commanded by Hunab K'u, we see and feel the living presence of our Mayan culture and receive the true teaching of our relig-ion and science. When we fully comprehend the meaning of this seven in the geometric pyramid, we will enter the mouth of the serpent as Mayan initiates. In so doing, we will fulfill the prophesies of the Itzaes when they return as *luk'umen tun ben can*, or "those absorbed by the serpent of the sacred knowledge." At that moment we will become buddhas, or as is said in Mayan, *butz hah*, "those filled with the truth of the essence," the ones who manage the seven powers. With our minds awakened to these powers of the mind and spirit, we will suffer no illness. We will live as the perfect beings created by Hunab K'u.

The Maya relate the human with the pyramid, saying, "You are the pyramid, and the pyramid is you." In *Mito y Realidad de Las Piramides*, (*Myths and Realities of the Pyramids*, published by YUG), professor G.J. Gon-zales Soto states:

> The pyramidal energy of the human being, the energy pro-duced as a result of a modification in the symmetry of a structural form, is obtained from the mechanism known as "controlled breath-ing" (Mayan Yoga), which when activated in the organism at a superficial or very profound level, results in a balance between the oxygen we inhale and the carbon dioxide we exhale; this generates the bioelectromagnetic energy which activates the cells, stimulates the heart, causes the liquids to flow throughout the organism, con-veys bioelectric current to the muscles, organs and bodily systems and keeps them alive.

This energy is called pyramidal because it is found principally in each of the molecules of water which constitute 75 percent of our bodies, and which possess triangular-pyramidal structure. The energy is released when there is a change in the angle of separation of hydrogen atoms on either side of the oxygen atom in the H_2O water molecule.

What we have learned from Professor Gonzales Soto is that when we practice Mayan Yoga, we function like the pyramids in processing energy. The Mayan masters teach that we are the integration of the seven powers of light, traveling in the form of the serpent, undulating eternally with movement and measure. In Mayan, the pyramid is called *k'u*, the root word for the sacred Hunab K'u, the Only Giver of Movement and Measure. Thus, when we see the seven triangles in Chichen Itza during the equinoxes, we are witnessing a demonstration of culture which pervades the atmosphere and the stones of this sacred place. With respect and humility we should kneel before the presence of Kukulcan or Quetzalcoatl. By so doing, we will begin to awaken our cosmic consciousness, allowing Hunab K'u to enter the sacred temples that are our bodies! The seven powers sleeping within us will awaken and, at that moment, we will cease to be poor Third World Mexicans. This applies to all the indigenous peoples of our distressed American continent.

Clearly, to attain such knowledge requires a disciplined apprenticeship in indigenous esoterica. Much of this information is ensconced in the sacred pyramids in those places where we are obliged to make rituals. There the great ancestral spirits wait to help us leap the barrier erected by Spanish colonialism after the conquest of Hanahuac. The temples, called pyramids, have been the abiding places of science/religion for thousands of years and will endure for thousands more. For this purpose they were created by our indigenous grandparents, whose spirits also reside in these sacred places.

We Maya have witnessed the passage of many cultures. And many more will come and go. But the Mayan and Nahua cultures will endure because they are founded on knowledge inspired by cosmic laws. For that reason, they will never become extinct. The permanence of our cultures is confirmed by the seven triangles seen at Chichen Itza and Mayapan. As we know, the conquering Spanish pillaged the lands of the Mayab, taking the gold from our continent and establishing their empire. They accumulated such material power that one of their rulers boasted that the sun never set on Spanish territories. But after a few centuries this empire vanished.

On the other hand, even now in the twentieth century, our astronomical science and mathematics are still operative at the sacred sites of Chichen Itza and Mayapan, and Mayan religion flourishes among those of us who are true to our indigenous heritage. To live with Mayan culture is to know art, religion, philosophy, etc. In this way we become children of time, as are our Mayan teachers, living as the essence of universal consciousness.

Today only a few people retain the millennial secrets of the corporal powers. Prominent among them are the Hindus of India. As we have related, this country received the teachings of the Naga Maya, including the lesson of the number seven. The preservation of this prehistoric knowledge represents a veritable treasure and can be related to cultural survivals among the Maya of the American continent.

Let us look at some of these surviving similarities between India and Mayan culture. The Hindi word *chakra* occurs in Mayan slightly modified as *chacla*. In Mayan, it relates to the symbol of the Milky Way in its graphic form and its movement. Seen from above, it has the form that appears next to the large number 2 in Figure 34. This is the form of *chakla* according to our Mayan teachers. Figure 34 was inspired by the monograph, "The Chakras," by C.W. Leadbeater (Orion, 1980) and is reproduced here to show where the author locates the bodily chakras. The primary or basic chakra is centered, according to the Hindus, at the base of the spine (Figure 34, Number 1). They say it radiates four primary forces. The Maya, interestingly, designate this area *k'ul*, from the etymological root *k'u*—"the sacred" or "God," and "L," the contraction of *lil*—"vibration." For the Maya, this part of the body is designated with four marks as in Figure 31. This recalls the word *can*, meaning "serpent" and the number "four." Thus while the Hindu sages teach us the value of four as a primary force, the Mayan culture provides a more comprehensive explanation.

We have thematic material here which requires much more study. God, vibration, serpent, four—these four words may be interpreted as follows: God is the intelligent energy of vibration in its four manifestations and the serpent is the form in which that energy travels. The Mayan word *chacla* also means "this my red," which implies that if we had the sensory capacity to do so, we would perceive the color of the primary center as red or orange. Initiates tell us that this center maintains our lives.

The Hindus relate chakras with flowers, and depict the basic chakra in floral form. The cultures of the Maya and Hindus converge into one teaching. When we analyze the Mayan word *lol*, meaning "flower," we again see the "L" contraction of *lil*—"vibration"—and the "O." This pronunciation and form of the latter was considered at length in Chapter 3; in summary, the use and sound of "O" is of Mayan origin.

We recall that this "O" represents consciousness combined with spirit. In the word *lol* it is augmented with the final "L" of vibration. This

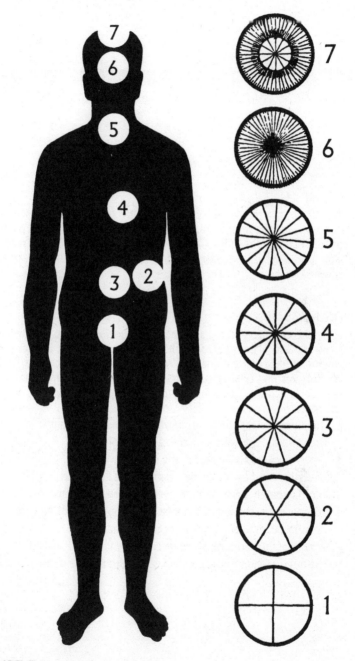

FIGURE 34.

FIGURE 34.

The Chakras, a monograph by C.W. Leadbeater, describes these points as the centers of the seven human forces. Several coincide with corporal focus points known to the Maya. Compare these with Figure 35, dear reader, and after due investigation you can draw your own conclusions about this knowledge.

FIGURE 35.

A life-size clay figure found at Etznah, Campeche, Mexico. Arrows indicate some of the focal points of forces that unite us with cosmic laws, or what the Hindus of India call our chakras. What follows is our interpretation of the symbolic features of this figure. Nevertheless, we are open to the contributions of other investigators in analyzing these points indicated by our Mayan ancestors.

1. The number eight represents universal harmony in duality.
2. The so-called third eye from the teachings of India.
3. This symbol may be related to the third eye.
4. Symbol of wind, air, or divine breath and its four directions.
5. Internal spirit in harmonious movement with the essence.
6. External spirit, expanding to make connection with universal law.
7. Celestial quadrature, to define locational parameters.
8. Symbol of the harmony of the seven bodily forces.
9. The number three of the pyramid which also represents internal spirit.

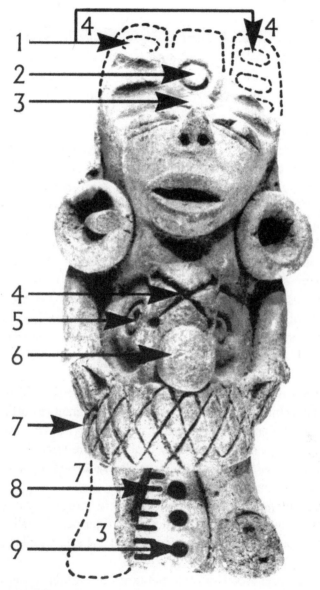

FIGURE 35.

conceptualization goes beyond the Hindu symbology of the flower with supplemental information in the representation of vibrational conscious spirit. The language of the Mayan initiates gives us this additional insight.

Thus we have the following words related to the seven forces: *k'ul, can, lol* (and additional words such as *tat, uac,* etc.). They refer to the sacred center at the base of the spine, the coccyx. These words help us develop our occult powers and become true reflections of Hunab K'u. This is the path to become Quetzalcoatl or Kukulcan. As we can see, these words are basic for awakening these dormant powers.

We recall from our lessons that *k'ul* is related to the sacred and its vibrations; *can* corresponds to the teachings and the symbology of how energy travels and the four manifestations of wave energy; *ol* signifies the basic relationship of vibration and spirit. The new word, *chacla*, is the red/orange force intimately related to the Milky Way.

The Maya understood not only the energies explained in Figure 34 but also other energies of the human body. Figure 35 shows some of these energy centers known to the Maya. Modern researchers should recognize these themes as part of Mexico's rich cultural heritage. To them we humbly offer this information. In Etznah, Campeche, Mexico, a small but significant clay figurine was found which appears in actual size in Figure 35. It helps us identify the points in the human body connected with sidereal energies. Please do not blindly follow the erroneous ideas started by friars such as Landa and his cohorts (children of evil), which have distorted the teachings of our Mayan culture. A flagrant distortion occurs with Landa's reference to the crown chakra, known in Mayan as *cizin*. For the Maya, *cizin* is radiating energy, but Landa referred to the crown chakra as the "devil." The ancient Maya clearly understood the function of this gland, as can be seen in Figure 35.

To become Quetzalcoatl is to know how to consciously use this radiation with all our awakened faculties. This figurine originally depicted the number four twice, once on either side of its head, yielding the magical, universal "eight."

The word *cizin* esoterically implies a manifestation of our energies, i.e., a practical application of knowledge. A flowering of radiation is visually represented by the serpent symbol of solar energy. The other extreme of *cizin* is in the coccyx, or the *k'ul*. Herein lie some of the secrets of Christ, the Jews, and other Catholic religious saints who exhibit auras surrounding their heads or bodies. It relates to what we saw in Figure 29, the meditating Mayan priest.

In Mayan culture, the aura is sometimes symbolized by feathers—a representation of the realized being. Let us recall the words of professor G.J. Gonzales Soto, who said, "In the pyramids, the human being can achieve an almost eternal life or reach a spirituality that will permit him to find the path to the creator."

To conclude this brief analysis of the magic seven and its importance, we will cite another Hindi word: *kundalini*. This word exists in Mayan in two forms: *k'ultanlilni* and *k'ulthanlilni*. This again demonstrates the fact that world culture had roots which we, the peninsular Maya of Mexico, helped establish thousands of years ago. The Hindi word *kundalini* is the derivative evidence.

In the sacred name of Hunab K'u, we offer this lesson so that our people can restore our true indigenous culture with the permission of the Only Giver of Movement and Measure, Hahal K'u. However, we cannot hope to convey all of the teachings of the seven energies of Quetzalcoatl or Kukulcan because, to do this, the apprentice must submit to a rigorous discipline. This apprentice needs great respect for all our indigenous sacred centers, must fast as described in the *Popol Vuh* and, finally, should practice ritual discipline before the pyramids. Sadly, much of the discipline of our Maya, Nahua, and Olmec heritage has been lost. One must also realize that these teachings can be used for evil purposes, and for this reason, care must be taken when conveying this knowledge.

It is important to review the teachings of Zuyua Mayan. Few people know that Suyua is the form in which Mayan priests codified the secrets of the most profound, enigmatic, and esoteric parts of words. Let us analyze the etymological, philosophical, and theosophical roots of the words *k'ulthanlilni* and *k'ultanlilni* as the Mayan priest/scientists knew and used them. We will employ one known aspect of the still mysterious Zuyua—based on my compilation from many years of assiduous study of the language. The esoteric word *Zuyua* is part of the profound structural understanding of the ancestral Mayan culture. The following information helps elucidate Zuyua Maya:

MAYAN WORD	MEANING
dziib	normal writing (written much like Spanish or English)
dziib zuhuy	virgin writing (the manner in which Hoil wrote the *Chilam Balam de Chumayel*)
dziib uoh	symbolic writing (glyphs and hieroglyphs)
dziib mucul	secret writing (written in cloistered places or for initiates)
dziib naat'te	writing for divination (for the most advanced initiates)

Now we will look at oral forms because, as some of us know, the Maya speak in several different ways.

MAYAN WORD	MEANING
than	to speak; common or popular speech
pach than	to speak in reverse
ca pach than	to speak twice in reverse

Keep in mind another expression of Suyua Mayan. In the Mayan language, certain words are spoken only by women or by men. For example, *al* in the sense of "to give birth" is used by women. The man uses *uihix mehen pal*, which means "ejaculated semen." These are components of the little-known Zuyua Mayan.

Continuing with our analysis of the words *k'ulthanlilni* and *k'ultanlilni*, we will try to discover new revelations through the Zuyua of *pach than*. As we just learned, in this form we use the words in reverse, i.e. *in lil nat luk'* and *in lil nath luk'*, and study them in the contexts of etymology, linguistics, symbology, religion, science, etc.

K'ULTANLILNI & K'ULTHANLILNI:

K'u—Sacred, God, and name of the pyramid; the first sound a human makes upon arriving in this world.

K'ul—Coccyx, the sacred place where solar energy is deposited at the base of the spine. It can also mean *k'u*—"sacred," "God," etc.—with the "L," contraction of *lil*, "vibration."

K'ultan—Literally, it means coccyx and its location. From *k'ul*, "coccyx," and *tan*, "place." This word also says *k'u*, "God" or "pyramid" of *lil*— "vibration," as seen above.

K'ulthan—Similar to above with the addition of *than*—"to speak." *K'ul*—"coccyx"; *than*—"to speak," or "to speak to the coccyx," "to God" or "to the pyramids," etc.

K'ultanlil—This word contains *k'u*—"God" or "pyramid"; "L"—"vibration"; *tan*—"place"; and *lil*—"vibration"; also *k'ul*—"coccyx," implying that the coccyx is the location of the vibration of Hunab K'u, the Sun God.

K'ulthanlil—Composed of *k'u*—"God," "pyramid"; "L"—"vibration"; *than*—"to speak"; and *lil*—"vibration." *K'ul* is also "coccyx"; in the coccyx we can address the vibration of Hunab K'u.

K'ultanlilni—Finally one of the two complete words. *K'u*—"God," "pyramid"; "L"—vibration; *tan*—"place"; *lil*—"vibration"; and *ni*— "nose"; also *k'ul*—"coccyx." The composite meaning—the coccyx as the place of vibration is directly related to the nose because it is where the breath of the Sun God enters.

K'ulthanlilni—Similar to the previous word except for one significant variation. It means *k'u*—"God," "pyramid"; "L"—vibration; *than*—"to speak"; *lil*—"vibration"; and *ni*—"nose"; also *k'ul*—"coccyx." Coccyx of vibration, speak to the vibration, and also know how to breath properly in order to generate movement of those faculties of Hunab K'u residing in the coccyx.

Through language, the Mayan culture instructs the people and enables them to develop the faculties which Hunab K'u placed in their bodies. Clearly, this process must become part of our consciousness so that we may become true Quetzalcoatls or Kukulcans. This process is uniquely expressed in our religious/scientific language, as we have demonstrated.

Now we shall discuss the second part of the explanation of these words. For the Mayan initiate, these words would be read in Zuyua.

IN LIL NAT LUK' & IN LIL NATH LUK':

Uk'—To take in swallows. Figuratively, it means "to take in small doses." This can refer to material or non-material things. If we analyze this word further, we can obtain a more ample understanding. *K'u* is "God," "pyramid," "human being." The inverted form, *uk'*, means "to take in small doses." Therefore, the Maya are saying that we must absorb Hunab K'u little by little. As we all know, the pyramid is a processor of energy. When we conduct rituals in the pyramids, the energy is first taken physically, and then it reaches the spirit at the moment when the essence of Hunab K'u is taken in.

Luk' — Swallow. This word most frequently occurs in the phrase; *luk'uben tun ben can*, which means "those absorbed by science." In many locations, *luk'* is exemplified by a man and woman coming out of the mouth of a serpent representing Quetzalcoatl or Kukulcan as "the one absorbed by knowledge." These four words of *k'ul*—"God," "vibration," "coccyx," "swallow"—are unified for the human being to use in initiation, and are thereby "swallowed" by the intelligent energy and consciousness of Hunab K'u, as the Only Giver of Movement and Measure.

Nat—Mount. The meaning of this word is complemented by using it together with its inverted form, *tan*, meaning "place." Thus, we learn that for everything we swallow, we must learn how to "mount" it in its place. Separately, the two words, *luk'* and *nat*, mean "swallow" and "mount," respectively. However, if we join them together, we get a figurative meaning for *luk' nat* teaching us that we need to mount or secure the sacred energy we have swallowed and absorbed into our consciousness. This is preferably accomplished by meditation.

Nath—Pliers. The significance of this word when used with its inverted form, *than*, is that it teaches us that a person who speaks can lock us into his or her grip. It can also mean that when we speak we can control a person we speak to, as if we are grasping them with pliers. Permit me to give another example. An actor in the theater can make us laugh or cry, depending on the play. This means that our innermost self has been reached. Speaking figuratively, this can be compared to using pliers. Adolf Hitler's strength was in his use of words. With words, he led the world into World War II. These examples shed some light on Zuyua Maya. When *k'ul* and *nath* are linked, we get the literal meaning, "swallow" and "grip." The Maya teach that we must grasp what we have swallowed, i.e., understand it consciously. Remember that God is implicit in this word, which also signifies "vibration," "speak," "pyramid," "apprenticeship"—the human being and the place where the sacred energy of the cosmos is deposited.

Lil—Vibration. Regardless of the direction in which this word is read, it always means the same thing. When a word of this type is encountered in Zuyua Maya, it means that the word is absolute truth. As everyone knows, scientifically, vibration is the same wherever it is found. Let us analyze the words *lilnatluk'* and *lilnathluk'*. The first indicates "vibration," "to mount," and "to swallow." Scientifically, all that we swallow is retained in the form of vibration. The second word indicates "vibration," "grip," and "swallow." This says that all the teachings we swallow seize us like pliers in some place, i.e., whatever enters us consciously or unconsciously, grips us for better or worse, depending on our preparation (as in the opposites of the actor and Adolph Hitler).

In—Personal pronoun, first person singular, "I." The greatest relationship between *in* and *ni* begins when we first arrive on planet Earth. In *ni*, meaning "nose," and *in*, meaning "I," the Maya imply that the divine breath of Hunab K'u enters through the nose. This is recognized by pediatric doctors, who know that when they spank a newborn, the infant takes a breath and begins life. The Maya show that the "I" (self) enters through the nose by using words that reflect this relationship. At Uxmal, Yucatan, this concept is exemplified by the Chacs, who have large noses that look like elephant trunks inscribed with signs and glyphs representing the wind and planets. The wind and planets, for the Maya, have a direct relationship as part of the creation of Hunab K'u. In summary, the nose, I, the wind, and the planets all have a direct cosmic relationship.

We will now summarize the English translations of these four sacred words known and used by the Maya in Suyua. In the name of Hunab K'u, with these words we give you part of the knowledge and understanding you need in the quest to become a true Quetzalcoatl or Kukulcan.

K'ultanlilni—God, pyramid, human being, coccyx, vibration, place, nose

K'ulthanlilni—God, pyramid, human being, coccyx, vibration, to speak, nose

Inlilnatluk'—I, vibration, mount, swallow, drink or take

Inlilnathluk' —I, vibration, grip, swallow, drink or take

All of these aspects of the kundalini relate to the seven forces of the human body and, subsequently, to sexual activity between man and woman, and reproduction as practiced by Mayan initiates. Figure 36 depicts a Mayan sexual scene. Here, a Mayan priest stands on a celestial band showing various planetary symbols. His erect sexual member displays seven circles which in Mayan are called *muluc*, meaning "the reunion of everything." The priest wears a type of headpiece called a "heavenly mat." In his hand is a vessel inscribed with the sacred "T," flanked by two dots. Above the vessel appears a serpent in movement. On the same celestial band, a woman is positioned to receive the virile member. She wears additional symbols on her head. This interesting "unknown" Mayan codex is from the collection of Mexican documents edited by Manuel Porrua.

For the Maya, sexual activity and propagation were governed by planetary knowledge and natural laws, as illustrated in Figure 36. Rituals were performed and the priests taught the responsibilities inherent in engendering children. To teach this knowledge, the priests used sacred calendrical calculations, especially from the sacred *tzolk'in*, in order to avoid unplanned children (as often occurs in our world today). The knowledge of sexual aspects was not exclusive to the Maya, as we can see in Figure 37 from the Chimu culture of Peru. It would appear that these indigenous relatives from ancient Peru have much to teach us regarding certain aspects of sexuality. As we can see from this clay figure, the male image has a serpent connected to his sexual member, and is apparently meditating in the yoga position which is well known in India. Remember, dear reader, that the serpent symbolizes wisdom, and is represented as such in all of the cultures of this continent of America.

The way the serpent is connected to this person's sexual organ is indicative of the profound relationship which exists between the sexual energies and *religare*, religion, and unity with God. This is the way to engender children in the consciousness of Hunab K'u, and to procreate Quetzalcoatls or Kukulcans.

The Spaniards who came to Hanahuac knew nothing of our understanding of sexuality. Even today, European culture ignores many aspects of sexual relations to the cosmos. For this reason and because of the

FIGURE 36.

FIGURE 36.

The *Unknown Mayan Codex*, published by Porrúa. This codex depicts a Mayan priest working with sexual powers. Here we see the lesson of the sacred seven on the male member. Also present are other symbols such as the "T" and a band of plants as inscribed on the base. It would be of some importance to hear the opinions of "official" scholars on this codex.

FIGURE 37.

A clay figure from the Chimu culture of Peru. Apparently, our Chimu Indian relatives of ancient Peru had much to teach us about sexual matters. This and the previous illustration from the Mayan Codex reveal a deep awareness of the use of sexuality among the indigenous peoples of the New World.

FIGURE 38.

Another page from the Porrúa Codex or pictorial manuscript. This drawing depicts the so-called "Cosmic Man," at the center, holding a serpent in his right hand, symbolizing energy. This serpent's nipples indicate feminine gender. A male serpent in the opposite hand completes the duality, the negative and positive energies of the process of creation in the context of cosmic laws.

FIGURE 37.

imposition of colonialism, Third World countries have remained in the dark. Even worse, Catholicism and other religions judge these sexual aspects as things of the devil.

Regarding sexuality, European culture has little to contribute to remove the darkness in which we live. It has even less to offer about the relationship between cosmic laws and sex. In contrast, the Maya and other peoples like the Chimu have sufficient sexual knowledge to produce children who will have the vocation and gender one desires.

Figure 38, taken from the "Pictorial Manuscript of the Mayan Culture," painted on animal skins, depicts the "Cosmic Being" and numerous symbols. We will deal only with the sexual aspect, because in this final chapter my intention is to discuss sex and its importance in begetting desired offspring. I want to show the Mexican people and the world that with this type of teaching we have much to learn from Mayan culture. Actually, Figure 38 contains a vast amount of symbolic information about the Cosmic Being. In the middle part of the drawing, the subject's right hand holds a serpent energy symbol with nipples, implying feminine gender. Another serpent held in the left hand indicates the dual polarity needed to engender children according to cosmic law. A detail (bottom) amplifies the sexual part to aid visual comprehension. The six lines or indications are called *uac*, meaning "to surge." They emanate from the point called *hun*. Let us analyze algebraically and sexually the *hun*, which in Mayan esoterica signifies "one" because of its direct link to the sacred Hunab K'u in its etymological roots. *Hun*—"one"—is the root of the sacred name of Hunab K'u, the Only Giver of Movement and Measure, represented by a circle and a square—the squaring of the circle. Hunab K'u, unnameable, unpronounceable, invisible, should be retained only in memory.

Hunab K'u for the Maya is the center of everything, including the sexual act when we engender children. Hunab K'u is here and there, the force around which everything moves. *Hun* is represented by a dot. Thus we have *Hun*-ab K'u as "one," or the dot as the manifestation of everything. This reasoning reveals that when the Mayan philosopher thought of the number *hun*, it was thought that in *hun* was everything, because Hunab K'u is in everything.

Below the dot is a symbol of the "G" or zero. It represents the cosmic egg. It would be good to review Chapter 1, in which we discuss the "G"

FIGURE 38.

and its religious and scientific manifestations. But here we have a new manifestation of the teachings of the sacred "G" and the relation of sexuality to its laws. Returning to Chapter 1, Figures 1, 2, 3, we should again study the symbolic "G" spiral. As we know, when a man begins to ejaculate semen, the sexual member moves in a spiral, which imprints cosmic information on the genes that form the future human being. As is evident in Figure 1, the Maya knew how to use the energies and movement of the Milky Way.

To conclude this section on sexuality, we would like to mention our gnostic brothers and sisters, who have much to teach on the subject of sex. We make special mention of Adolfo Migoni, founder and teacher at the Gnostic Association of Anthropological and Cultural Studies in Mexico. He can enlighten us about the sexual aspects of gnostic knowledge, and its relation to ancient cultures such as the Nahua and the Maya.

Mayan Solar Religion

Those who have traveled to diverse parts of the world, even to known places of unimaginable beauty, have been so impressed by the sacred lands of the Mayab, that they remain here or will always return. Those who remain in this land are motivated primarily by the rare and wonderful beauty of its vegetation and the wealth of symbols whose origin is lost in the obscurity of time. Those who return seek the knowledge enclosed in an infinite abundance of pyramids and monoliths.

Both divine and human beings know that the exalted Mayan race, without diminishing its own impressive development, is a repository for the elevated sciences of other civilizations (such as the positive polarity of Atlantis) which offer advantages over contemporary thinking.

Before delving into the theme of solar religion, we want to try to interpret the unique, little-known symbolism of Illustration 5 from the Unknown Mayan Codex (Figure 36) whose sexual nature is nevertheless profoundly religious, in accordance with the Hebraic kabala.

In this illustration, we have a priest of Balam with a religious miter bearing five feathers, representing the esoteric pentagram, the realization of humans on a spiritual plane. The left hand raises an offering receptacle with the inscription "T," symbolic of the sacred spirit tree, analogous to the Tree of Life which physically corresponds to the human spinal column through which the sacred fire rises according to Hindu philosophy (also the Inca serpent or Devi Kundalini). The two dots on this receptacle, known as *ca*, signify the duality of energies consisting of the sexual connection carried out without seminal ejaculation. This type of sexuality, known as Arcane of Mahituna, was practiced in the land of Kem (Egypt) in the days of the great pharaohs. It is still practiced in the highest schools of great mysteries. This, then, is a fundamental practice in the use of the third energy of creation. With this, the Maya obtained superior knowledge which connected them to the highest internal entities as well as with their deities. In this manner a morality and spirituality of the highest level was attained, as is demonstrated by the remainder of the work so admired in esoteric anthropology.

The serpent on the offering receptacle (*can*), the equivalent of the Grail of the Templars, signifies the cup of Hermes, with transmuted seminal energy being offered to the Father of all fatherhood. In another respect, the Mayan serpent signifies life, energy, solar substance, and *canil cuxtal*, "the serpent of life."

In these dark times we live in, when a couple marries, it is said that they go on a honeymoon. The symbol upon which the priestess sits is, in Mayan, called *zohol cib* or *cab*, and is translated as "honeycomb." It signifies the worldly sensations we should transcend to take true advantage of the most powerful energy in our bodies, the sexual energy. By administering it as the Maya did, we would be, instead of annihilating ourselves by wasting seminal fluid, exalting our moral and spiritual powers, giving our women the same attributes, and promoting lasting youth and beauty.

Before completing this work, it is necessary to praise the sublime knowledge of the Mayan race which coincides with universal knowledge. As a closing, we offer two Mayan prayers, one for reciting during the daylight, and one for reciting at night. It is very important to pronounce the words of the Mayan language correctly, as they are written. Remember that it is a mantric language. Using these prayers, dear reader, you will relive our Maya culture, and fulfill the prophecies. You will become a part of the divine cycle and a son or daughter of Hunab K'u in universal memory.

CUT TIP' IL K'INE C'K'AMIC A THAN YUM
With the rising of the Sun we receive your words, Master

TUMEL YETEL U ZAZILE C'AHAL C'PACTIC TU LACAL BAAL
Because with your light we awaken and contemplate everything.

C'ILICBA XANTUMEN A PALALOOB XAN
We also contemplate ourselves because we are your children.

LEBETICO CU ZAAZTALE C'K'UBICBA TECH
This is why at dawn we surrender ourselves to you

TIAL CA CALANTON. YETEL TOONE CANZAH TECH A MIATZIL
So that you may protect us and teach us your wisdom.

A UICH CU PACTICON CU YILCOOM, YUM
It is your visage which looks upon us and contemplates us, Master.

LEBETIC C'K UBICBA TI TECH TATA YETEL YUM HUNAB K'U
This is why we surrender to you, Father and Master Hunab K'u.

YETEL TECH CU CU K'UBIC C'PALALOOB
And we surrender our children

HEBIXTU K'UBAHOON C'YUMOOB TI TECH
Just as our parents surrendered us to you.

YUM HUNAB K'U A UOHEL BAAX CA BETIC TETEL
Master Hunab K'u, you know what you make of us

TOONEC C'K'ATICTECH YUM HUNAB K'U CA A CANZAHOOB
LE BEHO
We ask you, Master Hunab K'u, to show us the path.

ANTON YUM HUNAB K'U U TIAL CA ZUTNAG LE IN LAK'ECHO
Help us, Master Hunab K'u, to regain fraternal love.

C'K'ATICTECH C'YUM HUNAB K'U TIAL MA ZATAL.
OH, YUM HUNAB K'U!
We ask this of you, Master, Giver of Movement and Measure,
so that we do not lose ourselves. Oh Master, Hunab K'u!

For Nighttime

DZU BULUL H'YUM K'IN, DZU TIP'IL X'YUM AK'AB
Already the Master Sun has set, and the Mistress Night has risen.

PEPENOBE CU LEMBALOOB ICHIL U LOL CAAN
The butterflies shine amid the heavenly flowers.

C'TUCULE TIAN TI TECHE C'HUNAB K'U
Our thoughts are in you, dear God.

TUMEN TECHE C'AZAHOLAL, TA K'AB C'K'UBICBA
Because you are our hope; into your hands we surrender ourselves.

TECH A UOHEL BAAX CA MENTIC T'ETEL HUNAB K'U
You know what you will make of us, Hunab K'u.

AK'ABE HUNAB K'U, A K'AB CUK'ALALA
The night, Hunab K'u, is your hand which closes.

T'ICHILE CU YUCHIL TU LACAL
And within it everything happens.

HEBIX U TOP'OL NEK'E, HEBIX U HOK'OL YALCHE Y TIP'IL LOL
As the seed buds, as the flower emerges and blossoms.

BEYO HEBIX U ZIHIL LE WUINICE
In this way is born the human being.

BEL U YUCHUL TU LACAL TU K'AB HUNAB K'U
In this way everything occurs in God's hands.

CALANTEN IN HUNAB K'U! CALANTEN!
Take care of me, Giver of Movement and Measure! Take care of me!

TI TECH IN DZAMA IN WUINCLIL YETEL IN VOL.
To you I surrender my body and my spirit.

BIBLIOGRAPHY

Samael Aun Weor. *Magia Crística Azteca*, Iglesia Agnóstica Cristiana Universal, Editado por Asociación Gnóstica de Est. Antr. México, D.F. México, 1974.

Nelly Gutiérrez Solana y Susan K. Hamilton. *Las Esculturas en Terracota del Zapotal, Veracruz.* Editorial Universidad Nacional Autónoma de México. México, 1977.

Antonio Villacorta C. y Carlos A. Villacorta. *Códices Mayas.* Editor, Sociedad de Geografía e Historia de Guatemala. Guatemala, C.A., 1977.

Enigmas del Universo. *De los Atomos al Cosmos.* Ediciones, Daimon, Manuel Tamayo. Barcelona, España, 1979.

James Churchward. *El Continente Perdido de Mu.* Ediciones Nacionales Círculo de Lectores. Bogotá, Colombia, 1978.

C.W. Leadbeater. *Los Chakras, una monografía.* Editorial Orion, México, D.F. México, 1980.

La Santa Biblioa. *Antiguo y Nuevo Testamento.* Editorial Mundo Hispano. México, D.F. México, 1862 y 1909.

Domingo Martínez Paredes. *Desconocido Códice Maya.* Editorial Documentos Mexicanos Manuel Porrúa, México, D.F. México, 1978.

Ing. G.J. Gonzáles Soto. *Mito y Realidad de las Pirámides.* Editorial Yug. México, D.F. México, 1982.

Alberto Ruz Lhuillier. *El templo de las inscripciones Palenque.* Editado por: Instituto Nacional de Antropología e Historia. México, 1973.

Laurette Sejourne. *Pensamiento y Religión, en el México Antiguo.* Fondo de Cultura Económica. México.

Domingo Martínez Paredes. *Manuscrito Pictórico de la Cultura Maya.* Librería de Manuel Porrúa, S.A. México, D.F. México, 1953.

Julio de la Canal. *Breve Historia de la Literatura Universal.* Editorial Divulgación Literaría Mexicana. México D.F. México, 1961.

This Bibliography is reprinted exactly from the original Spanish edition of *Religión Ciencia Maya*; however, some of the above publications may be available in English.

Hunbatz Men is a Mayan daykeeper, artist, and authority on the history, chronology, and calendars of Mayan civilization. His lecture topics include Mayan mathematics, ceremonial centers, art, symbolism, ideography, iconography, astrology, astronomy, and philosophy. Hunbatz Men is founder of the Mayan Indigenous Community and a respected ceremonial leader.

BOOKS OF RELATED INTEREST

The 8 Calendars of the Maya
The Pleiadian Cycle and the Key to Destiny
by Hunbatz Men

The Mayan Code
Time Acceleration and Awakening the World Mind
by Barbara Hand Clow
Foreword by Carl Johan Calleman, Ph.D.

The Nine Waves of Creation
Quantum Physics, Holographic Evolution, and the Destiny of Humanity
by Carl Johan Calleman, Ph.D.
Foreword by Barbara Hand Clow

The Global Mind and the Rise of Civilization
The Quantum Evolution of Consciousness
by Carl Johan Calleman, Ph.D.

The Purposeful Universe
How Quantum Theory and Mayan Cosmology
Explain the Origin and Evolution of Life
by Carl Johan Calleman, Ph.D.

The Mayan Calendar and the Transformation of Consciousness
by Carl Johan Calleman, Ph.D.

The Mayan Factor
Path Beyond Technology
by José Argüelles

Time of the Quickening
Prophecies for the Coming Utopian Age
by Susan B. Martinez, Ph.D.

Inner Traditions • Bear & Company
P.O. Box 388
Rochester, VT 05767
1-800-246-8648
www.InnerTraditions.com

Or contact your local bookseller

Praise for *House of Thieves*

"Belfoure's sly, roguish writing opens a window to those living both gilded and tarnished lives. The architectural knowledge imparted will appeal even to those who are unable to differentiate between Queen Anne and IKEA. Best of all, Belfoure holds together each and every thread of the novel, resulting in a most memorable, evocative read."

—*Publishers Weekly*, Starred Review

"The world of old New York comes alive in this beguiling tale of mystery and intrigue. Danger and drama abide with vivid and dramatic description that allows the reader to easily conjure up the imaginary—as if watching a film—wrapped totally in the writer's world. Charles Belfoure definitely has the touch."

—Steve Berry, *New York Times* bestselling author of *The Patriot Threat* and *The Lincoln Myth*

"Fast-paced, uncompromising, with a winning and accessible prose style, *House of Thieves* grabs you from the first lines and explosive opening pages. Belfoure's fiction brings the dazzling and dangerous Gilded Age alive."

—Matthew Pearl, *New York Times* bestselling author of *The Dante Club*, *The Poe Shadow*, and *The Last Bookaneer*

"Charles Belfoure sees New York's Gilded Age with an architect's eye and evokes the atmosphere wonderfully. Familiar figures like the legendary Mrs. Astor and Stanford White help set the scene, but in no time at all a sinister intrigue begins, and Belfoure leads us on a splendid page-turner as a respectable family discovers its criminal side in old New York."

—Edward Rutherfurd, *New York Times* bestselling author of *Paris: The Novel* and *New York: The Novel*

"As in Belfoure's *The Paris Architect*, the author and architect artfully brings a city's streets to life with loving descriptions of its architecture, here capturing 1890s New York in all its opulence. A pulse-raising read for historical crime and historical thriller fans."

—*Library Journal*

"Charles Belfoure stocks *House of Thieves* with authentic architectural and historical grace notes. Of course he does! But he never loses sight of the story, which rockets along at full speed from one breathtaking scene to the next. I couldn't put *House of Thieves* down. I was so wrapped up in the plight of the reluctant hero, John Cross. And I wish I'd created the villain, James Kent, a man so evil I want to steal him for my own next book."

—Alex Grecian, national bestselling author of
The Yard and *Harvest Man*

"Charles Belfoure has written my favorite kind of novel. *House of Thieves* is the story of a family coming together in the most exceptional and peculiar way. Rich in mischief and populated by thieves and gamblers, gentry and rebels, it is as complex and ambitious as New York City itself. This is historical fiction at its best."

—Ariel Lawhon, author of the
The Wife, the Maid, and the Mistress

"*Gangs of New York* meets *The Age of Innocence* in *House of Thieves*. Charles Belfoure opens a (leaded-glass and arched) window on the upstairs-downstairs lives of New Yorkers at the end of the nineteenth century, as seen through the gimlet eye of architect, gentleman, and thief John Cross. As Cross navigates the manners and mores of both the Astors of the Knickerbocker Club and the Kingpins of the Tenderloin, we root for him and for his extraordinary family as well."

— Susan Elia MacNeal, New York Times bestselling
author of *Mr. Churchill's Secretary* (the Maggie Hope Series)

Praise for *The Paris Architect*

"I love that in *The Paris Architect*, a mercenary, talented man's passion for his creative work leads him down moral roads he never could have envisioned. The ingenious hiding spaces and the people in them infiltrated my imagination for weeks. I dreamed about this novel."

—Jenna Blum, *New York Times* bestselling author of *Those Who Save Us* and *The Stormchasers*

"A vivid, suspenseful story that keeps you gripped to the very last page. Charles Belfoure writes with great warmth, conjuring up an intriguing cast of characters and painting a fascinating picture of Paris under the Occupation, with all its contradictions—the opulence, and the fear."

—Margaret Leroy, author of *The Soldier's Wife*

"Belfoure writes like an up-and-coming Ken Follett."

—*Booklist*

"All novelists are architects. But are all architects novelists? Charles Belfoure in his impressive debut seems to have brought us the best of both worlds. Here is a novel to read alongside the latest Alan Furst. I hope there will be more."

—Alan Cheuse, NPR book commentator

"Belfoure's portrayal of Vichy France is both disturbing and captivating, and his beautiful tale demonstrates that while human beings are capable of great atrocities, they have a capacity for tremendous acts of courage as well."

—*Library Journal*, Starred Review

"Belfoure's characters are well-rounded and intricate. Heart, reluctant heroism, and art blend together in this spine-chilling page-turner."

—Publishers Weekly

"Architectural and historical details are closely rendered... a satisfyingly streamlined World War II thriller."

—Kirkus Reviews

"A gripping page-turner, *The Paris Architect* brings to life the dark and merciless streets of German-occupied France. Through elaborate designs of his characters' making, Charles Belfoure shines a light on the human heart—a complex maze of love, hope, and the yearning for redemption—and in doing so, provides a riveting reminder of sacrifices made by history's most unlikely heroes to triumph over evil."

—Kristina McMorris, author of *Bridge of Scarlet Leaves*

"Charles Belfoure's historical thriller delivers the suspense of *Schindler's List* and the German-occupied Paris of Alan Furst in this tense tale of an architect hiding Jews from the Nazis."

—Julie Kramer, author of *Shunning Sarah* and *Stalking Susan*

"Lucien Bernard, an up-and-coming French architect, is teetering on the edge of debt in German-occupied Paris in 1942. When a wealthy industrialist offers him an unusually large amount of money to design a hiding place for his Jewish friend, Lucien immediately refuses. But when an offer is added for Lucien to design a large factory where Germans will manufacture weapons for the war effort, Lucien soon finds himself caught up in a collaboration he cannot back away from. What is it then that changed the course of Lucien's life? This novel, which tells about a desperate time in the lives of Parisians affected by the Nazi's takeover of their city, is an emotionally stirring story about choices and sacrifices. Highly recommended."

—Carol Hicks, Bookshelf at Hooligan Rocks, Truckee, CA

HOUSE

of

THIEVES

a novel

CHARLES
BELFOURE

sourcebooks
landmark

Published by Sourcebooks Landmark, an imprint of Sourcebooks, Inc.

P.O. Box 4410, Naperville, Illinois 60567-4410
(630) 961-3900
Fax: (630) 961-2168
www.sourcebooks.com

Library of Congress Cataloging-in-Publication Data

Belfoure, Charles.
  House of thieves : a novel / Charles Belfoure.
     pages ; cm
  (hardcover : acid-free paper) 1. Architects--New York (State)--New York--Fiction. 2. Fathers and sons--Fiction. 3. Upper class--Fiction. 4. Gambling--Fiction. 5. New York (State)--Social life and customs--1865-1918--Fiction. I. Title.
  PS3602.E446H68 2015
  813'.6--dc23

                    2014048617

          Printed and bound in the United States of America.
              WOZ 10 9 8 7 6 5 4 3 2 1

Also by Charles Belfoure

The Paris Architect

For Chris.

1

———◆◆◆———

I T WAS A PERFECT DAY TO ROB A BANK.

The rain outside hammered the sidewalks like a monsoon. The river of delivery wagons, double-decker omnibuses, and carriages of all description that usually flowed in an unending torrent along West Thirty-Third Street had been reduced to a trickle. In place of the rush of pedestrians along the sidewalk, a few men with umbrellas hurried by the plate glass windows of the Manhattan Merchants & Trust Bank. Customers would hold off coming to the bank until the downpour stopped—and that wasn't going to happen for hours.

All of which meant fewer witnesses.

Stick Gleason looked down the barrel of his Colt Navy revolver at the people lying facedown on the shiny, white marble floor, then glanced over at Sam Potter, who was standing guard inside the massive oak-and-glass double doors of the front entrance. Potter nodded: things were going well. Though they both wore white muslin masks that hid their faces, Gleason knew Potter was smiling at him.

The woman on the floor in front of him started to whimper, reminding him of a hunting dog he'd once owned. When the dog wanted out of his crate, he'd give a high-pitched whine until Gleason couldn't stand the noise any longer and freed him. Gleason could only see the top of the woman's scarlet-colored hat, which had a slanted brim with a sort of high mound on top, like a beehive covered with yellow and green cloth flowers. Must have been a society lady.

"Keep quiet, ma'am. We'll be through in just a few minutes,"

Gleason said in a soothing tone, tapping the top of her hat with the barrel of his Colt. She shut up immediately.

He was getting anxious himself. "Come on, Red. How much longer?"

"Goddamn you, I told you never to rush me," Bannon said angrily, the words muffled by his muslin mask. He continued to pour the nitro-glycerin drop by drop from the small glass vial into the joints of the bank vault's hinges. Beads of sweat slipped down his forehead, sliding over his eyebrows and into his eyes, making him blink uncontrollably. He kept wiping them away with his left hand.

It was dead quiet in the bank. Then Gleason heard a faint noise building quickly toward a screech, like a boiling teakettle about to blow.

"Listen, woman, I told you…"

An ear-piercing scream exploded out of the society lady's mouth. Bannon flinched—and Stick watched in horror as the glass vial slipped from his fingers and fell to the marble.

The blast was like a white-hot fireball of a meteorite, streaking from the vault room to the front windows of the bank, incinerating everything in its path. Bannon was vaporized in a millisecond, along with Gleason, the society lady, four bank tellers, two customers, and the entire wood-and-marble interior of the banking hall. Potter was propelled like a rocket into West Thirty-Third Street and through a storefront window directly south across the road.

A delivery driver and his bay horse lay dead and bloody amid the wreckage of a dray wagon. A cast-iron electric light pole was bent parallel to the street. Windows and storefronts on the south side of West Thirty-Third were blown in too, leaving black holes that seemed to gape out at the newly silent street in astonishment.

❖ ❖ ❖

James T. Kent, standing under an umbrella on the flat roof of the eight-story Duckworth Building directly across from Manhattan Merchants

& Trust, watched as a great plume of black smoke billowed up from West Thirty-Third Street, drifting past him and blending into the gray sky. The street below was a mass of confusion, with people running toward the building from all directions. The clanging of fire wagons could be heard in the distance. *There won't be any need for them*, Kent thought. The blast had sucked the oxygen out of the space, which meant no fire.

From his vantage point, the men on the street looked like ants scurrying in and out of the blasted opening of the bank. *They'll find no bodies*, he thought. *Only tiny pieces of human flesh and bone.*

"Poor bastards," said Ben Culver, a short, stout, broad-shouldered man.

"It was the nitro," Kent said, not a shred of emotion in his voice. "Handling it is like trying to hold quicksilver—almost impossible. But still better than using dynamite. Remember Maritime National? The cash, negotiable bonds, and stock certificates, all burned to ashes by the blast. It took Red hours to sweat out that nitro from a dozen sticks of dynamite. He said blowing the vault would be the easy part."

"We'll never replace Bannon, Mr. Kent."

"No, we won't. Red was the best cracksman in New York." Kent took a cigar out of his gold case with his black-gloved hand and tapped it idly against his palm.

"These vaults are too damn hard to blow in the daytime, Mr. Kent. Bank jobs are just too risky anyhow. The Company has to…"

"Diversify?"

"Yeah, that's it."

"I agree," said Kent with a smile. "What do you suggest?"

Kent was a tall, thin man in his early forties, with graying hair and a commanding presence. He always wore a black frock coat with matching waistcoat and pearl-gray trousers, all ordered from Henry Poole & Co., the best tailor in London. He had schooled Culver, whose previous wardrobe could charitably be described as loud, in dress. A gentleman, he'd said, must always be so well dressed that his clothes are never observed at all.

Culver valued this advice almost as much as his cut from their jobs. These days, he was as elegantly clothed as his employer, though the juxtaposition of his battered and meaty red face with his fine, tailored outfits frequently struck one as very odd.

"The army's stopped guarding President Grant's grave in Riverside Park," he said, brimming over with his excitement at offering a new business proposition. "They just have a night watchman. They haven't started building the real tomb over it either, so we could snatch the body and hold it for ransom. Like they did with A. T. Stewart back in '78. His widow forked over twenty thousand dollars for the body. For a department store king! Think how much we'd get for a United States president."

"I can find only two things wrong with your plan," Kent said amiably. "First, I served proudly under Grant in the war. And second…it's incredibly stupid."

He smiled and patted Culver on the shoulder, as if to lessen the sting of his words. A disappointed expression twisted Culver's face, and he looked down at his expensive, black patent leather shoes—the ones Kent had advised him to purchase. Culver wasn't the brightest, but he was absolutely the most loyal employee of the Company, and Kent genuinely liked him.

"I know those men had families," he said, pulling out his tan pigskin wallet and removing ten one-hundred-dollar bills. "Please divide this among them."

"That's very kind of you, Mr. Kent."

Kent extracted his Gorham solid-gold pocket watch from his waistcoat and frowned. "The annual board of directors meeting for the Metropolitan Museum is at eleven. I'd best get going."

2

J OHN, YOU SHOULD BE DAMN PROUD OF THIS BOY OF YOURS."
John Cross turned and stared at his son, who stood next to him
in the entry foyer of Delmonico's. It was hard to believe that this was the
same toddler he'd once played with on the beach at Long Branch or taken
to Central Park to sail boats. George was strikingly handsome. He had
inherited his mother's dark complexion and straight black hair and was at
least three inches taller than his father. The twenty-two years of his son's
life blurred together in Cross's mind. When had his boy grown into a man?

"Thanks, Stanny. He turned out all right, I suppose."

Stanford White, a six-footer with red hair and a thick brush of a
mustache, roared with laughter. Beside him, Charles McKim, normally
a very reserved fellow, also burst out laughing. White's enthusiasm was
always infectious.

Cross had met White and McKim many years ago, when they all
worked for Henry Hobson Richardson as apprentice architects. Stanny
and Charlie remained his closest friends, and he was particularly happy
that they were there for his son's graduation party.

"Graduating from Harvard, captain of the baseball team. Not too
shabby," said McKim. "In fact, I'm jealous. I sat on the bench when I
played there."

"Yes, congratulations, Georgie. So, are you following in the old
man's footsteps and taking up architecture?" White asked, giving Cross
a wink.

"No, sir. Unfortunately, I didn't inherit my father's artistic talent.
I'm going to be a mathematics teacher at Saint David's this fall."

"George has been teaching part-time for the Children's Aid Society downtown since the winter. Then next year, after Saint David's, full-time at Columbia graduate school. On his way to becoming a brilliant professor," Cross said, voice full of pride.

"Not a bad place to begin your teaching career," said McKim. "Saint David's is the poshest school in town."

As White nodded with approval, his face broke into a sly smile. "Ah, behold. The beautiful Helen of Troy."

Cross's wife, Helen, walked up to join the men. She was mesmerizing in a crimson evening dress from Worth of Paris; a lovely pearl-and-diamond necklace set off its deep décolletage, and a pair of large diamond festoon earrings framed her high cheekbones. Few women in New York society could challenge her beauty and charm. At parties and balls, men swarmed around her like bees to honey, making Cross proud and nervous at the same time. Having a beautiful wife was a double-edged sword—Helen was the object of pride *and* possible scandal. But he knew he didn't have to worry about Stanny, whose preferences for female companionship tilted toward those below the age of fifteen.

Helen gave the group a steely look. "You gentlemen are blocking the way of Georgie's guests. Take your masculine good fellowship into the grand dining room, please. John and Georgie, you stay where you are."

White bowed, took her hand, and kissed it. "Whatever Helen of Troy commands."

Cross looked out, past the glass-front double doors of the restaurant. "Do you think she'll come?"

Helen rolled her eyes. "When she says she's going to do something," she snapped, "she always follows through. For heaven's sake, don't worry." She straightened George's white tie, brushed a bit of lint from his white silk waistcoat, and then ran her hands along the shoulders of the black cutaway tailcoat. Satisfied, she rose on her tiptoes and kissed him on the cheek.

"Later, I want you to be sure to talk to Granny—and Mary Morse."

"Oh, Mother."

For the next twenty minutes, the trio greeted more guests. Finally, Cross nodded toward the doorway and said in a low voice, "Here she is."

On Fifth Avenue, directly in front of Delmonico's, a shiny black brougham pulled by two sleek chestnut horses in gold-trimmed harness drew to a stop. The driver and attendant were dressed in gold and navy-blue livery and black top hats. The attendant hopped down from the box and opened the passenger door.

In the dusk of the warm July evening, a short, rather stout woman in a beautiful black silk brocade evening gown stepped out, holding on to the white-gloved hand of the attendant. She stepped onto the sidewalk into the circle of bright light cast by the new electric street-lights, which had recently replaced their much dimmer gaslight predecessors. The glow of the light reflected in tiny sunbursts off her tiara of diamond garlands and her dog-collar necklace of hundreds of tiny diamonds on a band of deep purple satin. As she rearranged her black lace shawl over her shoulders, a crowd gathered on the sidewalk to gawk at her.

Cross watched as she marched with regal ease and confidence through the glass doors of the restaurant. She moved as if she owned Delmonico's. And in a way, she did.

Caroline Astor was the undisputed queen—or despot, some felt—of New York society. She alone determined who belonged and who did not. If a person failed to meet her approval, he or she was condemned to social death.

In 1886, New York society had only two parts: old and new. The old, known as the Knickerbockers, were the descendants of the original Dutch founders of New Amsterdam, nicknamed for the knee-length breeches they once wore and headed by families with names like Schuyler, Schermerhorn, Van Cortlandt, and Van Rensselaer. There was also an old English flank of founders led by the Livingstons and the Phillipses. The rigid Knickerbocker social code demanded absolute propriety and strict conformity. They religiously obeyed this code, even dwelling in identical brownstones the color of chocolate sauce, driven by the paralyzing fear that they would be thought different and would thus become the subject of gossip.

Then there were the new, a *nouveau riche* class made up of millionaires who had made their fortune from businesses such as railroads, steel, or horse cars. Dirty, undignified pursuits, the Knickerbockers sniffed. The new displayed their wealth with outrageous extravagance, building luxurious mansions and amassing yachts, jewels, and clothing—luxuries universally condemned as vulgar by the old moneyed class. But undaunted, these parvenus came from all over America to New York City, where they stormed the walls of the Knickerbocker aristocracy.

Caroline Astor was a proud Schermerhorn, but she straddled the world of old and new by marrying the grandson of John Jacob Astor, a German-born fur trader who had become America's richest man. Helen Cross was a distant, relatively poor member of the Schermerhorn clan. John Cross, a distant and equally poor Livingston relative, helped cement the Knickerbocker connection. "Aunt" Caroline liked them both and watched over them like a mother hen, and they had been taken under her wing and safely ensconced in "new" New York society. She even insisted on paying for Helen's wardrobe and jewelry. They lived modestly, however, in a wide three-story brownstone at the corner of Madison Avenue and East Thirtieth Street and had only four servants. Cross likened his lifestyle to the architectural scale he used in his drawings; he lived at one hundredth the full-scale life of the Astors.

But to her credit, Caroline had opened doors to the advantages and privileges of society, to him and especially to George and John's other two children, Julia and Charlie. Thanks to her connections, Cross's architectural practice prospered. But Cross knew that if there were the tiniest hint of scandal about anyone in his family, she'd cut them off in a second and would have nothing to do with them again. These were the ironclad rules of their world. One malicious whisper could annihilate a family's reputation and banish them from society forever. Completely shunned—people who were once your closest friends would never talk to you again, even to your children.

"Aunt Caroline, thank you so much for coming," said Helen, meeting her at the door, arms outstretched. Helen was one of the very few people Aunt Caroline ever publicly hugged. She gloried in the fact that such an incredibly beautiful woman was a Schermerhorn.

"Tonight I must attend a tiresome charity performance at the Academy of Music," said Aunt Caroline, "but I knew I had to stop by to see Georgie. Where is that handsome boy of yours?"

"Aunt Caroline," said George, stepping forward, taking her hand with both of his and kissing her cheek.

"Here's a little something for my class of '86 man," she said, handing him a small box wrapped in silver paper. George unwrapped the present in front of her, knowing she would want to see his reaction.

Others had made their way to the foyer, eager to curry favor with Mrs. Astor. White, one of her architects, hovered about with Charles Crist Delmonico, the grandnephew of the founder who controlled the restaurant dynasty and had made it the best restaurant in the city.

Nestled in a wad of cotton was a magnificent gold pocket watch and chain. George pulled it out, eyes wide in wonder. Instead of the usual incised decoration, the tiniest of diamonds and rubies formed a sinuous, vine-like design on the watch's cover and sides. The inside cover featured a similar raised motif in a vortex swirl, with a large diamond at the center. The back of the watch was engraved: "To George, Harvard Class of 1886, From Aunt Caroline." Helen's and John's eyes met; their first reaction was not pride but fear. *What if George lost such a beautiful gift?*

Beside them, White let out a whistle. "That's incredible."

"You know that workmanship, Mr. White. I had Louis Comfort Tiffany design it specifically for Georgie," Mrs. Astor said.

White had just completed a commission for the Tiffany family, constructing a huge mansion of golden-brown brick at the corner of Madison Avenue and Seventy-Second Street.

"This is a work of art. Thank you so much." George bent to hug his aunt, who bear-hugged him right back.

"It's a pleasure, my dear boy. And now I must be off." Before anyone could bid her good-bye, Aunt Caroline turned, the train of her gown sweeping around, and marched triumphantly back to her carriage. Dozens of people were waiting to get a look at her and, more specifically, to see what she was wearing, for Caroline Astor also dictated New York fashion. If she decided to wear a Chinese coolie's straw hat to dinner, Fifth Avenue's shops would be flooded with them the next day.

As John and Helen stood at the front door, waving good-bye, Charles Crist Delmonico said, beaming with delight, "Ladies and gentlemen, dinner is served in the grand dining room."

✦ ✦ ✦

Only Caroline Astor could have persuaded Charles Eliot, president of Harvard University, to stop by to say a few words at George's graduation party. Eliot had been traveling through New York from Boston the day after commencement and couldn't say no, especially to such an immensely rich donor. Besides, George had been both an academic and athletic star at Harvard, so Eliot was pleased to visit.

So that he might leave in time to catch his train to Washington, Eliot spoke briefly before the meal started. He rose to his feet at the end of the long dinner table, a slight and unassuming man in his fifties, with a long nose and bushy sideburns, the leader of America's greatest university. The cacophony of the celebration was instantly silenced.

"Ladies and gentlemen, George Cross exemplifies the kind of man Harvard produces. During my tenure at the university, I've seen a change in the Harvard man's character. His sense of personal honor and self-respect has increased. Drunkenness has decreased. It still troubles me to see vices born of luxury and self-indulgence on the rise. But this doesn't touch George Cross. Not only does George exemplify academic brilliance, but he's also a man of great character and determination—as he showed last year at the Polo Grounds, when he drove in the winning run in the ninth inning against Yale."

The dining room erupted into wild cheering and applause, and George shyly rose and waved to his admirers. President Eliot shook his hand, bowed to the crowd, and left the room, a signal that the eating and drinking could begin. Because Helen and many other ladies were present—and because Caroline Astor had paid for the dinner—it was not a wild male bacchanal that such an occasion might have prompted, but rather a luxurious society event. More than one hundred diners sat at a table that stretched the length of the room. Down its center ran a deep trough bordered by high banks of beautiful summer flowers. In the trough swam three white swans, which glided up and down its length, oblivious to the diners on either side. The eight courses, served on silver, included consommé à l'Impériale, Maryland terrapin soup, red snapper, canvasback duck, fillet of beef, cold asparagus vinaigrette, a dish of sherbet to cleanse the palate, and then a saddle of mutton, truffled capon, and fresh vegetables of all kinds, followed by desserts and candies. Claret, Burgundies, Madeira, and champagne flowed into the guests' glasses as from a spigot; in the background, an eight-piece musical ensemble played on and on, light sounds to enliven but not disrupt the burble of conversation.

The party came to an end at about 2:00 a.m., when Cross found his son saying good-bye to Stanford White, always the very last to leave.

"George, your mother and I are going now," Cross said, clapping his son on the shoulder. "It was a wonderful party. Please be in touch in a few days."

"Thank you so much for tonight, Father. I'll never forget it." George clasped his father's hand, smiling.

"Helluva party, Georgie old boy," Stanny shouted as he left the restaurant with John and Helen. "The night's still young, and I know a place on East Forty-Fifth that's just beginning to heat up."

"We're not going anywhere with that blackguard," Helen hissed into Cross's ear as they made their way to a carriage on Fifth Avenue.

Cross just sighed. He had long since given up trying to change his wife's stubborn opinion of Stanford White's sybaritic character, especially his taste in women.

·◆· ·◆· ·◆·

His guests gone, George walked downstairs to the restaurant's open-air street café, settled into one of the carved wooden chairs, and lit a cigarette. After almost six hours in the dining room, the night air felt cool and refreshing. Fifth Avenue was deserted, and the pure silence soothed George after the hours of unending noise. He leaned back and closed his eyes, savoring the triumphant evening.

"Beautiful night, isn't it, George?"

The voice came from directly behind him. George smiled and swiveled around, expecting to see an admiring classmate. Then his face turned pale, and the cigarette dropped from his lips.

James T. Kent sat at a table a few yards away, dressed in elegant evening attire, smoking a cigar and sipping a glass of white wine.

"Just dropped in for a nightcap before heading home after the theater. But now that I'm here, maybe I could have a word with you. It's about a matter of some delicacy."

George rose from his seat and started toward the low wrought iron fence that enclosed the sidewalk cafe. But a short, broad-chested man stepped out of the shadows, moving to cut off his exit.

"I think you remember my business associate, Mr. Culver."

Culver smiled at George but said nothing.

"Why don't we take a little trip?" said Kent.

3

Oh, he floats through the air
With the greatest of ease,
This daring young man
On the flying trapeze;
His actions are graceful,
All girls he does please,
My love he has purloined away...

KENT GOT SUCH PLEASURE OUT OF SEEING HIS MEN ENJOY themselves. He hadn't realized Freddy Dugan had such a wonderful baritone voice. If he hadn't become an extortionist, the man could've made it on the stage.

Kent and ten of his employees were standing inside the new cable car power plant, currently under construction on the East Side. It was a huge brick and stone structure with tall, arched windows and a cavernous central room, where steam machinery would be installed to pull the coils of steel cables that wound and twisted beneath the city streets. Cable cars were the latest fad in New York, and the wise bet said they would soon replace the horse cars entirely. Kent saw it as a great investment. A cable car didn't have to be fed. It could work all day, and most importantly, it didn't deposit tons of shit and an ocean of piss onto the streets. When the Brooklyn Bridge had opened three years before, cable cars had been installed, and they'd been a great success.

But cable cars were still the future. The present object of his men's delight, George Cross's body, was swinging like a giant clock pendulum above the cement floor, bound and suspended upside down at the end of a thick rope whose other end was looped over a steel roof truss twenty feet above the men's heads. Culver held the end of the rope, and Tommy Flannigan pushed George's body, sending him in a wide arc. Back and forth he went. Kent's men sang and roared with laughter at each swing. Kent had never seen them have so much fun sober. When George threw up his banquet from Delmonico's, they whooped and howled.

Finally, Kent walked over to the swinging body and raised his hand, signaling for silence.

"For a mathematician, George," Kent said as the boy swung by, "I thought you'd have a better head for numbers." He pulled out a cigar and lit it, drawing in and exhaling the smoke with great pleasure. "Figuring in compounded interest, what you owe me is forty-eight thousand dollars. Quite a bit of money. Let me put it another way. A master carpenter makes about a thousand dollars a year. You owe me forty-eight years of carpenter wages."

"For God's sake, cut me down, Jim."

"I know you love to gamble, George. But if you lose, you *have* to pay up. I warned you about the interest that was accruing on your debt, but you ignored me. And you can't say I haven't been patient. Or generous. I gave you the opportunity to forgive the whole thing by putting the fix on the Harvard–Columbia baseball game…but you didn't come through, my boy. I lost on that bet, and I lost handily. You're lucky I didn't add it to your total."

"I tried! I swear I did! But you can't throw a game when no one else is in on it," George cried.

"I can't have you stiff me, George. It's bad for business. If people see that I let you slide, they won't have any respect for me, and they'll try to stiff me too."

"Give me one more chance, please," pleaded George.

Kent watched George swing. Then he signaled Flannigan to bring the body to a halt. Flannigan grabbed George on each pass to slow him down until the boy hung there, slowly turning around and around like a slab of beef on a hook. Kent motioned for Al Carney, a mountain of a man with broad shoulders and fists the size of hams, to come over.

"George, Al here once fought John L. Sullivan and lasted almost five rounds. Five rounds against the great John L. Imagine that. There was an article about it in the *Police Gazette*."

Carney's jowly face flushed red with embarrassment as he approached the hanging body. Then his fists let loose as if he was bashing a body bag in a gym. George cried out at each blow.

"I'm most sorry to have to do this to a society gentleman," Kent said, his tone sincerely apologetic. "But you have to understand, George, that I live in a world that also has a strict code of rules. Just like in New York society, when one breaks the rules, one must be punished. And as you may well imagine, that punishment can be…severe." He gave a sly smile. "Let me introduce you to Abe Gibbons. In his former life, Abe was a butcher."

A lanky, gray-haired man of about fifty walked over and placed a long knife to George's throat. Carney continued to punch, ignoring him; the ex-boxer was enjoying himself too much to stop.

"They'll find pieces of your body from the Bronx to Cape May, George."

"Please—no!" screamed George.

"There's no one you know who can pay off the debt?" Kent asked, more irritated than curious. "What about your family?"

"My family doesn't have that kind of money. My father's just an architect."

Kent's brow wrinkled, and he motioned for Carney to cease his pummeling.

"I didn't know your father was an architect. What does he design?"

"Office buildings. Like the Chandler Building on East Fourth."

"Indeed? That's a very handsome building. What else?" Kent sounded genuinely impressed.

"Empire State Life Assurance on Nassau Street. Saint Mary's Church. Lots of big houses up on Madison Avenue and Riverside Drive."

Kent turned and walked slowly across the power plant. He made a wide arc, returned to George's hanging body, and nodded at Gibbons, who lunged at George.

"God help me!" George screamed.

With a slash of the knife, the thick rope was severed. George fell hard and landed on his head with a groan that echoed throughout the empty plant. The men howled with laughter.

Kent walked over to Culver, who, relieved of holding the rope, was leaning against a wall, smoking a cigarette and enjoying the festivities.

"You remember George Leslie, don't you, Mr. Culver?"

"Sure. The king of bank robbers. Planned the Manhattan Savings job on Bleecker in '78. Got away with two *million*."

"Wasn't he an architect?"

"That's what they say. I heard that he could read them building drawings of banks, could even draw 'em up himself."

"And didn't they find him dead up in Yonkers?"

"Yep, said he was fooling around with one of his men's girls. The man was a genius. Shame to die because of a goddamned woman," Culver said, shaking his head.

Writhing in pain on the concrete floor, George yelled, "Just get it over with! Kill me and be done with it, you bastard."

"A *Harvard* man," Kent murmured, smirking. He turned to Flannigan.

"Mr. Flannigan, you're going to take George on a little vacation."

Visibly disappointed, Gibbons sheathed his blade.

"Yes, sir," muttered Flannigan.

"What are you going to do to me?" George shouted.

Flannigan took hold of George's feet.

"Wait," said Kent.

Kent pulled out a handsome leather billfold from George's inside pocket. He opened it, examined the contents, removed a card, and then returned the billfold. He nodded to Flannigan, who began dragging George out of the power plant.

"Mr. Culver, first thing tomorrow morning, I want you to deliver a message."

4

JOHN CROSS SAT IN THE UPPER DECK OF THE FIFTH AVENUE omnibus, the air already baked by the hot July sun. His eyes were vacant, his mind elsewhere as he mulled the strange events of the past two hours. He had never gotten new work in so peculiar a manner.

At around 9:00 a.m., a rough-looking man came into the office, asking to see him. The fellow had very crooked teeth but was dressed better than Cross, who felt himself taken aback when the man entered his private office. The clothes and the man seemed entirely at odds; it was like a pig wearing evening dress to the opera. The man explained that his boss admired Cross's work and would like to talk to him about designing a building. Because he was going out of town, however, they had to meet that day, at 11:00 a.m.

The economic boom of the 1880s had set off an enormous amount of construction in New York City. Cross had received his share of this new work entirely by word of mouth. Men he knew from the Union and Knickerbocker Clubs, the riding club, his Harvard classmates, gentlemen from Saint Thomas Episcopal and Newport—they all recommended him. But this fellow certainly didn't belong to that set.

The other requirement for the meeting was even odder. They were to meet in Saint Patrick's Cathedral on Fifth Avenue. This intrigued Cross. Perhaps the project was work for the Archdiocese, which oversaw a lucrative group of churches, parochial schools, and convents. Though he was a society High Episcopalian, he didn't mind designing for the Roman Papists, as his mother-in-law called them. Churches were a plum commission. Cross had designed just one, a Protestant church, early in his career, and he was eager for another opportunity.

The man tipped his expensive top hat and left. Cross left at once, walking from his office on Broadway and Eighth Street to Fifth Avenue, where he caught the omnibus. He enjoyed the ride; from the top, he had a grandstand view of the city.

Fifth Avenue was the backbone of his world. Its staid three- and four-story brownstones passed before his eyes, an unending line of high stoops, wrought iron railings, and striped canvas awnings extended out to block the summer sun. Cross watched as servants scurried in and out and families emerged from behind tall double doors of wood and glass. Broughams, hansoms, and victorias driven by men in top hats and black cutaway coats stood by the curbs, waiting for their owners. Dray carts carrying goods of all kinds slowly made their way up the avenue, making deliveries from house to house.

At Madison Square, where Fifth Avenue and Broadway collided then separated, the building style shifted and became a mix of commercial and residential. The Fifth Avenue Hotel, currently the city's most fashionable, stood on the left. The spire of the Marble Collegiate Church towered above Twenty-Ninth Street. Then, on the left, came a familiar sight: William Backhouse Astor II's wide brownstone. Aunt Caroline's home. To the south was a large walled garden that connected to her brother-in-law John Jacob Astor III's house.

The previous summer, Cross had stood in the garden with the Astors, looking over the high wall at President Grant's funeral procession. Now, as he passed Aunt Caroline's house, he smiled at its modesty. It was really only an extra-large brownstone, but that was the way it was supposed to be: unpretentious, dull, and respectable.

As the horse-drawn omnibus slowly rattled along on the cobblestones, halting to pick up and drop off passengers, Cross glimpsed the cathedral. Just north of Fiftieth Street, Saint Patrick's was complete but for its two spires, finally under construction after a hiatus of

almost eight years. Its architect was James Renwick Jr., a man Cross
greatly admired. Both were in the New York chapter of the American
Institute of Architects. When he got the commission, Renwick had
traveled around Europe for more than three years, observing and
sketching twin-spired churches. Finishing Saint Patrick's soaring
towers would complete a magnificent design that rivaled the cathe-
drals of the Old World.

The Knickerbockers, Protestant to the core, were shocked that
such a huge Catholic church could be built on Fifth Avenue. It
dwarfed nearby elite Protestant churches like Saint Thomas and Fifth
Avenue Presbyterian. Weren't there laws against such a thing, the
Knickerbockers protested. The fact that the church was paid for with
the nickels and dimes of Irish immigrants, the same trash that washed
the Knickerbockers' floors and dishes, was even more galling. There
was talk of building a Protestant cathedral on the West Side to put the
Catholics in their place.

Sighing, Cross shifted his gaze. The daily promenade by the fashionable had begun. Men in elegantly tailored frock coats accompanied
by women in beautiful walking dresses with tasseled parasols filled
Fifth Avenue's sidewalks. "Shoddyites," the Knickerbockers called
these "fashionable" new people. *They dress magnificently*, Cross thought,
making up in display what they lack in taste and education. He recognized
a client but made no effort to wave to him.

In front of the cathedral, Cross got off the omnibus and walked
inside. He'd been to the church many times, and on each visit, he marveled at the nave's breathtaking vaulted ceiling, supported by rows and
rows of Gothic arches. It ended at an altar in a full-height semicircular
apse, lit by tall windows of stained glass. He felt as if he were in France.
It was amazing how the thick stone walls of the church kept the interior so cool and refreshing, even on such a miserably hot day.

Most men hated what they did for a living—it was just a means to
pay the bills—but Cross genuinely loved being an architect. He was proud

that he'd chosen the right path in life and dreamed of being the best architect in the city (although he knew there was a lot of competition). He wanted someday to design something as magnificent as this cathedral, something that people would use for centuries after he was gone from this earth. Cross felt he had the talent to do it. He ran his hand over the cool stone of a column and smiled. *Yes*, he thought, *one day I'll do something truly great*. He turned and looked around for his new client.

His odd visitor had told him that a Mr. Kent would be waiting for him in the rear pew on the northwest corner. *It seems so mysterious*, Cross thought again, shaking his head. He walked toward the corner and saw a distinguished-looking man. He appeared to be about forty, clean-shaven, with swept-back hair and a sharp, almost hawk-like nose. Most encouraging, he looked like a very prosperous client.

"Mr. Kent?"

"It must be a wonderful thing to be an architect, Mr. Cross," Kent said, eyes fixed on the nave ceiling. "To think, you design and draw every square inch of a church like this. You decide what it will look like, down to the tiniest detail. Like that decoration atop that cluster of columns holding up the arch."

Cross took an instant liking to this fellow.

"Yes, it is wonderful," he said.

Kent stood and extended a hand, which Cross shook. "James T. Kent. Thank you for coming on such short notice."

"I'm glad to meet you, sir. I'm told you have a building you want designed?"

"Mr. Cross, although I do very much admire your work, I'm afraid you were brought here on a pretense."

A frown replaced the smile on Cross's face.

Kent continued. "I'll get to the point. This meeting involves a personal matter. I'm afraid that your son George has been doing business with me for the last year or so. Now he finds himself in serious financial difficulty. You see, he owes me a great deal of money."

"He—how much money?"

"Please sit down, Mr. Cross."

"How much?"

"About forty-eight thousand dollars."

Cross stood for a moment, dumbfounded, and then slumped into the pew as though someone had clubbed him. He rubbed his hand over his mouth, unable to speak. "I don't believe you," he finally forced out.

"I'm afraid you must, Mr. Cross. George will tell you himself that it's forty-eight thousand dollars—and that he has no way of paying it back."

"How could he owe you that much, for God's sake?"

"Of course, I suppose you don't know. George has a serious gambling habit, sir, and in very ungentlemanly places. The Bowery, the Tenderloin—you will see my meaning."

"No, no. That can't be," Cross said through tightly clenched teeth.

"Parents are always the last to know their children's shortcomings."

Cross stood, furious. "Who are you, scoundrel?"

"A businessman, sir. Who expects to be paid back."

"You're a criminal who took advantage of my son. There's no way he can pay you."

"Then George is going to die, Mr. Cross."

Cross sat back down, gazing in stunned silence at the padded leather kneeler of the pew. "You can't threaten me," he said at last, defiantly.

"It's not a threat, Mr. Cross. It's an ironclad guarantee. George will die if he does not pay me back."

"He's only twenty-two! He just graduated from Harvard. He—"

"And you must be very proud of him—at least until now," Kent said with a smile.

"I won't let you kill him, do you hear me?" Cross said, his voice rising above the accepted volume for the hushed solitude of a church. A woman praying over her rosary in a nearby pew gave him a disapproving look. Now he understood why Kent had wanted to meet him in a public place, and he clenched his fists.

"I know you won't," Kent said. "You're going to pay George's debt for him. You'll even pay the interest, which is accruing as we speak."

Cross laughed derisively. "Do you really suppose I've got forty-eight thousand dollars?"

"No, but you know where to get it—and more."

"What the hell are you talking about?"

"You're a successful architect, Mr. Cross. You've designed mansions for the rich, office buildings for all kinds of big companies and banks. Places that hold things of great value."

"You damn fool, you expect me to go and rob them?"

"Not at all. I expect you to help *me* rob them."

"You're mad."

"Am I? If you don't, pieces of George's body will be found floating around the island of Manhattan tomorrow. I give you my word on that. But for the present, George is my guest."

"That's a lie! He went home last night."

"Then how do I come to have this?" Kent smiled and handed a slip of paper to Cross, who let out a groan when he saw what it was—George's membership card to the Union League Club. "Impressive that someone so young is a member of the most prestigious club in the city, Mr. Cross. Myself, I belong to the New York Club."

Cross stood, grabbing Kent by the lapel of his frock coat. "You're bluffing. I'll go to the police about this, and you'll be thrown in prison, you damn rogue."

Unruffled, Kent gently removed Cross's hand. "I urge you not to do that, Mr. Cross. It will mean death for your son. In fact, I'll kill him in front of you and then kill you. Please believe me. I trust you'll understand that it's best you cooperate and pay back the debt. Then the whole matter will be settled. But until you agree, George will remain with me."

"You can go to hell!" Cross shouted and stomped out of Saint Patrick's, the echo of his footsteps bouncing off the white marble walls.

On Fifth Avenue, he stood in a daze in the middle of the sidewalk. A flood of pedestrians from either direction swept around him, like a stream around a boulder. His mind spun. He felt as if he were being sucked into a vortex, a horrible nightmare. If only he could wake up in his bed, begin the day anew, realize with a sob of relief that none of this had happened.

It can't be. This had to be some practical joke by George and his friends. *That's it!* Cross thought with a mixture of anger and happiness. It was a joke, and he had been taken in. His son was alive and safe. Perhaps Stanny was behind the charade. If so, he'd curse his old friend up and down for putting George up to such a thing.

A feeling of relief swept over Cross. His breathing returned almost to normal, and he started walking south. But when he came to Forty-Ninth Street, he stopped abruptly.

Suppose this wasn't a joke.

A man in a derby and dark gray frock coat collided with his back. "Damned idiot," the man muttered, stepping around him. Cross took no notice. With a sinking feeling, he replayed the events of the morning in his head. It was too cruel and elaborately staged to be a joke. But if it was all true—Kent wasn't bluffing—he couldn't stand by and let his son be murdered. He'd give his life in a second to save George or Julia or Charlie. The thought of losing his children was too horrible to bear.

Cross walked blindly, covering block after block as if in a trance. He crossed streets without looking, lucky not to be run over by the parade of wagons and carriages. All the while, his mind raced with terrible images of how Kent would murder George. How had his son gotten into such a fix?

In that instant, Cross realized he knew as much about George as one of these strangers next to him on the sidewalk. His son wasn't what he seemed. His handsome, charming facade masked deviant, illicit behavior. Cross had thought he'd been a model father. Well, the joke was on him. If what Kent had told him was true, then he'd failed miserably. His knees almost buckled under him, nearly sent him to the ground right there on Fifth Avenue. *A son's faults are his father's faults*, his mind repeated numbly.

He realized he couldn't face this alone, but he couldn't tell Helen. At heart, she was a weak-willed, status-obsessed woman who'd collapse into hysterics if he told her what their son had done. Cross kept walking, passed Aunt Caroline's house at Thirty-Fourth Street—and stopped dead in his tracks. Of course—he had the Astors, the most powerful force in the city, on his side. Surely they could save George.

Cross started sprinting up the front stoop but halted midway. What was he thinking? The thought of knocking on Caroline's door and telling her what had happened filled him with shame. George's dishonor would repulse her, and knowing Caroline, she'd slam the door on his family. If her son, Jack, had found himself in this kind of fix, it was merely a matter of writing a check and keeping the whole thing secret. But being poor, distantly related Schermerhorns and Livingstons only went so far. Society people walked on eggshells their whole lives to avoid the merest whiff of scandal. Cross had seen lives shattered by a mere whisper, no matter how untrue. And if it *was* true...

No, he couldn't go directly to Caroline. But perhaps he could reach out to someone in her circle of influence, a person he wasn't tied to by blood. Cross walked to the bottom of the stoop and thought for a while. Then he walked slowly downtown to Madison Square, oblivious to the scorching sun that beat down upon him. Continuing on Broadway, he stopped in front of the recently finished Lincoln Building at Fourteenth Street. The office of Thomas Griffith, the Astors' most trusted attorney, was located there. Griffith, the city's paragon of the legal profession, would tell Cross what to do, and he'd never breathe a word to the Astors.

Finally feeling a small measure of relief, Cross entered the towering, ten-story limestone building.

5

EVEN IF IT HADN'T BEEN A SWELTERING JULY NIGHT, CROSS wouldn't have been able to sleep. He was still too shaken and frightened by the day's revelations.

After tossing and turning for hours, he finally gave up and rose. Thankfully, he and Helen had separate bedrooms. If they'd slept in the same bed, his wife would have known immediately that something was wrong. Cross usually slept like a rock.

Putting on his dark green silk dressing gown, Cross sat on the settee in the parlor and smoked until dawn's light streamed in through the gap in the heavy velvet drapes hanging over the tall windows. He couldn't get his mind off what George had done. It didn't seem possible that Kent was talking about his son. Did George really live in a secret world, one unfathomable to Cross?

Of course Cross knew what gentlemen of his class did when away from the prying eyes of their families. Stanford White was the supreme example of a gentleman's penchant for extracurricular activities, and Cross was no saint himself. But even those debaucheries followed class boundaries. You'd never see White on the Bowery or in a Chinatown gambling den.

President Eliot's words from George's graduation party rang in Cross's ears: "...*vices born of luxury and self-indulgence on the rise.*" At the time, Cross had thought with self-righteous satisfaction that Eliot's words didn't apply to his boy. He'd seen high-society fathers destroy their sons with money, yachts, racehorses, and anything else they wanted—gifts that killed the boys' ambition. Despite his own past, Cross had avoided this path. Yes, he came from a society family with all the Knickerbocker advantages: elite private schools, summers in Newport and the Berkshires, riding, shooting, European tours, servants, balls. He'd gone to Harvard too. But then, defying the Knickerbocker business tradition, he went to Paris to train in architecture at the École des Beaux-Arts. After apprenticing for one of America's greatest architects, Henry Hobson Richardson, he'd set up his own practice. Cross had had a real goal in life. In turn, he wanted to set an example for his son. To his delight, George had great dreams too—to become a mathematician and teach, perhaps as a professor at Harvard. What the hell had happened?

None of that matters, Cross told himself. What mattered was keeping George alive. Speaking to Thomas Griffith yesterday had set Cross's mind somewhat at ease, if only because it allowed Cross to share his desperate burden.

To Cross's surprise, Griffith, a taciturn, granite-faced man of seventy, had turned ashen when he'd heard Kent's name. Kent, he explained to Cross, was a well-bred, Princeton-educated man from a wealthy mercantile family in Baltimore. Rumor had it that he'd originally trained to be a doctor. His connections at the highest levels of business and government in New York made him a man of great influence and power. Even Tammany Hall, the political machine that ran the city, did what he told them to do.

Kent was a man to be feared. Although he was already so rich he didn't need the money, he ran an extensive crime organization that committed any kind of depravity that would turn a profit. His gang was nicknamed "Kent's Gents" because they dressed like society gentlemen, down to their gold-capped walking sticks, which were used more frequently for beating people to death than strolling about.

The attorney made Cross repeat the conversation they'd had at Saint Patrick's word for word. Then, with a terrified look on his face, Griffith told Cross that they had to move quickly or George would indeed be killed. Kent did not make idle threats.

At these words, Cross groaned as if he'd been punched in the stomach and dropped his head, tears welling up in his eyes. Griffith went to the telephone on his office wall and asked for police headquarters on Mulberry Street. He was immediately connected to Thomas Byrnes, chief inspector of the New York City Police Department. From his tone, they seemed to be good friends. Griffith explained that he was calling on a matter of great urgency, and Byrnes agreed to see him first thing the next morning.

Cross had breathed a great sigh of relief when he heard the policeman's name. Byrnes was a ruthlessly efficient Irish cop who had transformed the New York City police, weeding out corruption and modernizing investigations with innovations like mug shots, which created a photographic gallery of known criminals. Before Byrnes's arrival, the New York underworld had seen the city's police force as a joke. But all that had changed. Wall Street, for instance, had always been a rich hunting ground for criminals, who preyed on bank messengers, robbing them of the bonds, securities, and cash they carried from bank to bank. Byrnes declared that Fulton Street, the northern boundary of Wall Street, would be a "dead line," below which all criminals would be arrested on sight. He was true to his word, and robberies on Wall Street soon dropped to zero.

Byrnes, Cross realized, was the only man who could save his son.

❖ ❖ ❖

It was 6:00 a.m. He heard Colleen, their maid, moving about in the kitchen on the ground floor, lighting the fire in the cast-iron stove and getting ready to set the table for breakfast. Mrs. Johnston, the housekeeper, and Mrs. O'Shea, the cook, would be down soon. Cross hadn't eaten anything since yesterday's meeting with Kent. Now, he found that his appetite had returned.

As Cross walked into the center hall to the stairs, he heard the telephone ring. Odd to get a call so early in the morning.

"It's for you, sir," said Colleen in her chipper Irish brogue as she passed him on the stair.

Cross picked up the receiver in the kitchen.

"Good morning, Mr. Cross," a man's voice said. "We wanted to let you know that we just made an ice delivery."

The phone clicked off. Cross turned to look at the icebox on the far wall of his kitchen, a thoroughly modern room with the latest in newfangled technology, befitting an architect. The icebox was clad in dark walnut and lined with cork insulation; it had extra shelves and a space at the top to hold a block of ice weighing about two hundred pounds. A little door in the back faced another matching door that Cross had cut into the outside brownstone wall on the Thirtieth Street side. The iceman could place the ice directly in the icebox without coming into the kitchen. But Mrs. O'Shea usually placed a card in the kitchen window to tell the iceman when ice was needed. It was odd that he would call the house.

Cross slowly walked to the icebox and opened it. He saw nothing unusual on the shelves, just the ordinary perishable foodstuffs. Cheese and lettuce. Puzzled, he opened the door of the top compartment— and stepped back with a gasp. Inside, encased in a block of ice, was the severed head of a man. After a few seconds, Cross recognized Thomas Griffith, the Astors' attorney. Griffith's eyes were wide with terror. His severed flesh was tinted bluish, the lips purple, his white hair floating above his skull like he was under water.

Heart pounding, Cross wheeled, made sure no one else was in the kitchen, and quickly pushed the door of the icebox shut. At that moment, the telephone rang again. He ran to it before Colleen could answer from upstairs.

"Mr. Cross? We must apologize. We delivered the wrong ice to you this morning. But don't worry. We'll replace it right away."

Cross slammed the receiver against the wall box and fell to the slate floor like a building collapsing in on itself. Crumpled and hyperventilating, he stared at the icebox in horror. As if from very far away, he heard the doors at the back open and then the sound of blocks of ice being moved about. The telephone rang for the third time. Cross stared at the dark oak telephone box for a long moment. Then he slowly reached for the receiver.

"Good morning, Mr. Cross. Please meet me at the Dakota today at three p.m. Apartment 7G." Cross recognized the voice of James Kent, who hung up abruptly.

Mrs. O'Shea, a gaunt Irish woman in a dark gray dress and white apron, came into the kitchen, humming to herself.

"Why, Mr. Cross, whatever are you doing down here this early?" Without waiting for his answer, she went right to the icebox and opened the top compartment to check the ice, as she did every morning.

The block of ice was crystal clear.

6

WHEN YOU PRESENT YOUR CALLING CARD TO THE BUTLER, JULIA, you must wait to see if the lady of the house will receive you. If the butler tells you, 'She's not at home to callers,' that's perfectly acceptable. Don't take it as a slight. Leaving your card fulfills your obligation. Now, if she does receive you, never stay for more than thirty minutes. And never pay a call before two or after four."

Helen Cross delivered her lecture in a stern schoolteacher's voice. Her daughter wrinkled her brow, took the calling card from her mother, and examined it.

"No lady *ever* leaves just her own card on the first visit. She must always include her husband's," Helen continued.

"This is so complicated, Mother. Why must I know all this absurd social arithmetic?" Julia asked, her tone a combination of scorn and amusement.

Her grandmother, a slender and graceful Knickerbocker matriarch who still retained her beauty after seventy years, took Julia by the shoulders and looked her in the eyes. "My child, calling cards are the alpha and omega of social intercourse. You *must* remember this."

"You won't get your own cards in your first season, mind. Your name will be on mine," Helen said. "It seems complicated, but you'll soon learn the rules. We all had to go through this."

"The most important rule to remember is that an unmarried woman never receives a gentleman caller without her mother or a chaperone present." Granny spoke with an earnestness that startled Julia. "A chaperone knows the world; a young girl doesn't."

Aunt Caroline Astor placed her arm around Julia. "Remember, my dear, you're a Schermerhorn. We're held to a higher standard."

"Why yes, of course, Aunt Caroline."

"You'll have the most brilliant coming-out ball in the city. At my place, of course. I'll see to *everything*." Aunt Caroline spoke confidentially to Helen, who beamed with delight. That meant that from now on, Caroline would pay for Julia's wardrobe. To Julia, she added, "You'll be the most beautiful debutante of the season."

"So much work to be done. We must make the list of guests, and then I'll make a personal call on every one," said Helen, who didn't consider this task work. She looked forward to seeing all two hundred people in advance of this, a truly special occasion in her life. A daughter's coming-out meant that the mother had decided she was ready to be accepted by the world as a fully mature woman—and more importantly, ready to receive homage from rich, eligible men.

"What about me? Where's my invitation?" asked Charlie Cross, Julia's ten-year-old blond brother, sliding down the black walnut banister of the front stair in the entrance hall of the Cross home, where the women stood.

"You, little boy, are not coming," said Julia with a frown.

"I wouldn't want to come to your dumb party. I bet no one shows up," Charlie said, dismounting before he collided with the ornate newel post. He leaped to the floor with the agility of an acrobat.

"Charlie, aren't you going to play in Madison Park?" his mother asked.

"On my way," yelled Charlie as he crashed through the front doors.

Julia's mentors were content to stay in the entrance hall, a wide, graceful space that ran the length of the house to the back stairs used by the servants. Its ten-foot-high walls were adorned with flowered brocade wallpaper and dark walnut wainscoting. A heavy, carved walnut hallstand with coat hooks, a large mirror, and a built-in seat dominated the space.

Granny pointed at the silver calling card stand next to the seat.

"The cards are left in the stand. You'll fill out this ledger stating when your visitors' cards were presented and by whom. It must *always* be up-to-date."

"Remember that a guest *must* pay a personal call within two days of a dinner party. For all other entertainments, leaving a card with the butler will do," Aunt Caroline added emphatically.

"I understand," said a bewildered Julia. "May I go upstairs, please, Mother?"

"Yes, dear. We'll start the list tonight." Helen spoke excitedly, like a child looking forward to her birthday party.

The women watched as Julia ran up the stairs.

"She's inherited your beauty, Helen, and that's important. A girl's beauty assures her brilliant future," Aunt Caroline said. "It's the most important possession a girl can have."

"But Julia, I think, has an independent streak," Granny said. She spoke disapprovingly, as if her granddaughter had done something reprehensible. "A girl *has* to conform. She must. And she needs a good chaperone."

"Hush, Mother. Julia would never do anything untoward. She's only seventeen."

"But what's this talk about her going to college? To Vassar?" Granny spoke incredulously, her tone bordering on panic. "A girl like her doesn't need college. She's already too educated. Men don't want a wife cleverer than they are."

Colleen stepped out of the front parlor and curtsied. "Tea is served, madam," she chirped.

"Thank you so much," Helen said. Granny frowned. Helen knew what was bothering her—Granny would think that Helen should have left off the "so much" or not even said a thank-you. Her mother thought familiarity with servants was vulgar and unwarranted. While servants were indispensable to society people, they had to know their place. This was why Americans were largely held to make terrible servants—they were too independent, expecting to have all sorts of *rights*. Absolutely the best way to run a household, Granny always said, was with dumb and subservient Irish servants, a spinster English housekeeper, or—if the house was big enough—an English butler.

The women settled into their chairs in the parlor, and Helen poured tea from a gleaming silver tea set on a mahogany tea table. Smiling, she passed a plate stacked with iced lemon cakes. Her front parlor, accessible through paneled sliding doors off the entrance hall, was "the best room" and served as the stage for important family events, as well as for entertaining. There, the lady of the house demonstrated her family's cultural refinement through her selection of the paintings and lithographs that adorned the blue damask walls. Like all society ladies, Helen had a fear of empty space. She filled every square inch of wall and floor with bric-a-brac. The deep-purple Belter chairs with their round backs, the scarlet velvet settee, the flowered rug, the forest-green drapes on the tall front windows—even the design of the lace doilies on the backs of the chairs were an aesthetic choice. She was proud of her parlor. It had to be the height of fashion, for soon it would be Julia's courting arena.

"Did you read, Caroline, that forty thousand workers have gone on strike in Chicago? It seems they want an eight-hour workday." Granny shook her head, appalled as ever by the changing times. "Fifteen thousand marched in Union Square to support them."

"All the meat packers, cigar makers, and leather workers in Chicago on strike. It's unbelievable. They already have a ten-hour day. Those fools should be grateful. It used to be twelve. I suppose that next they'll want Saturdays off." Caroline huffed. "William says the owners may call in Pinkertons to deal with them." A private army of policemen, the Pinkertons were detectives hired by rich businessmen to solve crimes and especially to put down strikes and labor protests the local authorities could not deal with. Considered much smarter than the regular police, the Pinkertons used brute force and bullets to get results.

"I hope they do. They know how to handle anarchists," Granny said with a smile.

"Then there's this talk of home rule for Ireland," Caroline said. "Every day, the front page of the *Tribune* has an article about the debates in Parliament."

"If the Irish we get as servants are any indication, it's madness to think they can rule themselves," Granny said. "They're no better than children."

"My Irish servants have gotten along rather well," said Helen, smiling. She knew what her mother would say next.

"You let your help walk all over you, Helen. It's a disgrace."

"I just happen to remember that they're human beings, Mother."

"When his mistress enters the room, a servant is supposed to turn away and avert his eyes," Granny said indignantly. "Yours speak to you without being spoken to first!"

"I'm glad to have the respect and loyalty of my servants," Helen said, reminded again how lucky she was that her mother still lived in her own massive brownstone on East Twenty-Fifth Street.

Caroline gracefully changed the subject. "Ellen Thackeray was a guest at President Cleveland's wedding reception last month. She said his bride, Frances Folsom, looked absolutely radiant in white lace."

"That man's old enough to be her father," Granny said.

There was a noise in the hall. *John coming down the stairs*, Helen thought. She rose and intercepted him in the entry hall before he made it to the front door.

"John, I thought you were ill. You said you weren't going to the office today."

She'd known something was wrong from the instant she'd laid eyes on her husband that morning. It was as though all the blood had drained from his face. Normally a robust man, he seemed listless and lethargic, unable to focus on her words.

"Helen, I must go out," John said.

But she blocked his path. "You look terrible, John. Go back to bed. I'll have Colleen bring you some tea."

"Goddamn it, I don't need any tea. I have an appointment, and I can't be late," Cross shouted.

His harsh tone made her jump out of his way. She watched in alarm as her husband grabbed his hat and stormed out the door. What could possibly be wrong?

7

"Mr. Cross, I want you to know that I'm not angry at you for what you did. But I will be less lenient if something like that should happen again."

Kent reminded Cross of a schoolmaster sitting in his wood-paneled office, reprimanding a recalcitrant student. Cross himself sat stiffly, balanced on the edge of the settee, watching Kent pour tea. Aunt Caroline would have envied the quality of the silver. In a multitiered stand on the tea table were a variety of pastries, but Cross had lost all appetite since the delivery of the ice that morning.

The Dakota was like a huge European château, a riot of steep gables, turrets, finials, and dormers clad in olive-colored stone and salmon-colored brick. Its sheer enormity was amplified by its position on the Upper West Side, surrounded by vacant lots and shacks. It gave the impression of a mountain that had risen out of nowhere. From Central Park, it reminded one of a fortress in the middle of an enchanted forest, like in a fairy tale.

Despite its far-flung location, it had quickly become a highly fashionable place to live. Kent's apartment was magnificent. He and Cross sat in a beautiful library lined with floor-to-ceiling bookshelves. A vista of Central Park stretched across the tall windows behind them.

"How many lumps do you take?"

"Two, no milk."

Kent handed him his cup and settled back in his green overstuffed velvet armchair. He sipped his tea with a look of great pleasure.

"Quite a place, Mr. Cross, hmm? Like living in a palace without having to own it."

Cross didn't reply.

At that moment, the front door to the apartment opened. A short, elegantly dressed woman with chestnut-colored hair followed by three small children walked past the open door of the library.

"Mr. Cross, meet my wife and children," Kent said in a jolly voice. "Hello, Millicent. How was the outing?"

"Oh, wonderful. The children so loved the ponies."

Cross rose and smiled at the beautiful woman, who beamed back at him.

"It's such a pleasure, Mr. Cross," Millicent said.

"Mr. Cross is a new business associate. And these rascals are Bill, Henry, and Abigail."

The children, all of whom were well dressed and well mannered, bowed to Cross and then raced off in three different directions.

"If you'll excuse us, my dear, Mr. Cross and I have business to discuss. Tonight at dinner, you must tell me all about your day. I wish I'd been there." Kent followed his wife out, closed the sliding doors, and returned to his seat. "I'm so glad we were able to come to an understanding, Mr. Cross," he said. "I'm sure we can do business together."

"Nothing is to happen to my son," Cross said.

"Or Helen, Granny, Charlie, and Julia—as long as you keep our agreement."

Cross was visibly shaken. After that morning, he knew what this man was capable of. Kent would kill his entire family without batting an eye. He was sure of it.

"I enjoy doing business with a family man," Kent said amiably. "There's so much collateral."

"Where is George?"

"In very pleasant circumstances. I'll notify him that his debt is forgiven, but I won't tell him of our arrangement. Don't worry—if you keep your end of the bargain, he'll never know. George will be back in his apartment in a few days. I just hope he can deal with his 'little weakness.' You do know there are hundreds of gambling dens in New York City besides mine. But that's your problem now."

Cross blinked. In all the confusion, he hadn't thought about that.

"Let me explain how our business arrangement will work," Kent said, setting down his teacup. "You will choose buildings you've designed that contain articles of great value—cash, stock certificates, gold, merchandise such as expensive clothing, fine linen, silverware, and jewelry. You will help me plan each robbery by giving me drawings of these places and telling me where items worth stealing can be found. And after each robbery, the value of the goods will be deducted from George's debt."

"Promise me that, once it's paid back, I'm free of this."

"Why of course. I don't think you're cut out for a life of crime, Mr. Cross." Kent gave him a wink. "But you are a talented architect. That Chandler Building—and those tall arches! I envy your talent. I wish I could do something like that."

Cross was silent. Coming from this merciless bastard, it hardly felt like a compliment.

"The next step will be for you to take some time—one week, say— to choose a building. Then we will meet to discuss whether your plan is feasible. It takes a criminal eye to evaluate these things," Kent said. "You'll want to pay off the debt immediately, of course. But for our first effort, let's choose something modest. And bring copies of the drawings. I understand that with the new blueprinting process, it will be easy for you."

Kent was sharp. Only a few years ago, copies of architectural drawings had to be traced over by hand, a long and tedious process. But with the introduction of blueprinting, all that had changed. Now, a photosensitive coating could be applied to a sheet of paper, which would be placed behind the original linen drawing. The contraption was put in a wood frame that sat out in the sun, developing a perfect image on the paper like a photograph.

"Yes," Cross said, nodding. "I can bring you your own copies of the drawings."

"From now on, it's better to meet elsewhere. You'll be told where to go and when." Kent rose from his chair. The meeting was over. "Please don't think me rude, but I have a Presbyterian Hospital board meeting in an hour over on East Seventy-Second," Kent said apologetically as he escorted Cross to the foyer. "But before you go, you must see my latest treasure."

He led Cross to a large oak table with carved legs and removed a heavy sheet of paper, revealing what looked like a very old, yellowed parchment.

"An early eighth-century illuminated manuscript from France. Isn't it magnificent?"

Though Cross didn't give a damn, he pretended to be impressed out of courtesy. After taking a respectful amount of time to examine the gold-leaf-flecked pages, he nodded and walked toward the library doors.

"Henceforth, Mr. Cross, you must learn to think like a criminal. Coming from your background, that may be difficult," Kent said as he slid open the paneled doors.

"It didn't seem to be an obstacle for you."

Kent gave a roar of laughter. "I suppose Griffith told you all about me. True, Princeton didn't give me much training for my line of work. You're a Harvard man?"

Cross nodded.

"A satisfactory school, but they have no eating clubs, unlike Princeton. So uncivilized," he said. "Do take a look around the building before you go. You'll find it most interesting."

"I walked through right before it opened. The architect, Henry Hardenbergh, is a friend of mine. It's a remarkable building," Cross said softly, looking up at the ceiling. "The best apartment building in the city. I wish I had done it."

8

I N THE COURTYARD OF THE DAKOTA, CROSS DREW A DEEP BREATH
and looked up at the four seven-story-high stone walls surrounding
him. He felt like a mouse trapped in a box.

At the corner of Seventy-Second Street, he walked across Eighth
Avenue into Central Park. The Transverse Road that cut across the
vast green space was filled with carriages. It was the time of day when,
rain or shine, society people paraded themselves. Various conveyances,
pulled by teams of sleek horses with two men in full livery atop the
box, traveled back and forth on the carriage drives. Every day without fail, hordes of onlookers lined the roadways of the park to watch
the Knickerbockers, the parvenus, and the famous pass by in unending
procession. Pure vanity, not fresh air, was what brought the society
women to Central Park each afternoon. Cross paid them no mind.
Instead, lost in thought, he veered off on one of the winding paths
through the trees.

George was safe, he told himself, and that was all that mattered. He
could do nothing to stop his own involvement with Kent; no one was
coming to rescue him. Griffith had been murdered before his meeting
with Byrnes in the police department. Cross was on his own.

He had no choice but to become a criminal in order to save not only
George's life, but the rest of his family's as well. With his loved ones
in danger, he shouldn't be doubting what he had to do. And still—still
he wavered. Was it out of some conviction that resorting to crime went
against all that he believed? It wasn't a matter of faith. Cross hadn't
been brought up in a religious family—society people went to church

every Sunday, Easter, and Christmas because it was expected of them, but it was all for show.

Was he afraid? Did he make a moral objection to committing crime as cover for this fear? *Yes*, Cross thought. He secretly knew this to be true. Deep down, he *was* a coward. More than twenty years ago, during the Civil War, he faced the decision of whether to fight. He hired a substitute to serve in his place. Not to pursue business or a professional career, like the other men of his class, but because the thought of being ripped apart by a volley of rifle or artillery fire in some far-off field terrified him.

War had seemed a noble and abstract concept to him. Then he saw Matthew Brady's photographs of the dead on the battlefield. No one had ever shown the cruel reality of war in such a way. The illustrated papers depicted only the victorious, marching to glory. Brady's pictures were unbelievably real, a harsh image of bullet-ridden corpses rotting in the sun. That was someone's son or brother lying there, Cross had thought, the soldier's eyes and mouth wide open and frozen in shock, hundreds of flies buzzing about the open wounds. Cross's mind transposed his own face onto one of the corpses, and he actually shook with fright.

It was his father who told him of the substitute law. He was secretly overjoyed. Though he put up a pretense of wanting to fight, his father, a successful businessman who didn't give a damn about slavery and saw the great profit to be made from the war, browbeat him into hiring a substitute. Cross was saved because his father could afford the three-hundred-dollar payment. But his older brother, Robert, refused to sit out the war. He volunteered immediately.

While the war raged, Cross gave his choice no mind. But the Union won, and the returning warriors were admired and worshiped. His brother and the others had probably been scared to death. Yet they chose to serve. Robert had even won a medal for gallantry in action, which made Cross feel even more a coward. Ever since, a sense of shame had dogged his heels. And he was still a coward; he had proved that with his vacillations. But no matter how scared he was, he *had* to do this. Even if it meant getting himself killed.

He needed to clear his mind and determine which place to rob. He came to the edge of the lake's south dogleg and sat on the grass bank, watching the fleet of snow-white swans gliding along the still surface. Forming a list of past projects in his head, Cross tried to visualize each one, tried to remember who the client was and where the building was located. But he'd been in practice for fourteen years; there were more buildings than he could recall with any clarity. All the offices, the apartments, Saint Mary's Church on West Sixty-Fourth Street, train stations in the suburbs, the Exchange Hotel, Manhattan Hospital and Dispensary, and scores of houses and cottages. He would have to go back to the office to refresh his memory.

Cross made his way back through the trees to the Transverse Road, following it east until he came to the wide stone steps that swept down from the Mall to the Bethesda Terrace. There, the great fountain stood by the edge of the lake. It was an unbearably hot July day, and dozens of people refreshed themselves in the fine spray carried off the fountain by the breeze. Children stood at the edge, splashing the water at one another. A few ragged urchins, contrary to park rules, were wading. Some society ladies holding brightly colored parasols to keep the heat at bay had even gotten out of their carriages to stroll the Terrace.

Cross stood at the top of the stairs, staring at the scene. Central Park had actually become the democratic meeting ground that its architects, Olmsted and Vaux, intended it to be. Below him, the wealthy rubbed elbows with the lowest of the low, immigrants from the Lower East Side and the Bowery. His class was never this close to such people, not unless they were shining shoes or washing floors. At any time they liked, the men and women of Cross's class could travel to the Berkshires, Newport, or Long Branch for fresh air and nature. But the convenience of Central Park drew them in. For the poor, Central Park was their oasis, easily reachable by horse car or elevated train. There, they could stretch out on the grass for a few hours before returning to the squalor of their everyday lives. Cross saw the park as a masterpiece, a work of art. Everything, save the large rock outcroppings, had been designed and placed by man.

With a sigh, Cross descended to the Terrace and circled the fountain. He was making his way back up when someone called his name. Turning, he saw an old client, William Cook.

"Playing hooky from work, old boy?" Cook was a short man in his early fifties, not fat but exceedingly well fed. A member of the new rich, he'd made tens of millions in the shoe business in Saint Louis. His wife had then forced him to move to New York to breech the walls of Aunt Caroline's high society. Many of the city's millionaires were originally from the Midwest or West Coast. Like the tens of thousands of poor immigrants who streamed through Castle Garden in the Battery, these wealthy people descended upon the city each year, seeking a new life.

While Cook was a "shoddyite," dressed in only the best suits, he was a good, decent man. He only flaunted his wealth as offensively as he did because he wanted to please his social climber of a wife.

"Hello, Bill. Yes, you've caught me. But why aren't you at work?"

"We're shutting up the house and taking the steamer to the cottage at Newport tonight. Alice loves that place you designed for us, John. I think she likes it more than the one you did in the city."

"That's kind of you to say." The "cottage" Cross had designed for the Cooks on Bellevue Avenue in Newport was a twenty-four-room, wood-frame house covered with shingles and surrounded by deep porches. Cross considered it one of the best things he'd done. He loved when a client told him how much they appreciated his work.

"Of course, I wanted to take a stroll in the park before we left. Nice thing about having a home on Fifth Avenue: Central Park is your front yard! I love walking about the place. Lot of good lookers on parade, if you know what I mean," Cook said and winked.

"Helen and I will be coming up later this month. I'll give you a call.

We can meet at the casino," Cross said, waving good-bye as he trotted up the stairs.

"That would be awfully jolly," Cook called.

Cross looked back and smiled. The new rich, Granny complained, were always using vulgar British phrases like that.

On Fifth Avenue, Cross walked along the inside of the low stone wall separating the park from the wide sidewalk. He stopped at East Seventy-Eighth Street and surveyed the Cook mansion from behind the trunk of an elm tree. He smiled when he saw the huge Renaissance Revival mansion.

The house looked impenetrable from the outside because a dry moat surrounded it on all four sides. After his first trip to England, Cook had become crazy about castles and moats and wanted one like a child covets a toy for Christmas. A real moat was out of the question for his new city mansion, but Cross had cleverly provided one without water, a stone-lined ditch that was fifteen feet wide and twenty feet deep. It actually had a practical purpose; it accommodated two stories of kitchens, storage rooms, and servants' quarters below the street level, with windows even. To Cook's delight, his architect added iron-and-wood drawbridges to span the moat to the front door and to the rear service entry. At night or when the house was empty, the drawbridges were raised, creating a wide, deep, protective chasm between the sidewalk and the house. But best of all, Cook felt that the unique design meant that he didn't need a night watchman while he was away.

Yes, this will do nicely, Cross thought.

9

THOUGH HE WAS A PRISONER, GEORGE HAD TO ADMIT THE JAIL WAS magnificent. Especially the views. To the south, you could see Kaaterskill High Peak; to the north, South Lake and North Mountain. George and his jailer, Tommy Flannigan, were taking a stroll along the front of the Kaaterskill Hotel, the finest in the Catskill Mountains. A four-hundred-foot-long building with three-story columns, it boasted six hundred rooms with steam radiators, running water, and electric service bells.

"You know what I like best about this place, Georgie? The air. It's so cool and refreshing. Not like bein' in that steam bath in Manhattan. I thought it might be more pleasant for us to spend some time together out here."

"Yes, it feels wonderful," George said. He hadn't given the weather a second's thought. It wasn't as important as knowing whether he would live or die.

It was a shrewd move on Kent's part, bringing him up there. If he'd kept him captive in Manhattan, George could have escaped and been on the next boat to China. But in the Catskills, one hundred thirty miles north of the city, he was in the middle of a wilderness with no place to run.

"Look at the size of this joint, will you? You know that it all got built on account of a fight over fried chicken?"

"What?"

"The owner, George Harding. He was staying over at the Catskill Hotel and wanted his daughter to have fried chicken, but they wouldn't give it to her because it wasn't on the day's menu. They told him to go build his own hotel if he wanted fried chicken. And that's what he did," said Flannigan with a braying laugh.

The sound reminded George of a jackass.

As they walked back to the main lobby, George watched Flannigan out of the corner of his eye. For years, he'd terrorized victims in the Five Points and the Bowery. Once, when he was arrested, the police found a price list for services in his pocket: nineteen dollars to break an arm; fifteen dollars to bite off an ear; ten dollars to break a nose and jaw; twenty-five dollars to stab or shoot in the leg. But for all these horrible acts of violence, Flannigan had a soft streak, and he'd been George's constant sympathetic companion for the previous two days. George could see that the genial bear of a man was downhearted about having to kill him.

"Come on, Georgie," he said, slapping George on the back with his big paw. "Things will work out. From what I hear, Mr. Kent may let the debt slide."

"After you break my arms and legs and poke out my eyes."

"Oh no, Georgie. I'd never do that to you. I've always had a hard time beating the hell out of really handsome guys like you. Seems like destroying God's best work."

"That's very noble of you, Tommy," George muttered.

The two men entered the hotel lobby, which was crowded with families waiting to check in and out. Since its opening in 1881, the Kaaterskill had become a fashionable destination for New York society. Like a Madrid bull, Flannigan rammed and pushed the well-dressed customers aside to get to the front desk. George waited in a sitting area, looking over a copy of the *Tribune*. Soon, he realized, his death might be a front-page article. Most murder victims in New York City were found floating in the East or Hudson Rivers, their bloated bodies bumping against the bulkheads of the wooden piers lining the island. He could imagine the police going to his home and asking his father to identify his rotting corpse. His family would be crushed. *It'd be better*, George thought grimly, *for my body to completely disappear.* Then no one would discover the ugly circumstances of his downfall. Kent was a gentleman—of a sort. Perhaps he would be amenable to such an arrangement.

"Mr. Cross."

George looked up to see Mary Morse, a pretty, blue-eyed brunette in a navy-blue walking dress and matching hat. Next to her was a small woman in her fifties, with beady eyes and an expressionless face. *The chaperone*, thought George. Every girl of Mary's set had one who followed her like a shadow.

"Hello, Miss Morse."

The lack of enthusiasm in George's voice brought a look of disappointment to Mary's face. She had hovered about him at his graduation party like a fly around horse manure—to his annoyance.

"It's so nice to see you here," she said brightly. "We're stopping for a few days before traveling to Newport. This afternoon, we're going on a walk in the Catskills to visit the waterfall. It's most beautiful. I do hope you might join us. Mrs. Rampling, my mother's great-aunt, will be with me."

Mrs. Rampling gave George the iciest of smiles. There would be no monkey business on her watch.

"I'm sorry, Miss Morse, but I've made other plans," George said. "Maybe later this week, if you're still here, I could call on you."

"Oh yes! We're in room—"

"Holy shit, I had a helluva time fightin' my fuckin' way up there to get the goddamn key. Oh, hello there," said Flannigan, trotting up to them.

"Miss Morse, this is Mr. Flannigan…a friend of mine," George managed.

"Damn glad to meet ya," Flannigan said, thrusting his broad red hand toward Mary. She shook it gingerly, as if it were dipped in blood. "And who's this other gorgeous dove?"

"Mrs. Rampling," snapped the chaperone, stepping back. Clearly she had no intention of touching Flannigan.

"Hey, what do you say we all have a drink in the bar, huh? I'm buying."

"Miss Morse was on her way to take a walk in the mountains, Mr. Flannigan. Maybe another time," George said.

"Sure. What's your room number? I can come by later to get you."

"I already asked them, but unfortunately, they've made plans for later."

"Oh, that's a goddamn shame."

"Miss Morse, maybe we'll run into each other again." George bowed and dragged Flannigan away by the arm.

"Good-looking babe, George. Were you making time with her? I hope I didn't butt into anything."

"No, Tommy. In fact, you rescued me, and I'm eternally grateful," George said, laughing.

Mary was like all the girls in his world. Marriage was their only vocation; it was what they were brought up for. With his looks and family background, he was a prime candidate—or victim—for their machinations.

Flannigan and George walked to their room on the sixth floor of the east tower, the best spot in the hotel. The room was large but not fancy. It had plain white walls, two beds, a chest of drawers, and a bright carpet. A green recamier stood in the corner; George flopped down onto it, rubbing his hands over his face. His mind was racing. When—and how—had his life changed?

George knew the answer. He could picture the winter night he'd first stepped through the door of Pendleton's, the most exclusive den of iniquity in the city. Some Harvard upperclassmen had taken him during Christmas holidays in '84. At Pendleton's, gentlemen of the highest pedigree could gamble, drink, and seduce chorus girls, free from the disapproving eyes of Aunt Caroline's New York society. Tucked away in a brownstone on East Forty-Fifth Street, the interior of the club was lavishly designed, with walnut-paneled walls, marble floors, and crystal chandeliers. In private gambling rooms, one could play faro, poker, baccarat, or roulette. Liquor and food flowed freely. It was as if George had opened a trapdoor and walked down a stair into a magical world of enchantment and pleasure.

Being a mathematician, George had an innate talent for gambling. He loved everything about it—analyzing the probabilities, calculating odds, counting cards, the throw of the dice. But it was the incredible rush of excitement when he won that thrilled him most. Pure euphoria. The sensation was even more pleasurable than sex, another pastime he was introduced to at Pendleton's. Soon, gambling became an obsession. It was all he could think about or wanted to do. At every second, he felt the uncontrollable urge to bet. He had no willpower, no control over his actions; the desire had taken hold of him, like a puppeteer manipulating the wires of a marionette.

At Pendleton's, George met James T. Kent. They took an instant liking to each other. Kent was one of George's own, a rich, dashing figure with a great deal of charm and intelligence. And the man knew how to enjoy himself.

If Pendleton's was the apogee of pleasure houses, however, below it swam a multitude of grimy, low-life establishments. Along the Bowery and Broadway were sleazy dance halls, whorehouses, and gambling dens that catered to the scum of the earth. In addition to games of chance like keno, dice, and craps, they offered wagers on cockfights, prizefights, dogfights, ratting, and horse racing. In addition to its opium dens, Chinatown had its own native gambling called fan-tan and pai gow.

George discovered these places by pure accident. A Harvard professor persuaded him to volunteer in the industrial school of the Children's Aid Society, and to George's delight, he discovered he had a gift for teaching. He loved working with children. But the mission was located in one of the city's vilest neighborhoods—the Lower East Side, which averaged four gambling dens per block. Like a little boy in a confectioner's shop, George couldn't help himself. And he could never walk away from the table when he was ahead—he had to keep playing.

In the fall of '85, his luck turned. A long losing streak began, one he couldn't pull himself out of. George found himself deep in debt, constantly chasing his losses. He drained his inheritance from his grandfather, which was meant to pay for his graduate studies at Columbia. It felt like he was running on an endless railroad track, trying to catch up with the last car of the train. He'd reach out and almost grab on, but then the train would accelerate at the last second and pull away, leaving him deep in debt again.

After a particularly catastrophic loss on a horse named Gray Ghost, George approached Kent for credit. That day began his fatal descent. Kent gladly extended loans and credit to him. For a while, some of George's luck returned, allowing him to repay Kent. This opened the door to more loans, and more again. Then the losing streak returned with a vengeance. It had continued until the day of George's reckoning at Delmonico's.

A knock sounded at the door.

"Damn you, Mary Morse. I don't want to go on a walk," George growled.

"Maybe they want that drink," Flannigan said, moving to open the door. Then, "Christ Almighty, Pretty Kitty McGowan, what the hell are you doing here?"

In the doorway stood a ravishingly beautiful woman with jet-black hair, a dark complexion, and large brown eyes. George thought she could have been described as Creole.

"On special assignment, Tommy. Here, take this double eagle and sample the goods in the bar." She deftly flipped up a coin. With equal dexterity, Flannigan snapped it out of the air and left the room.

"Kitty," gasped George. "Oh, Kitty." He ran over to her and took her in his arms. "Oh God, it's good to see you."

Kitty held George for a long time, burying her head against his chest. Finally, George took a step back and looked at her. Even amid all the fashionable ladies in the lobby, she was by far the most beautiful and elegant. No one would've suspected she was among the most desirable whores in New York, the darling of every scion, captain of industry, bank president, and Wall Street stockbroker.

George had met Kitty at Miss Jennie's, a discreet and handsomely furnished brothel that catered exclusively to the society set. The tinkling sound of a piano added a sophisticated note to its air, and champagne sold for ten dollars a bottle. The girls were clean, refined, and trained in the art of conversation. On Friday and Saturday nights, only clients in evening dress with bouquets of flowers were admitted. And, above all, Miss Jennie's was honestly run. In some of New York's brothels, called panel houses, a man would emerge from behind a detachable panel in the wainscoting and steal a man's wallet from his pants pocket while he was busy with a girl. Such a thing would never happen at Miss Jennie's. Nor did her girls use knockout drops to rob clients.

George was drawn to Kitty immediately. He didn't mind that other men coveted her too. In a short time, she paid George the highest compliment a whore can pay—she had sex with him without compensation in her off hours. The two soon fell in love with each other.

"Georgie, Kent sent me. I have wonderful news. He said to tell you he's calling off the debt. You're free, my love."

10

T AKE A DEEP BREATH AND HOLD IT."

Mrs. Johnston yanked hard on the laces of the corset, and Julia Cross groaned as the air was pushed out of her body. The English housekeeper, a stout old woman with beefy forearms, tied the corset as expertly as if she were wrapping a parcel.

"There," chirped Helen Cross. "You have the perfect figure for a princess gown. Long and narrow."

"Perfect," Mrs. Johnston agreed. "Next, you'll need the camisole trimmed in lace and ribbons, and the petticoat with the ruffle along the bottom edge."

Helen beamed with pride as the housekeeper continued to dress her daughter. She had waited for this moment for a long time. No longer would Julia wear her hair long and unpinned; it would be piled stylishly atop her head. In place of loose-fitting skirts hemmed six inches above her ankles, her dresses would be long and tapered, sweeping the floor. Above all, she could wear jewelry—as long as it had not been given to her by an unmarried man. Julia would finally be leaving her gawky, girlish days behind.

The housekeeper fastened a wire bustle atop Julia's buttocks. "Now for the dress," Mrs. Johnston said. Julia stepped into a beautiful, cornflower-blue gown, which the housekeeper rapidly fastened up at the back. Her mother stood behind her and looked at her in the mirror.

"You're a real beauty, Julia," she said, hugging her from behind. She lifted Julia's flowing hair and coiled it on top of her head. "I'll get some pins."

Fifteen minutes later, with the aid of eighteen hairpins, Helen had transformed Julia's hair. "Next week, you'll attend your first private teas. So many people to see. You know, the Beekmans' son just finished West Point," Helen said, smiling at Mrs. Johnston. The housekeeper also knew the social cachet of a West Point man from a Knickerbocker family.

"May I keep this on? Just for a bit, to get used to it?" Julia asked. Helen nodded.

"I have to finish some writing. But I'll be down for tea," Julia said.

Helen watched as her daughter skipped out of the room, her playful gait at odds with her newly grown-up look. By the ironclad rules of society, she was supposed to be raising her daughter as her mother had raised her. But Helen refused to practice the benign parental neglect expected of her class. Her mother had told her that she must see her children only on occasion and be "reasonably" acquainted with them. Helen defied her and fostered a close relationship with George, Julia, and Charlie. She'd made sure her husband did the same.

Julia's coming-out did not mean Helen was losing a daughter, of course. There was no rush to the altar; her daughter was only seventeen. Still, the whole journey was to be undertaken with great care. For Julia to have the highest value on the society matrimonial market, even the tiniest hint of scandal must be avoided. *The girl is lucky to have Aunt Caroline to give her counsel*, Helen thought. Caroline would help Julia avoid the misfortune of her own daughter's poor decisions.

Emily, Caroline's eldest, had fallen in love with James Van Alen, heir to millions from investments in the Illinois Central Railroad. An eccentric Anglophile who pretended to speak with an English accent, Van Alen was dubbed totally unsuitable by the Astors. William Backhouse Astor II, Caroline's husband, publicly stated that they would have nothing to do with the Van Alens. The groom's father, a Civil War general, challenged Astor to a duel; Astor backed out and apologized. The marriage took place, and the unhappiness began. After a succession of long, empty years, Emily died in 1881 while giving birth to her third child.

Caroline's own marriage, Helen knew, was an elaborate facade. Astor was content to let her spend his millions, but he'd pushed her out of his life long ago. He carried on with prostitutes and showgirls on his yacht, the aptly named *Light of the Harem*. Caroline, a master of ignoring unpleasant matters, pretended he was a loving and devoted husband but went to great lengths to keep him from her balls and dinners.

Her own marriage, Helen had to admit, followed similar rules.

⁌ ⁌ ⁌

As she often did when entering her bedroom, Julia got a running start and flopped onto her bed. This time, she let out a loud yelp. The corset jammed up under her newly full breasts, and the bustle rammed into the lower part of her back. Immediately, she jumped up again.

Sadness came over her in a wave. The adult way of dressing, she realized, ruled out relaxing and playing. She couldn't slide down the banister in this thing. Julia perched awkwardly at her rolltop desk, the corset forcing her to sit ramrod straight, the bustle keeping her at the edge of the seat. But her new posture didn't deter her from commencing her daily two hours of writing. She was working on a novel, a tale of love and adventure very much influenced by the work of Sir Walter Scott.

Julia was glad her parents hadn't listened to Granny and had her tutored at home. To their credit, they both wanted her to attend a day school—the elite and expensive Miss Spence's, where she could make friends with girls from her own class and get a first-rate education. There, she discovered her passion for literature and writing. In Granny's prehistoric world, too much education was dangerous; ladies only needed "ornamental knowledge" to win a husband. To placate Granny, Helen made sure Julia had lessons in painting, sketching, needlework, piano, and, most importantly, dancing. Now that she was coming out, the latter skill was essential.

There were other lessons too. Since all the men of her class were mad about horses and especially about racing, Julia had the requisite equestrian training from an early age. She went riding in Central Park—always sidesaddle, never astride—at least two times a week. Because her family spent every summer in Newport and the Berkshires, expertise in archery, lawn tennis, and croquet was also required. A girl should be proficient—but never good enough to beat a man.

In the past month, Julia had begun rigorous schooling in the intricate rules of etiquette. A dinner never starts earlier than nine, she was told. Sherry is always cooled but not red wine. Don't let two brown or white sauces follow each other in succession. Then there was the strict code of behavior. Two essential rules had been drilled into her: restrain all emotional outbursts in public, and any hint of scandal means disaster, for once a girl is talked about, she's done. Break these and it meant social extinction, Granny and her mother preached.

An eager student, Julia loved school. Now that colleges for women like Vassar and Wellesley existed, she eagerly looked forward to higher education. She wasn't sure if she'd be allowed to go—many Knickerbockers thought college was a colossal waste of time for society girls. Learning Greek wouldn't help her do important things like needlework, keeping the servants in line, or determining whether a room had been properly dusted.

"Why even bother?" Granny always said. "A woman's body is not equal to a man's, so it stands that her brain isn't equal either."

But Julia didn't want to be ornamental. Her mother was against college, but she could tell her father was on her side. As an architect, he had an innate thirst for knowledge and beauty, which she'd inherited.

Immersed in a description of her heroine's faithful nanny, Julia didn't notice Charlie stealing into the room until he plopped down on her bed.

"Why are you dressed like that?" he asked.

"From now on, I dress like an adult, little boy."

"What a bore."

"And adults prize their privacy. So get out, you little beast."

"I can't. I've to stay clear of Father."

"And why is that?"

"He's in a very peculiar mood."

11

HELEN CROSS WATCHED AS HER HUSBAND ABSENTMINDEDLY
picked at his saddle of lamb. It was usually his favorite dish.
But tonight, in thirty minutes, he'd eaten one bite. He'd not said more
than five words to her in that time either, but that was quite normal.
Monks who'd taken a vow of silence talked more than she and John did
at supper.

"Mrs. O'Shea's going to be upset to see all that food you've left on
your plate."

As was the custom of the Knickerbockers, except for Sunday and
holiday meals, the Crosses took the evening meal by themselves in the
formal dining room. Children younger than eighteen ate downstairs in
the kitchen with the servants.

Black walnut paneling covered every square inch of the walls and
ceiling of the dining room. The light of the four-armed, electric chandelier hanging above the table reflected off their expensive Wedgwood
dinnerware and gave the white linen tablecloth a warm glow.

Cross dropped his fork on his plate with a clatter. "Helen, I'm not
a child who has to be told to clean his plate."

A long moment of silence followed, interrupted only by the ticking
of the antique brass clock on the sideboard. Helen dabbed her lips with
her napkin and stared at her husband.

Six months after they married, they both realized they had nothing
in common. In their world, this was normal. After a year, they retreated
to different universes. Helen had hoped it wouldn't happen, but it was
a natural occurrence, really, like the coming of winter. It had happened

to her parents. Now, it was the same for her. Though she'd lost her husband's love early on and was resigned to the fact, sometimes, after all these years, it still pained her.

"I suppose you're going out tonight," she said. "You usually do when there's nothing on the social calendar."

"Let's not get into this, Helen. I'm in no mood."

"You could stay home and spend some time with me."

"I spent time with you last night," snapped Cross.

"That was across a ballroom at the Merricks'. And the night before, from the opposite end of a dinner table at the Linden-Travers'."

"Goddamn it, Helen, I told you: let it go. I'm a damn good husband who provides for his family."

"You are a good provider, yes. But there's more to being a husband than that."

"Like what?" shouted Cross. "You have everything you want."

His gaze slid to the wall. He'd designed a pass-through panel behind the sideboard; it allowed the maid to slide trays of food through from the kitchen. Tonight, Mrs. O'Shea was behind it. He knew she was listening in.

"It's true that I have every dress and bauble I might want. But did you ever think of my feelings? That perhaps I desire affection and attention more than I do another Dupret gown?"

"Really?" Cross asked, amused. "Affection? More than a Parisian gown?"

"Yes! You and I, sitting in the parlor *by ourselves*, you asking me how I'm feeling or how my day was or what I'm reading. Is that so inconceivable?"

"Helen, for God's sake. I always ask you about your day."

"No! You ask about running the house—preparing the meals, getting your underwear washed and folded, dealing with the servants, reminding you which social functions we're to attend. But you never ask about *me*."

"Stop this foolishness, now. I'm in no mood," thundered Cross, rising from his chair. "I won't allow it."

Helen stared down at her empty plate. "Just a tiny gesture of affection," she murmured.

"Then find yourself a better husband." Cross walked to the sliding doors of the dining room and opened them. "Yes, I am going out tonight. I'll be back late."

✧ ✧ ✧

"Here we are, sir: 158 Hester Street. Billy McGlory's joint." The carriage driver opened the door and added, as Cross was stepping out, "If you're going slumming tonight, sir, then Milligan's Hell on Broome is the place. The waiter girls there spread their legs as wide as the mighty Mississippi. Can take you there, if you'd like."

A look of shock came over Cross's face, followed by disgust. "No, thank you," he said politely, slapping the fare down into the driver's gloved hand.

Although it was nine o'clock at night, Hester Street was awash with pedestrians. In his neighborhood, the sidewalks were empty by seven, except for cats and the occasional stray dog. Cross surveyed the line of buildings on the north side of the street, which were still lit by old-fashioned gaslights. Five- and six-story brick tenements crowded together, the first floors given over to stores of every description. Nearly everyone had a Hebrew-sounding name on the awnings or the windows—Liebman, Pinsky. Every open upper-story window was filled with human faces, flushed and sweaty, hoping for relief from the oppressively humid July evening. People filled the sidewalks and the street as well from gutter to gutter, stopping at the curbside pushcarts to examine their goods and haggle with the vendors over the price. Wagons and carriages had to inch their way through the crowds, the drivers cursing constantly at pedestrians to move out of the way.

Cross looked down at the gutter and discovered he was standing in a pool of oozing, blackish-brown filth. Stepping up to the curb to scrape the mess off his shoes, he saw an unconscious drunk sprawled out no more than six feet away. His jacket and pants pockets had been turned out. The crowds of boisterous people, many of them men and women arm in arm, stepped over him as if he were a piece of litter.

Strange that McGlory's music hall would be such an unassuming building. Cross had expected something much fancier, a grand entry, perhaps. To his right, he heard the sound of a scuffle. Walking toward an obscured doorway, he was shocked to see a man holding a filthy handkerchief over a well-dressed fellow's nose. In the next instant, the latter collapsed, unconscious. With the help of another man, the thief took his wallet and began to strip off his clothes. The crowds continued to swarm along the sidewalk, completely ignoring them.

Stunned, Cross stumbled toward the dingy double doorway of 158 Hester. As he reached the door, two men burst out, dragging a third man by his armpits. They heaved his body out into the middle of Hester Street like a sack of flour and strode back inside. Trembling, Cross entered and found himself in a narrow, unlit corridor. Like a blind man, he felt along the walls for almost twenty feet until he saw a crack of light beneath an opaque door. Opening it, he was astonished to see a huge dance hall, brightly lit, with dozens of tables and chairs and a bar the length of a city block. The hall was two stories high; a balcony lined with curtain-covered cubicles ran along two sides. There had to be at least five hundred men in the space, all shouting and laughing above the screeching music played by a piano, cornet, and violin trio off to the side. Young girls in garish makeup and short red-and-white dresses moved through the crowd, singing and carrying trays of drinks. Their skirts exposed their legs up to their plump thighs.

At almost every table, even cheaper, more tawdry-looking women sat in the laps of the men, arms around their necks, laughing and kissing them full on the lips. To Cross's astonishment, one woman drained a large stein of lager in one try.

Did Kent really want to meet me here? Cross thought wildly. Shoving his way past the throng and weaving through the maze of tables, he finally found an empty seat. The second he settled down, two harpies were upon him. One plopped into his lap, and to his horror, Cross realized it was a man very unconvincingly dressed as a woman. His face was powdered white, his rouged cheeks as red as cherries.

"Buy me a drink, handsome," said the degenerate. Though Cross did not reply, two drinks appeared in front of him as if from nowhere. The fake female grabbed one of the drinks and disappeared into the crowd.

"Two dollars," a voice called out. To avoid any problems, Cross paid.

"How about some quarters in my stocking for good luck?" said the other woman, stretching a shapely, gartered leg in front of Cross. Again, he immediately obliged. She had hair the color of a Florida orange and seemed to be a genuine female. Pleased at his quick response, she whispered in his ear, "Why don't we go up to a private box, for a special cancan exhibition?" and she motioned toward the curtained alcoves lining the balcony.

Cross looked up and saw a man in evening dress buttoning his fly as he left one of the cubicles. "That's very tempting, young lady, but I'm here for a business appointment," he said apologetically. The constant noise and loud music were giving him a pounding headache.

The whore leaned over and wrapped her arms around Cross. "Surely a real gentleman like yourself can spare a little time for me."

In the next instant, the slut was yanked off him. A moon-faced man with a broken nose and a handlebar mustache roughly shoved her away by the wrist. "Mr. Kent will see you now, Mr. Cross. If you'll come this way," he said in the same polite tone Caroline Astor's butler would have used. He then grabbed the woman's other wrist and pulled a wallet from her hand. "And I believe this belongs to you, sir." He handed him the wallet and slapped the woman in the face. The blow was so hard, so punishing, that she fell, the back of her head slamming against the damp, sawdust-covered floor.

12

THE MAN ESCORTED CROSS THROUGH THE SMOKE AND CACOPHONY of the dance hall to a rickety wooden stair leading to the basement. In the low, dimly lit passage, Cross almost scraped his head on the underside of the floor joists. They reached a door that opened into a large room with newly plastered walls. At least ten men sat around a long oak table filled with liquor bottles, growlers of beer, and glasses. Cross spotted Kent, who stood and spread his arms in warm welcome, as if he were meeting a long-lost relative.

"Boys, meet John Cross. Our new business consultant."

Murmurs of polite welcome rose through the swirl of cigar and cigarette smoke that enveloped the room. Cross cringed at the sound of his name. Then he sank into an empty chair directly across from Kent and looked around the table. He'd never met any of these men at the Union League or the Knickerbocker Club. They were a mean-looking bunch, the scars of a rough and unhappy life permanently etched on their faces. One man's face looked as though it had been beaten with a cat-o'-nine-tails; another's was so pockmarked that it looked as if someone had hammered tacks into it. One man with a missing ear was nervously sticking a stiletto into the wood table, again and again, tiny, jabbing blows. Most of the noses present had been broken. Oddly, though, all the men were fashionably dressed in frock coats, waistcoats, and pinstriped trousers—most likely from Cross's own tailor, Brooks Brothers. Some had gold-topped canes by their sides.

At first, the only person Cross recognized was the man who'd paid a visit to his office. Then, to his surprise, he saw the man who'd held the handkerchief over the face of the fellow in the street. Some of the men were welcoming; a few remained expressionless, seemingly suspicious of the newcomer.

Sitting next to him was a gimlet-eyed hulk of a man with bright red hair. He was fingering a set of brass knuckles. Cross could see blood on them. A short, meek-looking man rose from his seat and handed Cross a shot of whiskey.

"Wet your whistle, Johnnie," he said.

Cross smiled and took the shot in a single swallow. His new friends nodded in approval. It was a good way of breaking down the barriers between them.

The man with the handkerchief smiled at him. "I believe I saw you on the street earlier tonight."

"Yes, I do recall seeing you. You seemed busy."

"I had a client."

"Pig McGurk's the best chloroform man in the city," said the skinny bald man next to him, slapping Pig on the back.

"Chloroform?" Cross asked.

"Yep. I can sneak up behind anyone, place a hanky of 'form over their face, knock 'em out, and strip 'em clean. Ten seconds or less."

"Each of these gentlemen brings a special talent to our company." Kent sounded as if he was boasting about his children. "Like you, Mr. Cross. I believe you have something to share with us."

From the side pocket of his frock coat, Cross removed a folded set of blueprints and flattened them out on the table so that Kent, who was sitting across from him, could see. He was about to speak but hesitated. It bothered him that so many people were in on Kent's scheme. He'd thought they'd be speaking alone. The expression "no honor among thieves" came to mind. Then he remembered the ice delivery, and he knew that none of these men would dare betray Kent.

"This is the Cook mansion. It's one of the first built on upper Fifth Avenue, on the corner of Seventy-Eighth." He showed the group the front elevation sheet, which displayed how palatial the house was, with its steep slate roof and tall chimneys, taking up half of the Fifth Avenue block. Cook owned the rest of the block, all the way up to Seventy-Ninth Street, allowing for a large open space behind the house for a yard and carriage access.

"That's a beautiful house. Indoor toilets, I bet," said McGurk.

"You better believe it! Imagine, living in a place like that and taking a shit out in an outhouse!" exclaimed the man with the missing ear.

"Hey, isn't that the house that has the big, wide ditch all around it?" asked another man.

Cross paused, smiled politely, and said, "That's exactly the house."

"Then how the hell are we getting in there?" countered the man.

"That ditch is called a dry moat, and I designed it, including the drawbridges. They are lowered and raised by a new type of electric motor and steel cables—the same kind they used on the Brooklyn Bridge," Cross answered, a note of pride in his voice. "I know how to operate them. So no one will see us from the street. We'll work in the rear. I'll lower the bridge, and then you'll break in through the back door."

The men all nodded their heads in admiration and exchanged smiles.

"Wait—after we crack this place, won't they know you used the bridge, since you thought of it?" asked McGurk.

The men stopped smiling and looked at Cross. All of them were thinking the same thing—if Cross was picked up by the police, he'd squeal on them in a second.

"Mr. McGurk," said Cross, "there were scores of workmen involved in constructing this building, plus all the servants who've seen how the bridges work. They'll be the prime suspects. And there's one more important point you have to understand—they'd *never* suspect a gentleman."

Kent smiled at this last observation.

"Now, let's move on," said Cross. "Here's the subbasement.

Right next to the wine room is a large vault that holds the silverware, chinaware, and, in an adjoining room, all the linens. The Cooks have an unusually large English silver service by Garrard and complete sets of real Dresden and Sèvres china. There are very expensive sets of embroidered Irish and Belgian lace linens in this separate cedar-lined room." Cross pointed to a space in the middle of the plan. "The door to the vault is hidden behind a wall rack of bottles. It swings out on hinges."

"Combination lock on the vault?" Kent asked.

"No, just a padlock that can be pried off with a crowbar."

The gang had risen from their seats and hunched over the plans. Cross wondered if any of them besides Kent could actually read them. Most of his rich, well-educated clients couldn't decipher the drawings. But intent on making a good first impression—and stealing the most he could, the better to repay George's debts—Cross laid out the second-floor plan on top of the basement plan.

"The second floor contains the family's private spaces—the bedrooms, study, a sitting room where they gather informally."

"That's goddamn amazing, a big place like this for one fuckin' family," said a rotund man in a dark-gray frock coat with an elegant pearl-gray waistcoat.

"In Mrs. Cook's bedroom is a safe. It holds all her jewels."

"The woman has her own bedroom?" McGurk said.

"Yes, all husbands and wives have separate bedrooms."

McGurk and his colleagues exchanged smiles at this arrangement.

"The family's up in Newport now, and a society woman never takes all her jewelry with her. She leaves the best for the social season that begins in mid-November. I happen to know that Mrs. Cook has a Cartier tiara. Five large diamonds, each mounted with a freshwater pearl. It'll be there."

"And the safe?" Kent asked. "Behind a painting?"

'That's where you'd expect it to be. So I put a false front of a safe behind a painting. The safe is actually right here." Cross pointed to a solid square drawn in the corner of the bedroom.

"What's that?" asked Kent.

"It's a Roman marble statue of Diana, goddess of the hunt. I put a small portable safe in its base with a removable panel at the back."

"The lock?"

"That has a combination lock. But the safe's not anchored to the floor. You can take it with you."

Grinning, the gang members started chattering among themselves, excited at the potential of such a big robbery. Cross looked down, conflict roiling in his belly. The Cooks had been excellent clients; they were down-to-earth and kindhearted, unlike most of the society folk he dealt with. Bill Cook had grown up dirt poor on a Missouri farm and had never forgotten his humble beginnings. Last month, he'd been kind enough to remember Charlie's birthday and had sent him an expensive present.

But Cross had no choice. The Cooks would survive. George might not.

And he had one more surprise for Kent's men.

"This room next to Mrs. Cook's bedroom is her dressing room. Here's the closet for her clothes."

"Christ, that's as big as her bedroom," said the red-haired man with the brass knuckles.

"It's bigger than this room we're in now," Cross agreed, eliciting whistles and a few "holy shits" from the gang. "It has to be, because society ladies change their clothes at least four times a day."

"Four times a day? Holy hell, my wife don't even change her underwear every day," said a man with unusually large ears and a pointy nose. He looked like an elf from a children's book.

"Morning dresses, afternoon dresses, tea dresses, riding habits, blouses, skirts. But the most expensive items are her evening dresses and ball gowns, which are in this cedar-lined closet here. Mrs. Cook's are from Worth's, the very best fashion house in Paris. Twice a year, she orders a completely new set of gowns and accessories. They're made from the most expensive silks, satins, brocade, velvets, and lace money can buy. The rest of the closet is filled with hats, shoes, gloves, silk lingerie, and furs." Cross tapped his finger on the dressing room image for dramatic emphasis. "*This* will be your biggest take, even more than the jewels and silver." He looked up to see Kent smiling appreciatively at him.

"Very impressive, Mr. Cross," he said. Many around the table raised their glasses in response.

But then a tall, physically imposing man with a haggard but handsome face rose. Cross had noticed him earlier, twisting a length of what looked like piano wire in his hands. He slammed his fist, which sported a large diamond ring, down hard on the table.

"How can we trust this goddamn swell?" he cried. "We don't know this guy from Adam. Suppose he's a Pinkerton?"

"For Christ's sake, calm down, Brady," one of the men yelled.

The smile vanished from Kent's face, and he turned to look at the dissenter. "We can trust him because I said we can, Mr. Brady." Kent's voice was icy. The man scowled but backed off. "One question, Mr. Cross," Kent said, the smile returning to his face. "Did the Cooks leave any staff behind?"

"No, they went to Newport with the family. And no watchman."

Cross didn't want to wait for any more questions. He wanted to get the hell out of there. "Well, gentlemen, it was a pleasure to meet you," he said, picking up his hat from the table. "You will no doubt want to examine the drawings further and discuss things, so I'll get out of your way. Good night to you all."

He was almost to the door when Kent intercepted him.

"Just a moment, Mr. Cross. Culver here will get you a carriage. I don't believe the Lower East Side is quite your milieu." Kent waved his gold-topped cane toward Culver. "Let's wait in here, shall we?"

Kent led Cross into another room, filled with what were probably the hall's excess tables and chairs. Most were damaged. As they waited, a slow trickle of ragged, dirty men and women entered. A blind beggar wearing black glasses and carrying a cane sat down at a table. He took off the glasses and began counting coins and paper money from a tin can. Another filthy-looking wretch wearing a leg prosthesis limped in—and took off the false limb, exposing a perfectly healthy leg. When he saw Cross's expression, Kent started laughing.

"Billy McGlory is kind enough to let these unfortunates do their day's accounting here."

"But that man can see as well as I can. And that man there is no cripple!" exclaimed Cross.

"Welcome to my world, Mr. Cross," Kent said, laughing uncontrollably. As more fake cripples straggled in, he continued to speak, tapping his palm with the head of his cane. "We're off to a good start," he said. "You did very well, made a good impression on the boys. We'll go over your drawings and start to prepare. Preparation is everything in this game, Mr. Cross."

"Where's my son?" Cross demanded, his patience worn thin. His voice drew curious glances from the cripples, but they quickly returned to their money.

"You delivered the goods tonight. I will keep up my end of the bargain and deliver George. He'll be home by late tomorrow morning."

When Culver appeared at the door, Cross started toward him. But Kent blocked his way with his cane.

"Before you go, there's one more small favor I'll ask of you."

·ŀ· ·ŀ· ·ŀ·

It was Ned Brady's habit to stop at the Hurdy Gurdy for a drink on the way home. Being a regular, he was given his own private cubicle at the back of the bar. Though he had a common-law wife at home, many women vied for his attention and affection. He was a strapping, good-looking man, generous with money. Only a select few were allowed his company, however.

But tonight, Brady desired no female companionship. He finished his shot of rye and left. As he walked west on Stanton Street, a filthy white-and-brown dog leaped from the shadow of a doorway. It attacked his leg viciously. Enraged, Brady shook the mutt off—and saw a ragged old man in his seventies standing nearby.

"Get your fuckin' mutt off me, you goddamn fool."

"Barleycorn knows a mean man when he sees 'im," the old man snarled.

Brady walked up to the man and smiled.

"You've got yourself a smart dog, then."

"Barleycorn's damn smart."

In a fraction of a second, Brady lunged at the man. He had a loop of piano wire around his neck before the old fellow could blink. With his powerful fists, he effortlessly pulled on both ends of the wire, garroting the man until his face turned gray-blue and his eyes bulged out.

With a sick thud, he dropped to the pavement.

"You're right. I *am* mean," Brady said to the dog. It whimpered and cowered back in the corner of the doorway.

13

—————◆—————

ADD THREE MORE TO THE TWO YOU ALREADY HAVE. HOW MANY is that?"

The nine children in the spartan classroom looked at George with blank expressions. When he'd first met his pupils, he'd been stunned. They were filthy, emaciated, and often seemed deaf and dumb. More like feral animals than children, and so different from his younger brother, Charlie. At first, George thought they were orphans, but he'd soon learned that almost all of them had been thrown out into the streets when their families could no longer support them. They were left to fend for themselves, stealing or working as bootblacks and newsies. The girls sold shoelaces and matches in the streets. Some worked in sweatshops, making envelopes or twine.

Before they came to the lodging house, all the children were homeless, forced to sleep in basements or alleys, to sprawl across steam gratings in the Five Points and the Bowery. Dr. Caldwell, the school's director, said that twenty thousand more roamed the streets of New York like rats. None of them had ever celebrated a Christmas or a birthday; most didn't even know when they had been born. To George, their reality came as a cruel shock.

"What about you, Tim? How many?"

The scrawny, freckle-faced child stared at the caramels that sat before him. Instead of toothpicks or matches, George used candy for his arithmetic lessons. These wretches didn't have the tiniest of pleasures. He meant to kill two birds with one stone. Chewing gum, licorice sticks, and boiled sweets became teaching tools.

Tim knit his brow and moved his lips, silently counting.

"Five?"

"As a reward for Tim's academic brilliance, the class may now eat today's lesson," George said.

Smiles broke out, and the children began unwrapping the caramels and popping them into their mouths. Initially, when George gave them candy, he expected them to devour every piece at once. He was surprised to see that most saved some to eat later. This, he discovered, was a survival instinct they'd learned on the streets.

It gave George great pleasure to see his class enjoy their treats. The longer he taught, the more it pained him that these children had absolutely nothing in life—no mother or father, no prospects for a bright future. It made him feel ashamed that he'd been given so much. And so, every week, George had come down by train from Cambridge to teach the urchins arithmetic. They weren't stupid. No, it was as if their minds were frozen on account of their mistreatment and neglect. Sometimes he tried to do something special for them, taking them on excursions to Central Park, the wax museum at Eden Musée, or a puppet show on Fourteenth Street. Dr. Caldwell had objected, but George convinced him the trips had a sound educational purpose.

"I'll see you next week," George said to his class with a wave of the hand, and the children bounded out of the classroom.

On his way out, he smiled at Miss Cavendish, the secretary, who blushed at such a handsome man's attention. The Children's Aid Society building on East Broadway was a massive brick-and-stone edifice designed by a friend of his father's, Calvert Vaux. It held dining facilities, classrooms, and dormitories for destitute children. Some people had even complained that it was too fancy for street urchins.

George walked north on Ludlow Street toward the Third Avenue Elevated Railroad. His new home at the Bradley, an apartment house on West Fifty-Ninth Street, right across from the park, awaited him. As a gift, Granny had paid the eighteen-hundred-dollar annual rent, even though she disapproved of apartment houses, calling them glorified tenements. They were just a fad, she said, because Anglo-Saxons would never share the same roof with strangers.

As he walked, George's thoughts kept returning to the day before. Something wasn't right. For Kent to forgive his debt—it seemed unthinkable. He'd been sure he was going to die, had even resigned himself to the fact. But there he was, back in the city as if nothing had happened. Kitty couldn't give him any details about Kent's decision, and to his dismay, Kent had flatly refused to talk to him.

It was frustrating. George wanted to tell Kent that he'd give him a percentage of his salary each week in appreciation for what he'd done. When he'd dropped him off at the curb, Flannigan had warned him to stay away from Kent's joints. George couldn't understand the reprieve, but he thanked God that his family hadn't found out. The shame would have destroyed them.

A block before Delancey Street was a basement dive called the House of Hell, a lowlife gambling den George had frequented many times. He stopped by the stair leading down to the basement and stared at the crude sign of a tiger above the battered wooden door, which meant the dump was a faro house. There was paper money in his pants pocket. He pulled it out. Six dollars. George bolted down the stairs—but stopped midway and climbed back up to the sidewalk. He closed his eyes, breathing heavily.

At times like this, he couldn't understand the universal forces at play. It was like he was made of pure iron, not flesh and blood, and the dive was a giant magnet, pulling him toward it with an unearthly power. He grasped the railing tightly, as if to prevent his body being yanked back down into the cellar. But there was no magnetic force emanating from the dive. The pull was coming from his brain, which was commanding his body to slap his six dollars on the green felt of the faro table. George wanted to feel that indescribable sensation of suspense in placing his bet, then the pure exhilaration of winning. He would never tell Kitty this, but the thrill was absolutely wonderful, more satisfying than any orgasm. With his mastery of numbers, he knew he could beat the house. Gambling was just a series of mathematical probabilities that had to be analyzed.

Feeling himself beginning to perspire, George tightened his grasp on the railing. Then, taking a deep breath, he let go and bolted down the sidewalk. He didn't look back. If he did, he knew he'd be lost.

⁘ ⁘ ⁘

Charlie Cross was determined to get the Crandall mini steam engine.

The gifts from his birthday last month had been disappointing, to say the least. He didn't give a damn about learning the value of money from card games like the "Amusing Game of the Corner Grocery" or the "Game of Banking." He'd been hoping for the engine or one of those new safety bicycles. The only decent present, a Mike Kelly base-ball bat, had come from George.

The Crandall mini steam engine. That was something special. You could actually sit on the thing and ride around. While looking at the sports pages of the *Tribune*, Charlie had seen an advertisement for the toy. It was sold at a store off Pearl Street and the Bowery, which, the ad emphasized in bold black letters, was conveniently located near the Second Avenue Elevated.

Having been on the Third Avenue line many times with his friends, Charlie felt he was ready to take the Second Avenue Elevated on his own. The one good thing about his parents was that they trusted him and gave him free rein to roam about the neighborhood. On foot, he and his pals had ventured all the way up to the park, as far south as Union Square, and east and west to each of the rivers.

He took his time on his way to the Thirty-Fourth Street and Second Avenue station, stopping to look in store windows, buying lic-orice, playing with a stray cat, and examining junk abandoned by the

curb. On the downtown train, he knelt on a seat, looking out at the
buildings as they rushed past. He loved being so high off the ground.
The colors and lettering styles of the signs that covered almost every
square foot of the building facades captivated him.

As his stop at Chatham Junction approached, Charlie turned to
face his fellow passengers. Dressed in odd clothing and chattering
in strange languages, they were nothing like the people on Fifth and
Madison Avenues. He found them as fascinating as characters in a sto-
rybook. One old man, dressed all in black with a broad-brimmed hat,
had a full, snow-white beard that flowed down to his chest and a long,
single curl of hair hanging from each ear. Farther down the car, there
was even a Chinaman in a scarlet-and-gold quilted jacket.

At Chatham Junction station, where the Second and Third Avenue
elevated lines crossed and formed a dramatic double-decker set of
tracks, Charlie scampered down the long stairway to the street. He
began walking east in search of Pearl Street and the Bowery but soon
found himself completely lost. Confused, he rounded a building and
was astonished to see the stone towers of the Brooklyn Bridge looming
above him. He'd never seen anything so tall. It dwarfed the buildings
around it, even the church steeples.

The net of cables attached to the bridge's towers reminded him of
giant spiderwebs. A flood of people, horses, and wagons was crossing
the bridge in both directions. Convinced he had gone the wrong way,
Charlie turned north and kept walking until he reached the corner of
Baxter and Worth Streets. It was as if he had walked onto another
planet. The sidewalks in front of the ramshackle two- and three-story
buildings were choked with people and strewn with foul-smelling
garbage. Instead of cobblestones, the streets were a mash of churned
rubble and horse manure. Two-wheeled delivery wagons and pushcarts
fought their way along. Charlie stared in amazement at the wide eyes
of a dead horse lying in the gutter, covered with green flies. Above
him, a withered old woman leaned out of a second-story window and

emptied a white porcelain-enameled chamber pot onto the sidewalk. The pedestrians dodged the airborne filth without batting an eye.

The shops along Baxter Street were unlike the neat and tidy ones in Charlie's neighborhood. Dark and dilapidated places, they displayed their stock in boxes and on long plank tables on the sidewalk. Most of it seemed to be used clothing. Their owners continually accosted pass-ersby, trying to physically drag them inside. Peddlers pushed rickety carts, calling out their wares. A fat woman smoking a long clay pipe was selling apples and gingerbread. Charlie was amazed to see little girls younger than him hawking wilted flowers and socks. Men without arms and legs sat on the sidewalk, selling shoelaces and buttons.

It was about ninety degrees, and the stink of the place was making Charlie dizzy. He leaned against a building. Its surface was coated with moldy, greenish slime. A greasy rat scurrying through the filth of the gutter stopped in front of Charlie and fixed him with its beady black gaze.

"Those are some real fancy duds you have on."

Two boys a couple years older than Charlie were standing perhaps three feet away. They wore filthy, torn canvas shirts and tattered black pants that stopped a few inches above their bare feet. Their faces and feet were smeared with dirt; it looked as if they'd been down a coal chute. Charlie dropped his chin to his chest to see what they were referring to. To please his mother, he had agreed to wear a velvet jacket and lace collar in the style made so popular by the story *Little Lord Fauntleroy*, which had just come out. At ten years old, Charlie had graduated to wearing long pants and refused to wear Lord Fauntleroy shorts or get his hair curled. The jacket was a compromise.

"Hey, we'll show ya somethin' neat," said one of the boys, smil-ing broadly and gesturing for Charlie to follow him into an adjacent alleyway filled with garbage. Charlie was about to politely decline the invitation, but before he could say a word, the larger of the two put his filthy hand on the back of Charlie's neck, his grip as tight as a vise, and shoved him into the alley. A few yards in, Charlie tried to twist away, but the boy's accomplice struck him full in the face. Down he went, and the two boys began to kick and pummel him. He was too shocked to utter a sound. As he lay on his back, stunned, he felt his attackers undressing him.

"This stuff's real velvet. And the shoes don't have no holes in 'em."

Like a carcass being picked over by vultures, Charlie was stripped to his underwear in seconds. He heard the scuffling of the boys' footsteps as they ran. His head was pounding with pain, and there was an excruciating ache in his stomach. He tried to fight back the tears, but they poured out in torrents. Pulling himself up from the filth of the alley, he grabbed on to a nearby rain barrel and tried to steady himself.

Out of the corner of his eye, he saw an older boy striding confidently toward him, holding each of his assailants by their ears. The thieves were howling in pain.

"Give 'em back," the boy said, lifting his arms up to stretch the boys' ears even farther. They screamed in agony, dropping the clothing and shoes on the ground.

"Kick 'em in the balls," the boy said.

Charlie shook his head. He didn't understand. "Balls?'

"Yeah, balls." With great agility, the boy swung his leg and kicked one of the boys between the legs. "Go ahead," he ordered.

Forgetting his pain, Charlie got a running start and kicked each of the thieves with all the force he could muster. Still holding them by the ears, the older boy smashed their skulls together with all his might. There was a loud crack, like someone splitting open a coconut. The boys collapsed to the ground and then stumbled away down the alley, clutching their heads.

"Let me help you." The boy held out Charlie's trousers so he could step into them.

"Thank you," peeped Charlie.

"So what brings you to the Five Points today?"

14

CROSS SAT IN A CARRIAGE AT FIFTH AVENUE AND EIGHTIETH Street, waiting to begin the Cook robbery. It was 2:00 a.m. on a moonless July night.

"You'll find the experience most interesting," said Kent, who was seated next to him.

Interesting? Terrifying, perhaps. Cross could hardly prevent himself from shaking with fear. His shirt was soaked with sweat.

Sitting across from Cross and Kent were Culver and Brady, the roughneck who'd been so reluctant to trust him. Brady toyed constantly with a length of piano wire, scowling at Cross all the while. The gang had a hierarchy of sorts, Cross had come to realize. Culver, the trusted right-hand man, and Brady, the henchman, were the two top members and thus sat in the boss's carriage.

Along the surrounding streets were scattered enclosed delivery wagons of all types—milk, grocery, bakery, lumber. They would transport the loot. Development on Fifth Avenue above Seventy-Sixth Street was just beginning, with construction proceeding in a checkerboard manner. With its many vacant lots, the area still had a desolate feel. It was deserted at night and rarely patrolled by the police, which was fine with Cross. No one was around to see them.

Kent, who had been puffing on a cigar, exhaled, filling the carriage with the thick, sweet aroma of a Havana premium. He pulled out his pocket watch.

"It's two fifteen, gentlemen," he said. His jolly tone reminded Cross of Charlie, bounding into their bedroom to tell them it was Christmas morning.

Kent, Brady, and Culver got out of the carriage. The plan was for two men to leave each wagon at one-minute intervals with one man remaining to drive. They would meet at the rear of the house. Other men would serve as lookouts.

Cross froze as if he were glued to his seat. His mind ordered him to get out of the carriage, but his body wouldn't obey.

"Time to go, Mr. Cross. It's your debut performance tonight," said Kent. "We can't be late."

Cross did not budge. Brady reached into the carriage, grabbed Cross by the lapels, and yanked him out. "Move," he said with a snarl.

"Please don't be embarrassed, Mr. Cross. Everyone gets stage fright on their first night," exclaimed Kent, beckoning Cross to come with a wave of his arm.

Cross's legs felt like gelatin, and he thought he was going to collapse. Somehow, though, he made it to the back of the mansion. A grand wrought iron gate was connected to the low fence that surrounded the fifteen-foot-wide dry moat. To Cross's surprise, the gate lock had already been picked.

Cross swallowed hard, took a deep breath, and slowly walked over to a paving stone right next to the gate. He placed all his weight on the side of it, and up popped the stone, revealing a little compartment below that contained what looked like the inner workings of a clock. His accomplices smiled at one another. He knelt down and turned a lever to the right.

The iron-and-wood drawbridge that covered the rear door slowly lowered with just a low murmur of cables and pulleys.

Everyone at once noticed a light come on at the far end of the basement level at the bottom of the moat. Cross stooped down and switched the lever to stop the bridge. It was only halfway down, at a diagonal to the face of the house. Kent and his men stood motionless, their eyes fixed on the light. A half a minute passed, then the light went out.

Brady turned an accusing eye on Cross and laughed, his voice harsh in the silence.

"I told you this little shit couldn't be trusted."

"It's a servant," Cross said in a calm voice, knowing exactly what room it was.

"Take care of it," Kent said to Brady in a matter-of-fact tone. He might have been telling him to shine his shoes.

Cross saw the smirk on Brady's face and knew what would happen next. "You can't," he yelled, grabbing the arm of Kent's well-tailored frock coat. Kent's eyes slowly traveled from his sleeve to Cross, who flushed with embarrassment, realizing his faux pas. But he couldn't keep silent. "No one's to be hurt!" he cried.

As Brady raised his fist to punch Cross in the face, Kent lifted a hand in silent command.

"I'm afraid that's going to be difficult, Mr. Cross. We certainly can't call the job off. You can see the position I'm in."

With Brady's hand still raised, Cross gathered his nerve. "Just let me peek in the window."

"What the hell good will that do?" Brady sneered.

"Maybe he didn't hear anything. Listen, I set up this job. You can at least give me ten minutes."

Kent nodded, though his eyes were skeptical. "All right, but you're wasting your time, Mr. Cross…and mine."

Brady bristled with anger at his boss's decision but didn't protest.

But Cross stopped and realized he had no way of getting down into the moat. No one brought ladders or ropes because he didn't think they'd be necessary. Then he remembered that the gray granite walls that lined the moat were rusticated—they had deep, wide joints between the stones that could act as hand and footholds. Cross swung his body over the iron fence and slowly climbed down the wall as if it were a ladder. When he reached the stone floor, he crept over to below the window and craned his neck until his eyes peered just over the very edge of the sill. The lower sash had been raised about a foot, allowing the servant to get some air in the cramped room. Cross let his eyes adjust to the darkness of the interior. He raised up further, until his entire head was through the opening.

The room was a typical servant's abode, with barely any furniture and no rug. Servants were not allowed to display personal items, and with its bare, white plaster walls, the space resembled a prison cell. Directly below Cross was a cast-iron bed. A young man in a white nightshirt slept soundly on his back. Cross had no idea why he was in the house. The entire domestic staff of city mansions always went to Newport in the summer.

He crouched back down and crawled away from the window, then sat against the stone wall of the house. He needed time to think. Kent waited impatiently above.

"Do you keep a bottle of that stuff on you?" Cross asked in a hushed voice to McGurk, who was standing next to Kent.

"The chloroform? Never leave the house without it," he said with a smile, patting the side pocket of his jacket.

Cross extended his arms and beckoned for McGurk to toss down the bottle, which he did.

"Mr. Culver, will you please go to the carriage and get the whip and the sponge in the horse's water bucket?"

Culver was puzzled by the request but trotted off. After a few minutes, he was back with the whip and sponge.

"What the fuck are you doing, swell? Time's a wasting," Brady hissed from the sidewalk above.

"Go to hell, you blackguard," Cross said, surprising himself with his nerve. He looked up at Kent and spoke directly. "You're not going to kill him."

Taking the oblong yellow sponge, he squeezed it out. With his penknife, he cut a slit in the end and inserted the long handle of the carriage whip into the space. He emptied the entire bottle onto the sponge. A pungent smell rose up in the warm night air.

Cross crept back and slowly threaded the carriage handle through the open window. Leaning his whole body into the opening, he lowered the sponge to the sleeping man's face, covering his nose. Two minutes passed. Cross pulled his head back and whispered up to McGurk, "Is this long enough?"

McGurk chuckled. "With the shot you gave 'im? He won't wake till tomorrow evening."

Cross pulled the carriage handle out and climbed back up the wall. "All right, let's get to it," he said to Kent, almost like an order.

Cross finished lowering the bridge. After Culver jimmied open the rear door, Cross took them first down to the subbasement, where they easily yanked off the padlock and entered the vault. He stood aside while they cleaned out the space, placing everything in canvas sacks. They worked quickly and efficiently, a well-oiled team. Even Brady threw himself into the effort. The vault was bare in minutes, the loot transported quickly across the drawbridge and piled into the wagons that waited in the rear yard.

Throughout the process, Kent stood, smoking a cigar and observing. He seemed to be enjoying every second of the experience and was a good leader, like a general at the front of his troops' charge into battle. His men respected that. And his eyes were sharp. As one man came out, Kent grabbed his arm. He reached into the man's jacket pocket, produced a bottle of wine, and ordered him to put it back.

Once the last of the loot was removed, the gang reassembled in the kitchen, and Cross led them up the servants' stairs to Mrs. Cook's bedroom. Once inside, they stood in stunned silence, gaping at the walls.

"Holy hell," McGurk whispered.

The walls of Mrs. Cook's bedroom were beautifully carved, gilt boiserie that sparkled in the light of the huge crystal chandelier. Cross hadn't designed this room. The interior was purchased from a Louis XVI palace in France and reassembled upon arrival in New York. At the far end, a gargantuan, ornately carved four-poster bed sat on a high platform fronted by a gilded balustrade, draped by a canopy of scarlet silk and dark-green velvet.

"A family of ten could sleep in that goddamn thing," McGurk said.

Eager to get the men's attention back to the job at hand, Cross pointed out the safe in the base of the statue of Diana. Two men eased it out and onto the maroon and gold carpet. Then a man brought in two lengths of wood, which were placed under the safe. They carried it out of the bedroom as though on a litter. They'd obviously done this many times before; it was all so amazingly fast.

Next came Mrs. Cook's clothes. Ball and evening gowns, furs, coats, dresses, riding habits, and hats of all description were swept from the closets and stuffed into more canvas sacks. Scores of shoes, scarves, gloves, silk petticoats, chemises, even whalebone corsets were taken. Then Cross escorted them to Mr. Cook's bedroom. The closets of London-tailored clothes were also stripped bare. The thieves reminded Cross of a horde of locusts, devouring a crop and leaving not a speck of grain behind.

As the robbery progressed, Cross realized that, to his surprise, he wasn't scared. Out in the carriage, he had been a nervous wreck, sweating like a pig. But once inside, he'd been so swept up in the excitement of the event that he actually had a feeling of giddy elation, like he'd drunk a bottle of champagne. He was alive with energy; an electrical current seemed to flow through his body.

The men worked in total silence. The gregariousness of that night at McGlory's had vanished, and not one word was exchanged. As they continued to scoop up more articles in Cook's bedroom, a great crash was heard from an adjacent room, like something breaking on the floor. The men froze. Almost at once, each man pulled a gun out of his side jacket pocket. Cross, who also stopped dead in his tracks, was momentarily fascinated at the variety of weapons drawn—derringers, short barrel revolvers, big Colt Navy revolvers, a western six-shooter.

A few seconds of deafening silence passed until McGurk slowly walked toward the wood-paneled door and pushed it wide open. Every man held their breath until he shined his lantern in to see a calico cat on the fireplace mantel and a Chinese vase lying in pieces below on the stone hearth. The cat jumped down and rubbed and purred against McGurk's pant leg. Laughter broke out, then the gang went back to work. McGurk picked up the cat, rubbed under its chin, and set it down gently. The room was Cook's private study, his inner sanctum, where he went to escape his wife and the world. In went the gang and out came his rare sixteenth-century dueling pistols and his beloved collection of ancient and medieval swords.

With an air of great satisfaction, Kent smoked and watched. Then he strolled around, taking a slow tour of the second floor. The long hallway was lined with green onyx stone and lit by five bronze chandeliers. At one end, it connected with a monumental staircase of gray marble. Eyes sweeping the space critically, Kent ordered that a Flemish tapestry depicting a battle from ancient Rome be carted away, along with two suits of armor that had been brought over from a Scottish castle. A man was even sent back to Mrs. Cook's bedroom to roll up her rug.

Finally, Kent came over to Cross and placed his hand on his shoulder. "Does Cook collect manuscripts?"

When Cross shook his head, a look of disappointment came over Kent's face. Sighing, he looked up at the coffered wood ceiling of the study. Even this was decorated in gold leaf.

"A private palace, this. The workmanship is amazing. One day, Mr. Cross, I'll have a place like this too. And you're going to design it. Millicent will love it."

Cross, whose heart normally leaped at the thought of a new commission, grimaced.

"These paintings," Kent said abruptly. "Any true masterpieces—Titians, Rembrandts?"

"No, they're all by popular French salon painters. Like that military scene over there—it's by Meissonier," Cross said, gesturing to a huge painting of Napoleon on horseback, directing his troops from a hilltop.

"Too bad they're so damn big. There's no room for them in the wagons."

Cross laughed. "To a society man, the bigger a painting, the more valuable it must be."

Culver signaled to Kent: they were finished. He and Cross walked toward the monumental staircase but paused when Brady called out to them.

"Kent!"

"Go on. I'll meet you in the back," Kent said to Cross, who started down the stair.

Brady was standing by a door at the end of the second-floor hall. "Look what I found," he said, yanking a skinny teenage girl out of the doorway. She had bright red hair and blue eyes and was dressed in a plain cotton nightgown. She shook violently in Brady's grasp, eyes wide in fright.

"I heard crying—found her hiding on the third-floor rear stair."

"Come here, young lady," Kent said in a kind, paternal voice. "Tell me, are you and the fellow downstairs the only ones in the house?"

The girl nodded.

"You know what happens to little girls who lie, don't you?"

"They go to hell. But I'm telling the truth, sir," she said, voice trembling.

"And why are you here?"

"I forgot to bring Mrs. Cook's cat with us," she said, lowering her head in shame. "Jamie came back with me to get him, and we decided to spend the night. Please don't tell her I forgot him. She'll be so cross with me."

"It's all right. I promise I won't tell anyone." Kent reached out to stroke her hair, smiled at Brady, and walked away.

15

---◆◆◆---

"THE HOUSE WINS AGAIN."

George stared at the green-felt faro table and the blue-ivory check that represented his twenty-five-dollar losing bet. The dealer, who sat behind the table with an assistant who tracked the house's card count, met his eyes, looking for a sign that he would continue to bet. But George turned and walked away from the table, Kitty on his arm.

He was down four thousand. Two hours ago, he had been ahead seven.

Less than a week after his debt was forgiven, George had caved in and resumed gambling. He couldn't help himself; the gambling dens reeled him in like a helpless fish. He fought with all his might, but it was useless. With college finished, George devoted more days to teaching. Doing so put him in constant proximity to the scores of gambling joints on the Lower East Side. Walking by them every day was torture. He was like a starving man walking by rows and rows of restaurants, smells of delicious food wafting out to tantalize him.

His brief hiatus had been hell. Like a drunk on the wagon, his body seemed to go through withdrawal. Smoking, pacing back and forth in his apartment, and going for long walks in Central Park were no help in shaking off the malaise. Even while making love to Kitty, he thought about the tables. But there would be no income until the fall, when he started teaching at Saint David's. The only money George had on hand was his weekly trust fund allowance, which he needed for living expenses. If he blew that, he'd have to live off Kitty—or worse, go to his parents. Inevitably, they would start asking questions.

One morning, he leaped out of bed and, without really thinking, took the graduation watch Aunt Caroline had given him to a pawnbroker on East Forty-Fourth Street, along with a few other valuable trinkets, such as a gold cigarette case. With a one-thousand-dollar stake burning a hole in his pocket, George's willpower vanished into thin air. Kitty begged him to stop with all her might, but it was like trying to halt a runaway locomotive. George could not be swayed.

Because Kitty insisted on going with him, George went to a respectable house instead of the lowlife joints, which had the lower stakes he preferred. Chamberlain's, a first-class gambling house that catered to society men, looked no different from the other brownstone mansions off the side streets of Broadway. The interior was magnificently furnished with expensive furniture, marble fireplaces, frescoed ceilings, and plush velvet carpets. Its front parlor was given over to the entertainment of guests, while the rear parlor was reserved for gambling. A large dining room beyond the rear parlor provided free meals, cigars, and liquor to the well-dressed patrons. Faro, the most popular game in the city, was played fairly in these first-class houses. George knew he wouldn't be cheated.

They sat down on a recamier in the front parlor, and Kitty laid her head on his shoulder.

"I can lend you some money to keep playing."

"No. You've given me too much already," George said. He kissed her cheek.

"Bad night, George?" asked a rotund, Havana-puffing man as he walked past.

"Just wasn't my night, Senator."

Chamberlain's boasted the most exclusive clientele in the city. Like Senator Philip Merrill of New Jersey. Two Congressmen, a city councilman, and an ex-governor were in attendance. The house's most frequent customers, though, were Wall Street speculators. They were in the enviable position of being able to lose five thousand in a night and then make eight thousand from deals the following day.

Merrill was standing next to Ned Chamberlain, the middle-aged proprietor. As the senator walked away, Chamberlain leaned in and spoke confidentially to George. "I'm sorry about tonight, Mr. Cross," he said apologetically. "I hope we can come to an understanding about tonight's setback. You're the last person I'd like to see something happen to." He bowed slightly and walked off.

Kitty shot a glance at George, who remained silent. "You have to ask your aunt for some money, Georgie."

George looked at her in astonishment. "For Christ's sake, Kitty, I could never do that. The shame it would bring on my family! They'd be ruined."

"Ruined? That's all you goddamned society people care about—your good name."

"You don't understand. You think society people live in a world of luxury and pleasure? Well, it comes at a price. There's an incredibly rigid code of behavior we have to obey, and if we break one single rule, we're subject to something worse than physical torture or death: expulsion from society. Forever. No forgiveness."

Kitty shook her head slowly from side to side. "You people just don't know how good you have it."

"And you just don't understand," George said, giving her a playful kiss on the cheek.

"It's four a.m. Come back to my place," she said, changing the subject abruptly.

"No. I have to go home and get cleaned up for class. I promised the students we'd go to Battery Park, and I can't let them down. Not after everyone else already has."

"I have to work this evening," said Kitty, "but I could come over to your place at two."

"I'll be at the Windsor Palace."

Kitty sat up and clutched George's arm. "For God's sake, Georgie, you can't go back there."

"They have a chuck-a-luck game going on, and I can win. I know I can," George said, determined. He had just been introduced to the dice game, which had become very popular on the Bowery. "I'll put down a fiver and let it ride."

"No, my love. Don't. Stay home and wait for me. I can cook you your favorite breakfast in the morning. Beefsteak and kidneys." She stroked his hair, gazing at him.

Kitty knew she could have any man in New York. She could be showered with wealth and diamonds, feted and adored. But she chose George. He didn't think of her as a mere sex object; he actually enjoyed her company. To Kitty, their conversations were the best part of their romance—long, engaging rambles about everything under the sun. Sometimes they'd talk into the night so enthusiastically that they'd forget about making love. They had gone to the Museum of Natural History and the theater at Niblo's Garden and strolled the boardwalk at Far Rockaway, arm in arm. Never was George embarrassed to be seen with her. *Not like my clients*, Kitty sometimes thought bitterly, who would avert their eyes if they happened to pass one another on the street. To them, she was still a whore, no matter how beautiful and poised she appeared. It delighted her that George was so nonjudgmental.

And never once did he ask her to give up her work. There was the practical side, of course—he couldn't support her yet, so she had to earn a living, making in one night what he would be making in a month as a teacher. And there was something very erotic to George that other men coveted his girl. George was never ashamed of what she did for a living, nor was she; in fact, she enjoyed it. Kitty was refreshingly open and comfortable about sex, and she knew how to give pleasure to a man. To the society girls George knew, sex was an unpleasant obligation in a well-arranged marriage. When it came to immorality, his world was unforgiving. He told her once about a classmate of his sister Julia's who had been hounded out of society because she sat beside a gentleman in a carriage instead of opposite. Her family was ruined. Even the slightest mention of sex in polite company was deeply inappropriate; a woman who exposed her ankle was dubbed a harlot.

But all this ostensible propriety, Kitty knew full well, was an elaborate facade. Men of George's class engaged in the most deviant sexual practices, sometimes with girls as young as ten. George had seen his father's friend, Stanford White, entertaining one no more than thirteen at Miss Jennie's. Half the buildings between Fifth and Seventh Avenues and Twenty-Fourth and Fortieth Streets were used for immoral goings-on, a veritable sexual playground for the rich and powerful. Sometimes it seemed that every society gentleman was a part of this secret world of indecency and vice. Kitty remembered a client telling her that a gentleman wouldn't be a real gentleman if he didn't have a dark secret, be it women, gambling, or little boys.

With the ample income she earned at Miss Jennie's, Kitty had acquired a nice apartment on East Nineteenth Street. It was there that George had noticed her sketches on the walls. He urged her to keep drawing, telling her she had real talent, and he told her about the Art Students League at Fifth Avenue and Fifteenth Street. Kitty took classes in her spare time, and her drawing did improve. Her newfound talent thrilled her, filled her with pride. George loved and *cared* for her as a real person, she'd think sometimes as she filled a blank sheet of paper with images, black lines moving across the expanse of white. It was this quality that had won her heart. One day, she hoped, they would travel to California, to a place where she had no past, and they'd start a new life together. Kitty loved George so much. Watching him destroy himself with his sickness was killing her.

"Please don't go out tonight, Georgie. Remember, you promised to wait up and pose for me."

George leaned over, kissed her cheek, and nodded. He saw Kitty to the door of her apartment. In the carriage, he called out to the driver, "Fifty-Ninth and Seventh."

But after a few minutes, he thumped the roof of the carriage and shouted, "Do you know the Windsor Palace on the Bowery?"

16

J ULIA LIKED TO THINK OF IT AS A RAGING RIVER OF WELL-DRESSED society women, flowing endlessly from Twenty-Third to Fourteenth Streets. Every day, enormous numbers of ladies in a rainbow array of velvets, silks, brocades, and satins, all wearing large hats topped with flowers and feathers, traveled along Ladies' Mile, the city's prime shopping district. Huge department stores lined block after block, their plate glass windows full of wonderful things to buy— from pet monkeys to French silk stockings to Peruvian hat feathers. Broadway, the spine of the district, was packed with carriages of all varieties, horse-drawn trolleys, and hordes of pedestrians crossing back and forth between them.

With her mother by her side, Julia was swept along in the current of shoppers. At Broadway and Nineteenth Street, they extracted themselves and entered the arched entrance of Lord & Taylor. The building, with its diagonal tower at the corner and a mansard roof (since childhood, her father had taught her architectural terms), had been built with cast iron. Julia's father loved cast iron and used it on his own buildings, but he said some critics thought it a phony material that only pretended to be stone. Still, whenever Julia walked past a cast-iron building, she rapped her knuckles on a column to hear the metallic sound.

Inside, they went into the double-height shopping space on the main floor. Although Julia's coming-out gowns had already been ordered from Worth's, there was still a whole new adult wardrobe to be selected. Dresses for mornings, afternoons, and evenings needed to be bought, each with dozens of accessories. The choices were daunting, and Julia felt a wave of envy for men, whose clothes were not meant to attract attention. A man who would dare wear a purple waistcoat, say, would be branded an outcast. But for society women, uniformity was a grave sin. Their wardrobes had to stand out and dazzle. The more extravagant, the better.

Julia was glad that her mother was there to guide her. She knew Helen was considered a great beauty, and her choice of clothes was admired by all. Julia was also happy that Granny had not accompanied them. Since beginning preparations for her coming-out, Julia had been bombarded by advice from Granny. Last night, she proclaimed, "Unless very, very well acquainted, a man who grins at a lady when he tips his hat is not a gentleman of good breeding."

Julia and Helen liked to tackle one store a day instead of racing up and down Broadway. Yesterday, they had shopped at Arnold Constable. Tomorrow, a day at B. Altman was planned. After making some selections on the main floor of Lord & Taylor, they took the steam elevator to the upper levels. Each floor was a riot of femininity, with salesgirls waiting on well-dressed women at counters and wrapping desks and running back and forth with parcels and change. Little Lord & Taylor boys in white shirts followed behind the female shoppers, carrying their purchases. There was hardly a man to be seen.

Mother and daughter patiently examined the wares, moving steadily up to the fifth floor with their bag boy. Finally, they descended to the luxurious reception room on the main floor where they ran into many friends and had tea while a woman played Brahms on the piano.

On the way out, Helen realized she had left her gloves in the reception room and left Julia to wait outside the main entrance. Amid the flow of humanity up and down Broadway, Julia noticed a boy on a safety bicycle, the new kind with identically sized wheels. He slowly rode south—then accelerated and intentionally ran into an elderly woman crossing the street, knocking her over. His bike tipped. The boy got up, yelling and cursing at the woman for her carelessness. In a second, a crowd of people gathered, blocking Julia's view. Straining to see, she made out a young man in his twenties, wearing a gray three-piece suit. He walked to the edge of the crowd, where a man was craning his neck, trying to see the commotion. In a fraction of a second, he stole the man's wallet from his pants pocket. The young man walked slowly along the perimeter of the crowd and stole a wallet from another distracted man; an instant later, he stuck his hand in a woman's blue velvet handbag and removed a leather change purse. He worked with lightning speed. Then he walked south on Broadway, as casually if he were taking an afternoon stroll. Julia was mesmerized, unable to believe what she'd just seen.

Helen came up behind her. Julia kept her eyes glued on the man.

"Mother, I just ran into Lavinia Stewart, and she asked me to go to Macy's with her and her mother to look at a dress. I'll take a hansom back home. Will that be all right?"

"I suppose. I wanted to pop into W & J Sloane to look at a rug for Charlie's bedroom. Don't be late for supper, dear."

Julia kissed her mother and disappeared into the crowd. Breathless, she walked quickly down Broadway; soon, she was just twenty feet behind the man. A sense of giddy excitement swept over her. A great admirer of Dickens, she had read *Oliver Twist* three times, fascinated by the story of Fagin and his gang. But while she'd read about pickpockets, she'd never seen one.

Near Broadway and Fifteenth Street, the boy on the bicycle reappeared and ran into an elderly man. A crowd formed, and the young man went to work. Julia stood in the doorway of a store and watched, grinning from ear to ear. When he finished, she kept following. The sidewalks were packed with shoppers. She knew she blended in with the crowd and wouldn't be noticed, even if he turned around.

The young man made his way to the Fourteenth Street station of the Sixth Avenue Elevated. The station, built of iron and covered with steep roofs capped by iron cresting and finials, straddled Fourteenth

Street like a huge crab. As Julia followed, she passed through dappled patterns of sunlight and shadow thrown onto the street by the lattice-like train tracks above.

Although her family's main means of transportation was carriages, her father had taken her and her brothers for rides on the Third Avenue Elevated. The whole experience was thus quite familiar. Staying a healthy distance behind the pickpocket, she paid the off-peak fare of ten cents and went into the waiting room, an elegantly appointed space done in black walnut and stained glass. Soon the rumble of an approaching train began to vibrate the station like an earthquake tremor, and dozens of waiting passengers went out onto the platform. The pickpocket was taking an uptown train. Julia hid behind one of the slender cast-iron columns that held up the platform roof, but she could still see the man.

The train's steam engine screeched and hissed as it pulled into the station. Julia took a seat at the opposite end of the pickpocket's car. The train lurched forward and picked up speed. Keeping one eye on the man, Julia looked out the window. The thing she liked most about riding the elevated was that you passed within a few feet of the apart-ment windows on the buildings lining the avenue, so close that she felt she could reach out and tap the inhabitants on the shoulders. It was better at night, of course. Then the apartments were lit up and you could secretly observe the intimacy of people living their lives: eating, reading, arguing. She'd see a mother feeding a baby, two lovers hold-ing hands on a sofa. It was like going to the theater, but with dozens of miniature stages stacked together. Julia was so caught up that she almost missed the pickpocket's stop at Thirty-Second Street.

After disembarking, the pickpocket walked down Sixth Avenue and stopped just south of Thirtieth Street, in front of a three-story brick building painted bright yellow. He went in, greeting the two men who were coming out. Julia cautiously approached the building, worried that he'd suddenly reappear. From the curb, she saw that the building was called the Haymarket Dance Hall. A sign by the door stated that women were admitted free, while men paid a twenty-five-cent admission. She went to the entrance to look inside, half expecting to see Fagin and his boys gathered around a table. Music emerged from within, and she stepped aside to let by a fat, middle-aged man holding the arm of a garishly dressed woman with rouge on her cheeks.

A man in a black frock coat and gray trousers walked up to her and smiled. "What do ya say…two dollars…for an hour? That's more than fair for a classy looker like you."

"I have no idea what you're talking about," Julia said.

"All right, three, then."

When Julia didn't reply, the man shrugged his shoulders and walked on. Confused, Julia stepped up into the doorway to get a better look.

"I wouldn't go in if I were you," said a voice directly behind her.

Startled, Julia spun around to face the pickpocket. Up close, she saw that he was in his early twenties and surprisingly handsome, with penetrating blue eyes. Regaining her composure, Julia put on a look of indignation. "Why ever not? The sign says women can enter for free."

Her reply made the pickpocket laugh out loud. "You're not that type of woman."

Baffled by his answer and angered by his laughter, Julia stiffened her spine and added ice to her voice. "Sir, I never talk to complete strangers on the street."

"But I'm not a stranger, am I? You've been following me since Fifteenth Street."

"That's absurd."

"You sat in the same car on the elevated."

"You're terribly mistaken."

"You'd be a rotten undercover detective—you're too beautiful. I spotted you a mile away."

Taken aback by the backhanded compliment, Julia paused, then went on the attack.

"You're a thief," she said in a shrill, accusatory tone. "I saw you."

"So you caught me. Why not turn me over to the police? Look, here's your chance." The pickpocket pointed to a barrel-chested police-man strolling down Sixth Avenue, twirling his billy club. "Go ahead."

Tongue-tied, Julia looked down at the slate sidewalk as the cop passed by.

"Dandy John Nolan's my name," said the pickpocket, tipping his bowler hat and grinning. Granny's admonition from last night came immediately to mind, and Julia looked away.

"Sir, we've not been formally introduced by our mothers."

"Who's been feeding you that malarkey? Listen, you've come all the way up here. Let me buy you a beer. You seem real interested in what's going on inside. I'll show you. Come on."

Julia looked at the handsome young man and then at the double doors of the Haymarket Dance Hall, perplexed. If Fagin was in there, she was determined to see him. She wasn't going to be afraid. Besides, didn't writers need to experience all aspects of life?

"I have never tasted beer," she said softly.

"Then you're in for a treat. It's the nectar of the gods." Nolan flashed her a smile, which Julia shyly returned. He held out his arm, and she hesitated for a moment, then took it.

Together, they went inside.

17

T HIS IS A GOLD MINE, JIMMY. A GODDAMN GOLD MINE."
Kent watched Bella Levine pick through the stack of gowns and dresses heaped on the plank floor of the warehouse.

"These are from Paris! *Paris*, Jimmy. The very best of the best. Look, see how they're stitched with real silver and gold threads?" She was beside herself with excitement.

Levine, a mountain of a woman who weighed more than three hundred pounds, let out a whoop of delight and flopped down face-first onto the huge pile of clothes.

"I'm swimming in dough, Jimmy. Where d'you get this stuff?" she asked, caressing a green silk brocade gown. "This is better'n finding Captain Kidd's treasure."

Kent smiled and blew a ring of cigar smoke into the stagnant air of the warehouse. "Yes, Bella, I've discovered a gold mine."

A professional thief with a great deal of stolen goods at hand is still poor. He can't sell them or take them to merchants on the open market without arousing suspicion. He needs a fence to dispose of stolen goods, and Bella Levine had owned New York City's best fencing operation for the last ten years. Bella handled millions of dollars in loot—for a hefty 50 percent fee, of course. But Kent knew it was worth it. Bella was honest and, above all, reliable. She and her husband lived in an opulently furnished three-story brownstone on East Twenty-Sixth Street from which she ran her fencing operation. Her business made her very rich and enabled her to bribe judges, police officers, and district attorneys into leaving her alone. She regularly entertained the city's power fraternity, including Tammany men, with eight-course dinners at her home. Bella was the city's foremost female criminal and greatly admired by other well-known female thieves like Kid Glove Rosey and Little Annie.

Kent appreciated her discretion. Unlike his former fence, Black Lena Kleinschmidt, who was arrested after wearing a stolen diamond ring to a party, Bella never kept stolen goods. She was wealthy enough to buy things as nice as the Vanderbilts'. Items to be fenced were never brought to her home but were examined at a warehouse tucked away on 448 Broome Street. The interior of the cast-iron building resembled the Arnold Constable department store: five floors crammed with every conceivable type of goods. Once, Kent had seen a dinosaur skeleton.

"And this silver!" Bella exclaimed, pointing to the goods on the floor. "That isn't American stuff. It's English, the absolute best."

"I'm glad you like my goods. Maybe because of the quality, you'll take 45 percent this time?"

A menacing scowl replaced the smile on Bella's face. Normally, she had a jolly personality as large as her immense body. Now, she resembled an angry bull elephant. She rose with difficulty from the heap of clothes and waddled over to Kent.

"Forty-eight. Then if you bring me more quality stuff, maybe forty-five. Maybe."

"Don't worry, my beautiful dove. There's a lot more where this came from."

Culver stepped off the freight elevator and motioned to his boss.

"Excuse me, Bella," Kent said. She was too engrossed in the piles of men's evening dress to hear. "Didn't I tell you not to disturb me?" Kent snapped at Culver.

"Bald Jack's been picked up. By Byrnes." Culver spoke in a quiet, worried voice, hoping Bella wouldn't overhear.

"What for?" Kent asked indignantly.

"Killing that bank messenger four years ago."

For years, banks had been in the foolish habit of sending messengers through the streets with substantial amounts of cash and securities. As the banks were too cheap to provide armed escorts, these men were easy prey for sneak thieves. Stealing from them yielded smaller amounts than could be had from vaults, but it was usually an easy job; the messengers always gave up the money without a fight. Save one Union Trust man who carried a pistol. He would have killed Bald Jack Sanders if Kent's man hadn't killed him first. Bald Jack had no choice in the matter. There had been no witnesses that day on Hudson Street, Kent recalled grimly. Someone must have informed on Bald Jack to win a lighter sentence.

"Is he in the Tombs?" Kent asked, referring to the city's main prison on Centre Street.

"No. Byrnes is taking no chances. He has him in Blackwell's Island. They're to ship him up to Sing Sing until the trial."

Kent lit a Havana and began to pace the warehouse in wide circles. If it had been anyone else, the solution would have been easy: have Bald Jack killed in prison. But the man was his top earner. An expert sneak thief, he consistently brought in more money than anyone else in the organization (Kent hated the word *gang*). He was fearless and robbed anything from anybody. In his finest professional moment, he'd hijacked four flatbed cars loaded with carriages from the New York Central Railroad at Tarrytown.

"Is he in the old or new part of Blackwell's?"

"The new addition, the one they finished in the spring."

Bella approached them. "What are you fellows whispering about? Bald Jack?"

Kent wasn't surprised. Bella knew everything that went on in the city a day before anyone else.

"Go see Hummel," she said.

✦ ✦ ✦

Abe Hummel may have looked like a deformed dwarf, but he and his partner, William Howe, were the most powerful criminal lawyers in New York. Since the early 1860s, Howe and Hummel had represented thousands of criminals. Once they got 250 out of 300 prisoners on Blackwell's released on a technicality. Their client list included entire gangs, like the Whyos and the Sheeny Mob, and celebrities like P. T. Barnum and Edwin Booth. Howe and Hummel were so effective that many gangs and criminals, including Bella Levine, kept them on a five-thousand-dollar annual retainer.

Kent went immediately to their office, located at Leonard and Centre Streets across from the Tombs, for a consultation.

"You've got a problem here, Jim," Hummel said. He sat behind his desk, obscured by a haze of cigar smoke. "Byrnes won't budge on this. He wants your man hanged."

"How much will it take to change his mind?"

"That's not gonna work this time. And bribing the guards is out."

Kent stared out the window at the Tombs. True to its name, it looked like an Egyptian mausoleum, framed by four massive stone columns trimmed with carvings of acanthus leaves. *Such an impressive and palatial building*, he thought, *to house the scum of the earth*. It had an execution yard between an inner and outer building, linked by a bridge of sighs across which the condemned took their last walk.

The Tombs usually housed New York's most serious criminals. It was unusual for Byrnes to move Bald Jack to Blackwell's, an island in the middle of the East River. But despite its formidable appearance, there had been many successful escapes from the Tombs. *Byrnes is being very careful indeed*, Kent thought, drumming his fingers idly on the desk.

"His cell is in the new addition, you say?"

Hummel nodded.

"I'll need to know the number," Kent said, rising from his chair.

18

W ELCOME TO MY HOUSE."
"This is incredible," Charlie cried.

Charlie's rescuer, Eddie Mooney, had graciously invited him to visit his home. He stood before the open hatch to a huge, unused steam boiler in an abandoned factory near the corner of Cherry Street and the East River. Together, they crawled inside an iron-lined compartment furnished with an old mattress, a table, and a chair. It was big enough to stand. Eddie lit a candle, throwing a spooky light against the rusty walls.

"Pretty cozy, eh?"

"I'll say. And it's all yours?"

"Yep. Until they tear down the building, which'll probably be never," Eddie said. "Have a seat."

Charlie had been so grateful to his rescuer that he'd given Eddie three dollars of the money he'd saved for the Crandall steam engine. Eddie, touched by this gesture, offered to buy Charlie a drink. To his amazement, Charlie didn't drink beer or whiskey, so he treated him to a sarsaparilla.

Eddie plopped down on his bed and pulled out a sack of tobacco. He rolled a cigarette for himself and his guest. He didn't dare think that Charlie didn't smoke. Everybody he knew smoked. He didn't want to offend the boy. Smiling, he lit Charlie's cigarette.

Charlie inhaled, coughed, and gagged a bit. "It's marvelous that your parents let you live here," he said when he was able to speak.

Eddie, who was skinny and bucktoothed, with a prominent cowlick of greasy hair, shot him a puzzled look. "My parents? I ain't seen 'em in five years. They kicked my ass out onto the streets when I was seven."

"Why'd they do that?"

"Couldn't afford to keep me, what with the five other tykes. My ol' man was a worthless ass drunk, and my ma was a drunk and a two-bit whore to boot. Every kid I know down here got kicked out like that. What about you? Your parents kick you out yet?"

"Well, no, not yet," said Charlie, surprised by the question.

"I used to sleep in doorways, cellars, on old barges. Slept in a carriage in a stable for a month before they found me. But I've had this place almost two years now. I got me a real padlock for the hatch so no one can take it away."

Charlie was distracted, replaying their conversation in his mind. "What's a whore?"

"A woman who fucks a stranger for money," Eddie said. It struck him as an odd question, like asking "What planet do we live on?" He smiled at his young guest. "Charlie, old boy, there's a lot of learning I gotta teach ya."

"So who takes care of you?" Charlie asked, still puzzled.

"I take care of myself," Eddie said indignantly. "I work as a newsboy…and some other things, to scrape up money."

Charlie had seen newsboys all over the city. They weren't much older than him, ragged-looking waifs standing at the entrances to elevated stations, on busy street corners, and in front of the department stores on Ladies' Mile, yelling out, begging people to buy their papers. "How much can you make?" he asked. He'd never earned a nickel of his own; he had to beg his parents for change or wait for birthdays and Christmas.

"On a good day, fifty cents. That's after overhead like buying the papers and paying for selling space. Mine's the Hanover Square Elevated—lot of Wall Street swells there. I do a good business. I used to pay this older kid, name of Mikey Harrigan, protection money, but he took half my profit. So last year when I got to be big, I got a lead plumbing pipe and beat the shit out of him. No more protection money," Eddie said.

Charlie was old enough to understand that he was related (in a distant way) to the Astor fortune. Somehow, though, Eddie's entrepreneurialism impressed him far more.

"It's getting late," Eddie said. "I gotta go down to Park Row and get my evening papers from the folding room at the *Sun*. That's my rag. Come along with me."

As Eddie locked up his abode, he patted the old boiler affectionately.

"I'll tell ya, it's a lot better living here than at the Newsboys' Lodging House. You can get a bed and meal for six cents each, but you know what they do? If you stay there a month, they ship your ass off to Kansas or some fuckin' place out west. Make you work on a goddamn farm like you're a nigger slave or somethin'. Can you imagine? You'd never make it back to New York. And New York's the best place in the world to live. You know that too, huh, Charlie?"

They walked up to Madison Avenue and headed east, Eddie chattering like a magpie.

"I used to clean pigpens. Then I shoveled coal for a while. Tried factory work, making twine and paper collars, but I couldn't stand being cooped up all day, and the pay was shit. A fella with the Little Daybreak Boys on the waterfront found me a place in the gang as a lookout on robberies. I crawled through the portholes of the ships docked at the piers to steal shit for 'em. But then I got too big to fit through, so I left."

The boys approached a grocery stand on the corner of Madison Avenue and Rutgers Street.

"Ya hungry, Charlie?" Before Charlie could answer, Eddie pulled him inside a doorway. "Well, I'm gonna show you a trick. See that old man in the apron? You go up to him and ask what's the best way to City Hall. Then pretend to be confused and ask him to repeat it."

Charlie felt a flush of excitement surge up his back. He casually strolled up to the man, who could see by his clothes that he wasn't the usual filthy guttersnipe. The old man was straining to see if the kid's mother was behind him when Charlie asked for directions. With the man's back turned, Eddie helped himself to generous amounts of fruit from the stand, stuffing them inside his tattered shirt. He crossed the street and continued up Madison Avenue. A moment or two later, Charlie caught up with him.

"Good job. Have a peach."

Charlie bit into the ripe fruit, wiping the juice from his mouth with his sleeve. It seemed to taste more delicious because it was stolen.

At the newspaper office, Eddie pushed his way through dozens of other newsboys to get his papers. They all seemed to know and like him. Charlie was proud to be with someone so popular. The two boys took the Second Avenue Elevated downtown to the Hanover Square station. During the ride, Eddie opened the *Sun* and scanned the pages.

"You know," he boasted, "I can read and write real good. And I can read big words too—like parliament." A moment later, he cried out, "Look, a man got bit by a rabid dog on Avenue A. That's what'll be our hook. Murders, animal attacks, fires, robberies. Those all sell papers. So you yell out, 'Man killed by rabid dog.'"

Charlie looked down at the article. "It says he was just bit. We'd be lying."

"Don't worry. He'll be dead before the week's out. The newspaper business, Charlie, is nothing but lies."

Eddie and Charlie each took a position at the bottom of the uptown and downtown stairs to the Hanover Square station and hawked their papers. As the crowds rushed by, Charlie screamed out the headline. To his delight, pennies were thrust into his hand until every paper was sold. When Eddie was finished, they met by the entrance to the nearby Hanover Bank.

"Here you go," Charlie said, proudly pouring his money into Eddie's hands.

"Hey, you're a born newsie."

"I have to get home, but I'll meet you at your place tomorrow morning," Charlie said and bounded up the station steps.

⁘ ⁘ ⁘

Eddie watched Charlie as he left and could see that he was beside himself with joy, which made Eddie feel happy and sad at the same time. That always happened when he thought about Harry, his little brother, and Charlie reminded him of Harry. Thinking about the fun times they'd had made Eddie feel so good, but then he would descend into a deep sadness.

Harry had been thrown out of the house at the same time as Eddie. Together, they fended for themselves on the streets. Harry would serve as lookout while Eddie lifted items from a store or warehouse. Sometimes, Harry would even squirm inside an open window and do the stealing himself. They were quite a team. But Harry wasn't as strong as Eddie, and the street life wore him down. He was sick all the time, coughing up blood and getting such bad night sweats that his body would shake convulsively, as though he were in a carriage moving over cobblestones.

Three years ago, they'd had one of the coldest winters on record. Shivering, Eddie woke one morning from a bed of rags at the bottom of a basement stair off an alley. His feet and fingers felt numb. He gave Harry a gentle shake, but his brother didn't stir. Pulling the filthy, torn blanket away, Eddie discovered that his brother had frozen to death. Harry was stiff as a board, his eyes staring up at the sky.

That morning, Eddie did something he hadn't done for years: cry. He sobbed for hours, hunched over by the side of his brother's body. He knew he couldn't call the police or a doctor. If he did, he'd wind up in an orphanage for sure. So he waited until dark, and then he wrapped his little brother up, carrying him to the front of a Methodist church a few blocks away. He knew the congregation would give Harry a real burial.

Walking away from Harry's body was one of the loneliest things Eddie had ever done. The feeling of that horrible day stayed with him.

19

Y OU'RE TELLING ME THAT THE DEBT IS ONLY REDUCED BY SIX thousand dollars?"

"Mr. Cross, you and George don't seem to understand the concept of compound interest. There's 15 percent interest accruing weekly on the principal."

"Fifteen percent a week? That's usury, you bastard," Cross yelled. "A damned Hebrew wouldn't charge that much!"

Brady came up from behind and grabbed Cross by the neck, placing his knee against Cross's buttocks and bending his back like an archery bow.

"That silver and linen was worth twenty thousand dollars, easily. The clothing had to be forty thousand dollars!" Cross cried, ignoring the choking pressure of Brady's stranglehold.

"The fence we use to dispose of the goods gets a 50 percent cut, Mr. Cross. The actual take from the robbery is thus greatly reduced," Kent said in a patient voice. "But don't worry—you'll soon learn the economics of our business."

Brady released Cross, who fell forward, gasping.

"Goddamn it, Kent," he rasped out. "This is an outrage. I planned this robbery and get a pittance in return."

"Why don't you complain to your congressman?" Brady said, erupting in laughter.

"You know the alternative, Mr. Cross. And I know you don't want that," Kent said softly.

Cross slumped down in a chair. They were in the basement room at McGlory's, but this time only Culver and Brady had joined Kent.

"Do you remember a very short, bald gentleman, Mr. Cross? From the robbery?"

Cross looked up at Kent, puzzled. "Yes, I do."

"That was Bald Jack Sanders, a very valuable member of our organization," Kent said.

Cross chuckled in spite of himself. "Why do you people in the netherworld have such colorful names? In architecture, we don't have monikers like Charming Charlie McKim or Racy Richard Morris Hunt."

Kent ignored the question. "Bald Jack has been arrested—and that means trouble for you."

"Me?"

"Bald Jack saw you at the robbery. Under duress, he might give you up."

"He might, but if he does, I can give you up."

Kent smiled and took a sip of whiskey. "I know you won't do that. Like I said before, family men come with a lot of collateral."

As he stared at Kent, Cross's mind raced, trying to sort out the various possibilities. Why was Kent trying to bluff him?

"Bald Jack is being held in the Blackwell's Island prison, in an addition I've learned was designed by your friend from the Dakota, Henry Hardenbergh."

Cross burst out laughing. "Give me the telephone, then. I'll ring him up and say, 'Oh, hello, Henry. I need your help springing a crook from prison.'"

"I was thinking along those lines," Kent said.

"Is it my imagination, or is James T. Kent showing loyalty toward a fellow human being? You must really like this man if you're willing to take such a risk instead of just having him killed."

"For a society man from Harvard, you show exceptional shrewdness. But for your own good, I insist you help me."

"For ten thousand off the debt."

"Four thousand."

✦ ✦ ✦

"It's very kind of you to meet me on such short notice, Henry."

"Not at all, John. I'm happy to help."

"I was down on Wall Street and saw your Astor Building. The entrance is wonderful. I wanted to see how you detailed that arch, the one with the columns? And that attic gable with the diaper-patterned terra-cotta facing."

"Thank you, John. That job came out well," Hardenbergh said, giving a brusque nod. He was a touch uncomfortable, Cross saw. After all, the building had been commissioned by the Astor family, and Cross was an Astor relative. Though there had been many referrals over the years, Cross had never gotten any work directly from the Astors.

"I have to be uptown for a dinner, so I can't stay. But Maxwell here will be glad to assist you."

Maxwell, a draftsman in his midtwenties, nodded, his face expressionless. Cross guessed he was irritated as hell to be kept after work.

Hardenbergh placed his top hat on his head, waved, and departed.

It was just after six, and there was no one left in the large, open studio. The poor illumination cast by the gaslight fixtures made it useless for architects and their draftsmen to try to work into the evening. Cross had recently installed electrical fixtures in his office and had seen a real improvement in the light level—to the dismay of his employees, who now had to work late.

"These are the Astor Building drawings," Maxwell said, pulling out the drawer of a flat file. He lifted a stack of thirty-by-forty-inch linen sheets, placed them on a table, and stood off to the side.

Cross flipped through them until he found the sheet he wanted. Pulling it from the pile, he turned to the draftsman and gave him an absent smile. "Maxwell, old man, do me a favor and go downstairs to that saloon on Forty-First. Get me a sandwich and a growler of beer." He handed Maxwell a five-dollar bill. "And keep the change for yourself."

Maxwell's eyes lit up like bonfires. The four dollars' worth of change was a dollar more than his average pay per day. "Thank you so much, sir," he cried and flew out the door.

Cross immediately went back to the flat file, found the drawer labeled Blackwell's Island Prison, and pulled it out. He flung the stack of drawings on the table and quickly sifted through them to the site plan showing the whole layout of the prison, all the way to the East River. Taking some sheets of tracing paper off a desk, he placed one over the drawing and started working. Flipping through more drawings, he traced the parts he needed. Fifteen minutes later, he was finished. He had just replaced the prison drawings and was back at the table, looking over the Astor details, when Maxwell returned with his food and drink.

20

Y OU SURE YOU WANT TO DO THIS?" NOLAN ASKED, REMOVING HIS derby and scratching his head.

"I'm absolutely sure," Julia said. "I'm dying to see it. Please."

This was the second time Julia had met Nolan in the Tenderloin since their introduction at the Haymarket Dance Hall the previous week, and she felt like Alice, falling down the rabbit hole into Wonderland. Somehow she had stumbled into an exciting world of fantasy and revulsion. Even the name of the neighborhood, "the Tenderloin," had a magical sound.

At their first meeting, Nolan had showed her what a concert saloon was. Men would come to meet ladies of the evening—Nolan had explained them too—to dance and make friends. Julia thought the music was tinny but quite entertaining, and the whole joint—another term learned from Nolan—was gay and lively. The owner, William McMahon, was a genial, well-dressed gentleman who didn't allow swearing or close dancing and forbade the girls exposing their ankles. Huge behemoths of men called bouncers threw any rowdy customers into the gutter.

The curtained-off cubicles at the side of the hall, Julia was told, were for private dances, in which some girls performed naked. There was a secret tunnel from the hall to an adjacent hotel for more intimate liaisons, Nolan added.

At home, Julia hadn't gotten a wink of sleep. Her head was swimming, awash with the incredible sights she'd seen. The next morning, she decided to shelve her old novel and start a new one, based on the new world she'd discovered. To meet Nolan again, she told her mother she was going out with her school friend, Lavinia. She delighted in coming up with these lies. As a writer, she realized, she had a great talent for altering the truth.

"Shouldn't we be going? You said it starts at one on the dot," she said.

Nolan frowned, seemingly unsure. But when he saw Julia's pretty face and looked into her brown eyes, the size of silver dollars, he relented. "It's on Twenty-Seventh Street."

The Tenderloin had its own specific geography, she learned. West Twenty-Eighth Street was for high-end gambling, West Twenty-Seventh Street for low-end. West Twenty-Ninth Street was exclusively row houses for the ladies of the evening. She and Nolan passed the Cairo Dance Hall, where they'd gone the day before yesterday. Julia didn't think it was as nice as the Haymarket. The Cairo, Nolan told her, was a clip joint—it watered down the drinks.

All the streets had saloons. They'd visited two: the Star and Garter and the Ruins. Each had a long bar to the side with a mirror behind it, sawdust-covered floors, a pot-bellied stove, and chromolithographs of prize fighters and plump nude women on the walls. All women had to be escorted, and if you had two beers, a free sandwich lunch was offered, which Julia found delicious but quite salty. In her society world, a saloon was considered low class. But it was really a club, she learned, a second home for the men who played cards or pool and argued about politics and sports. In a way, it was no different from her father going to the Union League or Knickerbocker clubs.

Nolan was delighted to show her the sights and had proudly escorted her by the arm into dance halls and saloons. On the streets, he pointed out colorful local characters like Dan the Dude, a knockout drop artist—although Julia didn't quite understand what that was yet. Nolan was also flattered to be asked about his profession, and Julia laughed delightedly when she discovered that he'd been trained in a

Fagin school right out of *Oliver Twist*. Nolan spilled trade secrets about how to distract a mark and then pull a wallet or purse. The bicycle trick she'd seen was taught to him by one Crazy Bob, who had even trained his dog, Whiskey, to snatch purses!

Nolan hadn't hesitated to show her anything—until now. They stopped at the Last Hope. From the outside, it looked like any other saloon. "Here we are," he said.

"Lead the way, Mr. Nolan," Julia chirped. They addressed each other as mister and miss because, as etiquette dictated, they hadn't known each other since childhood.

Nolan smiled and took her by the arm. They strode into the saloon, past the patrons with their shot glasses and mugs of beer. The men and women looked up, surprised by the sight of Julia, who wore a stylish blue afternoon dress.

When they reached the rear of the first floor, Julia gasped, "Just like ancient Greece."

In front of her was a wooden amphitheater that stretched down into the basement. The benches were filled almost completely with men, some of whom had gaudily dressed women at their sides. Nolan paid the attendant four dollars and guided Julia down the steep steps. They found seats near the arena floor. Men called out greetings to Nolan, who raised his derby in return, proud that they were admiring Julia.

The wall surrounding the arena was about four feet high and lined with zinc sheets. The floor was packed earth and gave off a damp, moldy smell. Off to the side stood a man in a green three-piece suit. He held an excited fox terrier on a leather leash.

"How does this work?" Julia asked above the din of the spectators.

"Fifty in a twenty-minute limit and three-to-one odds on Sampson, the mutt."

"What should we bet?" asked Julia, removing a bill from her red and gold embroidered purse. "I've got a five," she said, handing it to Nolan.

He caught the attention of a bookie standing at the top row behind them and nodded. "Get ready," he yelled.

A gate opened at the side of the arena wall. In one fluid motion, two burly men set a large wooden box on the dirt floor and opened a front flap. Out came dozens of rats, scurrying like mad around the arena. The men pulled the box in and closed the gate. At that moment, a whistle blew. The man in the green suit released the dog and climbed over the wall, taking a seat.

The fox terrier ran into the mass of rats, grabbed one by the neck, sank his white teeth into him, shook him violently, and flung the dead carcass away. Then he attacked another, and another. At each kill, the crowd roared with delight. The dog killed systematically, with great discipline. He didn't waste a second chasing the rats about. The spectators cheered raucously, urging Sampson on.

Seated on a bench near the floor was a man holding a pocket watch. A man next to him held a slate, on which he made a chalk mark for each kill. As the tally mounted, the crowd went into a frenzy. The dirty gray rats formed a vortex in the arena, colliding with one another, leaping over the dead bodies of their comrades. The man holding the watch yelled out, "Ten minutes left! Twenty-nine kills."

Julia found herself screaming Sampson's name. At five minutes left and forty-one kills, the volume of the cheering increased fourfold. The dog kept attacking without the tiniest sign of fatigue. Julia thought dizzily that he must be enjoying himself. But some rats evaded him, scattering here and there, making him race around the arena to run them down. Only three remained, and they were determined to live. Sampson sat back and waited for one rat to run right into him. Two left. The dog chose his first victim and went in for the kill.

"One minute!" yelled the timer, and the crowd went mad. The last rat was not only fast but wily, as if he knew the remaining time. In a burst of speed, Sampson caught up with him and hurled his body to the ground as the timer yelled out, "Time!"

Some of the crowd was ecstatic; others were angry and disgusted. Julia and Nolan threw their arms up in victory. "We won fifteen dollars," Nolan yelled.

Sampson's handler had him back on the leash. He paraded him in front of the cheering crowd like a gladiator in a Roman arena. The white curly fur around the terrier's mouth was bloodstained, but Sampson was triumphant. To the delight of his fans, he stopped, picked up a dead rat, shook it, and threw it to the floor.

A few moments later, Julia and Nolan found themselves back on the sidewalk of West Twenty-Seventh Street.

"That was exciting, Mr. Nolan," Julia said breathlessly. "Thank you for taking me."

"Would you believe the record is one hundred in fifteen minutes, Miss Cross?"

"One hundred in fifteen minutes? That's amazing!"

"I must be honest: I didn't know if you'd like it."

"Oh, Mr. Nolan, rats are evil. Did you know that they spread the Black Death in the fourteenth century? The plague killed half of Europe!"

It was a hot July afternoon, and Julia was fanning herself.

"Would you like something to drink, Miss Cross? Perhaps a cold sarsaparilla?"

"No, I must be getting back. I told my mother I was at the Natural History Museum with Lavinia."

"I suppose you did get to see some animals."

Julia gave an unexpected burble of laughter. "And they weren't stuffed."

"I had a wonderful time, Miss Cross."

"Next Tuesday at ten a.m.?" Julia asked, shaking his hand and smiling.

21

S ITTING IN A ROWBOAT IN THE EAST RIVER ACROSS FROM Blackwell's Island at 2:00 a.m., Cross was surprised by how cool and refreshing the air was.

A strong wind swept up the river. In Manhattan, the August night had been unbearably hot and humid; to feel the wind was a sweet relief. All day, he'd dreaded this moment. He hadn't bothered to ask whether he would accompany Kent's men tonight. He knew his presence would be mandatory.

The three men sat in a long rowboat tied to an overhanging tree. They were hidden in the shadows on the banks of the river at Long Island City, less than a thousand feet from Blackwell's. To avoid detection by people on Manhattan's piers, it was safer to approach from the less-populated Queens County side in the east.

"Here they come," Brady whispered, nodding to a passing guard boat. "It won't be back for another two hours."

The steam-powered prison patrol boats continuously circled the twelve-mile-long, cigar-shaped island. As this one passed, a barrel-chested man named Wild Jimmy Coogan untied the line and began rowing them to the island. The prison, a forbidding stone fortress topped with castle-like crenellations, was located near the southern end of the island, just north of the smallpox and municipal hospitals. Coogan expertly guided them across, taking advantage of the speedy south current. Cross guessed he must have been a seaman before embarking on a career in crime. To Cross's relief, they encountered no other boats. No one said a word during the trip, and only the sound of the oars cutting softly through the water could be heard.

From the middle of the river, the men could see a few lights on in the prison.

Coogan continued rowing until they were fifty yards away from the sloping granite seawall that circled the island.

"What now, Mr. Engineer?" whispered Brady.

Cross took out his tracings. It was a moonless night and hard to read. He struck a match and looked up at the seawall.

"I'm an architect, not an engineer," he whispered indignantly.

"Goddamn you, which way?" Brady snarled, punching Cross hard in the right arm.

"Head about twenty yards to the south," Cross said, trying not to grimace from the pain. After a minute, he called out, "That's it."

A circular opening in the seawall appeared before them, and Coogan steered toward it. If it had been high tide, they never would have seen the sewer tunnel, which sloped up almost 150 feet to the new addition at the prison's south end. When Kent told Cross about Hardenbergh's addition, Cross had remembered an article he'd seen in the trade journal *American Architect and Building News*. Back at his office, he'd looked it up. Instead of having a slop bucket in each cell for the prisoners to relieve themselves, the men had unenclosed toilets that dumped into waste lines between the two hundred back-to-back cells. During the day, a huge cistern on the roof of the addition periodically flushed the lines into a sewer tunnel, which dumped into the river. The addition had been designed according to the wishes of the Prison Reform Society, a do-gooder group that lobbied the state legislature for more humane prison conditions.

To Cross's surprise, Hardenbergh's drawings showed no iron gate over the opening. The state had skimped on money, he guessed, and never installed it. All the better. They wouldn't have to saw off a padlock.

About ten feet from the opening, Brady grabbed Coogan's arm and pointed along the top of the seawall. They saw a single light by the edge, coming toward them from about twenty feet away. It swung to and fro as it moved.

"It's a guard," Brady hissed, and the men immediately crouched low in the boat. With several powerful stokes of the oars, Coogan slid the craft inside the opening as the guard stopped directly above them. They froze and waited, listening to the river lap against the walls of the tunnel. With an oar, Coogan steadied the boat, keeping it from drifting out of the tunnel.

After five minutes, Brady nodded, and the men started to gather their equipment. Without the gate, there was no place to tie up the boat. It took several minutes to concoct a mooring. The distinct sound of streaming water interrupted their work. Brady raised his hand as the signal to halt, and the men froze again, struggling to meet one another's eyes in the darkness.

Outside the tunnel, they saw a thin jet of liquid falling from above the opening. The stream began to taper off, and someone said, "Ah." A minute later, a cigar butt was tossed into the water. Brady and Coogan exchanged smiles. Brady lit a lantern and ordered Cross to lead the way.

The diameter of the tunnel was only four feet, but it was big enough to bend over and walk through. Past the point at which high tide rinsed the tunnel clean, a powerful putrid odor hit them like a shovel to the face.

"Keep your mouths open and you won't smell it," whispered Cross. Looking down, he realized he shouldn't have worn his good shoes.

The tunnel sloped at a very steep angle. Good for drainage but tiring for walking. About fifty feet from the prison, they heard a rumbling.

"Brace yourselves and don't let go of the bag," Cross yelled.

A few seconds later, a wall of brown water crashed into them.

"Christ, I'm covered in shit," Coogan screamed as the torrent swept around his waist.

"Goddamn you, Cross," Brady hissed, clutching the bag of tools to his chest.

"How the hell should I know when they flush the lines?" Cross snapped, thinking he shouldn't have worn his Brooks Brothers trousers either.

Stinking and angry, the men kept walking until they reached the exterior prison wall. They climbed through a hatch into a plumbing cavity in the addition, a towering three-story space filled from top to bottom with waste lines from each cell. The space was barely four feet wide. Cross pulled the drawings from inside his soaking shirt. Brady raised the lantern.

"He's in cell twenty-four, second tier," whispered Cross. He started pacing off a small distance to his right, trying to find the actual position of the cell as displayed on the drawing. "Right up there."

Using the labyrinth of piping like a ladder, Brady began climbing up to the cell, his dirty canvas bag of tools bouncing against his side. When he grabbed for an upper piece of lead pipe, it pulled out of its joint and crashed to the cement floor. The sound reverberated through the space like a pistol shot. The men froze, waiting for a reaction.

The minutes passed like months. Cross's wet body was drenched in sweat. He tried to imagine how he would explain his presence. Nothing he thought of was very convincing. He could see the front-page article in the *Tribune*, imagine the ruin that would befall his family.

But there was nothing but silence. Brady, still above them, took another route to the second tier. Coogan followed. To provide ventilation, each cell had a two-foot-square grille made of wide bands of iron; it looked like the weave of a basket. Above them, in the roof over the cavity, ventilators drew in fresh air. Hardenbergh was no fool; he knew the grilles could be escape routes, and he took great care in detailing their anchorage to the massive stone walls. Huge bolts and iron plates secured them to the inside face of the cavity wall. There was no way a prisoner could unfasten them from inside the cell, but from the outside, it was a simple matter of unbolting—as Brady was about to do with the huge wrench he'd brought along.

"Sanders, we're here to get you out," he whispered through the vent grille.

"I'll keep watch by the bars while you work," a voice said.

Brady placed the spanner on the first bolt and threw his weight on the handle. The bolt loosened with a tiny squeak. He quickly attacked the other three. Once loosened, he unscrewed them, placed them in his bag, pulled out the vent, and handed it to Coogan, who was perched on the pipes. The shiny, round pate of Bald Jack appeared in the opening. Being skinny and small, he squirmed through without difficulty.

"Good evening, Mr. Brady," whispered Bald Jack. He wore a gray-and-black-striped prison uniform of rough wool but otherwise looked much the same.

As Brady and Coogan helped Bald Jack keep his balance on the piping, a head of red hair appeared. "Who the fuck is this?" hissed Brady, watching the man wriggle his shoulders and arms through the opening.

"That's Gordon, my cell mate," Bald Jack said. "This isn't the Fifth Avenue Hotel. I don't get my own goddamn room."

"And I'm coming too. Ya ain't leaving me behind," Gordon snarled. He bulled his way through to his waist, and then Bald Jack and Brady pulled him the rest of the way out.

Brady carefully inserted the vent into place and tightened the bolts.

"They'll think we vanished into thin air," said Bald Jack with a smile.

"Let's move," said Coogan, leading the way down.

"Who the hell is he?" asked Cross, who had been waiting for them at the bottom of the plumbing cavity.

"Never you mind," said Brady, who took the lead as they moved back into the sewer tunnel.

"Holy shit, it stinks," Gordon said.

"Shit smells like shit," said Coogan with a smile.

The five men splashed through the tunnel to the boat. Brady

scanned the seawall for guards. Satisfied, he gave Coogan the signal to shove off.

"You know, the grub wasn't bad in there. Ya got a pound of meat for dinner every day," Bald Jack said, looking back at the prison as they rowed away.

"And a whole quart of vegetable soup," added Gordon.

"We can turn around and take you back if you liked the place so much," said Coogan.

"Shit no. You know the worst part of bein' in there? They *made* you go to evening school," Bald Jack said.

Brady laughed. "Hell, let's take 'em back. You would've finally learned to read and write at the age of forty."

The rowboat silently made its way back across the river. To Cross's relief, there wasn't a boat to be seen. Just a few hundred yards more, and they'd be safe on the Queens side.

"So what were you in for, Gordon?" Brady asked.

"Got caught robbing Saint Jerome's Rectory on East Forty-Seventh Street."

"Tough break," Brady said sympathetically. "Lotta silver in those places."

"You bet. When I get back to Manhattan, I'll get set up, maybe go back to the same place and try again."

"That's a real smart idea. They won't expect you to hit it twice in a row," said Brady, nodding in approval.

They reached the bank of the river and tied up. As he stepped out of the boat, Gordon laid his hand on Bald Jack's shoulder. "It was real white of ya to let me come along, and I won't forget it. You should look me up at the Black and Tan on Bleecker. That's my joint."

"Sure thing, Gordie," said Bald Jack, extending his hand.

As Gordon reached out to take it, Coogan and Brady grabbed him from behind and flung him facedown into the river. They held him under, Cross watching in horror as the man struggled with all his might to free himself, arms and legs flailing, splashing against the dark water. After two agonizing minutes, his body went completely still. Bald Jack watched impassively as Brady tugged the floating body by the back of the collar, gently guiding it into the fast-moving current. The black-and-gray form was carried away silently into the night.

"You bastard," screamed Cross, his voice shattering the silence.

In a second, his own head was underwater. Gulping down what seemed like a gallon of river water, he felt hands forcing him down, down. He flailed his arms in panic.

Suddenly, he was released. He stumbled to the river bank, coughing and gagging.

"It's late. Time to go home, Cross," said Brady, watching him with impassive eyes.

22

THERE'S A FELLOW OUT FRONT WHO WANTS TO SEE YOU, MR. CROSS. Says he's your brother."

Cross put down his pencil. He'd been working on a design for an office building on Broadway and Spring Street. Like his former master, H. H. Richardson, he would make a rough sketch of an idea and then hand it off to his assistants to refine and develop. But an avalanche of work had descended upon the office in the last month, and he was behind. He hadn't even started the design for the new orphan asylum up in Westchester.

When he did sit down to work, he couldn't keep his mind off of Gordon's body, floating away into the night. It wasn't so much the image of his corpse as the fact that Cross had watched him be murdered. Brady and Coogan had done it with such ease, such absolute lack of emotion. Still, Gordon's death had a positive side. It had almost completely erased his anxiety over getting caught for the Cook robbery—what was a little jail time when he could be dead?

Cross approached the office reception room slowly, trying to see if it really was his brother or one of Kent's men with a message. A week after the jailbreak, he'd received a call telling him he had a week to prepare the next job. Had Kent's men come early?

But no. Standing there was Robert, his older brother, someone he hadn't seen in years. Cross smiled when he saw how fit and well Robert looked. His full head of dark hair was showing some gray, but he still cut an imposing figure. Cross looked up to his older brother still, even though their father thought Robert a failure. He'd dropped out of

Harvard after one year and drifted around the East Coast until the out-break of the Civil War. He joined the Union Army, rising to the rank of captain and winning a medal at Gettysburg. His heroism had made Cross proud but at the same time ashamed for having sat out the war.

"Robert," Cross cried, and every draftsman lifted his head and looked up. They embraced, and Cross found that he had tears in his eyes.

"You blackguard, I haven't seen you in three years," Robert said. "Before you start jabbering on about your architecture, tell me how Helen and the children are."

"Fine, just fine. George graduated, Charlie's ten and constantly in motion, and Julia's about to make her debut."

"Already? She was so little when I last saw her."

"All grown up. Though she can't stand wearing a corset."

"I can't wait to see them all. How's the beautiful Helen?"

"Running around like mad, preparing for Julia's coming-out ball."

Robert checked his pocket watch. "It's getting close to noon. Stop slaving away on those drawings and come out to lunch with me."

"You're in luck. I'm meeting George at Delmonico's on Fourteenth Street for lunch. And you're coming too," Cross said, almost giddy with happiness. "He'll be surprised as hell to see you."

Seeing his brother was the best medicine he could have imagined. Growing up, Cross had adored his big brother, who always welcomed his company, unlike many older brothers who would tell their young siblings to get lost. Robert was a far bigger influence in his life than his aloof father, often giving him advice on how to play baseball or ride a horse, how to avoid getting bullied by classmates at prep school, and on the best methods to woo the opposite sex. Robert had the knack of knowing when something was troubling his brother and would imme-diately offer counsel on how to deal with sadness, disappointment, or anger over a particular problem. It bothered Cross that they had drifted apart over the last few years.

As it was a beautiful August day, they decided to walk from Broadway and Grand Street up to the restaurant. Robert had always been a good listener, and now he asked his brother insightful questions about his business. Because they had time on their hands, he graciously asked if there were any of Cross's buildings nearby. There were, and the brothers took a detour toward a publishing company at Lafayette and Bond Streets.

"Damn, Johnny," Robert said, staring up at the facade. "I wish I had talent like yours. To figure out all that decoration on those arches? That's really something."

Ever since he was a boy, Cross had loved his older brother's praise. This time, the words gave him pause—the admiration suddenly reminded him of Kent's.

"Does Aunt Caroline ever throw you work?" Robert asked with a sly smile.

"Lots of referrals, but no real Astor work."

"Always keep on the old girl's good side, Johnny," Robert said. "Remember how she said I was acting common when she caught me smoking that cigar?"

"In her formal parlor! And you were ten," Cross said, laughing.

They turned north on Fifth Avenue. Before Cross could ask about his brother's life, Robert said, "The thing I envy most about you is your family. Sometimes I wish I had one."

"Nonsense. There's still time."

"Not pushing fifty and in my line of work."

"What are you doing now? Last I heard, you worked for the Remington Arms Company."

"I'm a Pinkerton man."

"Since when?"

"About two years ago. I ran into a man from my old regiment who was a Pinkerton. Said that with my military background, he could get me a job, and he did, in Buffalo. That's where I've been all this time. But they transferred me to New York last week."

"Do you like the work?" To Cross, being a detective sounded exciting and romantic, though in recent years, the working classes had come to think of the Pinkertons as a ruthless mercenary army used to break strikes. But society people loved them, for they kept the commoners in their place.

"I've finally found my calling," said Robert, nodding. He slapped his brother on the shoulder and resumed walking.

"And you're based in New York permanently?" Cross couldn't keep the excitement from his voice.

"Yes. I've been promoted to the main office. I'm staying at the Hotel Brunswick for now. Perhaps you can help me find an apartment?"

"Of course. That's wonderful, Rob. I can recommend a few places."

"Wonderful. I've been assigned a very interesting case, you see. A rich fellow named Cook—of Cook Shoes, out of Saint Louis? Perhaps you heard of him. Had his place on Fifth Avenue completely cleaned out a few weeks ago. Never seen so thorough a job. The criminals strangled an unfortunate servant girl who happened to be there. The police found her body in the river."

Robert looked to his side, but Cross wasn't there. He turned and saw his brother, standing still as a statue in the middle of the sidewalk.

"What's wrong, Johnny?" Robert asked, alarmed.

At first, Cross didn't answer. He just stared off into space. His head was swimming; he thought he was going to faint.

Concerned, Robert walked up to him.

"I never saw anything about it in the papers," Cross whispered, trying to pull himself together.

"Cook was embarrassed. He didn't want any publicity. That's why they called us in."

"Any leads?"

"Not a one. Come on, I'm starving. I could eat a bear."

⁘ ⁘ ⁘

This would be the first time since the graduation party that he'd seen George—and the first time since he'd found out about his debt. Despite his anguish regarding his son's secret life, Cross had been looking forward to it. His anger toward his son had diminished, and he was slowly beginning to forgive him. *A son's faults are the father's faults*, he kept reminding himself. And every time he thought of leaving Kent, he saw his son's corpse.

But Kent's warnings about his son's "weakness" haunted him. Although Cross was closer to his son than most society fathers, a wide gulf still yawned between them. Though he might wish it otherwise, and while he desperately wanted to believe George was staying out of trouble, he really had no idea if the boy had kept gambling.

Down deep, he didn't want to know. The thought terrified him. He pushed it away, viciously sublimating it. *Like Aunt Caroline*, he thought grimly. *Always ignoring anything unpleasant.*

So, after all these weeks, the sight of George did not brighten Cross's spirits. The news his brother had delivered crushed him; his mind reeled. While his son and brother chattered away, he kept thinking of the girl's body, floating in the water. Just like Gordon.

Had she been like Colleen, the Cross's servant girl? Pretty and sweet-natured, straight off the boat from Ireland? Girls like that spent their entire lives bent over washtubs and ironing boards, but incredibly, they still had a cheerful outlook on life. They were happy just to be in America. Cross thought back to that night in the carriage, watching Brady play with the length of piano wire. It wasn't a nervous affectation.

Cross hadn't touched his terrapin soup or the lamb chops. He swallowed hard and looked over at George, laughing and happy.

"John...John. Are you still with us, old man?" Robert asked.

Cross snapped out of his trance. "Why yes, yes, of course. What were you talking about?"

"That it's incredible George played in the Polo Grounds in front of all those people."

"He's too modest to tell you he hit the game-winning home run against Yale."

"Damn, I wish I would've seen that. And against those bastards from Yale too!"

But as Cross watched them speak and exchange easy smiles, his whole feeling toward his son shifted with the abruptness of a switch being thrown. He'd been fooling himself all this time. His family's calamity was the result of George's foolishness. Cross stared at his son, the brilliant Harvard academic scholar. It was all a facade, shielding a terrible secret. At that moment, there was not a shred of fatherly love in him. He felt like reaching across the table and throttling George. A father wasn't supposed to hate his own son. Cross hated *himself* for feeling this way, but he couldn't help it. He averted his eyes.

"Now that I live in New York," Robert was saying, "we can go to the Polo Grounds to see the Giants."

"Charlie's going to love that," said George.

"Robert," said Cross. His voice was unusually loud and halted the conversation. "Please come to dinner tomorrow night to meet the rest of the family. George, I hope you can make it."

"I'm sorry, Father. I've made plans."

Cross glared at his son. An uneasy silence fell upon the table. A waiter came to take dessert orders and serve the coffee and brandy. Robert tried to resurrect the conversation, to no avail. After Cross saw his brother off in a carriage, he hailed one for himself.

"I'll drop you off uptown, George."

"I wasn't heading that way, but…"

"Get in," Cross snapped.

They sat in silence as the horses clip-clopped up Fifth Avenue. Progress through the morass of afternoon traffic was slow. As he stared at his son, anger built up within Cross like red-hot magma in the throat of a volcano. He took a deep breath and turned his head to look at the stream of pedestrians on the sidewalk. Not one of them, he thought, could have as great a burden as the one he shouldered at that moment.

"So you have plans for tomorrow. Do they involve numbers?"

"No, Father. I don't have to teach."

"What about numbers on playing cards? The five of diamonds, the three of spades?"

Cross saw the puzzled look on George's face change to panic. His son shifted his body uncomfortably on the leather bench seat of the carriage.

"Even as a child, you had an affinity for numbers. You could do the most complicated puzzles, add large sums in your head. I was so damn proud of you. I knew you'd become a scholar—and you did." Cross spoke without looking at George. His gaze was fixed on the passing storefronts along the street.

"Yes, I was always fascinated by numbers," George said, his eyes full of worry and suspicion.

"I suppose there's one number that's of particular fascination—forty-eight thousand."

For a second, Cross thought George would throw open the carriage door and bolt. But the boy froze in his seat and looked his father straight in the eye.

"I have a gambling debt of forty-eight thousand dollars," he said in a loud, clear voice.

Instead of exploding in anger, Cross was actually pleased by his son's candor. He could tell George was shaken down to his boots, but he was fighting hard to put up a brave front. It was impressive.

"You *did* have a gambling debt of forty-eight thousand dollars. I paid it. Mr. Kent and I have reached an agreement that ensures no harm will come to you."

George's brave facade crumbled. His hands covered his face. He bent over as though the shame had punched him in the stomach.

"No one in the family knows of this—and they never will."

Still bent double, George began to sob. "I'm so sorry, Father. I—"

"I don't understand how you got mixed up in this. You're an adult, and I respect that. I would not attempt to meddle in your personal life. But you can never gamble again, George. It's over. It has to be!"

George looked up at his father. "Thank you so much," he said in a trembling voice. "You don't know how grateful I am. I'm…so sorry for what I've done to you."

Cross could see the shame and embarrassment breaking his son in two. It was painful to watch, but he had no intention of letting up. "It's what you've done to *yourself*. You don't know how close you came to destroying your life—and your family's. You have a brilliant academic career ahead of you, George. I won't allow you to throw that away. We'll put this behind us, but I *forbid* you to gamble again. You must promise me, son."

"Yes, yes. Of course. I know what I did was foolish. I swear to you, it won't happen again. I swear."

When the carriage reached the corner of Fifty-Ninth Street and Fifth Avenue, George reached over and hugged his father, pulling him close. Cross embraced his son, tears filling his eyes. He didn't want to let him go. It was like George was six years old again. He wanted to hold him, to protect him from all the bad things in life.

As George walked away, he turned and waved to his father. Cross's anger toward his son vanished. He loved George with all his heart. He would do anything to save him.

⊹ ⊹ ⊹

George walked to the north side of the street and into Central Park. Running off the stone path, he stumbled into the undergrowth, fell to his knees, and threw up his lunch. His head was spinning. He turned onto his back, looking up through the canopy of trees at the cloudless sky.

His worst fear had been realized—his father had discovered his secret. He wished Kent had killed him that night in the power plant. The shame and humiliation of what had happened ate away at George's insides like a horrible pain, the likes of which he'd never felt in his life. In their world, fathers and sons weren't supposed to be close, but George and his father were, which made the revelation all the more unbearable.

He was lucky, George knew. A tyrannical father would have exposed him and cast him out of the family forever. Instead, his father had forgiven him. He was even giving him another chance—as long as he gave up gambling.

George wanted to keep his promise with all his heart, but he knew it was almost impossible. There was an illness inside him. He hadn't attempted to explain that to his father in the carriage; he knew people didn't understand, that they thought gambling a moral failing. But it was a sickness, he thought wildly, one that caused men and women to destroy themselves like a drunk or drug addict would. He didn't know if he had the strength to withstand it.

Where did my father get forty-eight thousand dollars? he wondered, staring up at the trees. His first thought was Aunt Caroline, but he knew his father could never go to her; such a request would have meant certain expulsion from her world. Did his father borrow from friends or clients, sell the house on Madison, or even place a bet? The amount was easily three years of his income as an architect.

Wherever he'd gotten the money, George swore he'd pay him back—after he wiped out the nine thousand he still owed.

23

C HARLIE, MEET MY FRIEND, INJUN SAM KELLY."
Charlie, who had never met an Indian, stared at the boy, looking for some trace of Indian blood. But he seemed to be completely white, a pale, blond-haired boy of about eight. He wore a man's plaid shirt that hung past his knees.

"Glad to know ya, Charlie. Call me Sam."

"So what have ya been up to?" Eddie asked the boy.

"Doin' lookout work for the Whyos," Sam said, voice brimming with pride.

"The Whyos are the toughest gang in town, next to Kent's Gents," Eddie told Charlie. "When they're robbing a store at night, Sam here keeps an eye out for the cops."

"Also been robbin' Protestant churches." As an aside to Charlie, Sam said, "We're all Irish down here, so we hate Protestants."

"That's way better than what you used to do—pretending to be the kid of that wop organ grinder on Mulberry and gathering up the pennies people threw at him," Eddie said, smiling at the memory.

Sam rolled his eyes—then lit up with an idea. "Say, I know a warehouse at the end of Grand where there's boxes full of bridles and horse stuff. We can get in real easy. What d'ya say? We sell it and split it three ways."

"Later. Charlie and me's goin' uptown to do a little wranglin'."

✦ ✦ ✦

Carrying a large canvas U.S. Post Office mailbag and a wooden billy club, Eddie led Charlie along Twelfth Avenue. Charlie had freed up his whole afternoon by telling his parents he'd be at dancing class. Last Thursday, he'd supposedly attended drawing lessons. Charlie's new-found interest in the arts had delighted his parents. Praising his enthu-siasm, they'd given him money—which Charlie had promptly pocketed for other ventures. *Science classes at the Museum of Natural History will be next*, he thought, smiling.

"It's coming up on the right. All these places along the docks are good huntin'," Eddie said with an air of authority. "But I've had the best luck here."

They stopped in front of an abandoned four-story brick ware-house, once used to store cargo unloaded from the ships that docked across the street. Eddie pointed to the arched entry that no longer had a door, and they entered. Inside was an open space, the plank floor completely covered with debris and broken glass. The tall windows allowed enough daylight for the boys to see their way around.

Eddie positioned Charlie near the rear wall and handed him the club. "When I tell you, start banging this club like crazy all over the floor," he whispered.

Eddie walked to a door in the rear wall and out into a tiny yard. Near the corner of the building, a small basement window with missing glass stood open. Spreading the mailbag wide, he covered the entire opening. "Start banging!"

At the signal, Charlie began to pummel the floor with the club. The sound was like pistol reports, echoing throughout the building.

Eddie heard the scurrying of tiny feet and high-pitched squeaking from the basement below. Then objects started hurling themselves into the bag from the window opening with great velocity, as if someone was throwing rocks.

The bag filled up fast, until it looked like a single, vibrating mass.

"Stop," Eddie yelled. He yanked the bag to an upright position and pulled the drawstrings tight. Dozens of gray rats with long, pink tails raced past his feet into the yard.

Club in hand, Charlie ran to the back. "There must be a hundred in there," he said, delighted.

"I dunno. I sure as hell ain't putting my hand in to count 'em. Rat bites hurt like hell, and you can get rabies from 'em. Start foaming at the mouth like a mad dog."

Eddie tied the drawstring around the neck of the bag, ensuring there would be no escapees. The bag was pulsating with rats, struggling in a mad frenzy. He took the club from Charlie and started beating on the canvas. "That'll keep 'em in line," he said.

The boys took hold of the bag and dragged it through the warehouse and onto the sidewalk.

"We don't have far to go. The place is just a few blocks up, on West Twenty-Seventh," he said.

"How much do you think we'll get?" Charlie asked eagerly.

"The going rate is twelve cents a head, and I ain't gonna take a penny less."

Taking a rest every block, the boys finally made it to a saloon whose front was painted a bright blue. They dragged the bag through an alley on the left-hand side to a rear yard.

"Wait here, and I'll get Nardello."

Eddie eventually returned with a lean, swarthy man who had greasy black hair. "Put 'em in the corral for the count," he ordered.

At the rear of the yard was a walled enclosure of wood boards almost four feet high. At the bottom was a sliding panel, which Nardello opened with his foot.

"All right, let 'em out."

Eddie untied the drawstring, shoved the bag into the opening, and kicked the rear until every rat was out.

"Eleven cents a head."

"Fuck you and the horse you came in on. Twelve, you dago bastard. Look at the quality there. Nice and fast," Eddie yelled.

Charlie gaped at him. He had never seen a child talk to an adult in such a manner.

"Twelve, then. So I can get rid of your ass."

Eddie hung over the top of the wall and began counting with his index figure, jabbing at the air.

Nardello did as well.

"I got forty-eight," said Nardello.

"I got fifty-three," snapped Eddie.

"Fifty, then," Nardello said.

Eddie nodded.

The man counted six one-dollar bills into Eddie's palm, and the boys exchanged triumphant smiles.

"We're about to start. If you want to watch, I'll let you in for free," Nardello said.

"Nah, we gotta get downtown to get our papers," Eddie said, placing three dollars in Charlie's hand.

As Charlie and Eddie came out of the alley, Julia and Nolan entered through the front door of the saloon.

24

G EORGE HATED COOKING FOR HIMSELF. HIS BACHELOR APARTMENT on West Fifty-Ninth Street had a small kitchen off the parlor, but he rarely set foot in it. If Kitty didn't fix him a meal at her place, he'd eat in a restaurant or buy a sandwich. He could always go home to eat—his mother begged him constantly to come for dinner—but that would mean facing his father, and he just couldn't bring himself to do it. He'd thought the shame would diminish with time, but it had increased instead. Over and over, he relived the confrontation with his father. He felt physically sick every time he thought of it.

He loved his father more than anything. John Cross had spent many hours talking and playing with him. He was always there to help George when he was troubled. Although he was busy with his architectural practice, he never used it as an excuse not to spend time with his son. He was like that with Julia and Charlie too. All three children had a close bond with their parents, unlike most of George's friends, whose nannies were more like their mothers.

Dodging his father meant not seeing his brother or sister, and this too gave George a profound feeling of emptiness. He enjoyed discussing literature with Julia and baseball with Charlie. He'd promised to take his little brother to the Polo Grounds to see a Giants game this summer, and he wasn't going to let him down. He resolved to call him when he got home.

The question of where his father had found forty-eight thousand dollars to pay his debt was also deeply troubling. This weighed on George, a mystery he couldn't solve. His determination to repay his father had become all consuming—and this intensified his gambling sickness. But he kept losing.

"Why, George Cross, haven't seen you in a coon's age. How's my Harvard man?" a voice behind him called out.

George spun around to face Jack Bacon, a collector for Turk Holden, who owned the Silver Slipper gambling den on Houston Street.

"Good to see you, Jack," said George, resisting the overpowering impulse to start running in the other direction. "What are you doing in this neighborhood?"

"Just conducting a little business for Holden," the broad-chested thug replied. "You know, Georgie, why don't you come with me? You might find it fun."

"Well, Jack, I was just…"

"Only take a few minutes. Come on, old boy, keep me company," he said in a cheerful tone.

Jack took hold of George's elbow and steered him along Fifty-Sixth Street. While they walked, Jack chattered on about baseball and how well Brooklyn was doing, rattling off the season's statistics and scores. He led George to a well-to-do apartment house. On the fifth floor, Jack knocked on a door.

A well-dressed, middle-aged woman answered. A look of sheer terror convulsed her face when she saw Jack.

"Good afternoon, Mrs. Todd. Is William about?" he asked in the politest of voices.

"No, I'm sorry. He…"

Jack placed his shovel-size hand in the center of the woman's forehead and shoved her violently to the floor. He walked through the doorway, turned, and beckoned George to follow him, smiling broadly.

The apartment was well furnished. The spacious parlor had a grand round table in the center, adorned with ornaments and a sculpture. Jack deliberately walked into it, sending it crashing to the ground. The woman cried out.

"Oops. So clumsy of me. My apologies." Still smiling, he reached over and pulled a glass-fronted bookcase forward. It hit the floor with a resounding crash. While the woman wailed, Jack went from room to room in the apartment, looking under beds and in closets. George followed behind, unsure what else to do.

Sitting deep in the rear of the kitchen pantry, Jack found a paunchy, bald man of about fifty.

"So good to see you again, William," Jack said, yanking the man out by his ankle.

"I'll have something for you tomorrow, I swear! I swear," William screamed.

Jack kicked the man full in the face, if he were punting a football. Then he kicked him repeatedly in the stomach while William's wife screamed continuously from the front parlor. Pulling William upright, Jack leaned him against the kitchen wall and pummeled his face until blood splattered in all directions. William screamed for mercy, reaching desperately into his pockets to produce some money, but Jack was unmoved. He started working on his midsection.

Pressed hard against the opposite wall, George stood cringing at the sight.

Mrs. Todd came rushing into the kitchen to intervene, but as she approached Jack, he swung out his left arm and swatted her to the polished wooden floor with no more effort than he would have taken to strike a fly.

Growing tired of the effort, he let go of William, who slumped to the floor, and looked around the kitchen. Taking a knife from the kitchen counter, Jack placed the blade inside William's left nostril and flicked up. Blood gushed like a geyser. Jack stood over him, viewing his handiwork, then shook his head and cut the other nostril. Satisfied, he kicked William hard in the groin as a parting gesture.

"I'm coming back tomorrow, and you better have my six hundred dollars, William. If you don't, I'm going to have to hurt you," Jack said over his shoulder as he walked toward the door. To the right of the entry, an expensive-looking vase sat on a console table. Jack grabbed it and smashed it against the wall.

At the door, George stopped and turned to view the carnage. Husband and wife were screaming in agony; blood covered the kitchen floor. It looked as though someone had slopped a bucket of red paint from one end of the room to the other. George felt faint. He steadied himself against the foyer wall, trying to breathe. An instant later, he started violently as Jack slapped his paw on his shoulder, guiding him down the iron and stone stairs.

"Now, like I was sayin', Jeffries of Brooklyn is just as good a player as anyone the Giants got."

25

CROSS DIDN'T WANT TO GO TO THE LEES' DINNER PARTY, BUT HE and Helen had already accepted the invitation. A popular saying held that if a man who had accepted a dinner invitation died, his executor had to take his place.

Hand-lettered invitations on thick, white vellum arrived a full three weeks before the event. At the same time, flowers had been ordered, a French chef had chosen the menu, and Mrs. Lee had purchased a new silver service. Society parties were expected to be a show of magnificent ostentation, and the hostesses never failed to live up to this obligation.

The Crosses' carriage pulled up to the Lee mansion the customary thirty minutes prior to the eight o'clock meal time. Located on the corner of Fifth Avenue and Sixty-First Street, the house was a wide, four-story, French Empire model with an English basement. *A dull, uninspired design*, Cross thought. Footmen outfitted in black-and-gold livery stood by the red carpet that ran from the curb to the front door, opening the carriage doors and bowing to the guests, all of whom were dressed the same: men in white tie and tails, women in light summer evening gowns with long gloves. Honoria Lee, a middle-aged woman whose beauty had barely faded over the years, stood in the gilt-paneled reception hall, greeting her guests.

"Helen, how beautiful you look," she gushed. It pleased Cross that instead of his wife having to flatter, she was always flattered herself. "And, John. So lovely to see you. Go see who you're escorting."

Cross walked to a table where small white envelopes inscribed with the names of the gentlemen guests were arranged. Locating his, he opened it to find a card: Elizabeth Burnham. The wife of an insurance company owner, she was beautiful, with raven hair and piercing blue eyes, but exceedingly insipid and dull. It would be like talking to a rock all evening. Still, in society, beauty excused a great many failings. And it was bad form for a gentleman to complain about his escort. Cross strolled into the drawing room, a palatial space adorned with Chinese vases full of red roses, mahogany paneling, a white marble floor, and a sparkling crystal chandelier.

A crowd had assembled around the Tarletons, the guests of honor, who had recently arrived from London. Everyone in Cross's set was a rabid Anglophile, loving every intricacy of British aristocratic life, from cricket to pheasant shooting to tweed suits. Sir Henry was regaling the crowd with descriptions of the renovation to Castle Twickham, his ancestral home. Tarleton, John understood, was one of the few British elites who still had a substantial fortune. Many British lords had seen their riches frittered away by prior generations and had had to sink to the humiliating state of marrying young American heiresses—"dollar princesses," the press called them—who might rejuvenate their fortunes and save their estates.

Sir Henry and his plump wife, Deidre, were basking in the glow of New York society's admiration. They interrupted their boasting to meet Helen, with whom the couple was immediately captivated.

On the outskirts, Cross milled about, nodding to people he knew, paying compliments to ladies, and conducting an informal architectural survey of the house. He enjoyed appraising the proportions, detailing, and finishes of all the houses he was invited into.

He felt a tap on his shoulder, and there was Stanford White.

"Hello, Stanny. I knew you'd be here. You did their place in Newport, I recall?"

"Oh yes. And I never turn down a good meal," White said, patting his belly. It had grown considerably since the two men had worked together at H. H. Richardson's office.

"What are you currently working on?" Cross asked.

"Christ, I just came from Columbia Bank, a job I did on Fifth Avenue and Forty-Second. They want alterations to the banking hall. Idiots. It's fine the way it is."

Cross nodded. All of White's buildings were special. Though he envied his friend's incredible talent, he had long ago acknowledged that he could never surpass him as a designer. The bank building was unique and original—all Stanny's work was. Done in the Classical Revival style, it had a pair of balconies covered by flat roofs and supported by slender Ionic columns, which gave the big building a wonderful sense of lightness.

"Where'd you put the vault?"

"They wanted it in a subbasement. That's where the safe-deposit boxes are."

"Is the vault all steel or encased in cement?"

"Steel."

"Did you put in one of those new alarm systems?"

"It's just an electric line connecting to a police precinct. Why? You got a bank project?"

"Ah, yes…I'm looking into any new vault systems," Cross said. He added in a low voice, "Maybe I could look at your drawings?"

Avery Lee, their host, approached. Beside him was a man sporting a magnificent waxed mustache.

"Gentlemen, this is Count Sergei Aleksandrov, of the court of the Czar in Saint Petersburg. I'm privileged to have him as my house guest."

Both men bowed, impressed by the man's aristocratic bearing. The count was the very model of what an aristocrat should look like—very tall, lean, and strikingly handsome.

"Count, these are two of New York's finest architects. Perhaps they might design a home for your visits to America?"

"That would be wonderful. Much more pleasurable than imposing on friends or living in a hotel," the count said in perfect but heavily accented English. Bowing, he excused himself.

"Stanny, John, have you heard about these robberies in the city?" Lee growled as soon as the count was out of earshot. "It's unbelievable. A whole mansion cleaned out! Where the hell are the police?"

Cross stared down at the polished marble floor.

"What do you make of it, Mr. Cross?" Lee asked.

A butler called out, "Madame, dinner is served," saving Cross from having to answer. He and the other men in the room scurried about like mice, looking for the women they had been assigned to escort. As per strict custom, Mr. Lee led the way into the dining room with Lady Tarleton. The rest of the guests followed, with Mrs. Lee and Sir Henry entering last. On the dinner table sat twenty-four place cards, arranged to ensure that husbands and wives were well separated and that the guest of honor, Sir Henry, sat to Mrs. Lee's right.

Cross thought the table impressive, even by New York standards. Down its center and raised a few inches above the white embroidered damask tablecloth was a continuous sheet of plate glass. Beneath it, dozens of tiny electric lights glowed, giving the cut-glass bowls of carnations spaced every three feet a magical aura. Each seat had a setting of Sèvres china, laid with ten pieces of engraved silver from Gorham that included a fork for oysters, a fork for fruit, and separate knives for bread, fish, and meat. Five different kinds of glasses for the sparkling water, wines, champagne, hock, and claret flanked the setting.

Cross pulled out a chair for Mrs. Burnham and then seated himself, unfolding his napkin, which held a dinner roll. Next to his plate was the usual small party favor—tonight, a silver cigarette case. His dinner companion found a jeweled brooch. Cross examined the handwritten menu, inscribed on gilt-edged vellum. Chesapeake Bay oysters on the half shell to start, chicken consommé à l'Italienne, Spanish mackerel à la Maître d'Hôtel served with hock, soft shell crab farcies with Johannisberger sparkling wine, and perdrix aux truffes. Honoria always put forth a good spread. French chefs were more prized than jewels in New York society, and the Lees had one of the finest. Everything was cooked at home instead of catered, which made a vast difference in quality.

Cross set about engaging Mrs. Burnham in conversation. He decided to set the bar high and work down to banalities about the weather.

"Do you think Parliament will grant home rule to Ireland, Mrs. Burnham?"

"I...wouldn't really know, Mr. Cross."

A footman appeared at his left with a plate of oysters. All dinner parties were served à la russe. The footmen stood by the side of each guest, offering him or her each course instead of passing platters of food on the table, *à la française*. Without the clutter of multiple dishes, society dinners could boast elaborate centerpieces of the sort on Honoria's table.

Cross changed tactics and tried something he knew was closer to Mrs. Burnham's heart.

"Tell me, Mrs. Burnham. Which do you feel are superior—gowns from Worth or gowns from Pingat?"

She lit up at the question. "Worth, Mr. Cross, always Worth. In fact, I just received a trunk last week. We had visited the showroom in Paris in the spring to place the order, and I tell you, Mr. Cross, we weren't disappointed."

"That gown looks magnificent on you." The expected response.

Mrs. Burnham blushed. For the next twenty minutes, she spoke enthusiastically about her clothes, only stopping to offer an aside about how handsome Count Aleksandrov was.

The white-gloved footmen continued to serve the food and pour the alcoholic beverages. Finally, desserts of pudding, ices, Bavarian creams, petits fours, and glaces aux marrons were offered, along with a fruit-and-cheese course. By this time, Cross had given up trying to engage Mrs. Burnham in conversation and had begun talking to Marmaduke Scott, who sat across the table.

Scott had made a fortune importing beef from the West in the new refrigerated railroad cars. Cross hoped the conversation would swing to possible architectural commissions, like a summer place in the Berkshires, where it was much cooler. These dinners were often a gold mine for new jobs. But Scott was in a foul mood.

"It took an hour to go four blocks in my carriage on Broadway this morning," he growled, wolfing down strawberries drenched in sweet wine. "Four blocks. Traffic crawled like a slug, I tell you. It's damn impossible to get anywhere in New York."

"And the dust and the manure is shocking," Mrs. Burnham said.

"They said the elevated trains would reduce traffic by half. What a lot of nonsense. Traffic is ten times worse. We need new ways of traveling. Perhaps under the ground."

"Exactly," Mrs. Burnham said. "Years ago, I remember my father taking me for a ride on Mr. Beach's underground railway on Broadway. It was so wonderful. Such a shame it went bankrupt."

Cross's eyes widened, and the spoonful of Bavarian cream that was about to enter his mouth stopped in midair. Setting down his gold dessert spoon, he turned to Mrs. Burnham and smiled.

"Elizabeth Burnham, you are an amazing, magnificent creature."

26

———◆◆◆———

I ASSUME THIS MUST BE URGENT, AS YOU'VE SUMMONED ME DOWN here at two a.m." Kent was in evening dress and top hat, his expression frosty.

"I'm glad I didn't get you out of bed," Cross said. He'd made the call when the gentlemen at the Lees' party had retired to the smoking room for brandy and cigars.

Kent frowned. "Millicent and I had just walked in the door from a dinner party at Sherry's—very tired, mind you—when you called."

They were standing in the shadows of the huge U.S. Post Office, south of city hall on the east side of Broadway. There was barely a breeze, but the night air felt good after the hot day.

"I designed Fidelity National across the street," Cross said, pointing to a narrow, six-story brick building, its huge, arched entry supported by polished granite columns.

"A very handsome bank, I'm sure. But unfortunately, I experienced a recent mishap robbing a bank in the daytime," Kent said. "It's made me cautious."

"It was you who tried to blow the vault at Manhattan Merchants & Trust," Cross said, shocked in spite of himself.

"With very poor results. Houses of society people are more lucrative—and less of a risk."

"Suppose you robbed a bank over a weekend."

"Please continue, Mr. Cross."

"Back in '70, a man named Alfred Beach, the editor of *Scientific*

American, had a new idea for public transportation. His train traveled not aboveground, but below," Cross said.

"I remember. He built an experimental underground tunnel with his own money so the Tweed Ring wouldn't find out."

"For an underground pneumatic railway, propelled by blasts of compressed air."

"Where was it?"

Cross pointed directly in front of them, at Broadway. "There. In front of my bank."

Kent walked to the curb and looked down at the cobblestone street. It was brightly illuminated by the electric streetlights.

"It's a ten-foot-wide, brick-lined tunnel that went one block, along Broadway from Murray Street on your left to Warren Street on your right. After the panic in '73, Beach couldn't get financing to continue it and went bust. He rented the thing out as a wine cellar and shooting gallery. Then he gave up and sealed it in '74."

"So it's still down there," Kent said with a smile.

"There's a sealed plate around the corner on Warren where the entrance was. Come on."

At this hour, Cross thought they'd be alone, but the area was thick with streetwalkers. They walked to the west side of Broadway and past the bank. "Where's the vault?" Kent asked.

"In the basement toward the front of the building—in line with the bottom of the tunnel."

As they walked, the whores called out in low voices, "Fifty cents, fifty cents for a fine time." Most of the women were poorly dressed hags. Drink, opium, and violence had eaten away any trace of beauty they'd once possessed. But their vulgarity and coarseness were what most offended Cross. New York had a strict hierarchy of whoredom, from the first-class parlor houses in the West Twenties to the street-walkers at Broadway and Twenty-Fourth, who almost resembled fashionable ladies and brought their clients to respectable quarters to transact business. Then there were these disgusting creatures at the bottom. Only the most depraved and desperate were out this late.

A gap-toothed wench in a torn and soiled dress brazenly confronted Kent.

"Fifty cents for a handsome gentleman like you. What do you say?" she croaked.

With astonishing speed and viciousness, Kent struck her on the head with his cane. She dropped to the sidewalk, crying out in pain. Kent grabbed the gold head of the cane, pulling out a long blade, and held it against her throat. "Stay away from me, you filthy bitch," he snarled.

Wide-eyed and shaking with fright, the whore crawled away from him, holding the side of her head.

Kent sheathed the blade and continued walking. "How wide did you say the tunnel was?" he asked. He spoke casually, as though he'd just shooed away a gnat.

"Not more than ten feet in diameter. There was only one set of tracks. The air blew the train in one direction and then sucked it back."

Turning the corner at Warren, they saw the iron plate set in the street. Kent bent and poked at it with his cane. "You're right. This is likely where the station was."

Rising, he walked quickly around the corner back to Broadway. This time, the whores who saw him coming gave him a wide berth. Kent stopped in front of the bank and smiled at Cross, rubbing the head of his cane with his white-gloved fingers.

"Yes, Mr. Cross, this has great possibilities. I must look into it more closely. Preparation, preparation, preparation. As always, the key to this game of ours. You'll be hearing from me." He turned to leave.

"Kent."

Kent stopped.

Cross walked up to him, closer, and closer again. Their faces were six inches apart. "Fidelity National handles big accounts. Edison Electric, Atlantic & Pacific Steamship, B. Altman. The owners were on the bank board that hired me, so I know. There's a good bit of money in there."

"And I'm sure it'll go far in reducing your son's debt. Good night, Mr. Cross."

✛ ✛ ✛

Honoria Lee laid her head on Count Aleksandrov's shoulder, toying with the soft hair on his chest. "Sergei, you're wonderful," she cooed.

"And you, my love, are more passionate than any woman in Saint Petersburg."

"I have everything in life a woman would want—money, houses, clothes—except passion," Mrs. Lee said forlornly.

"A woman of your quality needs passion, every night."

"Ha. Avery Lee knows what a 6 percent return on a Pennsylvania Railroad bond will bring, but he knows nothing about passion."

Aleksandrov laughed. "Mr. Lee is a good provider. That's what matters most."

"Oh, I suppose." Mrs. Lee raised herself up to look at the clock on the fireplace mantel. "It's almost five a.m., my dear. You must get back to your room before the servants are about."

Aleksandrov kissed her on the cheek and rose from the bed, reaching for his robe. He opened the bedroom door a crack to check the hallway, waved, and was gone.

The electric lights were off in the long carpeted corridor, but daylight was creeping in through the windows. Aleksandrov stopped at a door and opened it. Before going in, he took off his leather slippers.

From their breathing, he could tell the Tartletons were sleeping soundly. The guests of honor were housed in a magnificent room with an adjoining sitting parlor. Aleksandrov smiled at the sight of the couple. They probably hadn't slept in the same bed in years, but their hosts had been afraid of offending them by providing separate rooms.

Aleksandrov crept silently to the dresser where Sir Henry's handsome leather billfold sat. Opening it, he found several hundred American dollars, of which he borrowed three-quarters. Rich men like this never kept track of their cash. He spotted the lady's dressing table and quietly slid open the drawers until he found Lady Deidre's jewel case. With an expert's eye, he laid aside the choicest piece, an emerald-and-pearl necklace, and slipped a small ruby brooch inset with tiny diamonds into the pocket of his robe.

Smiling, Aleksandrov left the bedroom.

27

O N ARRIVING AT THE BALL, THE GUESTS WILL FIND YOU STANDING at your mother's right. She will do the introducing. Then you will dance the German with the gentleman *she* selects to lead."

"Yes, Granny."

Julia and Granny were walking along Broadway together. They would always be together from this point on, for Julia's coming-out meant that she needed a chaperone. And, to her horror, her mother had designated Granny, not a maiden aunt, for this grave responsibility. Granny had taken up her duties with an enthusiasm bordering on mania. Her granddaughter's well-being and social worth were at stake; the task was not to be left to an amateur.

"A chaperone is the guardian angel of a well-bred girl," Granny declared. "She must always be by her side."

Julia had a very difficult time concealing her anguish.

A widow in her seventies, Granny lived alone in a three-story brownstone overlooking Madison Square. It was the heart of what Julia called Knickerbocker Land. When she wasn't at the Cross house interfering in the family's lives, Granny spent her days sitting at the tall window in the front parlor, surrounded by at least a dozen cats, watching the world go by. It was like staring at an aquarium, a source of constant fascination for her.

This morning, Julia had told her mother she was to meet Lavinia Stewart on West Thirty-Second Street to look at a crystal punch bowl at Fernbach's. This wasn't quite true. First, she had an appointment with John Nolan. Then she would see the punch bowl. Granny's accompaniment threw her plans into disarray. There was no possible way of getting rid of her.

"Above all," Granny said, "never paint your cheeks. Complexion comes from within."

"I promise I won't."

They passed storefronts stocked with every kind of product, protected from the hot August sun by striped awnings. The streets brimmed with the usual flood of carriages, horse-drawn trolleys, and wagons. The stench of horse manure and urine was particularly pungent for so early in the day.

"It is perfectly correct for you to refuse an offer of a dance with a man, but you *must* then sit that dance out. Never accept another offer for the same dance. It *just* isn't done."

Julia ignored that, as she'd done for all the advice she'd been given for the last eight blocks, consumed by the question of what to do about her rendezvous with Nolan. Reluctant to stand him up, she decided to steer her grandmother in the right direction and then improvise.

"Granny, let's turn at Thirtieth. I want to see something in a shop window."

This didn't interrupt Granny's discourse in the least. She continued to lecture on about taking cold baths every morning. Julia saw a hat shop window on the northwest corner of Sixth under the elevated railroad and crossed the street. Above, a train thundered past, and Granny stopped talking for almost ten seconds. She had never ridden on an elevated railroad and she never would, she exclaimed when it was gone. They threaded their way through the crowds to the shop, and Julia pretended to be interested in its wares, sweeping the streets with her eyes.

"Excuse me, ma'am. I believe you dropped this." A young man handed Granny her rose-colored velvet purse with a smile.

"My goodness, yes," Granny exclaimed, bewildered. "I can't understand how I lost it. It was tucked in my handbag."

"Why, Mr. Nolan, how good to see you again," Julia said cheerfully.

Confused, Granny turned her head from Julia to Nolan and back to Julia. "You know this man, Julia?" It was her sworn duty to keep Julia from making improper acquaintances.

"Of course. You remember the Nolans on East Twenty-Sixth Street. Very close friends with the Roosevelts," Julia said with a big smile, shooting a wink at Nolan. "Their son, Theodore, is going to run for mayor."

Once Granny heard a familiar Knickerbocker name like Roosevelt, she began to calm down.

"Young John here was with me at Doddsworth Dancing Academy. In fact, that's where you met him, Granny. You said that you'd never seen a young boy dance a more elegant German. You must remember."

Granny looked at the boy. Julia knew she was thinking that he *was* quite handsome and well dressed.

"Thank you so much, Mr. Nolan. You came around at exactly the right time. There were four hundred dollars in that little purse," Granny said in a surprisingly friendly voice.

Julia saw Nolan frown. "Mr. Nolan, this is my grandmother, Mrs. Arabella Rutherford."

Recovering, he shook Granny's hand. "A great pleasure, ma'am."

"We're just doing some shopping," said Julia.

"For Miss Cross's coming-out ball," Granny added proudly.

"A ball for Miss Cross? How nice. Please, let me escort you. So many wonderful things to buy in this district. It would be an honor to carry your parcels."

"Indeed, yes, I love to shop here," Granny gushed. Julia could see she was falling for Nolan's charm and good looks.

"What's your favorite thing in the world, Mrs. Rutherford? Something you don't have enough of, I mean?"

"Cats."

"You're a cat lover! So am I," Nolan said. "It just so happens that I know where there's the most incredible collection of cats—and all for sale."

"Really?" There was obvious pleasure in Granny's voice. Without any children left in her house, cats had become her surrogates, offering endless unconditional love. She'd had scores of them over the years and lavished attention on them. It was such a paradox to Julia: Granny, so rock hard and uncompromising in her feelings toward humans, was so loving and affectionate to her cats. In her will, her surviving animals were due a sizable bequest. Her cats would have a higher yearly income than 99 percent of New York.

"The place is just on the next block, on Thirty-First. Would you like to see?"

"Oh, yes."

"Tell me more about the plans for Miss Cross's ball."

As they walked, Granny rattled off the details, down to the pattern on the Dresden china settings. Nolan listened with great curiosity, peppering her with questions. They stopped in front of an ordinary-looking brownstone, and Nolan led the way in.

The first thing Julia noticed was the odd smell. Not noxious, but almost alluring—rich and smoky. Instead of the usual layout of rooms off the central hallway, there were cubicles furnished with small plush sofas. Each one held a little round table and an oriental rug. Very respectable-looking men and women lay inside, smoking what looked like a pipe. The windows were shuttered from within, making the interior very dark. But throughout there were dozens and dozens of cats of all different colors and sizes, perched on tables and the arms of sofas, sleeping on the cushions, pacing the hallway.

"My goodness, so many beautiful cats," Granny exclaimed and began to walk around, petting and caressing the cats. Granny was so distracted that she didn't seem to notice the people lying about.

A smiling Chinaman wearing a blue-and-gold quilted jacket with shiny black pantaloons approached. "Lady like kitties," he said.

To Julia's astonishment, Granny returned the smile and nodded. As far as Julia knew, she had always found anything different from

Knickerbocker society vulgar and disgusting. Yet she treated the Chinaman as though he was a Van Rensselaer.

"Oh, yes. Are any for sale?"

"All kitties for sale. Which one you like?"

"Oh dear, there's too many to choose. That calico is amazing, and that tortie! Adorable."

"No hurry. You sit here." The Chinaman pointed to a sofa. He began to gather cats and arrange them like throw pillows. "You sit, lady, here. I bring you *Li Yuen*. That 'Fountain of Beauty' in English."

Granny perched primly on the sofa and began to caress the cats, which purred loudly as they rubbed against her. "They're so friendly," she said with glee.

At Julia's side, Nolan beamed with pride.

Instead of bringing tea, which Julia had thought Fountain of Beauty was, the Chinaman brought her aunt a long ivory pipe, a little box, and what looked like a lamp.

"This *yen tsiang*," he said, pointing to the pipe, and then holding up the box. "This *yen hop*." He pointed to himself. "And I Wah Kee."

He took a tiny blob of what looked like grease from the *yen hop*, put it in the jade bowl of the pipe, and lit the lamp. Then he placed the pipe in Granny's hand, motioning her to hold the pipe bowl over the lamp and inhale.

"Granny, you really shouldn't be doing this," said Julia, alarmed.

"Fiddlesticks, Julia," snapped Granny. "My Uncle Hector was in the opium trade with Warren Delano. Made a fortune. Warren's daughter, Sarah, married James Roosevelt up in Hyde Park a few years back, and I was at the wedding. Uncle Hector told me the smoke had definite medicinal qualities. It might be just the thing for my lumbago."

Granny lay back on the sofa and calmly inhaled, then coughed.

"Take in slow, hold, let out slow," tutored Wah Kee, giving her a solicitous smile.

"Besides," Granny continued, a stern gaze fixed on her

granddaughter, "this is good manners. Like smoking a peace pipe in an Indian village. It's a token of this yellow devil's gratitude for buying his cats."

Granny looked over at the cubicle directly across from her. "Isn't that the mother of your schoolmate, Ellen Bentley?"

Indeed, a woman in a royal-blue princess dress, puffing away on a sofa, was Ellen's mother. She seemed to be in a state of hazy bliss, her eyelids drifting down with each inhale.

Closing her eyes, Granny continued to smoke. The cats snuggled up around her.

"It's almost noon, Miss Cross," Nolan whispered in Julia's ear. "The cockfight will be starting soon. If we leave now, we can make it. Remember, the bird that won for you last time, General Sherman, is fighting."

Julia nodded and moved toward her grandmother, extending a hand to bring the elderly woman to her feet. Granny looked up, annoyed, a glassy look in her eyes.

"My child, I am not ready to leave, and I won't be rushed into making a decision as to which cats I want. If you must run an errand, I shall allow Mr. Nolan to accompany you. You did say he's a close friend of Theodore Roosevelt's family?"

Julia nodded and whispered to Nolan, "Wah Kee will look after her, won't he?"

The Chinaman nodded. "Lady be fine, Mr. Johnnie. You go. She buy cats—two dollar for cat. Good price."

"Don't worry," Nolan said to Julia. "We'll be back in an hour."

G EORGE RESTED HIS HEAD AGAINST THE WINDOW OF THE TRAIN. Only five minutes out from Grand Central Station, he was struck by how fast the buildings disappeared. An empty landscape met his gaze, vacant lots punctuating the grid of streets. A few isolated brick buildings stood alone, as if they had sprung up from the earth like weeds. The builders, it seemed, were patiently waiting for development to flow north to their doors and increase the value of their property.

Each of the twelve children in his class had a window seat. Their small faces were pressed against the windows, peering out eagerly. None of them, George knew, had ever taken a train ride out of the city. Their world had been a ten-block radius, filled with tenements packed cheek by jowl onto the filthy, crowded streets. It was as if they were on a rocket to the moon. The smallest detail fascinated the children, and it delighted George to see them so excited.

Many of the lots had jumbles of rundown shanties on them, with open fires and chickens, cows, and goats milling around. The children pointed out the animals to one another, laughing happily.

"Look, a castle," cried Fred Enman.

The vacant blocks had given way to the open countryside of northern Manhattan, which was dotted with farm buildings and the occasional estate and imposing mansion, some of which looked like medieval castles.

Fifteen minutes later, the train crossed the Harlem River into the Bronx.

"Fordham Station. Next station, Fordham Station," the conductor called.

The train slowed to a stop. George gathered his charges and jumped down to the platform. Joining the crowd of hundreds of race fans, the group climbed Kingsbridge Road up the long hill to the Jerome Park Racetrack. It was a beautiful August afternoon, warm but not hot. The children followed George and passed through the huge, double-arched main gate into a field with a racetrack, bordered on its farside by a hundred-yard-long, two-story grandstand. It was filled to capacity on both tiers, with spectators crowding the rail in front of the building.

The children were stopping to point out anything that interested them. Like a cowboy herding cattle, George directed them across the track to the grass infield. He saw Jonah Kissel carefully gather up a fistful of the soft, reddish dirt and put it in his pocket.

The infield directly across from the grandstand was filled with every imaginable type of expensive carriage and coach. Top-hatted society gentlemen in black frock coats and gray trousers picnicked with attractive young women in brilliant princess dresses. Spread out on the lush, green grass were white linen tablecloths and huge wicker picnic baskets filled with cold food and bottles of chilled wine and champagne. All the teams had been unhitched, and some people ate on the roofs of their carriages to get a better view. The drivers ate off by themselves but within earshot of their masters.

Up on a bluff overlooking the track and grandstand was the clubhouse, the home of the American Jockey Club. It was a white wooden mansion with a red slate mansard roof. It offered luxurious hotel accommodations so that horse owners could entertain guests at lavish balls, put them up for the night, then have breakfast and watch the morning workouts. In the past, George had spent many a wondrous afternoon there.

"George, old boy! Come join us," yelled a young, red-haired man in a top hat, waving a champagne glass.

"Yes, please come, George," pleaded his companion, a girl holding a yellow parasol.

Smiling, George tipped his hat and continued on with the children to a large empty area toward the south end of the infield. He put down his picnic basket and told the class to find seats on the grass.

As a child, he'd always taken grass for granted. He was amazed at the effect it had on the children. Whenever he took them to Central Park, they loved rolling around, yanking out clumps, even just touching it. Their world was confined to hard surfaces—stone sidewalks and cobblestone streets. Grass was a revelation.

Sandwiches, apples, and bottles of sarsaparilla were distributed. After passing out cookies, George pulled a deck of cards from his jacket pocket. With thirty minutes before post time, there was room for a lesson. Every outing, he assured Dr. Bennett, had educational value— although he didn't tell him he was taking his students to the track. Bennett would have had an apoplectic fit.

With a deft hand, George flashed a two of spades and placed a four of spades next to it.

"Now, how many spades do I have altogether?"

Hands shot up in the air, but Andy Clayton shouted out "Six!" before anyone else could answer.

"You're supposed to be called on, you idiot," snarled Ginny Talbot.

"Your turn, Ginny. If I have the nine of diamonds but take away four, I'll have...?"

"Five," she screamed with glee.

Nothing gave George more pleasure than seeing his class progress. Each day, they improved. The reformers had thought them underprivileged dolts, rendered hopeless by cruelty and neglect. But George knew better; he had unearthed bright minds.

"Let's go back to multiplication. There's a special kind of multiplication we use at the racetrack. It's called odds, and it's a way of predicting whether a horse will win. If you have a horse at three-to-one odds, and you place a two-dollar bet and it wins, then you multiply two times the three and you win six dollars."

"Six whole dollars?" Davey Hill exclaimed.

"Indeed. But if you put down five dollars, how much would you win?"

"Fifteen?" Tom O'Hara said.

"Exactly. Tom, you have the makings of a mathematician," George said with a smile. He glanced at his pocket watch and motioned Sarah Shulski forward. At fourteen, she was the oldest and most mature, the big sister to the group.

"Sarah, I have to see someone, but I'll be back in five minutes. Give them these peppermint sticks and keep an eye on them, will you?"

Sarah, a pretty, dark-haired Jewess, smiled and took the candy. George trotted off to an open-air, wood-framed pavilion on the inside rail of the track. People were crowded eight deep around the round structure, shouting at bookies who were furiously taking down bets on scraps of paper. George fought his way through the crowd to the pooling stand. A lanky man with a black waxed mustache waved and went down the stair to meet him.

"Georgie, I ain't supposed to take bets from you unless it's just two dollars. Toby warned me if I did," he said. On either side, people yelled and cursed at the bookie for ignoring them.

"A thousand dollars on Sam Brown to win in the first, Jake."

Jake looked at him in disbelief. "Christ, Georgie, did you say a thousand?"

"A thousand on the nose."

"He's a five–to-one shot in a mile and a furlong, Georgie."

"Jimmy McLaughlin's still riding him, right? And he's the best jock in America, right?"

"Well, yeah. But one thousand dollars? Toby told me not to take any more big bets from you. You're goin' to get my ass in trouble."

"Write it down, Jake," George said and walked away.

Returning to the class, he motioned them to follow. The children ran after him, laughing and shouting. He brought them up to the thick, white wooden rail lining the track. Most were so short that they had to look out from below it. The children screamed with delight as the horses for the first race were brought up to the starting line, about thirty yards to their left. The horses snorted and stomped and swung their heads up and down and side to side, impatient to run. One reared up, pitching its jockey off.

Heart in his throat, George watched Sam Brown approach the line. He was a two-year-old descendant of a sire in Pierre Lorillard's stable, the finest in America. With racing's best jockey aboard, George's tip from last night told him, the horse was due for a big win.

"I like the brown one," shouted Andy.

"Nah, the gray one's gonna win," Sam Mostel yelled.

"The one we want to win has the scarlet and black colors," George said, pointing out the jet-black thoroughbred. "Cheer with all your might for Sam Brown—that's his name."

The official starter came alongside the horses, and the jockeys turned their heads in his direction. He raised his right hand, held it there for ten seconds, and then dropped his red flag to signal the start. A dozen horses thundered off, their hooves pounding the dirt track like drums. George could see McLaughlin guide Sam Brown immediately to the front. He meant to control the pace from the start and run the race on his terms.

When the horses flew by, the children went wild with excitement. Sam Brown roared down the track like a locomotive.

"Come on, Sammy," screamed Andy.

As the field rounded into the final turn for the home stretch, the black thoroughbred led by three lengths. A wonderful feeling of elation seemed to lift George a finger's breadth above the infield grass. Then, ever so slowly, Sam Brown slowed down. It looked as if he were running in reverse. Buckstone caught up and passed him, and George's heart sank like a rock.

But fifty yards from the finish, Sam Brown put on a burst of speed and surged ahead to win by half a length. Crazy with joy, George picked up Sam Mostel and swung him through the air like a rag doll. Seeing their teacher's elation, the class exploded with delight, jumping up and down and hugging one another.

"Wait here with them, Sarah. I'll be right back," George shouted as he ran off.

As Jake counted out the winnings into George's hand, George slipped a hundred-dollar bill into his pocket. He'd celebrate his good luck by taking the children to a nice dinner and a show. Giving the bookie a smile, George said, "Put the rest on Night Train to win in…"

A hand clamped onto the back of his neck, squeezing like a vise. George thought his head was going to be ripped from his shoulders. Twisting around, he saw Mike Donovan, a red-haired giant, towering above him. Donovan snatched the cash from George's hand with a grim smile.

"Now you only owe Harrigan three thousand, Georgie."

———◆◆◆———

29

"Tell Mrs. O'Shea what a fine meal that was. No one does salmon à la reine better."

As Cross would be away on Sunday, his family ate together that Saturday night. He looked around the dinner table at his family, a perfect portrait of warm domestic bliss. Only he knew the terrible danger they were in. Each of them had their own sword of Damocles, dangling by the thinnest of threads over their heads, and only he could prevent Kent from snapping them.

Despite the dread welling in his chest, Cross tried to put on a cheerful face.

"I bet you're looking forward to the Giants game, Charlie."

"It's Tuesday afternoon. You said you'd be back on Monday," Charlie said with a worried expression. "Uncle Robert is going."

"I'll be back Monday afternoon at the latest. It's just a short trip to Albany to see about a museum project," Cross said. He turned to his daughter and smiled. "I haven't read your novel in ages, Julia." He was immensely proud of her love for literature and real talent for writing. To his relief, she wasn't growing up to be an empty-headed socialite.

"I'm afraid I haven't done much writing lately," Julia said. "I haven't had the time." She bit her lip and added, "And, in fact, I may have come across a new subject."

"With all these preparations for the ball, of course she hasn't had the time," Helen said, ignoring Julia's latter comment.

Cross smiled. He knew his wife thought her daughter's literary aspirations a serious impediment to a successful marriage.

"Well then, I'm off. Everyone come give the papa bear a kiss good-bye so I can catch my train."

Julia and Charlie jumped up and ran to their father, hugging and kissing him. Helen sat where she was, hands folded in her lap.

In the entry foyer, Cross picked up his leather bag and went out to hail a carriage. But instead of telling the driver to take him to Grand Central, he asked for the Union League Club. He smoked and read the papers until Culver picked him up.

Preparations for the robbery had taken three long weeks. The robbers would tunnel twenty-five feet from the side of the underground tunnel to the basement wall of Fidelity National, break through, crack the vault, and loot the safe-deposit boxes. Cross was not expected to do any digging, but his presence would be required when they reached the basement wall.

The corner of Warren Street and Broadway was deserted when the carriage pulled up to the iron plate in the street. The whores had gone to wherever it was the poor wretches lived—in the cellars or alleys. There would be no prying eyes tonight.

Cross and Culver knelt on the floor of the carriage. Culver removed a false panel, took an iron bar with a hook at its end, reached down, and pulled up the plate. *A clever way to bring the digging equipment into the tunnel without being noticed*, Cross thought.

"Down ya go, Mr. Cross," Culver said.

Below the plate were stone steps. Cross descended slowly. To his amazement, he found himself in an opulent waiting room, fitted out like a luxury hotel lobby, with a cut-glass chandelier, wood paneling, and a marble floor. An empty stone fountain stood in its center. Except for a layer of dust, the room looked exactly as it must have when Beach opened his underground railway.

A rough man in an expensive suit and derby was waiting.

"I'm Dago Frank," he said, not extending his hand.

Cross nodded and followed him to the far end of the waiting room, where the pneumatic tunnel began.

Frank held up his lantern. There stood the abandoned tubular train car, which had been pushed through the tunnel by the huge blower fan. They entered the car's front door, then walked down the ten-foot aisle flanked by plush leather bench seats and out the rear. Even in the swaying light of the lantern, Cross noted how well engineered the tunnel was. A perfect cylinder constructed of painted white brick, it showed no sign of deterioration or leaking water. Beach, he knew, had invented a flexible hydraulic shield that could cut through the earth without cave-ins. Kent would not have that luxury tonight. He'd have to tunnel through the sandy soil by hand and shore up the sides and top with planks. The whole job had been planned to the letter, only it still could be doomed by a cave-in.

After walking about forty yards, Cross saw light ahead. The men had broken through the brick wall of the Beach tunnel and begun excavating. He stopped by the opening and peered in. The tunnel was already twenty feet long. His first impression was that Kent had hired real coal miners to do the excavation, but then he recognized the regular gang, hard at work. Even Brady was there. The twelve-man team consisted of diggers with picks and shovels, haulers who took away the dirt in small wheelbarrows, and men who shored the tunnel. Instead of their customary suits, Kent's men were dressed in work clothes and covered with dirt. Their efficiency reminded Cross of an ant colony he'd had as a boy.

Kent emerged out of the shadows, dressed in his usual elegant attire, twirling his cane.

"Just a few more feet and we'll hit the basement wall, Mr. Cross."

"Then you have four feet of solid brick foundation to get through," Cross said.

"We have the tools we need. Your drawings were very helpful. May I offer you some food and drink?"

In spite of himself, Cross was hungry. He followed Kent down the tunnel to a pile of wooden boxes containing sandwiches and bottles of sarsaparilla. "Clever not to provide alcohol on the job," he said with a smile.

"Some of my men are too fond of it, and it can impair their judgment," Kent said, picking out a sandwich for himself. He sat on the box and ate.

"Remember our discussion," Cross said. "Tonight's proceeds should forgive my debt."

"I certainly do. And as I said, it's a possibility."

"I want to be present when you do the accounting."

Kent did not answer.

They ate and drank in silence. More than an hour passed. Cross listened as the picks beat against the brick foundation wall. He looked to the right and saw a small wooden box with red Xs painted on the top and sides. His heart sank. Kent was going to try nitro again.

Without thinking, Cross asked, "Why does a man like you do this sort of thing? You certainly don't need the money."

Kent smiled. He didn't seem at all offended by the question. "Mr. Cross, you can't imagine the feeling of exhilaration I get when committing a robbery. Whether it's cracking a bank vault or stealing valuables from a house, there's a sense of intense ecstasy, a sensation like no other." He paused, grinning from ear to ear. "The excitement comes from the fact that at any second, I might be caught. I love that feeling more than any other. You're right; I don't need the money. But I *want* that feeling."

Cross looked at him incredulously. He'd never met a man like this before. "Is it true that you studied to be a doctor?"

"I *am* a doctor. Graduated from Columbia University College of Physicians and Surgeons."

"But how—"

"Whether we like it or not, our lives are dictated by pure circumstance, Mr. Cross. One night, there was a knock on my office door. A man told me his friend was badly hurt. When I grabbed my bag and went with him, I found a man shot through the gut and bleeding to death. I saved his life. His name was Ben McGarrigle. At the time, he was one of the most feared underworld bosses in the city. In gratitude, he paid me ten times my usual fee, took me under his wing, and treated me like a son. He was more of a father to me than my real one in Baltimore. With his help, I descended into the underworld. It's a separate universe, Mr. Cross. It has its own rules and values, and it doesn't have to answer to anyone. I admired that. But I didn't give up my privileged life in society. I didn't have to. I simply took on a secret life. And after a time, I gave up my practice and went into a more lucrative line of work—crime. I've never regretted it. You see, there was another thing I found out about myself. Instead of saving life, I like taking it away."

Culver approached, out of breath, but with a smile on his face.

"We've broken through."

30

THE GANG GATHERED AROUND THE JAGGED OPENING IN THE brick wall, and the first two men passed through, holding lanterns. All the men were in a boisterous mood, laughing and talking among themselves.

While some banks housed their vaults in full view on the banking floor, most preferred to hide them in the lower bowels of the building, where they would be harder to rob. The safe itself was some forty feet into the basement in its own room, fronted by an ornate iron gate Cross had designed. Beside it was a room lined with safe-deposit boxes. There was no alarm system installed. Fidelity National hadn't thought they'd need one. They were too cheap to even hire a watchman. The police came by to check the front door while on their night rounds.

Two more men stepped inside the hole in the basement wall as Kent and Cross approached.

"Make way for Mr. Kent," came the command.

As the men began to part, a voice from within the darkness of the basement yelled out, "Hands up. You're under arrest. Stay where you are."

The voice hit them like a thunderbolt. Cross and Kent froze, as did the rest of the gang. In an instant, the basement was flooded by another source of light—the electric lights on the walls and ceiling, illuminating the space in stark tones.

"Pinkertons!" someone cried out in panic.

"That's right, gentlemen, and you're under arrest."

The voice hit Cross in the stomach like a prizefighter's punch, almost knocking the wind out of him. Robert had a rich, deep baritone like that. Cross crouched and looked through the mass of men to see his brother, standing in the basement, holding a revolver. "Damn you. I said hands up!" Robert Cross roared.

Kent's men stood frozen in place. Cross felt like he was about to pass out. Staggering backward, he leaned against the tunnel wall to keep himself from falling. Then he began running like a madman. As he pumped his legs and struggled to breathe, he kept thinking about explaining the tawdry story to his brother from inside a jail cell.

Back in Beach's tunnel, he turned right and sped to the nitro box. He removed his handkerchief and tied it around his face. Carefully lifting the lid, he saw that the box was packed with cotton. Fishing his hand around in the stuff, he found the glass vial of nitro. Cradling it in the wad of cotton like a newborn, he ran back into the tunnel, toward the basement of the bank.

As he ran, he heard shots ring out. Kent and his gang were pressed against the wood shoring of the tunnel walls, guns drawn. One man was down, holding his leg and screaming in pain.

"Put your guns down or I'll give you this nitro!" Cross screamed in a raspy voice he prayed his brother wouldn't recognize.

His words were met by dead silence.

Cross dropped the wad of cotton and walked to the opening, holding the vial above his head.

"You men, get out of there," he commanded the gang members already inside the basement.

The men obeyed. Robert, along with the other Pinkertons, lowered his gun and backed slowly away.

"Stay where you are or I'll throw this!" Cross shouted. The Pinkertons didn't move.

Cross stayed where he was too. Behind him, the entire gang inched out of the tunnel. Two men picked up the wounded robber and dragged him out.

Cross started backing down the tunnel. Under his voice, to no one in particular, he said, "Cave it in."

As men on either side yanked out the wall shoring, Cross turned and ran. The ceiling came down hard; in an instant, tons of yellowish-brown earth filled the opening. Safely beyond the cave-in's range, Cross carefully set the nitro vial on the soft dirt, happy to leave it behind.

Kent met him at the intersection with Beach's tunnel. "They'll be waiting for us at Warren Street. Come this way," he yelled.

Instead of going north, the gang ran to the south. Cross heard shouting from the railway tunnel; far in the distance, he saw men with lanterns running toward them. Brady and Coogan stopped running. As if reading each other's minds, each man grabbed handfuls of the dozens of canvas sacks meant to transport the money, piled them in the middle of the tunnel, and threw four lanterns onto the stack. There was the whoosh of spreading flames, and a wall of fire blocked the entire tunnel diameter.

At the Murray Street end of the tunnel, Dago Frank pulled open a heavy iron hatch on the right wall. Men flew into the opening like rats jumping into a ship's porthole. The passageway opened up into a tiny service alley. One by one, the men disappeared into the darkness.

❖ ❖ ❖

"You tipped off the Pinkertons, you son of a bitch."

Cross couldn't believe this was happening. As the gang had scattered into the night three hours earlier, Brady had collared him and dragged him into a carriage. Throughout the fifteen-minute trip to McGlory's, as Cross lay helpless on the floor of the carriage, Brady pummeled him with his fists.

Cross was standing on a chair, a wire noose around his neck. Instead of being hailed as a hero for his quick thinking, the gang seemed ready to kill him for being a traitor.

"Don't lie to us, you shit. You told them!" Brady screamed.

Kent wasn't watching. Calmly smoking a Havana, he was bandaging the leg of Bill Crabb. The white gauze was wrapped neatly and tied off with a sure hand. "Haven't lost my touch," Kent said to himself, smiling.

"Who else have you told?" Brady had his foot on the rickety wooden chair. With each outburst, he shook the chair until it was about to topple over—and then stopped.

"Goddamn you, I didn't tell a soul!" Cross was red in the face with anger. "Why the hell would I do that? One of you betrayed us, can't you see that?"

"Bullshit. No one ever informs. Ever," Brady hissed.

"The police could've picked up one of your men. Maybe he turned on you."

"The men waiting for us were Pinkertons, not the police," Kent said in a quiet voice.

"I'm telling you: I didn't say a word to anyone. Why would I do that?" Cross pleaded.

Brady began to shake the chair again.

Cross was breathing heavily, his heart pounding like a drum. At any second, Kent would announce that his brother, the Pinkerton, was one of the men waiting for them, and his fate would be sealed. Brady would yank out the chair with glee.

"They'd catch the gang in one shot, and you'd be in the clear," said Coogan, looking up at Cross, his hands on his hips.

"And suppose just one of the gang wasn't down there. He'd find out I was the turncoat and kill my whole family in front of me," Cross said.

Kent laughed. "Mr. Cross, you're beginning to understand how we think in this line of work."

"Good God, man, you'd be sitting in the Tombs right now if it weren't for me. I saved you. Where's your goddamn gratitude?" A wall of silence met his question. "There's a traitor. Goddamn it, don't you see? All of us are at risk."

"None of my men is a traitor—they know what the consequences would be," Kent said. He circled the chair, smoking his cigar, deep in thought. "All right. I'll give you a second chance, Mr. Cross. We lost a good deal of money tonight, so you'll have to make it up to us. Find another house. No more banks, not for a while."

"But there's a traitor. No matter what move we make, the Pinkertons will be on to us."

"Then from now on, we will be more cautious. You'll only deal with me," Kent said and nodded to Brady, who, with a disappointed expression, stepped up on the chair, removed the noose, and shoved Cross to the floor.

Y OU'RE BACK SO EARLY."

  Cross's and Helen's separate but adjoining bedrooms allowed Cross to come in at all hours of the night without waking his wife. It also ensured that she kept out of his private life. But they shared a spacious bathroom, specially designed by Cross, with all the latest plumbing features, including the Deeco flushing toilet.

It was just past midnight. The going-over Brady had given Cross in the carriage had produced a noticeable swelling on his right cheekbone. He was patting it with a wet washcloth when Helen slammed open the door.

"What on earth happened to you, John?" she cried in an almost hysterical voice that made Cross cringe.

"I fell from the carriage on the way home, Helen. That's all."

She came forward and studied his face. Some of Brady's other handiwork had resulted in small, angry red blotches.

"No, you've been in a fight." Helen's eyes widened in horror. Men in society attacked with insults and cutting sarcasm, never their fists. Physical brutality was something ruffians on the Lower East Side did to one another, or to their wives and children. She put her hand over mouth, looking at her husband as though he had contracted leprosy.

Cross grew angrier by the second—at Helen and at the fact that he hadn't thought to design them separate bathrooms.

"Damn it, Helen, I'm fine. Leave me the hell alone," he said.

But Helen stood her ground. She placed her hand under his chin, rotating his head side to side. "No, John. Someone beat the hell out of you."

Instead of shouting at her, Cross stomped away to the other side of the bathroom, fighting the rage welling in his gut. Helen followed.

"Tell me what happened."

"Nothing. I was set upon by robbers. That's all."

Unexpectedly, Helen reached around Cross's side and felt for her husband's wallet. "They did all this to you, but they didn't take your wallet?"

"I...I got away from them."

"All those men attacked you, and you escaped?"

"I just told you what happened," snapped Cross, his back still toward her. "You will listen to me."

"Tell me what *really* happened, John," Helen said.

Despite his anger, Cross was touched by her concern. He bent his head, eyes on the black-and-white-tiled floor.

In his fraternity of society gentlemen, a man who faced a crisis or financial disaster would never tell his wife. Even if he went dead broke, his wife and family would know nothing—until the day the bank came to repossess the house and throw the children out into the street. The reasons for such silence would be the gentleman's sense of shame and the general perception of society ladies as overly emotional, useless dolts. A gentleman would confide in his friends at the club, his valet, or his favorite bartender, never his wife. The only woman to whom a man might tell his tale of woe was his mistress.

But in this matter, there was no one in whom Cross might confide, no one to turn to. He was hopelessly alone. Every day, he woke with a sense of dread—this would be his family's last day on earth; something would go wrong and force Kent to kill them. The pressure sometimes seemed unbearable. He didn't know how much longer he could stand it. And there was no way out. If he went to the police, his family would be dead within the hour. Griffith's frozen head had taught him that.

Robert's new involvement put the Crosses in even greater danger.

Once Kent discovered who his brother was, he'd be out for blood. Cross had thought of confiding in Robert, but that would almost certainly mean his death. The fact that he was a Pinkerton wouldn't deter Kent.

He was lost, and he was alone. He looked into Helen's eyes, and the urge to tell her was overpowering.

Helen knew something was terribly wrong. She instinctively knew her husband's moods and feelings. "Please tell me," she whispered.

Cross closed his eyes. At first, the words wouldn't come out. Was he doing the right thing, or was he condemning Helen to death? "We're in great trouble, my dear."

"When you have bad news, it's best to get it out quickly," Helen said.

"George has a gambling problem," Cross said. "He owes thousands to a man who threatened to kill him if he didn't pay."

Helen stepped backward, pressing her body against the sink. She gripped the edge of the marble counter until her knuckles turned white. "How much?"

"More than forty thousand dollars."

Helen gasped and covered her face with her hands.

"When George couldn't pay, these men came to me to make good on his debt."

"But we don't have that kind of money!"

"They knew that. They wanted me to help them rob the houses and businesses of my clients."

Helen looked at him in astonishment. "We have no choice but to go to the police, John. They can arrest these criminals, and then we'll be safe."

"I tried, but it didn't work. I know this beyond a shadow of a doubt: if I go to the police, all of us—you, me, George, Julia, Charlie, even your mother—all of us will be dead. These people aren't bluffing, Helen. They're cold-blooded murderers."

Helen shook her head violently from side to side, her eyes filling with tears. "No, I won't let anyone hurt my family. Aunt Caroline can help. She knows powerful people, people who can help us. I'm going to call her right now."

Helen ran from the bathroom into her bedroom, but Cross was on her in a flash. He grabbed her from behind, threw her on the bed, and pinned her down by her shoulders. "If you call Caroline—or Robert or anyone—we're dead!" he shouted, his face pressed close to hers. "Do you hear me? Dead!"

She looked into his eyes with a pleading, helpless look and asked in a low voice, "Then what can we do, John? What can we possibly do?"

Cross released Helen and sat next to her on the bed. "Until I can think of some other way out, I have no choice but to do what they say."

Helen lay on the bed for a few moments, her body shaking with sobs. Then, as if gathering her will, she sat up and put her arms around Cross's waist. She pulled him close, settling her head against his shoulder. "Until *we* can think of some other way out," she said.

Cross smiled and kissed her on the cheek. "I've had a long day, Helen. I need to get some sleep. Tomorrow, I must find a new place to rob." He raked his fingers through his hair. "I confess, though: I'm drawing a blank."

Helen's eyes met his, and he saw in her gaze a flash of unexpected excitement. "Remember the Greenes on Fifth and Sixty-Fifth? They're up in the Berkshires for the month, and, John, Edith Greene just bought a tiara with a diamond the size of an almond!"

32

D ID YOUR SHOT HIT THE ROBBER, UNCLE ROBERT?"
Annoyed that Charlie was more interested in Robert's account of the bank robbery than the baseball game, Cross said, "What did you think about that putout Dude Esterbrook just made at third, Charlie?"

"Sorry, Father, I missed it. Did any Pinkertons get shot, Uncle Robert?"

It was a perfect, sunny day at the Polo Grounds. Cross had kept his promise to go to the game with his son and brother, to please Charlie—and to get information from Robert.

The crowd cheered like mad as Smiling Mickey Welch struck out the Detroit batter to end the inning. It was an important game: the Giants were two behind the Detroit Wolverines, so if they won that game and the next, they'd be tied for first. The three-year-old stadium, directly across from the northeast corner of Central Park, stretched from 110th to 112th Streets and was filled to capacity with ten thousand rowdy fans. Along 112th Street, people stood atop their carriages, straining to see. As yet, very few buildings had been constructed so far up Fifth Avenue. The few taller ones near the ballpark also had spectators on their roofs.

"Did you see that fastball Welch threw?"

"I wasn't watching… Did any of your men get hurt, Uncle Robert?" Charlie repeated.

"No, Charlie, none of our men were hurt. One fellow sucked in too much smoke when the gang set a fire in the tunnel, but he's all right now."

"Charlie, your uncle is here to enjoy the game. He doesn't want to keep talking about the robbery. Look, Ewing's the first batter up," Cross said, winking at his brother.

"But it's so exciting. *My* uncle stopped a bank robbery. I can't wait to tell my friends."

"Turn around and watch the game," Cross said, exasperated.

Charlie did as he was told and was soon caught up in the action. Ewing, the catcher, rapped a single to right, and the crowd roared. Chip Ward advanced him to second on a bunt, and a single by Dorgan, the right fielder, sent Ewing home for a 1–0 lead. The Giants protected the lead with great fielding and scored again in the sixth on a three-run homer.

But soon Detroit had two men on. The crowd fell quiet. Could their star pitcher, Mickey Welch, throw his way out of the jam?

In the momentary lull, Cross slipped in a veiled question to his brother. "I'm glad you're all right, Robert. That must have been a close call."

"It didn't turn out the way I'd hoped," Robert said. "We had them dead to rights, John, but every single one got away."

"Were you able to see who they were?"

"No one I recognized. We're going through the rogue's gallery to see if any turn up. But I'm not optimistic. The clever bastard who saved them wore a mask. The one threatening to throw the nitro, I mean. If he hadn't had the nerve to do that, they'd all be in jail."

"Was it really nitroglycerin?"

"Indeed. Luckily, we found the vial in the tunnel before anyone stepped on it. It would have blown the underground railway tunnel to bits and taken us along too."

"A daring robbery."

"It was a brilliant piece of planning. Would've worked like a dream if we hadn't gotten a tip."

Cross stiffened in his seat.

The next batter up hammered the ball, bouncing it off the

McCann's Celebrated Hats billboard in the center-field bleachers for a three-run homer. The crowd inside the stadium groaned. But several pitches later, Welch finally got the third out with a strike.

"Charlie, go down and get yourself a pretzel," Cross said, handing his son a nickel.

"I don't want a pretzel."

"Well, go get something else you like," he snapped.

"How about a beer?" Robert said. He and Charlie burst out laughing. Cross glared ruefully at his son as he ran off to the concession counter under the stands.

"Who tipped you off?" Cross asked in a matter-of-fact voice, looking straight ahead at the field. "One of the gang?"

"I don't know. Someone telephoned on Saturday afternoon and told us about the robbery."

Robert sounded evasive. Cross wondered if his brother was keeping the information close to the vest for professional reasons. Until he discovered the informant's identity, Cross knew he was in danger at every moment.

Connor, Ewing, and Ward all grounded out, and the Wolverines came up for their last at bat. Charlie returned with a bag of popcorn in time to see Welch get three quick outs to retire the side, and the game was over.

"Great game, huh, Charlie?" Robert said, clapping the boy on the back. "We win tomorrow, and we're tied for first! Let's do this again next week. What do you say?"

He's so happy to be with family, Cross thought. The joy fairly radiated off of him. When he'd come to dinner for the first time, Robert had enjoyed himself immensely, chattering on with Helen, Julia, and Charlie, interested in every detail of their lives. He seemed to want to stay forever. Robert had since gone with them to social events and spent many quiet evenings at their home. Cross's children and wife were even pestering him to have Robert come live with them.

Charlie had liked his uncle from the beginning, but the robbery had sent Robert's stock soaring. He beamed up at him and said, "They play Boston next week. The Giants will beat the shit out of them."

"Charlie," Cross scolded.

Swear words had become a more frequent part of his son's vocabulary in recent weeks. Cross didn't know where Charlie picked it up. Probably the footman of that Mackay boy he'd been playing with.

"Let's look at the schedule by the ticket window," Robert said.

At 109th Street, they tried to hail a carriage with little success. While they waited, Cross asked his brother about his rooms at the Benedick, an apartment house designed by Charlie McKim. They were most satisfactory, Robert said.

"It's good you've found a nice place to live. You can relax, perhaps get your mind off the robbery," Cross said.

Robert smiled at him. "Little Brother, I'm obsessed with the robbery. And I guarantee you: I will catch that bastard with the nitro."

33

THE FAILURE OF THE BANK ROBBERY HAD BITTERLY DISAPPOINTED Cross. He knew he should be grateful for their skin-of-the-teeth escape from Robert and the Pinkertons, but he'd been counting on the take from the job to wipe out his son's debt. Without it, he needed new victims. And as Helen had suggested, the Greene mansion on Fifth Avenue and Sixty-Fifth Street was perfect. Not only were the Greenes rich and away for the summer, but they also weren't former clients.

The time would come, Cross knew, when Robert would discover that his brother had designed both the Cook mansion and the bank. He'd start asking questions. Henceforth, Cross's own clients had to be avoided in favor of his architect friends' rich clients. There was a good selection: McKim, White, and another successful colleague, Bruce Price, had a slew of them. The Greenes had been clients of James Ware, an architect Cross knew from the New York chapter of the American Institute of Architects. Having made a fortune in steamships that plied the Gulf of Mexico, Andrew Greene was another classic parvenu, come to New York to buy his way into society. For his part, Ware was a talented architect who'd achieved national fame by winning a design competition for a new tenement model that allowed more light and air into the units. The tenements in the Lower East Side were unbelievably foul, inhumane hovels. Ware's design was nicknamed "the dumbbell plan," because its squeezed-in form resembled an exercise dumbbell.

Cross called Ware to see if he could look at the plans. He was going to do some tenement work, he told him, and he greatly admired the dumbbell design. Architects loved to be flattered, and Ware enthusiastically agreed. Cross used the same ruse on Ware's draftsman as he had on Hardenbergh's, and paired with Helen's personal knowledge of the Greenes' wealth, he determined where everything of value was located in the house.

But at every moment, Cross was cautious. Someone was watching— and waiting to tip off the Pinkertons again. Cross had reconnoitered the Greene mansion in the middle of the night and insisted that Kent not tell his gang the next target until right before the job. Not wanting to repeat the violence of the Cook robbery, Cross took great care in determining that no servants had been left behind.

On a sultry August night, Kent and his men cleaned out the Greene house. They stole Belgian and Irish linens, Gorham silver, and seventeenth-century Sèvres china. Helen told Cross that the wives of parvenus loved to show off their jewelry to fellow society ladies, so she knew where Mrs. Greene's jewels were hidden. The Crosses had been there just a month prior. Mrs. Greene's prized tiara and the rest of her valuables were hidden in a secret compartment below the stone hearth of a fireplace in her bedroom. A long piece of marble was cleverly hinged so it blended in with the rest of the stone, unseen. By just tapping on it, it popped up like a jack-in-the-box, revealing a deep-purple, velvet-lined box. Cross thanked God for his wife's powers of observation. The hiding place wasn't shown on the drawings, and they never would have found it.

When Kent's men opened the compartment, it was like lifting the lid of Captain Kidd's treasure chest. Even the usually cool and calm Kent almost fainted when he saw the flash of gems and metals.

Every stitch of Mr. and Mrs. Greene's clothing was taken, including their silk underwear. This time, Kent made sure he had larger wagons to haul away the huge Meissonier paintings of epic Napoleonic battle scenes. Not one bottle of vintage wine was left in the wine racks. Every one of Mr. Greene's rare black-and-red ancient Greek vases was taken. To his delight, in Greene's immense, wood-paneled library, Cross discovered four priceless tapestries made at Gobelin, the official design studio of the French kings; along with three exquisite Persian rugs, these found a place in Kent's wagons. Cross had a solid knowledge of antique furniture, and he directed Kent's gang to take away the choicest seventeenth- and eighteenth-century French pieces.

Helen also knew that Mr. Greene's secret safe was located in the back of his medicine cabinet. His wife bragged that no thief would look there. Kent's men took his horde of cash and negotiable bonds, plus all his imported French cologne.

Strangely, Cross found he was enjoying himself. Walking about and barking orders gave him a power he'd never experienced before, a feeling of indescribable elation, and he liked it. In a way, he thought, architects were well-paid servants of the rich, complying with their every whim, no matter how stupid. They had to bow and scrape to get jobs and be paid. Clients often compromised Cross's design with ridiculous demands, catering to the momentary whims of their wives. How many times had Cross wanted to tell them to go to hell? But he didn't have the guts. He just smiled and took it.

This night was different. This night, he was in command.

❖ ❖ ❖

Cross was not alone. Hidden in the shadows of the trees on Sixty-Fifth Street, Helen watched the loot from the Greene mansion being carted off. Seeing the robbery gave her an unexpected feeling of exhilaration, like drinking three glasses of champagne one after the other.

Walking north to Sixty-Sixth Street and over to Madison Avenue to hail a carriage home, Helen skipped along the pavement like a ten-year-old. She hadn't felt this alive in years.

❖ ❖ ❖

Despite the rich haul, Cross discovered when he met with Kent that the debt had been reduced by only ten thousand dollars. Without losing his temper, he detailed the incredible value of the tapestries and the jewelry. Kent laughed in his face. If they'd stolen Michelangelo's *David*, he said, it'd still be sold at only a millionth of its true cost.

"This wasn't an auction at Christie's, Mr. Cross," he added.

Cross demanded to know where his debt stood. A man with a head for figures, Kent scratched out some numbers on a scrap of paper and handed it to Cross, whose jaw dropped.

"Christ Almighty, man. Still twenty-six thousand dollars?"

"You keep forgetting the 15 percent weekly interest," Kent said contemptuously. "I'd have thought an architect would better understand numbers. So tell me: What's the next job?"

There was no use arguing. Cross knew that when Helen heard about the amount of the outstanding debt, she would fly into a rage and want to confront Kent, but he'd convince her that to do so would be madness. To ensure her safety, Kent could never know she was aware of their business arrangement.

Besides, Cross thought, *Kent is being tough on the debt because he still believes that I informed on them.* If he told Kent it had been an anonymous tip, the man would ask who'd given Cross that information and grow even more suspicious.

In the days after the robbery, there was no mention of the crime in the papers. Greene, like Cook, wanted no publicity about the burglary of his home. The Pinkertons, and probably Robert, would be on this case as well, but Cross had no choice. He had to continue. He had to get out from under George's debt.

After meeting with Kent, he was in a foul temper. Instead of going home, he walked to the Union League Club on the corner of Fifth Avenue and Thirty-Ninth Street. As he approached the building, he felt some of the weight on his shoulders lessen, and he smiled. His entry hadn't won the design competition, but he admired the domestic quality of Peabody & Stearns's Queen Anne building. It was much nicer than the renovated house of the rival Knickerbocker Club. *A club should have a homey feel*, Cross thought. After all, it was a gentleman's home away from home.

Built of beautiful, red, pressed brick and Belleville brownstone, the building featured a huge dormer window with a Tiffany glass oculus on the Fifth Avenue side. Cross entered and went directly to the reading room, the main social space on the second floor. It stretched the length of the Fifth Avenue facade and was also called the "ogling room," as it allowed members to sit and watch the young female passersby. Cross settled into a large leather armchair and stared out the window. Members came and went, some using the adjacent smoking rooms or the bowling alley in the basement. Some had just finished dinner in the main dining room on the fourth floor and settled into a favorite chair in the reading room.

Many of the men, Cross knew, rarely went home. They lived in various bedrooms in a separate wing of the building. The club was their inner sanctum and was never violated by a woman's presence. Even the highest quality ladies of the evening were not allowed. The furniture was arranged in groups, allowing men to do what they loved most while in a club: bond in male comradeship and bonhomie. With servants fetching glasses of brandy and cigars, the members chattered on like the women they sought to avoid.

"It was Shelby's idea," said a portly, middle-aged man with a brush mustache.

"And a grand one. A private banquet for our horses! It's never been done before," said another man.

"Robertson will bring Storm Cloud."

"What a horse. Paid twenty thousand for the animal, but he's paid off twice as much in purses," said a scrawny man holding a glass of brandy and a cigar.

"I saw him run at Brighton Beach just last week. Won by eight lengths."

"We've picked a place on West Forty-Ninth. The dinner will be catered by Delmonico's—canvasback duck and quail, oysters, roast sirloin."

"Blue Day, who you'll recall won the Westminster Derby at Jerome Park, is coming. And Buckshot, Lemon Drop—the finest horseflesh in the land will be there."

Though he pretended to look out the window, Cross was listening with great interest.

34

HELEN MADE SURE TO PUT THE JEWELRY BOX BACK EXACTLY AS she'd found it.

With a contented smile on her beautiful face, she continued to survey Mrs. Elizabeth Ogden's dressing table for items of exceptional value. Finding nothing else, she turned her attention to the dressing room, which was the size of a parlor at the Crosses'. With an expert's eye, Helen assessed the quality of Mrs. Ogden's gowns. The absolute finest, but she had expected no less. Mrs. Ogden's husband owned the biggest copper-mining company in America.

There was a joint in the cedar-lined closet wall behind the gowns, barely visible unless one looked closely. Pushing the clothes aside, Helen found a secret door, which opened by a recessed brass latch. Inside was a lead-walled room filled with racks of beautiful Russian sable and mink furs. Running her hands over them and pressing them against her cheek was a most wonderful sensation.

Leaving the dressing room, Helen moved to the enormous Tudor four-poster bed, which had been imported from Dottington Hall in England, took out her little red leather notebook and a gold pencil, and cataloged her findings. She was not nervous or scared, nor did she feel the slightest guilt about going through another society woman's possessions.

At first, she'd only cared about helping John steal enough to pay down her son's debt. Like a tigress protecting her cubs, she told herself, a mother must do anything for her children. Her family, the center of her existence, would not be harmed. But another feeling was competing with her biological instinct—she *enjoyed* doing this. She loved the intense thrill of the robberies. Though she was forbidden from accompanying her husband on jobs, it gave her an enormous sense of excitement to help plan them.

In the wake of John's devastating news about George, Helen's visits to the guests who would attend Julia's upcoming ball had taken on new meaning. Among the fifty families that remained to be seen, there would be many nice things for "future acquisition." To Helen, a good Knickerbocker Episcopalian, the seventh commandment no longer had meaning.

It had been perhaps fifteen minutes since she had excused herself to go the bathroom. Not an excessive amount of time, given the difficulty of lifting one's long dresses up around the waist and lowering the many layers of underwear. Many women resigned themselves to suffering and postponed going.

Smiling, Helen rose from the bed and walked downstairs to rejoin the tea.

⁘ ⁘ ⁘

"Will you be going to the opera this season, Miss Cross? *Faust* will be the first production at the Metropolitan," Alfred Wharton asked, balancing a cup and saucer expertly on his knee.

"Yes, Mr. Wharton, I plan to attend," Julia said.

This was no idle chitchat. Julia did enjoy the opera, especially the Italian productions. But for her, operagoing would be different. When she sat in Aunt Caroline's box in the Diamond Horseshoe tier at the Met, she saw with great disgust that society women attended not to appreciate the music but to show off their latest Parisian gowns and jewelry. Going to the opera on Thursdays was the most important event of the social season, which began in mid-November and ran until mid-February. The Met's huge gold-and-white auditorium glittered with the flash of diamond tiaras, earrings, and chokers.

Julia thought the worst thing was that no society person ever arrived on time. They always came in the middle of the first act. When Aunt Caroline arrived, not one person paid attention to the performance, craning their necks instead to see what she was wearing. The audience talked constantly and left for supper before the end of the second act. When Julia told Caroline that one day she hoped to attend an opera from beginning to end, her aunt laughed uncontrollably.

"We have a box in the second parterre," Wharton said. "Perhaps after your coming-out, my family can have the pleasure of your company in our box."

The Whartons were among the old society people who'd made the switch to the Met. When the parvenus couldn't get boxes at the Academy of Music, society's old opera house on Fourteenth Street, the Vanderbilts, Whitneys, and Morgans decided to build their own on the corner of Broadway and Thirty-Ninth Street. The Academy of Music couldn't compete and had made the switch from opera to musicals. The Knickerbockers, with Aunt Caroline leading the way, decamped with the "new people" to the luxury boxes of the Met.

"That's very kind of you, Mr. Wharton. I'd like that very much."

This was Julia's fifth visit to an at-home tea. Society ladies like Elizabeth Ogden sent out cards with "Thursdays in August, tea at four o'clock" handwritten in the corner. On that day of the week, they would accept visitors. Attending these teas was an informal way of introducing Julia and allowing her to practice her social skills. She had also had one at-home tea at her house. Because the men were working, the guests were predominately female. A few fellows, like Wharton, took time off specifically to see Julia. She was fast becoming the most admired debutante of the season. That day, at least two dozen visitors filled the Ogdens' opulent parlor.

"We're going to the Thalia to see that new Gilbert and Sullivan production, The Mikado. They say it's first-rate," Wharton said.

Granny, sitting next to Julia and waiting to intercept an improper advance, interrupted.

"I'm doing research for the book now."

Granny smiled at Julia, the signal that she should get up and mingle with the rest of the guests. But before Julia could rise from her chair, Helen approached, a tall young man with chestnut hair at her side.

"Mr. Van Cortlandt, this is my daughter, Julia."

"A great pleasure, Miss Cross," said the young man.

"Mr. Van Cortlandt. You know Mr. Wharton?" Julia asked, knowing full well that all the children of the Knickerbockers knew one another. They went to the same dancing and riding schools, to the same prep schools.

"Hello, Wharton. How are your beloved dinosaur bones doing? The fellows at Yale call Wharton here 'Bonehead,' Miss Cross," said Van Cortlandt, laughing heartily at his joke.

Julia scowled at him. "Mr. Wharton will be a famous scientist one day," she said indignantly.

Granny shot Helen a withering look, and Helen smoothly redirected the conversation to another guest at Julia's right, a handsome gentleman named John Beekman.

"Julia, Mr. Beekman has just graduated from West Point. He's going to join General Miles's staff in Arizona and will help hunt down that Apache savage Geronimo," Helen said.

John beamed with pride. "Since he escaped from the reservation at San Carlos, Miss Cross, Geronimo's killed a dozen Americans and hundreds of Mexicans. We're going into the mountains to bring him back, dead or alive."

"It sounds *so* dangerous. The *Tribune* has been full of stories about that heathen Indian," Helen said in a hushed voice.

"He's a killer, Mrs. Cross. No doubt about that."

"Geronimo fights because he refuses to accept America's occupation of the West. Not to mention the terrible conditions on the reservation," Julia said and took a sip of tea.

A moment of awkward silence ensued. Only the sound of Julia's spoon stirring sugar into her tea could be heard. Hours seemed to pass before anyone dared speak.

"Julia…reads the newspapers daily," said a very embarrassed Helen. John Beekman stared into his teacup.

"Will you gentlemen excuse us for a moment?" Helen said, giving them a radiant smile. In the hall, she grabbed the back of her daughter's white princess dress, pulling it so tight that Julia gasped for breath. The talking-to was finished within a minute, and then they were back in the parlor. Julia was steered back toward Van Cortlandt, then on to Charles Whitney and Frederick MacKay.

When the tea concluded two hours later, Julia threw herself on the recamier in the parlor at home and looked resentfully at her mother.

"When do I have to pay a call after that shindig?"

"Don't use slang, Julia. And how many times have I told you? A guest does not pay a call after a tea."

Julia looked at her mother curiously. She sounded deeply annoyed. Julia had noticed that in the past weeks, Helen had taken far less pleasure in these calls than she had when they'd started. She'd become testy and irritated too, and sometimes Julia would see her staring off into space. But when she asked if anything was wrong, her mother put on a cheerful face and insisted everything was fine.

Granny sat down next to Julia and whispered, "I'm surprised Mrs. Ogden didn't invite that nice Mr. Nolan today."

Julia was at a loss for words. "I…I think he had a business engagement."

"Such a shame. You know, dear, the next time we go shopping, I was hoping we could go back to Wah Kee's to look at more cats."

35

At around 7:00 P.M., TWENTY WAGONS, EACH TRANSPORTING A single horse, pulled off West Forty-Ninth Street into an alley beside an L-shaped, five-story, cast-iron-fronted warehouse.

One by one, the beautifully groomed horses, which had been saddled and tacked up, were led to a freight elevator at the end of the alley. The elevator took two horses and two stable boys at a time up to the fourth floor.

The doors opened on a bizarre sight. The empty warehouse floor had been transformed into a rural scene, as if transposed from the Long Island countryside. The wood plank floor was completely carpeted with real green turf. Attached to the ten-foot ceiling was a twenty-foot-diameter dome constructed of plaster. Its underside was painted dark blue and festooned with strings of tiny twinkling electric lights, creating the impression of a night sky. The columns of the space had been altered to resemble pine trees. A forest had been created using huge potted trees and mature shrubbery. Dozens of real birds flew from tree to tree.

Directly under the dome was a circular, white wood plank fence with twenty separate hitching posts, each with its own trough of hay and water. After the horses were led from the elevator, servants dressed as jockeys fitted them with special trays attached to the front of the saddle and a pair of saddlebags that contained champagne bottles in ice buckets. Off to the side stood a group of distinguished middle-aged men, all dressed in cutaway coats, white ties, and gloves. They smoked and talked among themselves.

One by one, each gentleman mounted his horse and walked it to its assigned hitching post. Soon twenty horses circled the fence. Between every second horse, servants placed a small carpeted staircase. When everyone was in place, a six-piece band began to play "Camptown Races." One of the men on horseback raised his hand and spoke.

"My fellow horsemen. Welcome to the First Annual Horseback Banquet. Tonight we honor the greatest and finest racehorses in the entire world."

The men applauded, roaring with delight. The horses were too busy eating from their troughs to take notice.

"Let the festivities commence," the master of ceremonies yelled.

Twenty servants carrying platters of food rushed to each of the horsemen, climbed the little staircases, and placed food on the special trays. Each guest pulled out a champagne bottle and popped it open, producing a twenty-gun salute of flying corks. In place of glasses, they sipped the champagne through long rubber tubes. As the band played on, the gentlemen ate and drank with gusto. Twenty more stable boys with small shovels carried out cleanup from behind when required. Smoking, laughing, joking, and bragging about their steeds, a spirit of goodwill and fellowship spun around the circle like a ring of fire. In the general gaiety, the stench of gallons of urine soaking into the turf wasn't noticed.

After a modest eight-course dinner, a dessert of chocolate-covered strawberries with whipped cream was delivered. Then the master of ceremonies raised his hand.

"Gentlemen, may I present Amos and his Dancing Darkies!"

Into the inner circle came three white men in blackface, dressed in white evening clothes and top hats, carrying banjos. The performers bowed and began to strut around the circle. The crowd cheered like mad. "Better than real coons," someone yelled out.

More champagne was placed in the saddlebags as the evening wore on. After three bottles, Clarence Post fell off Eclipse onto the turf and had to be reseated.

Out of respect for their beloved horses, the banquet ended after three hours.

✦ ✦ ✦

"You here for Mr. Robertson?"

"Yeah, what about you?"

The drivers of the wagons stood in the dark night, waiting for the festivities to end and the horses to be loaded. They were in a rotten mood. Upstairs, the horses ate to their hearts' content. Down in the alley, no one had had the courtesy to offer the men refreshments.

"I'm waitin' on Mr. Shelby. Hey, how 'bout a drink while we wait?"

"I never refuse a free drink."

Lefty Montgomery pulled out a flask and poured two shots.

"How about those whores out there on Forty-Ninth?" he said, nodding toward the street. "Wish I didn't have to work tonight."

The driver followed his gaze to the parade of streetwalkers. "That one in the purple dress looks mighty good." He knocked back the shot in a single gulp. "Thanks," he said, grimacing at the strong taste.

Ten seconds later, the driver fell to the ground in a heap. Montgomery looked around; the coast was clear. He quickly pushed the man's body off the bench, onto the floor of the wagon. There was no better knockout drop man in New York than Lefty Montgomery, a master at sneaking chloral hydrate into a drink in a fraction of a second. He'd had twenty years' experience knocking victims out, robbing and stripping them, and dumping them in alleys. He believed using chloral hydrate was an art. A fifty-grain dose was best for knocking out a burly man the size of the driver. Too much would paralyze the heart and lungs, and you'd have a corpse on your hands.

As the horses were led off the freight elevator, Montgomery hopped onto the driver's seat and reached down to put on his victim's hat. Taking the reins, he waited five minutes, until he heard the horse being loaded in the back of the wagon by Mr. Robertson's groom. From behind, there came the sound of a scuffle. Pig McGurk, who'd been hiding in the hay bin inside the stall, came out, chloroformed the boy, and dumped him in the wagon. Three sharp knocks sounded. Montgomery snapped the reins to get the two dray horses moving.

At an abandoned building off West Nineteenth Street and Eleventh Avenue, the men dumped the two unconscious bodies in a basement and then proceeded to South Street on the East Side. The wagon was met at the pier by Cross and Kent. Montgomery backed in toward the gangplank, and McGurk flung open the rear doors and led the horse out by its bridle.

Cross was delighted to see the wagon. He had been so angry at Kent's refusal to reduce the debt, and then the idea for this robbery had fallen into his lap purely by accident. It was a quick and easy way to make a big killing. It didn't have the usual risks of breaking into a building or needing elaborate planning. He thought of it all by himself. The job had a wonderful simplicity to it—just wait for the horse to be loaded in the wagon for you, then drive off.

Cross took two steps toward the horse—and froze.

"That isn't Storm Cloud," he shouted. Kent ran up beside him.

"What the hell are you talking about?"

"This is a chestnut, not a bay, and it has a blaze on its head. Storm Cloud doesn't have a blaze," Cross said, panicked. He went to the side of the wagon and examined the coat of arms painted on its side: two crossed golden sabers on a circle of blue. "It's the right wagon. Goddamn it, they must have loaded the wrong horse."

"It's still a first-rate thoroughbred. What does it matter?" Montgomery snarled.

"It matters to my buyer," Kent said. "He's paying an arm and a leg for Storm Cloud—and only him."

Cross and Kent looked at each other and seemed to read each other's minds.

"We have to search the other wagons. It's only been fifteen minutes.

They're likely still on the street." Kent turned and called for his men, who were milling about the pier.

"Most of the stables are in Jersey, so they'll be heading for the Hoboken ferry," Cross said. On either side, pairs of gang members got into carriages or mounted horses and tore off into the night. "He's got socks on his two front legs," Cross yelled after them.

"Five hundred to the men who find him," Kent shouted.

An elderly man, his face weathered to the texture of leather, walked up to Kent. "This ship leaves at the tide in two hours and waits for no one," he growled.

In a smooth movement, Kent whipped his blade from his cane and held the tip to the man's throat. "Rest assured, Captain," he said softly. "Our cargo will be aboard by then."

"Might as well load this one," Cross said, gesturing to the chestnut.

Kent ran his gloved hand across the horse's muzzle. "He's beautiful. My children will love him. It's time they learned to ride."

From a carriage a block away, Helen watched in amazement as men ran in all directions from the dock.

✦ ✦ ✦

As McGurk held a pistol to the driver's forehead, Montgomery yanked open the door of the horse transport.

"Shit, it ain't him," he barked, imagining his share of the five hundred flying away as if on wings. The two men hopped into their carriage and sped off.

✦ ✦ ✦

At King and Greenwich Streets, a masked man pulled the driver and groom off their seats onto the street; another ran to the back of the wagon and unlatched the door.

In the darkness, a dappled gray with a mouthful of hay turned to look at the visitor. With a huff, he went back to eating his meal.

✦ ✦ ✦

"That's my boy," shouted Flannigan, peering under the horse's belly to see its two front white socks. A block from the Hoboken ferry slip, he'd found his prize. He danced a crude Irish jig as he went back to the front of the wagon and signaled Jenkins to begin pistol-whipping the driver. He took care of the groom, and they dragged the unconscious bodies into a doorway off of Barclay Street and West Broadway.

36

T HIS IS A VERY SPECIAL TRANSACTION I'M OFFERING, MR. SPRINGER.
To buy gold bullion at this price is most unusual. But you're an
astute businessman who knows a good opportunity."

George Cross watched as Herbert Springer, a prosperous grain
merchant from Toledo, Ohio, ran his hand over the gold bar on the sitting room table. The initials *U. S.* were stamped on the top and bottom.
As Springer picked it up to look more closely, it gleamed in the sunlight
streaming through the window of his room at the Grand Hotel.

Springer had come to the city for a week to attend the National
Grain Dealers Association convention, held at Chickering Hall on Fifth
Avenue. The night before, George, posing as a Mr. George Candler,
had shown him the pleasures and sights of the Tenderloin. The appreciative Springer was more than willing to listen to his investment pitch.

"Gold is a rock-solid investment in times like these, Mr. Springer.
It will *always* rise in price," George said.

"Indeed, Mr. Candler. But you understand that I need to verify the
quality of the metal," Springer said, setting the bar back down.

"Of course. That's why Mr. Bertram Johnson, chief assayer of the
Manhattan Guaranty & Trust Company, has joined us today."

Mr. Johnson, a plump gentleman with wire-rim spectacles, smiled
and bowed from the waist. From a leather bag on the table, he removed
a glass vial of clear solution and an empty steel cup. Impressed, Springer
stepped aside and let him get to work. Johnson took the dropper out of
the vial, paused, and explained in a professorial manner, "This, sir, is
nitric acid, the test for true gold." He put a drop on the gold bar. "If the

solution turns green, it means this is gold plated. If there's no reaction, it's true, 100 percent gold."

Springer's eyes were glued to the bar. When he saw no reaction, he broke into a wide grin.

"I assure you, Mr. Springer, that all the bullion is of this quality," George said.

"Very well then. You're right, Mr. Candler, you can't go wrong with gold. Silver is for pansy-picking fops." Springer pulled out a cigar and picked up the heavy bar. He paced the sitting room, tossing the gold into the air and catching it with one hand. A strapping man in his forties, he did it with ease. But on the third try, the bar slipped from his hand and landed on the stone hearth of the fireplace. Springer stooped to retrieve it—and froze.

He looked at George with cold eyes. Slowly, he pointed to a grayish gash on the edge of the bar. Taking his penknife, he started to scratch away at another part of the bar, scraping off a film of gold to reveal a dark gray surface. At the spot where the solution had been applied, he found a quarter-inch plug of solid gold.

"You blackguard! This a goddamn lead bar," Springer cried, dropping the bar to the wood floor with a thump.

George stood paralyzed with fear as Springer pulled a derringer from his frock coat pocket.

"You thought I was some dumbass hick you could swindle," he said in a hurt voice, raising his arm to aim the weapon.

"Yes, as a matter of fact, I did," George said. With the agility of the former athlete he was, he scooped up the bar in a fluid motion and smashed Springer on the head with it.

The businessman tumbled to the ground and lay still.

"Let's get the hell out of here, George," Johnson yelled, grabbing his bag.

George took a step toward the door—then halted. He went back to Springer and took his billfold.

He and Johnson were out on the street in less than a minute. "Don't run. Walk," George hissed. The two men paced up Broadway and turned right on Thirty-First Street. They walked eight blocks along Sixth Avenue before slipping into a saloon. George downed two mugs of beer, his throat as dry as a bale of cotton.

"Christ, that was close, George," Johnson said. "What are you going to do now?"

George was counting the money in the billfold. "Only four hundred," he said dejectedly.

"How much are you down?"

"Four thousand. I could've gotten that for the one bar," George said, rubbing his hands up and down his face.

"At least we still have the bar. But we'll have to get it replated."

"That bar's been good to us, Henry. It's paid off eight thousand by now."

"Still. It's best to lie low for a while. You're going to have to give them something soon, Georgie, or they'll come looking for you again."

George ignored Henry's words. Staring into space, he muttered under his breath, "With this four hundred, I can get even tonight. I know I can."

37

I BELIEVE THE FIRST DANCE IS MINE, MRS. CROSS."

"Don't be such an ass, Wilberforce, I've called for the first dance."

Horace Wilberforce and Clinton Collingwood stood forehead to forehead with looks of rage on their red, leathery faces.

Helen Cross inserted her long, white-gloved arm between the pot-bellies of her two admirers, but they paid no mind. They still glared at each other, seconds away from launching into combat like two elks locking antlers in mating season.

In a quiet, soothing voice, Helen said, "Mr. Wilberforce has the first dance, but you may have the next one, Mr. Collingwood."

Collingwood snorted and stepped back, angry at Wilberforce's smug look. The full orchestra in the balcony of the great ballroom struck up a Strauss waltz. Helen took Wilberforce's plump, gloved hand and glided effortlessly onto the dance floor. The old man beamed with joy as though he had been transformed into the young man he had been in 1858. The couple spun gracefully across the beautiful, black marble floor of the ballroom with all eyes fastened on Helen in her white, low-cut ball gown. When Helen spotted her husband standing by himself, near one of the gilded cast-iron columns that held up the horseshoe-shaped balcony, she smiled, and he walked out of the room.

Out in the high-ceilinged foyer, Cross ran into his friend, Bruce Price.

"Not leaving so soon, old boy," admonished Price in a pretend scolding.

"Just wanted to get a smoke and gaze at the ocean from the piazza of your magnificent building."

Price smiled at the compliment.

"This may be your best work of all. What a palace. There's never been a hotel like this," said Cross with genuine feeling. He always admired—and at the same time was jealous of—Price's tremendous talent. The man never failed to do something innovative in each of his buildings, and that was the true mark of artistic genius. Cross tried to do the same in his commissions but never pulled it off. His projects always turned out to be a rehash of a previous design. He needed to break through that creative wall to do something special.

Cross pulled out his gold cigarette case as Price turned and entered the wide double doors to the ballroom. "I'll be right back. Catch up with you inside."

Though Newport was the center of the summer season, there were important events held elsewhere. All of society's elite were at the charity ball at the new Oceanside Hotel in Long Branch, New Jersey. It was an invitation no one would turn down. The hotel, through the tobacco heir Pierre Lorillard's patronage, had become fashionable very quickly. Cross wasn't lying when he said no other hotel was like it. It was massive, stretching along the beach for two hundred yards at least. But instead of housing hundreds of small rooms, the hotel offered only fifty, all huge suites. The owner's strategy was shrewd, like the Metropolitan Opera's, which kept its elite seating to a minimum to drive up demand. Along the entire rear of the building was a deep porch where one could enjoy the views and walk on a wooden bridge over the dunes to the private beach. Servants in cutaway coats would serve guests on the sand, bringing buckets of champagne and iced platters of Blue Point oysters.

The hotel was also unusual in its method of construction. Instead of being built of wood with a shingled exterior, it was made entirely of stone, giving it a strong, massive stature rising up out of the sand dunes like a fortress. No hurricane would ever budge it from its place. Its sense of majesty made it seem very elite and special to the rich—a place they *had* to visit.

Cross puffed away on his cigarette as he walked down the thickly carpeted hallway flanked by paneled walls of African mahogany with onyx wainscoting. At the end of the long hall, he turned around to see if anyway else was about. But with the ball going on, the rest of the hotel was completely deserted. He put out his cigarette in an ashtray on a side table and walked to a door located just before the window in the end wall of the hallway. Through the door was a service room where there was an open dumbwaiter. In his white tails, Cross hopped into the dumbwaiter, sat down cross-legged, and pushed the switch to send it up. It rose along iron rails in its wooden enclosed shaft, slowly passing identical service rooms on each floor. At the fourth floor, it came to a stop, but instead of getting off, Cross stood up and gave a low whistle. Above him was an opening in the ceiling, and Culver's head appeared. He reached down to Cross to help pull him up into the opening.

Aside from being a great work of design, Price's hotel had included an engineering innovation that no hotel had ever employed. All other hotels followed the same layout—a central corridor on each floor, lined on both sides with rooms about fifteen feet in depth. The Oceanside used huge, wood and iron roof trusses that spanned its stone walls for a distance of seventy feet, allowing the rooms to measure over thirty feet and giving them a palatial feel. No one had ever before used such colossal trusses, other than for the roofs of great railroad sheds.

Cross stood with eight other members of Kent's gang. In front of them were row after row of the great timber trusses, giant triangles latticed with iron and wood struts. Directly below them was the ceiling of the fourth floor, which was attached to the bottoms of the trusses. And that was where the top-floor luxury suites were located—brimming with expensive jewels, clothing, and cash. All the gang had to do was walk along and break through the ceiling into each suite. Instead of plaster ceilings, the rooms had ornate pressed metal. By just tapping on the ceiling panels from above, they could quietly remove a section and lower themselves down into the room. No messy plaster and lath to deal with, and no risk of being seen entering from the corridor.

"This will be a snap, Mr. Engineer," said Culver, slapping Cross on the back. After each successful robbery, Cross had been more and more accepted into the gang until he was pretty much considered one of the fellows—except by Brady, who mercifully wasn't present tonight.

"I'm actually an architect, Mr. Culver. There's a big difference."

Cross was trembling with excitement, not only because of the potential take, but also because he alone would direct this robbery. Millicent, Kent's beloved wife, was quite ill, and Kent wouldn't leave her bedside, so he'd entrusted the entire operation to Cross. Kent really had no choice. The job was planned for the night of the gala ball and couldn't be postponed. Cross had to prove he was up to the task. When Helen had smiled at him from the dance floor, that was the signal that every top-floor guest was in the ballroom. The men who were carrying canvas bags and small hammers took their positions so they were lined up over the rooms and waited for Cross's cue. From the floor plans, Cross knew how the rooms were spaced out and where each man should stand. He felt like a general about to give the command to attack. Cross took a breath, grinned, and waved his troops into battle.

"Nice and easy. You just tap and the ceiling comes loose," reminded Cross.

Using the wooden end of the hammers, they lightly tapped and pushed down the metal ceiling panels and, like rabbits hopping into their burrows, dropped down into the rooms using narrow rope ladders tied to the trusses. Cross followed Culver down and went along with him as he scooped up every piece of clothing and grabbed objects off dressing room tables. Each room had a small safe that Cross thought would be invulnerable, but with a pry bar, Culver made easy work of it and emptied the safe out. The rooms were luxuriously decorated with beautiful rugs, chandeliers, and French period furniture. Bedrooms flanked a massive sitting room. Cross went over to one of the huge picture windows to look at the ocean and smiled.

"All done," whispered Culver, who started climbing up the ladder. Two men were left above to pull up the bulging bags from below. Cross followed him, and they hit another room. Soon the truss space was filled with bags. Down the gang went into room after room. Cross grew tired of following Culver down and waited for him above, hoisting up the bag of loot. There were a dozen suites and, by Cross's count, four more to go. The truss space was pitch-black, so Cross was shocked when it was suddenly filled with bright light. He was confused, and his eyes opened wide in panic. The other men froze in place. They looked around, expecting to see police shining lanterns at them with guns drawn. But Cross finally discovered the source of light. It was coming from one of the ceilings they had lifted—the lights were on in a room below.

Cross crept over, knelt by the hole, and cautiously peeked into it. His head jerked back in fear as he heard voices.

"Edith, I couldn't keep my eyes off you. I want you so badly," a man cried.

"Gerald, we can't do this—it's madness. We'll be missed," said a woman, not very convincingly.

"The hell with them. They're too busy dancing. It'll be an hour before they notice we're gone."

There was a brief silence and a woman's low moan.

"Take me to the bedroom," cried the woman.

"No, here," ordered the man.

With great care, Cross had decided where in the ceiling to enter, so rope ladders would be off to the side in the sitting rooms, away from the entries. But this ladder seemed to be not more than ten feet away from the couple. It would be seen immediately if either one of them glanced upward. Cross slowly raised the ladder and tucked it up safely in the truss space.

"I want to kiss every square inch of your body," commanded the man.

"Do it," pleaded the woman. "But be careful of my gown—it's a Pingat."

"I'll buy you ten gowns. I'm going to rip this off your body. I want you naked."

The woman gave out another low, passionate moan.

All of a sudden, Cross recognized the voices—it was Gerald Davenport and Edith Trevelyan, who were both married, but not to each other. To his knowledge, they had never even spoken. Cross was temporarily transfixed by this discovery of infidelity. He knew that many married individuals cheated on their spouses in his set but was amazed that these two were lovers. Who could have imagined it? Although Helen had probably known all along.

The other men had come up from below and were standing around him. Cross propped his arms on both sides of the opening and slowly lowered his head through. Not more than ten feet away were two completely naked people, fornicating with incredible animal energy. True to his word, Davenport couldn't wait and had taken Edith right on one of the matching sitting room sofas. Sounds of such intense passion came floating up and out of the opening that Cross was embarrassed. His gang members were mesmerized.

Cross kept watching, but out of the corner of his eye, he saw something move under the opposite sofa. He pulled himself up and started taking an inventory of the gang. "Where's Culver?" he hissed.

The other men shook their heads.

In horror, Cross looked down and saw movement again under the sofa across from the lovers. He looked back at the couple, who had increased the vigor and intensity of their lovemaking and seemed to be in no hurry to finish. Cross began to panic. He could imagine Kent berating him for fouling up the job. It might be an hour before the two of them called it quits, and that would be an unbearable wait for Cross. He just couldn't chance it; he had to stick to the timetable he'd set. The longer they were up there, the greater the possibility of being detected.

In a low voice, he ordered the men to begin to bring down the bags on the dumbwaiter. Cross lowered his head again and saw Culver peeking out from under the sofa and up at the ceiling. Cross looked over at the couple to make sure they were still preoccupied, then waved at Culver to get his attention. A decision had to be made quickly. Should they wait it out until they finished and returned to the ball? But that could take some time, and when they were putting their clothes back on, would they spot Culver?

Cross gestured to Culver to come up. Culver's eyes were full of fear at this command, and he glanced over at the man and woman. He suddenly slithered out and crawled on his hands and knees across the Oriental rug, holding the bag of loot on his back like Santa Claus. Cross lowered the rope ladder through the hole, and Culver scampered up like hounds were on his tail. Up in the truss space, he was breathing heavily and calmed himself by taking a long swig from a small, amber-colored bottle.

Cross and Culver went down the dumbwaiter to the basement where two bound and chloroformed hotel servants lay motionless on the stone floor. After helping Culver out the basement door with the bag, Cross returned to the ballroom and asked Sybil Davenport, Gerald's wife, to dance.

38

"THIS PLACE IS ONE GIANT TREASURE CHEST," HELEN EXCLAIMED. She had been in incredibly high spirits since the Oceanside heist last week. It delighted Helen that all of New York society was in an outrage over the robbery. That's all they talked about. She couldn't wait to plan the next job. It became her consuming passion, even more important than Julia's coming-out ball.

On a table before them lay a map of Newport. Helen had marked the houses with the greatest potential for loot with red Xs. The marks concentrated on either side of Bellevue Avenue, the main thoroughfare for the town's richest neighborhood.

For ten weeks in the summer, this narrow stretch of land overlooking the Atlantic Ocean became New York society's social Mecca. At a staggering cost, balls, dinner parties, yachting fetes, and concerts were thrown, each family trying to outshine the other. Bellevue, Daily, and Ocean Avenues were jammed with a promenade of magnificent carriages, carrying beautiful women who wanted to be seen and admired while their husbands raced yachts and played polo. Aunt Caroline's mansion, Beechwood, recently renovated by Richard Morris Hunt at a cost of two million dollars, was the brightest star in Newport's social firmament. During the summer season, Helen and John had a standing invitation to stay there anytime they wanted.

"How about Watts-Sherman? He's a banker," Cross said. "Remember, I worked on that house for Richardson. I may still have a set of plans."

Helen smiled at her husband. "Of course I remember. You were a young architect, so happy to be learning from the master. Those were happy days. Lean, but happy."

"True. I was just getting started, but you know, those were some of the best days for us. George had just been born. Do you remember? I didn't think I'd like having a child, but I was wrong. It was a joy."

"We'd take him along the Cliff Walk to that little beach near the point. He'd get knocked down by the waves, but he'd always get up and run back in," Helen said, smiling.

"George was always headstrong," Cross said. "But those were wonderful times." He placed his hand on his wife's. "What do you think?"

"Watts-Sherman's place has nothing special. There are more lucrative targets."

Cross smiled. Helen's tenacity amazed him. She could have been a general or an admiral, planning a battle.

"Kingscote, Chateau-sur-Mer... What about the Belmonts' place—By-the-Sea?"

"Maybe Beechwood?" Cross asked, knowing what his wife's response would be.

"Blood is thicker than water, sir. Aunt Caroline is off limits. She's family," Helen said, giving his hand a little slap and laughing.

"The problem is the servants. These places can have up to a dozen, and they're always there. It's too many to tie up or lock in the wine cellar," Cross said. Helen nodded. "What about Isaac Bell?" he continued. "I can get the drawings from Stanny."

"No, too poor," Helen said. She ran her finger along the red marks, pausing to take inventory of each house. It had amazed Cross to discover that his wife had a near photographic memory when it came to valuable objects, recalling where every priceless vase or necklace was located. Her reconnaissance of Julia's coming-out guests' homes had been quite impressive.

"The Millards are a possibility. So are the Christies. The Van Alens' house is all by itself, and he's always in London on business. Do you know, he actually keeps his horses on the first floor and lives above them!" Helen said, amused by this eccentricity.

"No more horses for me," Cross said. "Too damn much trouble."

At that moment, Helen's bedroom door swung open. Charlie dashed in, grinning.

"It seems you've forgotten the rule about knocking," Cross said.

"I didn't know that applied to me."

"It especially applies to you."

Sucking on a lemon stick, Charlie sidled up to the table and looked at the map.

"What's going on here?" he asked with mock curiosity.

"We're marking all the places in Newport to which we've been invited this summer," Helen said.

"Great guns, you're popular. Glad I don't have to go. So dull."

"We certainly don't want to bore you. That's why you're staying behind with Mrs. Johnston," his father said, patting him on the shoulder.

"I'm most grateful," said Charlie. "Now, do you want to see my dancing steps?"

Though his parents were plainly preoccupied, they nodded. If they indulged him, they might get rid of him more quickly.

Charlie started to hum a tune, and with dainty, nimble steps, he performed a little dance. When he was finished, Cross and Helen politely applauded. Charlie was smiling from ear to ear—not because his parents were pleased with his performance, but because the dance he'd made up on the spot had been a success.

"I'll need one dollar for next week's lesson," he said brightly.

"I thought it was always fifty cents," protested his father.

"Special double session. We're learning the latest mazurka."

Cross doled out the money, and Charlie skipped out of the room. Next week, he'd demonstrate his progress in art class by showing them some drawings his classmate, Fred Truscott, would provide him for five cents apiece.

The Crosses returned to the map. The logistics of the job greatly depended on the location of the house, so they paid particular attention to the entry and exit points. Helen wrote the names of potential victims on a sheet of stationery. She went down the list, giving her husband the pros and cons of each. When the cons outweighed the pros, she crossed off the name.

"John, the Van Duncans have this unusual stair just for the use of the servants," Helen noted with excitement. "So Henry and Lily don't have to run into the servants in the hallways, they had an inner stair built so the help can get into the rooms through secret doors. The stair is entered from the basement and leads all the way up to the fourth floor. We get in there, and we can clean out the place when they are having a dinner party."

Helen's beautiful face lit up at the thought. Cross had never seen his wife look so radiant.

"But Henry's had some financial setbacks lately, so they're not nearly as rich as they used to be," Helen said and crossed the Van Duncans' name off the list.

As they worked, Cross marveled at the ways in which his wife had surprised him. After he'd told her about Kent, she had thrown herself into the project with incredible energy. He'd thought she would fold under the heartbreak, but to his amazement—and admiration—she'd displayed an iron will. Cross felt he had no choice but to tell Helen that Robert was assigned to investigate the robberies, but she showed no panic at all. In fact, at dinners with her brother-in-law, she carefully probed to find out what he was up to. From the typical, cloistered society woman, content to dedicate her life to household responsibilities and children, she'd undergone a remarkable transformation.

Unlike her husband, though, Helen never condemned George for causing their calamity. *She doesn't understand the shadowy side of our son,* Cross thought. *Neither do I, as a matter of fact.* Father and son had

avoided each other since their confrontation in the carriage, unsure of
what to say.

Helen spoke of nothing but the planning of the robberies whenever they were alone together. For the first time in years, they spent
evenings in the same room, selecting potential targets and weighing
the merits of each job. They hadn't talked so much in the last decade.
Cross had a new regard for his wife, for the clarity of her analytical
thought. He actually enjoyed her company. Helen's mind, he realized,
was razor sharp.

She already knew where the owners would be on a certain day
throughout the summer; the Newport social calendar was set in stone
weeks before the season began. Some would be sailing yachts far out
on the ocean; others would spend the afternoon at a polo match and
attend a party after. Next to the names of the most likely victims, Helen
made an inventory of assets that could be taken. The more she spoke,
the more mesmerized Cross became. He could imagine her as the head
of a giant company, barking orders to a board of directors.

Each name on the list reminded the Crosses of parties they had
attended or gossip they had heard. As the evening wore on, they spent
more time reminiscing than planning the robbery.

"Old man Ogden thought he had me trapped, but since you
designed his house, I knew where the dumbwaiter was. I escaped his
grasp and down I went. He spent an hour searching for me upstairs.
You know, that dumbwaiter of Ogden's could be quite useful if we
decided to hit them, a wonderful way to get all the loot down—just like
at Oceanside." Helen was laughing uncontrollably, and Cross couldn't
help joining in.

Abruptly, though, he stopped and looked at his wife's face. It was
lovelier at forty than it had ever been before. He reached out and put
his hand on the back of her slender neck. Gently, he pulled her toward
him. Giving her a long, passionate kiss, he whispered, "I've been quite
the fool." With his arm around her waist, he led her to her bed.

◆ ◆ ◆

In the darkness, Cross gazed at his wife's naked body as she walked to the bathroom. She *was* like Helen of Troy, with the sort of beautiful body one saw on statues from antiquity—perfectly conceived, without the tiniest flaw. Her long black hair cascaded down her back, swaying as she walked.

When she returned, Helen snuggled up against Cross's chest. He wrapped his arm around her, pulling her close as he drifted into a wonderfully peaceful sleep.

He awakened abruptly to a cry from his wife.

"My God, what have I done?" Helen sat up in the bed.

Alarmed and disoriented, Cross sat up too.

"The Goelets. I completely forgot about the Goelets. *They'll* be our next job," Helen said triumphantly.

39

H URRY THE HELL UP, CHARLIE, OR WE'LL BE LATE."
Charlie had had to take the unfamiliar Ninth Avenue
Elevated to meet Eddie, and it had taken longer to get across town
than he'd thought. His friend was impatiently waiting at the bottom of
the stair at Cortlandt Street. He grabbed Charlie's arm and pulled him
in the direction of the West Side piers.

Crossing West Street, Charlie saw hundreds of screaming boys
crowded around a pier where a white steamboat was moored. A
fast-moving stream of boys was running up the gangplank onto the
ship. Once aboard, they raced around the decks, shouting and waving
to the boys still on the pier.

"What the hell's this?" Charlie shouted above the din. Cursing had
become second nature to him, a fact he took great pride in, as it allowed
him to blend with the rest of Eddie's set.

"It's the annual newsboys' picnic. They're taking us on a boat ride
up the Hudson River to the Palisades," Eddie yelled, waving to friends
already on board.

Together, he and Charlie squirmed their way to the front of the
crowd and sprinted up the gangplank, butting up against the backs of
the boys ahead of them.

"Come on. Get your asses movin'," Eddie screamed, pushing
them forward.

One boy fell on his face, and Eddie and Charlie hurtled over him.
On board, they raced to the bow of the boat.

"The rich people feel sorry for the newsies, so they try to do somethin' nice for us," Eddie said, climbing onto the ship's railing and spreading out his arms for balance. "Same do-gooders who built the lodging houses, so we don't have to be out on the street. But you know you'll never get me in one of those joints."

"They'll send your ass out west to work on a farm, right?"

"That's right, Charlie, my boy. Eddie Mooney ain't gonna be no farmer with cow shit on his shoes. I'll step in the horse shit on the streets of Manhattan any day."

The boat was fully loaded, hundreds of crazed, filthy newsboys racing back and forth on the decks like wild animals let out of cages at the zoo. The children were delirious with excitement and impossible to control. The crew members, dressed in smart, navy-blue uniforms with red piping on the sleeves and legs, were cursing and yelling at their new passengers, but corralling them was an impossible task, and they quickly gave up. Soon, every painted-cork life preserver was around a dirty neck, and the restroom was a pigsty, the toilets impossibly backed up. When the newsies discovered the steel stair to the bridge and started their ascent, the captain, a nautical-looking elderly man in a double-breasted tunic with gold buttons, ordered the door to the bridge barred.

The *Blue Angel* cast off, the engine thrown into reverse as it backed away from the pier.

"Come on," Eddie shouted to Charlie. "They're going to give out candy."

At the stern, a table was set up. Well-dressed, middle-aged men were arranging brown paper bags on its surface, but the newsboys descended like locusts, grabbing the bags as fast as the men could set them out.

"One to a boy. One to a boy," screamed one of the benefactors.

The bags contained abundant amounts of wrapped caramels, bon-bons, and a variety of hard candies, which were immediately stuffed into salivating mouths. When their stomachs no longer had room, the boys did what came naturally: they threw candy at one another. Once the first boy began flinging sweets about, another followed suit. In an instant, three hundred newsboys were pelting one another and the crew with projectiles. The crew, outgunned and helpless, retreated below-decks, locking the hatches behind them. They were paid to be sailors, they huffed, not attendants in a zoo.

The captain and helmsman, captive on the bridge, watched the spectacle in horror. As the boat steamed slowly north, the frenzy increased. The children seemed mad with delight.

In an attempt to entertain them, the Society for the Prevention of Cruelty to Children, which had officially sponsored the excursion, had hired a small brass band. The society believed that the unfortunate children had never been exposed to music, though in fact every boy present likely frequented saloons and heard music daily. Undaunted, the musicians set up on the lower deck at the bow; in the belief that the show must go on, they played stirring military marches, which only seemed to intensify the madness spinning about them. Soon the newsies turned on them too, bombarding them with candy. With its widemouthed horn, the tuba was a favorite target. It soon filled with candy, making it impossible to play. Charlie caught the percussionist in the back of the head with a peppermint ball. The band had no choice but to retreat.

Finally, the captain could take no more abuse. He charged from the bridge like a wounded rhino and made his way below deck to a private cabin. Entering, he was amazed by an incongruous sight: society ladies and gentlemen from the Society for the Prevention of Cruelty to Children, having tea.

"So nice of you to take the time to accompany us today, Mr. Cross," Mrs. Isabella Beekman was saying as she poured tea into George's cup. "Captain, George recently graduated from Harvard and is teaching at the Children's Aid Society school this summer. His students have made wonderful progress."

George, who had been shanghaied into coming by Dr. Caldwell, gave a meek smile and took a sip of his tea.

Cap in hand, the captain walked up to a distinguished matron in a hat bedecked with artificial flowers.

"Mrs. Beekman, do you have any idea what those little beasts are doing to my boat?"

The woman took a long sip of tea and patted her lips with a linen napkin. "I do hope the children are enjoying themselves. Those poor unfortunates deserve some pleasure in their lives," she said.

Around the table, her companions nodded earnestly.

"Madame, I'm turning this boat around. We are going back to Manhattan."

"You shall do nothing of the sort," Mrs. Beekman said. Her voice implied that the captain was a feeble-minded Irish servant of the very lowest sort. "You have been paid to land us at the picnic grounds at the foot of the Palisades and then take us back. *That's* what you'll do, sir."

"I'll land you and leave these animals there," the captain thundered.

"That would be a mistake indeed, sir. Do you know of my family?"

Reminded of the Beekmans' sway, the captain cowered like a beaten dog and left the cabin.

At the Palisades, each boy received a large box lunch as he disembarked. Inside was a thick roast beef sandwich with pickles, two hard-boiled eggs, a generous slice of chocolate cake, a bottle of sarsaparilla, and an apple. The newsboys' hunger had returned, and the food was devoured in minutes, save the apples. They became handy projectiles as the boys cavorted happily across the picnic grounds. The hot summer air was full of delicious red missiles.

Like many of the boys, Eddie had no interest in games. With Charlie at his side, he was eager to explore the woods. Eddie prowled about with great interest. It was a completely alien world to him. He had been to Central Park, of course, but always to steal purses, and he didn't have much time to enjoy nature.

The captain, who had raised the gangplank so that the boys would be forced to stay ashore, ordered the crew to feed river water through a fire hose to wash off the decks. If need be, he vowed, he'd turn the hose on the boys on the return trip.

From the upper deck of the bow, Mrs. Beekman and her fellow members of the Society watched the fun the boys were having with great pleasure.

"Remember that we are child savers," Mrs. Beekman said. "Though I maintain that these wretches would be better off with farm families, breathing the good, clean country air of the Midwest."

"But some have parents. They'd never see them again," a dissenting voice murmured.

"You call those vile creatures *parents*? A cat would make a better mother or father," Mrs. Beekman said, voice dripping with disdain.

After two hours, the steamboat's whistle blew, signaling the return to the boat. To the crew's relief, gorging themselves and running around had worn the boys out. Most stood at the ship railings and quietly watched the Palisades to the west and Manhattan to the east slip by. A few even fell asleep on the decks.

As the gangplank was lowered, Mrs. Beekman and other Society members gathered at the top of the gangway to hand out an informative pamphlet entitled "God Loves a Clean and Moral Boy." It was forced into the newsies' hands before they could descend the gangplank.

"Here. I think this will do you some real good, Charlie Cross."

Charlie's heart dropped like a stone. He looked up and saw his big brother standing above him, a very amused look on his face.

"Let's have a talk onshore, Little Brother," said George.

40

"JOHN. SO GOOD TO SEE YOU, OLD MAN," STANFORD WHITE bellowed. "I was wondering when you and Helen would make it up to Newport."

"With Helen preparing for Julia's coming-out ball and all the work that's come into the office of late, it's been hard to get away," Cross said.

"I'm eager to see your design for the theater."

"You'll see it in *American Architect and Building News* next month," Cross said.

"John Cross here is one of the city's best architects, Bob," White said to the tall man standing next to him. "You know Robert Goelet, John?"

"Yes, we've met several times," Cross said, nodding to Goelet.

"Mr. Cross, always a pleasure," Goelet said. "Quite a crowd tonight, eh?"

The horseshoe-shaped porch at the rear of the Newport Casino was packed with women, whose vibrant summer gowns stood in stark contrast to the black evening wear of the men. The casino, on Bellevue Avenue, was the social center of the summer Newport season. It had been designed by Charlie McKim for James Gordon Bennett Jr., owner of the *New York Herald*. Bennett's friend had gotten kicked out of the Newport Reading Room, the resort's former social center, after Bennett dared him to ride a horse inside. Outraged, Bennett bought land and built his own club. It was a wonderfully creative building, covered in wood shingles, its porch clad in a screen of lattice and spindles. White, who'd decorated the rooms, added a domed clock tower. Lawn tennis courts were added shortly after the building was completed, and McKim included a sizable theater on the second floor.

Tonight, there was to be a performance by a well-known tenor from Italy.

"Stanny designed a wonderful house for you, Mr. Goelet," Cross said.

After the Astors, the Goelets were the biggest landlords in New York, collecting millions in rent. Goelet and his brother, Ogden, had inherited the business from their father and uncle. Of late, real estate had become the most lucrative business in the city. If he'd known how valuable the land would become, John Jacob Astor was fond of saying, he would have bought up the entire island of Manhattan.

Two years before, Stanny had done a huge shingled house for Robert Goelet on Narragansett Avenue, near the cliff overlooking the Atlantic. The project cost more than eighty thousand dollars. The house's rear facade, facing the ocean, had a porch that stretched the width of the house, supported by the slender, Japanese-inspired columns Stanny so admired.

"We love Southside. Sitting on the porch, seeing the sun rise over the ocean…it's my favorite place in the world," Goelet said, smiling at Stanny.

To create a house in which a client loved to spend his time—that was one of the best things about being an architect. It wasn't just four walls and a roof; it was a home and a refuge, a place where one might feel safe from the unfairness and cruelty of the world. Cross wished he could design a country house of his own. He could escape there and take his family with them, spiriting them away from harm.

It was seven o'clock. The crowd began to make its way toward the theater. Cross excused himself and went to look for Helen. He found her in the café, surrounded as usual by male admirers. One of them, a distinguished man with an aquiline nose and a mane of swept-back hair, he'd seen somewhere before.

"John, you remember Count Aleksandrov?"

"Of course. We met at Honoria's party. How are you, Count?"

"In the presence of such beauty, I always feel elated," the count said in heavily accented English, nodding toward Helen.

Cross smiled at the compliment. Then he excused himself and pulled Helen aside.

"Remember, you've got just two hours," she said urgently. "Once the performance is over, I don't know if I'll be able to hold Goelet here until you get back."

"If anyone asks where I am, tell them I hate Italian opera and went out for a smoke," Cross said. He knew no one would miss him. The men would kill for the honor of sitting next to Helen and be glad that he was out of the way.

"The necklace with eight hundred pearls is in the safe under the floorboards, in her private study on the second floor in front of the bay window," Helen reminded him. "You have to lift the rug. And Goelet's ninth-century gold chalice is behind a panel on the fourth bookshelf from the top in his library."

Cross nodded. Then he drifted to the rear of the crowd filing into the theater. As the last person entered, he slipped down the stairs to the entry hall and left. Walking two blocks north, Cross turned into an alley where a boy held the reins of a bay. Giving him a dollar, Cross mounted and headed east, making his way through backstreets until he came to Narragansett Avenue. As he rode, he couldn't help wondering if—or when—the informant would strike again. Would he be riding into a trap? Would he find the Pinkertons and his brother waiting for him?

No. He had to put his fears out of his mind and concentrate on the task ahead.

Finally, he reached a large house on the right. There, the road dead-ended at the cliff. Tying the horse up behind a large holly bush, Cross opened the saddle bag and pulled out a folded sheet of paper. He checked his pocket watch—7:15 p.m.—and walked up the drive.

As he reached the front porch, Kent emerged from the front door. "Such a nice summer house. I'll keep the details in mind when you design one for me," he said, puffing away on his Havana.

Cross cursed him under his breath but gave only a strained smile. "What about those servants?"

"Fast asleep. Montgomery has sprinkled his fairy dust," Kent said.

Though it wouldn't have bothered his conscience, Kent had thought killing six to eight servants too time-consuming. Another method had to be employed to get them out of the way. Luckily, the large houses always needed extra help in the summer. By lying through his teeth, Montgomery secured a job as a gardener's assistant for the week before the robbery. He showed himself a hard and dedicated worker and was quickly accepted into the Goelet household. His fellow servants liked his jovial personality. Mrs. Hopkins, the widowed head housekeeper, had already taken a fancy to him.

Two hours earlier, as the servants prepared to have their tea, Montgomery kindly offered to help—and put an expert dose of chloral hydrate in the pot. In the servants' dining hall, Cross saw all seven fast asleep, heads resting on the long oak table. They looked like school-children, fallen asleep atop their desks. The head butler was snoring so loudly that Cross burst out laughing. Shaking his head, he walked back to the twenty-four-foot-high entry hall White had designed. Kent's men had already begun to work. Priceless Japanese and Chinese pottery was snatched up and bagged. Paintings came off the walls. With a blueprint he'd secured from White's office, Cross directed them to a secret compartment behind a wall in Goelet's dressing room that held jewelry, rare coins, and stacks of cash. His wife's closets were cleaned out, as well as the china and silver service. Helen's keen eye led them to the floor safe, where Mrs. Goelet kept her priceless necklace, and to the gold chalice.

Watching the buzz of activity, that same incredible sense of exhilaration swept over Cross like an ocean wave. He felt as if he were walking on air, floating a foot above the floor.

He strolled through the house, as much to admire Stanny's interior decoration skills as to supervise the men. On each successive job, Stanny outdid himself—a hard thing for an architect to accomplish. But Stanny had yet to reach his artistic zenith. While Cross didn't like robbing a friend's client, he knew from conversations with Robert that he had to pick different marks. Mansions in the city were no longer safe. That made Newport the next most lucrative target.

The men were working their way through the eight bedrooms on the second floor. As Montgomery opened a wide, paneled oak door, a deafening explosion rang out, and he fell to the hall carpet, clutching his right leg.

"I've been shot," he cried and launched into a tirade of expletives. Dozens of tiny bloodstains appeared on his light gray Brooks Brothers trousers. His leg, the gang realized as they clustered around, had been blasted by buckshot.

Another blast exploded above their heads, and the men dove for the floor.

From inside the bedroom, an angry, high-pitched voice called out, "General Jackson, the British have commenced the attack! They're advancing in force against the earthworks."

Another blast followed. The men scattered to either side of the bedroom door, trying to see inside. Kent joined them. In the dim light streaming through the bedroom shutters, he could make out a withered old man, sitting on the bed, reloading a double-barreled shotgun.

"We have them on the run," the old man shouted. "The bastards are falling back." He raised the shotgun and unloaded both barrels at the door.

Cross came up behind Kent. "What the hell is going on? This racket's going to alarm the neighbors."

Kent frowned at him. "It's a family member, I believe, who thinks he's under attack."

"General Jackson, the fog is lifting. We can pick them off like squirrels!"

Cross peeked in. "The old fool thinks he's back with Stonewall Jackson?"

"Not Stonewall—Andrew Jackson. At the Battle of New Orleans, if I'm not mistaken."

Cross was dumbfounded. "What should we do?"

"You men finish up—and don't forget that tapestry in the library," Kent yelled.

Another blast boomed forth. Cross and Kent ducked behind the wall, exchanging uneasy glances. Then Kent got down on his hands and knees and crawled into the bedroom.

"Cease fire, cease fire! The Redcoats are retreating. We've got them on the run, boys!" Kent yelled with great dramatic effect, as if he were on a stage. Cautiously, he made his way to the side of the bed, stood up, and slapped the old man on the shoulder.

"Good work, good work. We've won. I'm proud of you, son."

The old man laughed, waving the shotgun above his bald, wrinkled head.

"We did it, General. We thumped those goddamn Britishers."

Kent smiled and gently removed the gun from the old man's hands. Gently, he eased him back against the pillow.

"You've had a rough day, son. Take a rest."

The old man smiled and closed his eyes. "We did it, sir," he mumbled. "We whooped the hell out of 'em."

A bottle of soothing syrup stood on the nightstand. Kent picked it up and examined its contents. Seeing that it contained cocaine and had an 80 percent alcohol content, he gave the old man three tablespoons.

"Sweet dreams, soldier."

Kent set the gun under the bed and left the bedroom. In the hallway, he met Cross, who was shouting orders, trying to get the men out. Montgomery was being helped down the stairs, still cursing his head off.

The house had a corner turret. Cross ran to one of its tall windows and looked down Narragansett Avenue.

"Gather the rest of the loot and get the hell out of here," he yelled. "It's the police!"

Galloping down the street were two black-helmeted constables. If it had been a workingman's house instead of a millionaire's, Cross thought, the police would have taken hours to respond to the call.

"Let 'em in the front door, and I'll take care of 'em," Brady said

Kent turned to face him. "Get downstairs, lock the front doors, and rip out the telephone," he commanded.

Cross ran into the hallway. "Come on, goddamn it, get a move on. We haven't got much time." From a window in the entry hall, he saw the two policemen tethering their horses at the hitching post.

"Everybody out. Now!" yelled Kent.

Men dragging long, white canvas bags ran past him to the rear of the house.

The constables started knocking on the front door in a polite but insistent manner. One tried the doorknob.

"This is the police! Open up!" One of the constables finally lost patience and pounded his fist on the glass-and-wood door.

Knowing that the transport of so much loot through Newport would attract unwanted attention, Kent had devised an ingenious scheme. Goelet's backyard overlooked the ocean. It was easy to move the booty down the steep cliff path to the rocky beach, where three rowboats were waiting, ready to take the loot to a small steamship anchored out beyond the breaking waves. Kent's men bounded out the back door and down the path to the beach.

The police were shouting and pounding with all their might on the door.

With the police at the front door, Cross and Kent ran down the hallway to the rear servants' stair that led to the kitchen. Suddenly, Kent stopped and faced the wall on his left.

"My God, that's a manuscript from 900 A.D.! A Muslim work from *Spain*. Look!"

On the wall were four framed, illuminated manuscript pages, done in gold and silver with brilliant purple and red.

"These are priceless," shouted Kent, as he began to take them off the walls.

Cross stood in shock for a second, then ran to the top of the main stair and saw only one constable trying to force the door. He knew the other had headed for the back door. The constable smashed the leaded glass of the door and reached his hand in to unlock the door.

"Christ almighty, Kent, we have to go," screamed Cross, grabbing Kent by his sleeve. He had the four framed manuscript pages under his arm. Cross could hear the policeman running through the first floor like a crazed man, in and out of every room. When they got down the servants' stair, they heard the other policeman break through the back door, and they retreated up the stairs.

Kent knew the severity of their predicament. Cross watched with horror as Kent pulled a small pistol from the side pocket of his linen suit.

"No," hissed Cross, who looked about the hallway and yanked Kent by his lapels into a bedroom. He pulled him to what looked like a closet protruding from the wall. Opening the door, he shoved Kent in and followed behind. In a second, they were sliding down a corkscrew slide made up of polished sheet metal. Around and around they slid until they crashed into a door at its bottom. It opened up to the side yard, and out they ran to the beach path.

"What the hell was that?" asked Kent in amazement.

"Goelet's aunt is scared of burning to death in a fire, so he had Stanford White put in a spiral fire escape slide just for her. It's compact and better-looking than sticking a stair on the side of the house," huffed Cross as they ran.

At the path at the top of the cliff, he halted while Kent ran down, still clinging to his precious manuscripts. Cross saw that two rowboats were almost to the steamship. The last one was waiting for Kent on the beach. Luckily, the ocean was calm.

With the police inside in the house, Cross circled around to the front yard and back to his horse. He was mentally and physically exhausted but managed to ride back to the casino without pitching off. He slipped into the rear of the theater as the audience rose to give the Italian howler a standing ovation. The crowd filed down into the courtyard, where Cross found his wife standing with the Goelets and a crowd of other guests.

"I hope you enjoyed tonight's performance, John," said Helen in a soft, mocking tone.

"I did. The evening was an unqualified success. We must do this again."

"Oh, and John," Helen said. "Mr. Goelet has invited us back to his home for a late dinner."

"How kind. I've been dying to see the house."

41

Y OU RED DEVIL, YOU'LL NEVER HAVE ME!"
    "You'll be the first of all my wives in my lodge, white woman!"
"Never, you beast!"
"But first you must be made to obey!"

As the war-bonneted warrior chief hefted his tomahawk, ready to rain down a crushing blow upon the scantily clad white maiden, an explosion sounded outside the log cabin. Through the windows came the roar and crackle of reddish-yellow flames.

A bugle call rang out, followed by a volley of earsplitting gunshots. The Indians inside the log cabin ran to the windows, pointed their Winchesters, and fired.

"Holy shit, Eddie, they're using real bullets!" Charlie screamed.

Amid the chaos of the attack, the Indian chief leered at the white girl, lowered his weapon, and ripped her white lace bodice, exposing a plump, pink breast. The girl screamed, cowering back.

"He's going to fuck her right there," yelled Eddie.

The audience was in a frenzy, screaming and cursing the Indian for what he was about to do. The girl fainted, dropping limply to the floor, and people gasped, realizing that the redskin would easily have his way with her.

"Leave her alone, you red shit!" someone in the audience screamed.

Then the tide seemed to turn. The Indians at the windows began to fall like tenpins, grasping their chests where the bullets had pierced them. More explosions followed.

With an evil smirk, the chief knelt over the helpless girl and lowered her dress to her waist.

"Ya dirty Injun bastard, don't you touch her," bellowed a woman wearing a floppy hat ringed with fake yellow flowers.

With a resounding crash, the crude wooden door of the log cabin slammed open, and a young cavalry officer with flowing blond hair thrust his way inside. Seeing the chief, his eyes widened in shock, and he lunged forward, ramming his saber through the Indian. The chief staggered back, holding his hands over his wound, and dropped to the floor. The crowd went mad with joy, cheering and clapping.

More cavalry soldiers poured in, killing off the rest of the Indians. The officer lifted up the white maiden and embraced her. The men at the bar at the rear of the Baxter Street Playhouse raised their schooners of beer in honor of the brave soldiers, throwing amber-colored foam in all directions. The crowd rose to its feet, giving the heroes a standing ovation.

The actors proudly took their bows. When the one who played the chief took off his headdress and bowed, the audience hissed and cursed the actor, who smiled broadly. It was proof he'd given a convincing performance.

In the midst of the crowd, George, Charlie, and Eddie clapped and screamed their heads off. George had never had so much fun at the Metropolitan Opera House. He was always bored to death and couldn't understand a word of the German or Italian being spouted by the singers. Not that it mattered. The opera was merely a place for society women to show off their gowns and jewelry, and they gabbed through the entirety of the performance.

Since he'd started teaching on the Lower East Side, George had made it a habit to attend musicals and theater near the sleazy dumps where he gambled. It was wonderfully refreshing to see something so improper and salacious. The plays were always the same: a villain punished for his evil deeds, a nearly nude heroine rescued by a handsome hero.

As the audience filed out, George smiled down at Charlie and Eddie as they chattered away excitedly about the play. He had taken them to four others, but *The Savage's Lust* was definitely the most exciting. The

"While Miss Cross cannot go out without a chaperone, perhaps you and she will happen to attend the same performance." Julia smiled at her grandmother, knowing she had to protect Julia yet steer her toward acceptable Knickerbocker men. Wharton was handsome, wealthy, and without a stain of scandal—a very good catch.

"Yes," Wharton said enthusiastically, "I could let you know in advance when we're going."

"What are you studying at Yale, Mr. Wharton?" Julia asked. She wanted to know if he was a serious scholar or the usual society college boy, who drank all the time and never opened a book.

"Paleontology, Miss Cross. The study of dinosaurs at the Peabody Museum of Natural History."

This so impressed Julia that she put down her cup of tea.

"I'm just back from a summer expedition in the Southwest," Wharton continued. "We found eight new species of dinosaur bones and twelve tons of vertebrate fossils."

"How exciting, Mr. Wharton! I'd like to see those."

Wharton was pleased to have found something to spark Julia's interest. It gave him an advantage over the other handsome young suitors in attendance. "One day in the fall, you must come up to New Haven, and I can show you."

"This will be my last year at Miss Spence's," Julia said proudly. "Then I'm off to Vassar." Holding her breath, she awaited his reaction. Would Wharton frown at the prospect of a girl going to college, or would he be supportive?

"That's wonderful, Miss Cross. What will you study?"

Wharton has possibilities, Julia thought, smiling. "English literature."

"And become a teacher?'

"No, a writer. In fact, I'm working on a novel. A young girl, born in the lowest and cruelest depths of poverty in the Bowery, rises up and becomes a doctor."

"How fascinating."

use of special effects was unparalleled, and while most heroines were in a state of perpetual undress, this menaced maiden exceeded the others by a long shot. It would be a very popular production indeed.

Out in the street, they followed their established after-theater ritual and headed for a restaurant.

"I tell you, they were using real bullets. Don't you think so, George?" Charlie asked.

"Sure sounded like the real thing."

They tore into plates of beefsteak and fried potatoes. As they ate, George couldn't stop smiling at his brother. He was very pleased that Charlie had found a new world for himself, a universe free of the deadening Knickerbocker propriety they'd been brought up in. Charlie was so happy. Eddie, George had learned, was a good and loyal friend. In a way, it made George envious. He had no such person in his life.

"Her tits were popping out of that dress, did you see?" Eddie exclaimed. "We should go back tomorrow tonight!"

Perhaps we will, George thought.

42

NOLAN SAT IN HIS ARMCHAIR, STARING AT THE INVITATION HE'D lifted from Julia's handbag at the cockfight.

Mr. & Mrs. John Cross
request the pleasure of introducing their daughter
Julia Claire Cross

to

Monday evening, September 24, at half past nine
at the residence of Mr. William B. Astor II
424 Fifth Avenue

From a side table drawer, he pulled out a pen and ink pot. In careful, flowing cursive, he wrote "John Evan Nolan" on the blank line. He blew on the ink until it dried.

Walking over to the window, Nolan looked out onto Morton Street. He liked where he lived. Greenwich Village was quiet. He was far from the bustle of the Tenderloin and the filth of the Five Points and the Bowery, where most of his fellow gang members resided. Having a nice, well-furnished flat was a point of pride for him. It might have been the home of a college man or a law clerk.

Although his parents had cast him out into the streets at the age of nine, Nolan had developed a middle-class sense of thriftiness in contrast to the "live today, gone tomorrow" philosophy of the netherworld he inhabited. He had been brought up in a savage and unforgiving jungle where only the strong and wily survived. Death from violence and disease always lurked around the corner, choosing its victims with cruel randomness. At twenty-two, Nolan had seen scores of men and women die before age thirty. To them, such constant threat meant enjoying the moment and never thinking about the future. A dollar made was a dollar instantly spent—on drink, food, gambling, or whores.

Such a life was not for Nolan. He had vowed to save his money. Of the eight hundred dollars he'd recently stolen, three hundred went to the gang, leaving him a five-hundred-dollar share. Eighty percent, or four hundred dollars, went immediately into his account at the Emigrant Savings Bank on Chambers Street. Even if he only came away from a job with ten dollars, eight went into the bank. For six years, he had faithfully built up his fortune. The gang chided him constantly for his frugality, even accusing him of having Jew blood, which he always angrily denied—to their delight. But one hundred dollars was more than enough for the basic necessities and for entertainment, which he enjoyed as much as the next crook. On a good day, he could bring in at least one hundred dollars for himself, or what a bank clerk made in a month.

Nolan went to the table in the center of the parlor and picked up a slim, leather-bound volume. As he settled into his armchair, his black cat, Jupiter, settled in his lap. Nolan opened the book to the title page: *The Book of New York Social Etiquette—A Description of Our Customs as Taught & Practiced by the Superior Families of New York City*, by *Humphrey L. Oglander.*

The introduction read, "As to the unfortunates who have been reared at remote distances from the centers of civilization, there is nothing left for them to do but to make a careful study of unquestionable authority in those matters of etiquette that prevail among the most refined people." Nolan had no argument with this statement. While the world of the Bowery and the Five Points was separated by only two miles from Fifth Avenue and Twenty-Third Street, it might as well have been as distant as Mars.

Nolan moved on to the first chapter, "The Young Man Who Desires to Enter Society." It proved a good primer on the basics, including attire for a ball: black broadcloth dress coat, white waistcoat, pantaloons, faultless linen, and a white cravat. No jewelry except plain finger rings, and one's nails must be beautifully cut and trimmed, "like Lord Byron's." White gloves were essential, as they prevented perspiration from ruining the back of a lady's gown.

Nolan read every chapter carefully, pausing on "A Young Lady's Entrance into Society." But chapter 10, "Giving and Attending Parties, Balls, and Germans," was the most informative. First were the instructions on eating properly: the napkin in your lap, never tucked in at the collar; the fork always in the right hand, except when cutting meat. Above all, never bring the knife into contact with the lips. When arriving, a girl and her parents must stand near the entrance of the drawing room, where she is introduced to the guests. A gentleman bows to them, but not excessively.

The dinner at a debutante's coming-out ball comes first, with dancing to follow, but ending no later than 1:00 a.m. A gentleman can only ask the girl for one dance. After the dance is over, he brings her back to where her mother is sitting. He may converse with her for only a minute or two. He then continues to dance with the other ladies who have him reserved on their dance cards. A gentleman never smokes in the presence of ladies but retreats to a library or smoking room in the house.

It was almost eight o'clock when Nolan finished. It was a lot to absorb in one sitting, but there was time to reread before the ball.

He'd just finished fixing himself something to eat when he heard a knock at the door.

"Hello, Bernie," he said, greeting a small, florid-faced man in his sixties.

"Johnny, my lad. Are you ready for your lesson?" the man asked in a refined British accent.

"Let's start," Nolan said, waving him in. "Want a drink?"

"Best to wait on that until after our lesson, son," he replied with a chuckle and a wink.

Bernard Covington, formerly of Birmingham, had been head butler in some of England's finest homes. Because New York society idolized anything English, he'd had his pick of jobs in the city and chose the Pembroke-Joneses, one of the richest families.

But Bernie had the curse. While cleaning up after dinner parties, he would drain every glass on the table, drinking any molecule of wine, claret, hock, or sherry left in them. At first, his master ignored his habit. Only when Bernie was found dead drunk in the wine cellar, surrounded by empty wine bottles of priceless vintage, was he given the sack. The scandal of his dismissal prevented him from landing another job, and he embarked on a new career as a con man. With his British accent and gentlemanly manner, he'd fooled many an out-of-town rube into buying fake stock certificates.

"Now, the first dance will be a quadrille, and we've already gone over that. Then a waltz, a polka, and a mazurka. Do you remember the steps for the mazurka?"

The two men clasped hands and danced the correct steps while Bernie hummed a tune.

"Good boy. Now, at a debutante's ball, there may be what they call a German, which is a circle dance led by a leader and his partner. The leader will motion for a few couples to join in what they call a *tour de valse* around the ballroom. When it's finished, he'll motion for two more couples and so on until everyone has danced. The ball will end with *les bouquets*. For that, they bring a flower cart filled with favors. After each *tour de valse*, a couple picks a favor and offers it to a new partner. It continues until everyone has danced and everyone has a favor."

Bernie laughed at the perplexed look on Nolan's face and slapped him hard on the back. "You're right, lad, it's confusing, but I'll teach you. *And* give you some good tips. With all those people, it's going to get hot as hell in the ballroom. Take extra starched collars and exchange the sweaty ones for fresh in the bathroom."

The lesson continued on into the night, with Bernie demonstrating steps for more dances in the German. Finally he flopped onto the sofa.

"All right, lad, I'm ready for that drink."

43

CROSS AND HELEN HAD BEEN WAITING FOR THIS DAY FOR WEEKS. He'd received a call from Kent that morning, asking him to come down to McGlory's at 7:00 p.m. He knew that Kent was going to tell him the debt was paid after the Goelet job. His family was out of danger. He would never have to see Kent again. The relief was so strong he could almost taste it.

The last months had seemed like a nightmare from which Cross couldn't wake up. What he had been forced to do was reprehensible, but he'd had no choice. And the people he'd helped rob were so rich that they could replace the stolen goods within a week.

But his mind always returned to the image of the Cook's servant girl. Staring out the window of the carriage, unseeing, he chastised himself for being squeamish. This was the price that had to be paid for saving his family. Would he rather see Charlie or George murdered?

At Hester Street, the usual evening depravity was underway. A man lay in the gutter; a filthy stray dog licked eagerly at his face. Whores leaned out of doorways, hectoring passersby. Cross passed through the noise and chaos of McGlory's concert saloon, ignoring the tarts who pressed him to drink with them. He made his way down to the basement corridor. The parade of fake cripples and blind men was beginning to assemble. Without knocking, Cross went into the gang's room and found Kent, Brady, and Coogan seated around the table.

Kent raised his hand in welcome. "Please sit, Mr. Cross," he said, gesturing to the chair directly across from him.

Cross smiled and sat. On the way there, he'd decided he would control the conversation.

"I suppose my debt, including the interest payments, has finally been satisfied?" he said, using a formal, stentorian voice to show Kent that he meant business.

"Except for a thousand or two, which I forgave out of appreciation for your fine efforts."

"Then if you and I are finished with our business, I'll bid you farewell, Mr. Kent," Cross said, beginning to rise from his seat. "I can't honestly say I enjoyed it, but it's been an experience. I think it's best we never meet again."

"Finished? It's just starting. Mr. Cross, we're going to make more money together. Lots more," Kent said, rising to his feet and pointing enthusiastically with his gold cane.

"Like hell we are."

"I'm afraid you've been under a misapprehension, Mr. Cross."

"What the hell do you mean?" The smiles on the faces of all three men horrified him.

"In the brief time you've worked for us, you've been a gold mine for our organization. We've never cleared so much revenue."

"I'm glad to have helped. But our business is finished."

"*You* don't understand. We've decided to let you into our organization on a permanent basis. We'll give you a 7 percent cut of the take. That's very generous. And it's a great deal of money. Far more than you'd make in a year as an architect."

The three men stood beaming, proud as hell to have bestowed such an honor on Cross.

"Damn you, I don't want to be part of your gang!" Cross cried.

"Organization, Mr. Cross," Kent said.

"He don't seem to be very appreciative of this offer, does he?" Coogan said.

"No, he doesn't," Brady said. "I don't think you really have a choice, Cross."

"You'd be more of a consultant, really. You'll be able to continue your architecture practice. A man as talented as you should be allowed to create. I wasn't joking about having you design a summer home for me," Kent said, smiling at Cross.

Cross felt his knees weaken beneath him. He took hold of the back of the chair. "You said once I repaid the debt, I was out," he whispered.

"I might have misled you. I'm sorry. But you're just too damn valuable to let go, Mr. Cross."

"You've got a real talent for this line of work," Coogan added.

"You'll make us all rich," Brady said.

"And I suppose I have no say in the matter."

"Of course you do. All those in favor of Mr. Cross joining our organization, raise your hands," Kent said. He, Coogan, and Brady raised their hands. "There you have it. Three to one—democracy in action."

Cross sat in the chair, eyes fixed on the floor.

"You see, Mr. Cross, in our world, once you're in, you can never leave. No retirement. That's the rule. And if you try to break it, you must be punished—severely." Kent's tone was that a pastor might use with a wayward congregant.

"You mean my family."

Brady walked up to him and stooped, bringing his eyes level with Cross's. "Every Tuesday," he said, "Helen goes to Arnold Constable. Anything can happen to her on the way. She gets in the way of a runaway carriage. Maybe she falls under a horse car and gets trampled to death." He pulled out a length of piano wire and wrapped it around his hand, critically examining its length.

"Julia and Charlie go back to school in a few weeks," said Coogan.

"And then there's George. Poor hapless boy," Brady said. At his words, Coogan burst out laughing. "But we don't have to worry about George. Someone else will wind up killing him."

Cross jerked his head toward Coogan but said nothing. He had a vague idea of what he was referring to but didn't want to think about it. Things were going badly enough. It was Kent who broke the silence.

"I'm glad we've come to an understanding. Let's drink to our new partner, gentlemen."

44

NOLAN STOOD AT THE BACK OF THE ROOM WITH HIS BEST FRIEND, Pickle Nose Johnson, an expert forger. Their gang, the East Side Cowboys, rarely held official meetings. The leader, Spike Milligan, detested all authority. He ran the gang in a very autocratic manner and preferred to meet members individually. Nolan thought it must be a serious matter for them to gather like this in the rear of the gang's saloon, the Bucket of Blood.

As one of the finest pickpockets in New York City, Nolan was highly regarded by the gang. Milligan liked him because he was respectful and a good, consistent earner. He never tried to cheat the gang out of its share either. In return, the gang provided protection from other gangs that might intrude on Nolan's territory, the Ladies' Mile. Fourteenth to Twenty-Third Streets offered a rich hunting ground, with many silk purses just waiting to be picked. Christmastime was the most lucrative season, but the area was a temptation year-round.

The Cowboys, who numbered around sixty, sat knocking back shots of Irish whiskey and draining schooners of beer. Lunch had been set out; they devoured sandwiches of rye bread, liverwurst, and salami slathered with brown mustard. Times were good for gangs in New York. The docks were full of good things to steal, and out-of-town hicks were flocking to town, ready to be robbed. The Cowboys couldn't have been happier.

Milligan walked to the front of the room, and the noise instantly ceased. "Boys, somethin's been bothering the hell outta me," he announced. Milligan was a barrel-chested man with flaming red hair and a long pointy nose. He squinted accusingly at his men. "I don't like it when another gang gets rich and we don't. It jest ain't fair."

The men in the room murmured in agreement.

"There've been some real big heists in the last couple of months. You all heard about the Cook and Greene houses gettin' knocked off." Milligan paused for dramatic effect, then growled contemptuously, "I know it was Kent's Gents that did those jobs. I just heard that they stole some valuable horses from some rich bastards too. Those three jobs took in what we clear in a whole goddamn year!" He slammed his big fist down onto the table, upsetting a schooner of beer.

The gang put down their drinks and sandwiches and started talking among themselves. Nolan stayed silent, his mind whirling. He knew that Milligan hated Gentleman Jim Kent. Milligan hated everyone who was better bred, better educated, and smarter than he. His hatred was also fueled by his unshakable belief that street crime was the province of the poverty-stricken underclass, not college-educated swells who smoked Cuban cigars and ate at Delmonico's. It was this crossing of class lines that upset Milligan most.

"Now," Milligan shouted, silencing the crowd. "I found out that they have an inside man who set those jobs up. I don't know his name yet, but they call him the Engineer."

The gang all seemed to think this was less than sporting.

"We have to find this man and make him an offer to join up with us. Pay 'im more than that cheapskate Kent," Milligan said. "Every man has his price, and we'll learn his."

"What if he won't switch sides?" a man shouted.

Milligan smiled and shook his head. "Well, we can't allow the competition to have an unfair advantage, can we?"

45

CROSS KNEW WHAT AN ANIMAL FELT LIKE WHEN IT WAS CAUGHT IN a steel trap. No matter how hard he struggled, short of chewing off his own leg, he couldn't get free.

A week had passed since he'd been forcibly made a permanent member of Kent's Gents. Until he thought of a way out, he had to cooperate. That meant planning the next job.

When he'd returned home after his meeting with Kent, he'd found Helen waiting up to celebrate the end of their indenture. She had baked a Lady Baltimore cake, his favorite dessert. When he told her it wasn't over, Helen had almost fallen to her knees, as if she were physically crushed by the news. Nothing had changed, she said; her children and husband were still in danger. There was no end in sight.

But instead of weeping, she'd sat in an armchair and stared out into space, almost as if she were in a trance. Cross had stared at her, unsure what to think.

After a few minutes, she'd stood and said in a calm, determined voice, "The Whitmans will be away in Long Branch for two weeks, starting on Tuesday."

◈ ◈ ◈

If he could ignore his unwanted partnership with Kent, times couldn't have been better for Cross. He'd been getting so much new work that he'd had to hire three more draftsmen. He was at the height of his career, yet his predicament canceled out any happiness he might have felt.

One of his new commissions was a theater on Longacre Square. It was a prestigious job, but since he'd never designed a theater, Cross began doing research, attending numerous shows. Instead of sitting and enjoying the performances, he paid close attention to the seating, the interior detailing, the staging logistics, bathrooms, and circulation. At the end of a show, he waited, watching how the patrons exited. He noted sight lines, measured how wide the seats were and how much leg room there was. Every night for a week, he'd attended the theater by himself. He was glad for the immersive nature of the experience. It took his mind off his problems.

Tonight, he was walking home from a revival of *The Telephone Girl* at the Casino Theater on the corner of Broadway and Thirty-Ninth Street. The building, designed by his friend Francis Kimball, was only four years old and offered the city's most up-to-date theater design. Kimball had given him a set of drawings to study and had asked the owner to let Cross walk around backstage. It was a beautiful building, done in a Moorish style that gave it exotic appeal. The theater, which sat thirteen hundred, had a six-story, domed tower anchoring the corner. Still, its most novel feature was a roof garden, the first in the city. The garden served as a separate space, had seating to serve alcohol and food, and offered a small stage for entertainment. It was lit by thousands of electric lights and packed every night. Cross hoped he could design something half as good.

It was late September. The nights were finally getting cooler. Cross took his time, smoking and enjoying the evening. In his mind, he worked out the basic shape of his theater on its midblock site. He wanted a dramatic entry with a long canopy to protect theatergoers from the weather as they waited for their carriages. *It should be bigger than the one at the Academy of Music*, he thought.

"Excuse me, sir. Can I get a light?"

A rough man in an ill-fitting green suit stood next to Cross. Jolted out of his reverie, Cross said, "Certainly," and pulled out a box of matches. Smiling, he lit the man's cigar.

"Beautiful night, isn't it?" said the man.

Cross was anxious to be on his way but didn't want to be rude. With a sigh, he answered. "Yes, but fall will be here soon. I prefer the cooler weather."

"Me too. It's been hotter than a nigger's ass this summer, hasn't it?"

"Yes, there were some hot days." Cross nodded good-bye and started to walk on.

"Hey, don't I know you?"

"No, I don't think we've ever met," said Cross over his shoulder.

"Sure, sure, you work for Gentleman Jim Kent, don't you?"

Cross stopped dead in his tracks and turned to look at the man. He knew every face in Kent's gang, but he had never seen this man before.

A sense of panic enveloped Cross. How did this piece of scum know about him? It was no good to pretend ignorance. "How the hell did you know that?" he snarled.

"Oh, I hear things."

"Like what?"

"Like you're called the Engineer."

Cross was about to correct the man but stopped. "What else have you heard?"

"That you're a smart fellow. An expert planner who knows where the big money is."

Cross smiled. "I'm afraid you're mistaken, my good man."

"Nope, that's who you are."

"What do you want of me?" Cross blurted. He was tired of beating around the bush. "Out with it, damn it."

"You're shortchanging yourself, working for Kent. You could do better. I know a way you could make a lot more money. And work for people you can trust—not a murdering shit like Kent."

The puzzle pieces of this mysterious encounter were slowly fitting into place. Cross was being recruited by a rival gang. Which meant someone else knew what he'd been doing.

Oddly, in a roundabout way, he was flattered by the offer. He remembered working in the office of H. H. Richardson when an architect from Stephen Hatch's office approaching him, asking him to jump ship. Hatch had done many prominent buildings in the city, including Bryant's Opera House. Cross, then a young man not long out of the École des Beaux-Arts, had been flattered to be asked to join his firm. The promises of more pay and design responsibility were tempting, and he gave the proposition a great deal of consideration. But in the end, he stayed with Richardson, wanting to learn from a master.

This was different. Richardson wouldn't have had him murdered for leaving. There could be only one response.

"Thank whoever sent you for the offer, but I'm staying put," he said.

"Just think about it," the man urged. "And take this. Little token of our esteem."

The man placed a very expensive pearl-and-gold tie stud in his hand. Cross didn't protest; he didn't want to insult the man and risk a beating—or worse. *Who had the stud once belonged to?* he wondered. Maybe someone he knew.

"Thank you. But—"

"Just think about it," the man repeated. "We'll talk again."

46

━━━━━◆◆◆━━━━━

J ESUS CHRIST, GEORGIE! YOU DID IT! WE'RE IN THE CLEAR!"
On the edge of the green felt of the faro table lay nine thousand dollars in greenbacks. Kitty had lost control, hugging and kissing George ecstatically. She grabbed a handful of bills, closed her eyes, and rubbed them against her high, rouged cheekbone. No perfume had a sweeter smell. The crowd around the table was cheering the way people had cheered when George hit the winning home run at the Polo Grounds.

George was floating somewhere in the stratosphere. He'd chased this feeling for so long. Kitty began gathering the stacks of bills and placing them in the envelope the house attendant handed her. With the money tucked safely inside his frock coat pocket, George took Kitty by the arm, bowed to the adoring crowd, and walked out of Benfield's.

On Forty-Sixth Street, Kitty gave him a long, passionate kiss, not giving a damn what the passersby thought. George patted the bulge on his left side, smiling down at her.

"I knew I'd hit a lucky streak. Mathematics all comes down to probabilities," he said.

"We're going straight to Mallory to pay him off," Kitty said, looking George square in the eye.

"We have more than enough," George said. "We should go get you a special gift first and celebrate at Sherry's."

"After."

"Then let's get a carriage," George shouted with glee, grabbing her arm. Across the street, a conveyance was discharging a passenger. But as they got closer, someone else commandeered it. George looked up and down Forty-Sixth Street but saw no other carriages.

"We'll go down to Forty-Second and get one."

As they walked down Sixth Avenue, they passed a large toy store with huge, plate-glass windows. George stopped in his tracks. Without saying a word, he tugged Kitty's arm, drawing her inside.

"Why are we here?" she asked, casting him a puzzled look.

"I want to share my good luck with the children at school," he said, already perusing the shelves. "The girls would love china dolls, and the boys like cast-iron toys—like that locomotive there."

Overhearing his wish, the proprietor appeared with a hearty, "May I help you, sir?"

Though she was annoyed by the detour, Kitty decided not to make a fuss. Playing the good sport, she inspected the wide variety of dolls, ready to make some selections and get the hell out. George examined the trains and horses. As he mulled his choices, his eye stopped on a blue bicycle leaning against the wall of the shop. It was one of the new safety bikes and had equally sized wheels instead of the huge front wheel that made older models almost impossible to ride. The new design had spawned a bicycling craze all over America. It was the best gift one could get.

"How much is that bicycle?" he asked.

"Twenty-five dollars, sir, and they come in a range of colors," the proprietor said, rubbing his delicate white hands together.

George stared at the bicycle and then grinned. "I want fifteen of them," he said.

"George! No!"

The proprietor frowned at Kitty's protest but beamed a smile at George. "Certainly, sir. We only have four in stock here, but there are many more in our warehouse on Murray Street."

"Get me a variety of colors. The address is 112 East Broadway," George said, counting out the money.

"They'll be there tomorrow," said the very happy shop owner.

"For God's sake, George, you can't give everyone a bicycle," Kitty said. "It's too extravagant. What will Dr. Caldwell say?"

"Dr. Caldwell can go straight to hell. His family was rich, and he never wanted for anything," George said bitterly.

The proprietor pressed the receipt into George's hand before Kitty could change his mind.

"That's enough, then," she said firmly. "Don't buy anything else."

Irritated, George thrust the envelope toward Kitty. "You hold the money then."

On the street, though, Kitty saw the happiness radiating from George. He was smiling from ear to ear. She wasn't going to chastise him again, she resolved. After all, it was only a tiny portion of the money.

Instead of hailing a carriage, they walked down Sixth Avenue. Catching hold of his arm, Kitty matched George's brisk pace along the sidewalk. Occasionally, she looked up at his handsome face. He smiled at her but said nothing. It was a beautiful summer afternoon, with a warm breeze sweeping the avenue. Kitty felt so happy, as if her heart might burst.

As they neared the corner of Thirty-Eighth Street and Sixth Avenue, George came to a halt. He turned west and walked a few doors to a wide brownstone with forest-green canvas awnings on every window. Kitty knew this address. She took a step back, heart sinking in her breast.

"Please give me my money," George said gently.

Kitty looked at him incredulously.

"I need my money," he repeated.

"I'm not going to give it to you," she said, shaking her head.

George's eyes narrowed. "You don't understand."

"Don't understand what?" Kitty asked, looking not at him but at a porter across the street, sweeping off a stoop in slow, steady strokes.

"My good luck is bound to go on. I have to take advantage of it.

It's like a strong wind behind a ship. You don't fold your sails—you keep going as far as you can, because you never know when the wind might die."

"That's nonsense, George. We're taking the money to Mallory," Kitty said, looking unflinchingly into George's eyes. "It's taken us too long to get this. You can't blow it now."

"Trust me," George said soothingly, extending his hand. "I can double this."

"No, goddamn it."

George's face grew dark, and he swallowed hard. He moved closer.

"Please, George, for God's sake, don't do this," Kitty pleaded, tears welling in her eyes. "Let's get away from here. We'll have a wonderful dinner after we see Mallory, maybe go to a show."

"Now," he commanded loudly.

"There's no way in hell I'm going to let you do this," she said defiantly, holding the purse behind her back.

George's blue eyes seemed full of fire as he lunged at her. Kitty backed away, but he caught her by the arm, which she tried with all her might to keep locked behind her back. George jerked her around, putting her back to him.

"No, no, don't do this," she yelled. Passersby noticed the commotion but did nothing to intervene. Kitty was sobbing, tears running down her cheeks. "Don't you know you're going to lose?" she cried.

This enraged George. He easily twisted her arm until the purse fell to the sidewalk. Picking it up, he removed the envelope and handed the purse back, smiling amiably.

"There's nothing to worry about, my love. You'll see." George began to climb the high stoop of the brownstone, the fire still burning in his blue eyes. "Come along."

Kitty sprang forward, grabbing his pant leg. She fell onto the stoop and sat on the bottom step, holding George's leg in a bear hug. He tried to wriggle free, but she clung tightly to him. Furious, he took hold of her hand, roughly yanked it away, and resumed his ascent. Kitty collapsed into hysterics, lying flat on the step, bawling her eyes out. This was George's sickness, taking over his mind and soul. He was powerless to prevent it. And so was she.

A group of people paused to ask if they could help, but Kitty waved them away. She lay there for fifteen minutes, then sat up and wiped the tears that had streamed down her face like rivers, destroying her powder and rouge. Still sobbing, she stood and looked up at the glass-and-wood doors of the brownstone. She didn't want to be there when George came out.

Slowly, Kitty walked away.

47

I T'S INTERESTING. YOU NEVER MENTIONED THAT YOU DESIGNED Cook's house...and the Fidelity National Bank."

Cross sat across from his brother at a table at the Park Restaurant on East Sixty-First Street. He and Robert had gotten into the habit of lunching together once a week. They also went to ball games and the theater and sometimes took walks together in Central Park. For the first time in their lives, they lived near each other, and they were developing a deeper personal connection, even discussing their feelings about their parents, especially their father, and growing up in society. Cross felt a sense of relief and comfort when he confided in his brother about the past. He knew Robert felt the same way.

He wasn't shocked by Robert's question. He'd been expecting it. He was only surprised that it took so long in coming.

"I thought I told you I'd designed Cook's place."

"No, I would've remembered that."

"Mmm, thought I did. I don't think I mentioned the bank."

"Quite a coincidence."

Cross held his hands above his head and widened his eyes. "I confess! I robbed them both," he wailed. He stuck out his hands, as if to receive handcuffs.

Robert roared with laughter. Around the restaurant, curious patrons looked up from their meals.

"I've designed lots of buildings in the city over the years," Cross added. "So many that I sometimes forget about them."

"There've been other big robberies of mansions."

"Not my clients."

"No, but the places were cleaned out in the same manner, probably by the same gang."

"What are the Pinkertons going to do?"

"We've set up a network of informants that covers Fifth Avenue and the Upper East Side. They'll keep watch for us at night. And after so many massive robberies, the rich are running scared. They've hired watchmen to patrol their properties, whether they're at home or away."

"And the banks?"

"We met with the New York City Commercial Bankers' Association to convince the cheap bastards to hire guards. I think most of them will. But we have people keeping an eye on some of the bigger ones nonetheless."

Cross took a sip of his coffee and a bite of apple pie.

"You've got a real crime wave on your hands," he observed. "No more help from your informant?"

As Robert paused, Cross watched carefully, trying to read his brother's reaction. If only he knew the man's name! The identity of the informant tormented Cross.

"Not a peep. And that's not the whole of it. Some prize racehorses have been stolen too. That's upset the hell out of the parvenus—more than the robberies even. You can rob his mansion, kidnap his wife and children, but you never steal a man's horse." Robert gave a barking laugh. "It isn't sporting."

"That's incredible. Any news about the horses?"

"They're probably somewhere in Europe. Their identities would never be discovered over there. We'll never find them."

Cross finished his dessert, called for the check, and lit a cigarette.

"As if the crime wave wasn't enough, we have to coordinate gold bullion shipments for Kidder, Peabody & Co., the big Wall Street investment company."

"They handle gold?"

"They act as brokers on gold exports out of the country. To countries like Spain or Italy. Say, how's George getting along? I never see him. Whenever I ask him out, he's busy." Robert sounded disappointed.

Cross's family had truly become the center of his brother's life, Cross thought. To his dismay, Helen had even been playing match-maker for his brother, introducing him to an assortment of wealthy widows and young heiresses. Robert played along good-naturedly, pla-cating his sister-in-law by socializing. He'd even been to a tea at their house that Aunt Caroline attended. To Cross's surprise, the fact that Robert was a Pinkerton didn't bother her. She seemed to be very proud of him and steered several eligible ladies his way herself.

"I never see him either. George lives his own life. It upsets Helen."

"Oh, he just wants to be on his own. You should be proud. He'll be a brilliant professor."

"Yes. I should be," Cross said, voice barely audible. He still hadn't been able to force himself to find out whether George was gambling again. He was a coward. Whatever the truth, he didn't want to face it. A father wants to believe he can trust his son.

"And Charlie. What a special kid! You should be proud of him too."

✦ ✦ ✦

Over the summer, Charlie had become an expert at stripping naked at a run and jumping off the pier into the East River. The most exciting part was leaping off the edge and being suspended in midair—it felt like he was flying—before crashing into the cold water of the river. On a hot day, it was as refreshing as a drink of cold beer, which he greatly enjoyed thanks to Eddie's tutelage.

It was a warm September day, one of the few Charlie had left before school resumed. He was determined to fill every remaining minute with fun. The rotting pier off Cherry Street was filled with skinny naked boys, either diving or pushing one another into the river. Charlie sprinted along beside Eddie, and together they flew off the pier and hit the water, just missing a floating hog carcass. The East River sported a continuous parade of dead creatures through its currents, including the occasional human body. The water was filthy with oil slicks, dead rats, floating garbage, and human and horse feces, but the cold water felt so good that one ignored such minor distractions.

"How about some rat wrangling today?" Eddie asked, his head bobbing up and down in the dark waters. "We can get thirteen cents a head."

"We should try that warehouse on Thirty-Second. You can hear them squirming around from the sidewalk," Charlie said, trying to float on his back. A partially decomposed horse drifted by a few feet away.

"Then let's get going." They swam back to the pier and hoisted themselves up. Some boys were lying in the sun on the pier; others were soaping themselves down and then diving in to rinse off in the filthy water. This was the only time they got anything close to a bath.

After dressing, the boys stopped off at Eddie's to get the mailbag and club. It was a good haul, about eighty rats, exceptionally energetic and fast. The bag was heavy to pull, and Charlie had to continually beat the vermin about the head to prevent them from escaping. Despite his best efforts, three squeezed out, causing a woman on West Twenty-Ninth Street to scream.

"I hope one bites ya on yer tit," Eddie yelled after her.

At the rat pit, Eddie haggled with Nardello over the price, calling him a dirty wop until he relented and agreed to thirteen cents.

"I got a tip for ya," said Nardello as they readied themselves to leave. "We got a new dog named Mustard. A ten-to-one shot, but I seen 'em. He's a killer—can do fifty in eight minutes. You got time to lay down a bet. The action starts in five minutes."

Eddie and Charlie looked at each other and smiled, doing the math in their heads. They went in through the back door to the amphitheater, which was filled to capacity. After Eddie placed two bets, they found seats in the second row from the bottom. The crowd was noisy and happy, impatient for the games to begin. Mustard was tugging hard on his leash, almost yanking his handler's shoulder out of its socket. His coloring looked like any fox terrier's: brown and black, with no sign of the yellowish color indicated by his name.

The chute opened, and the rats came flying into the arena in their usual frenzy. The crowd roared with delight as Mustard went to work, tearing into the rats with glee. It almost seemed as if he were smiling. With astonishing speed, he killed rat after rat, flinging the dirty gray carcasses through the air onto the dirt floor of the arena. At seven minutes in, he'd finished off an astounding forty-eight rats. He'd have gotten more than fifty kills if he hadn't run out of victims. Most people threw down their betting chits in disgust, defeated by the long odds.

Ecstatic, Charlie was hugging Eddie when he looked to his right. At the end of the row, he saw his sister, Julia. At that exact moment, Julia saw him. Looks of utter bewilderment gave way, slowly, to smiles. They both burst out laughing.

An instant later, Charlie ran up to Julia and hugged her.

48

"WHEN ROME WAS JUST A SWAMP, CHILDREN, THE ANCIENT Egyptians were beginning their greatest period. They built the mightiest and richest empire in the world, the New Kingdom, along the great Nile River."

"Is that how they got this diamond?" Henry Kent asked.

The Kent family stood in front of the glass case housing the Pharaoh Blue Diamond, a huge gem with a mysterious blue-green glow. On loan to the Manhattan Institute of Science and Technology from the Alexandria Museum of Antiquities, thousands of New Yorkers had stood in lines that summer to see it. But because Kent was a member of the board of trustees, he and his family didn't have to wait in line.

"What a marvelous color," said Millicent with awe. "It could hypnotize you."

"It's so big," gushed Bill Kent.

"Maybe the biggest in the whole world," Kent said, affectionately mussing his son's hair.

◆ ◆ ◆

Cross looked up into the night sky. Thick storm clouds were gathering; he heard thunder rumbling in the distance. Normally, a downpour would be just the thing to cool off after an unusually hot autumn day. But later, at 2:00 a.m., on the roof of the Manhattan Institute of Science and Technology, it wouldn't be welcome at all.

A week earlier, Kent had summoned Cross to a meeting and given him the plans for the building. As a trustee, Kent had been given a set of construction drawings when the Institute was built five years before. It was the first time since they had started working together that Kent had actually set up a job, and to his bemusement, Cross realized that instead of being relieved, he was miffed.

By setting up a job himself, Cross could foresee the dozens of ways the theft might foul up and get him arrested. Before a robbery, along with studying the drawings, Cross would prepare himself by standing near the building and just looking at it for at least an hour. Using his imagination, Cross transported himself inside and conducted the robbery step-by-step, then asked himself what could possibly go wrong at each step. Would a lantern be seen from across the street? He studied the entry point and envisioned the escape route. Was there enough cover at the exit, or could the neighbors see them leaving the building? Right off, he could see a few negatives about tonight's project—like what if someone had insomnia in the ten-story apartment building behind them, looked out their window, and saw men on the roof at two in the morning?

But with Kent running the show, Cross had no control over how the job was run. And there was another thing that bothered him. He *wanted* to plan the jobs. It gave him a sense of satisfaction and enjoyment—and Kent had taken that pleasure away.

For all his acumen, though, Kent couldn't read the drawings. He relied on Cross to figure out a way of getting the coveted prize: the Pharaoh Blue Diamond. When Kent told him about the job, Cross thought he'd gone mad. Stealing such a famous gem? It was crazy. But trying to talk Kent out of it was useless; he had no choice but to cooperate.

"Always steal in a way that's admired, Mr. Cross," Kent had told him sanguinely.

Because of the enormous value of the diamond and its provenance in another country, armed guards sat in a carriage directly opposite the Institute twenty-four hours a day. The rear of the building, on

Forty-Sixth Street, was watched as well. Such a guard was easy to get around, though. The institute was a hundred-foot-wide, four-story, marble structure that sat midblock, flanked by buildings of about the same height. The gang would enter a building two doors down, go up to its roof, and cross over to the institute.

Kent, Brady, Cross, Culver, and another gang member named Lacey were standing on the flat tar roof. Next to them was a fifty-foot-long pitched skylight. Kent, not Cross, had decided this would be the easiest entry point, though not the safest. The skylight was twenty feet above the gallery floor.

Carefully, Cross opened one of the skylight's pivoting glass panels. He fastened the hooked end of a rope ladder to the edge of the opening and lowered it to the floor below. Based on the drawings, Cross knew exactly how long the ladder had to be.

Lacey, a lithe bantamweight, climbed down with the agility of a circus acrobat. On the gallery floor, he steadied the ladder for the others to descend. Cross made his way down slowly, causing Brady to curse him viciously. The ladder swayed back and forth, and Cross had to hold on for dear life. The others followed with little difficulty, which embarrassed him.

The institute was a science and technology museum. Tall glass cases containing all manner of scientific and archaeological displays lined the walls. Down the center of the gallery stood long display tables topped with flat glass.

Lighting a match, Kent looked at his pocket watch. "Right on schedule, gentlemen. We need to be on the third floor," he said, nodding at Cross, who knew the layout by memory and led the way.

In pitch darkness, they waited in an alcove off the hallway. Down the hall came a flickering light, moving slowly toward them. The men backed into the alcove as a rotund night watchman of about sixty passed by, carrying a newspaper. He shuffled to the end of the hallway and opened a door.

"Good old Collins. You could set your watch by his bowel move-ments," Kent whispered.

Culver walked to the door. From a canvas sack, he pulled out a flat iron bar and wedged it into both sides of the doorjamb. "He's not goin' anywhere for a while," he whispered, rejoining the group.

Cross led the men down to the second floor and through a corridor to the south side of the building. "We're going to drop down from here into the main heating duct that's hidden in the south wall of the gem room on the first floor," he said over his shoulder. "And then pop out the heating grille near the floor, and we're in."

From the drawings, he knew the building had a new kind of heat-ing system in place. Instead of sending the heat from a huge cast-iron furnace in the basement through the building by gravity via floor grat-ings, the furnace used sheet metal ductwork to transfer heat. These ducts were big enough for a man to fit through. When he got to a point down the corridor, Cross stopped in his tracks. He walked farther down the hall and then back again.

"I was positive the duct opening was here. This is where we were supposed to enter the main duct and go down," he said.

The men looked at him but said nothing. Sighing, Culver lit a small kerosene lantern and handed it over. A circular pattern of yellow-ish light washed the walls of the corridor.

"Where the hell did it go?" Cross asked no one in particular. He turned to Kent. "When did you get those drawings?"

"Before we started construction," Kent said, annoyed.

"But were any changes made?"

Kent thought for a moment. "Well, yes. The damn architect came in with a cost so far over budget that we had to make some cuts."

"Did you ever get a set of revised drawings?"

"That was the only set I got."

"Then those weren't the final drawings," snapped Cross. "They don't show what was actually built. I'll wager the heating system was changed back to a gravity system to save money—which means there's no goddamn ductwork."

"So what?" growled Brady.

"So what? That was how we were getting into the gem room—through the ducts," Cross said.

His revelation was met by silence. All of them knew they were stuck, and Cross knew that they expected him to think up a solution, even though this wasn't his fault.

Running his hand through his hair, he leaned back against the white plaster wall. Minutes passed like hours as he racked his brain for an answer. As he paced back and forth, he inadvertently swung the lantern up, shining the light onto the ceiling.

"Come on. We're going to the first floor," he announced.

The institute had a large interior room on the first floor used exclusively for special exhibits. It was there the diamond was kept. Trying to breach its double bronze-fronted doors would have been useless; they were as strong as the doors to a bank. Blowing them with nitro would bring the guards in from the street.

Cross led them into a room to the left of the exhibit hall. He lifted the lantern toward the ceiling. "See that truss?"

Above them was a five-foot-deep iron truss that spanned the entire width of the building. It was one of six supporting the load of the second floor, like a very wide ladder laid on its side, with diagonals connecting the rails. Its ironwork was exquisitely crafted and had beautiful ornamentation on every segment. Because this was a museum devoted to science and technology, the architect had deliberately exposed the trusses to show the engineering structure.

"We're going to get up there, walk along the bottom edge, break through where the truss intersects the wall, and get inside the gem room. There's only a thin infill around the truss penetration there." Cross spoke like a general barking out orders for battle. He would not brook any dissent. "Mr. Lacey, there has to be a ladder in the basement. Mr. Culver, we'll need that ax and length of rope you brought along."

The men did as exactly as they were told.

A ladder was placed against the wall, and Cross climbed up, then carefully inched along the edge of the truss, holding on to the struts. Where the truss intersected the wall, he chopped a small hole in the plaster infill, inserted the saw, and began to cut a hole the height of the truss. Plaster dust showered down. Having cut a rectangular shape barely wide enough for a man to fit through, he pulled it out and let it fall to the floor.

"All right, follow me," he commanded.

One by one, the four men climbed the ladder onto the truss. Because the bottom edge was only six inches wide and it was almost fifteen feet down to the marble floor, they crept along cautiously to the opening Cross had cut.

Somehow, Cross was experiencing no fear at all, only that wonderful sense of exhilaration he got while thieving. He was a circus acrobat on a high wire, no net beneath him. His confidence seemed to propel him along like a steam engine.

They were in the gem room. Cross took the lantern from Culver, lowering it toward the floor. Below them was the Pharaoh Diamond, enclosed in a small glass box on a tall, stone pedestal in the center of the exhibition room. The multifaceted gem caught the light of the lantern, throwing off a brilliant iridescence. The men turned to one another, smiling and nodding in appreciation.

"She's a beauty," whispered Culver. "A real beauty."

"The glass case is fastened to the top of the pedestal. We'll have to unscrew it," Kent said, eyes fixed on his prize.

Without being told, Lacey tied a length of thick ship's rope to one of the struts of the truss. With a screwdriver in his pocket, he began to shimmy down toward the floor. *He must have been handpicked for this assignment*, Cross thought. He was nimble and quick, unlike the generally stout, heavyset members of the gang.

Lacey was almost to the end of the rope, which dangled about two feet above the floor. Cross's heart leaped into his throat.

"Stop," he yelled. "Don't go any farther."

"What the hell is your problem?" Brady said, grabbing him roughly by the shoulder and almost making him lose his balance.

Cross crouched on the bottom of the truss and lowered the lantern as far as he could, staring at the floor. "Something's wrong," he said, swinging the lantern back and forth. "Don't drop down yet."

An annoyed Lacey stayed where he was, about three feet from the end of the rope.

"The floor doesn't look right," Cross murmured.

"What the hell do you mean?" Kent asked.

"A marble floor wouldn't reflect light like that. Look: it's almost as if it's wet."

And indeed, the men saw an odd reflective sheen coming off the floor, which had a kind of rippled texture. Cross swung the lantern, trying to throw more light.

"There," he said, pointing. Beneath the spot where he had cut through the wall, he could see tiny fragments of plaster bobbing gently up and down.

"It's covered with water. Why the hell did they do that?" Brady hissed.

Lacey looked down and laughed derisively. "Yeah, it's water, but it's barely an inch deep. It ain't like I'm gonna drown." He resumed his descent.

Above, Cross walked the length of the truss to the opposite wall, lowering the lantern as much as he could. He stopped abruptly and turned back toward the gang.

"Lacey, if you don't want to die, get back up here. Now!"

49

S EE THAT?"
The men, including Lacey, had inched across the truss until they were next to Cross. He pointed down to the bottom of the wall. In the dim light thrown by the lantern, they saw a thick wire protruding from the wall and extending about a foot onto the marble floor.

"What the hell is that?" Kent demanded. Cross knew he was greatly upset by the delay.

"It's an electric wire," Cross said.

"So?"

Electricity was a fairly new phenomenon. It had been less than a decade since Edison's invention of the lightbulb. New York was rapidly replacing gaslight with electric, stringing miles of wire along the streets. As an architect, Cross knew about the other properties of this new medium.

"When you insert a live electrical wire into water," he explained, speaking slowly, as if they were five-year-olds, "and step into that water, you will be electrocuted."

The four gang members stared down at the floor in astonishment.

"It's to discourage people like us from stealing the diamond."

"Shit" was the only reply.

"My guess is that they flood the floor with a half inch of water at closing time and then unplug a hole to drain it out in the morning."

Lacey looked at Cross with new appreciation and clung more tightly to the struts of the truss.

"They say Edison's come up with a new way to execute people

using electric current. Supposed to be more humane than hangin',"
said Culver.

"I'll take hangin' any day," Brady said.

The men looked at the diamond. They had come too far to give up.
Even more slowly, they edged back to the center of the room, directly
above the gem.

"Move the rope so it'll hang right over the pedestal," Kent ordered.

Everyone knew what he was going to say next.

"Down you go, Mr. Lacey. Stay off the floor, and you'll be just fine."

Staring down at the floor, Lacey swallowed hard.

"Don't worry. I'll include some hazard pay in your cut," Kent said,
patting his shoulder.

"Better tie a big knot at the end so his feet can rest on something,"
Cross said. He'd been lucky in his entry point. The truss he had chosen
to follow was close to the center of the room. Still, Lacey would have to
reach over a few feet to get the diamond. In the flickering light of the lantern, Cross could see rivulets of sweat traveling down Lacey's forehead.

The rope was ready. Lacey paused for a few seconds to build up his
nerve and then started down. They could all see how scared he was. He
looked straight ahead and stopped once to wipe sweat from his eyes.

When he got to the level of the pedestal, he was too far away to
reach over to the glass.

"How are you doing, Mr. Lacey?" Kent called.

"Just fine, sir." But even as the words left Lacey's lips, his sweaty
hands slipped on the rope. Down he went—but he grabbed and held
on at the last possible moment. The toe of his fashionable black shoe
stopped two inches above the surface of the water.

In unison, all four men watching above exhaled an audible sigh
of relief.

Lacey looked up at his companions, smiled wanly, and said nothing. He climbed back to the right height and began to sway his body
side to side, slowly gaining momentum. After four swings, he made it,

wrapping his legs around the pedestal. Using just his arms, he pulled himself up the rope until he could stand atop the stone column. The pedestal was about three feet square, with the six-inch square glass box sitting on its center. Lacey had plenty of room to stand.

Wrapping the rope securely across his chest, Lacey took out the screwdriver and went to work removing the glass case. The four screws at the corners came out easily. Cross was thrilled, his body bursting with excitement as he watched. *It's that feeling of absolute ecstasy Kent once described*, he thought, casting the criminal mastermind a sideways glance.

Tilting the glass box on its left edge, Lacey placed his hand beneath it to get the diamond, which sat on a small purple velvet cushion. Without hesitation, he grabbed it. At that instant, the handles on the bronze doors to the room made a slight rattling sound, as though someone was jiggling them. In the dead silence of the exhibition room, the noise had the effect of a pistol shot, and Lacey was so startled that he lost hold of the diamond. It dropped onto the pedestal top, bounced, and rolled toward the edge. Lacey fell to his knees and lunged for it as it dropped off the pedestal, snatching it in midair. But in doing so, he lost his balance and pitched to the side. The men above watched, wide-eyed with terror.

With lightning-quick reflexes, Lacey grabbed the rope with one hand, swinging to and fro like a zoo monkey. Then he placed the diamond in his jacket pocket, gasping for air as if someone had him by the throat. It took almost a minute for him to compose himself. Then he said, looking over at the doors, "I thought the watchman couldn't get out of the john."

"That wasn't him. The guards stationed outside probably came in and checked the doors," Kent said. "They've likely gone back to their posts."

"I sure as hell hope so," Lacey said and began to climb the rope. At the truss, Brady and Culver hoisted him up by the armpits. Lacey handed the diamond to Kent, who barely looked at it for fear of dropping it. Quickly, he stuck it in his pants pocket.

The men walked along the truss to the opening in the wall. On the way back up to the fourth-floor gallery, Culver checked the bathroom.

"He hasn't finished taking his shit," he said with a big smile.

This time, Cross scampered up the rope ladder like a squirrel. Culver, who had been steadying the ladder as they climbed, was last to ascend. About ten feet off the floor, he tried to shift the sack of tools he was carrying from one shoulder to the other and lost his grip. As he tried desperately to grab for the sack, his feet slipped off the rope rungs of the ladder.

In a sickening instant, Culver plummeted to the floor. Instead of falling straight down, he came off the ladder at an angle, crashing onto one of the display tables in the center of the gallery. At the sound, the men, who were waiting on the roof in the midst of a downpour, rushed back to the skylight window. Beneath them, they saw Culver writhing in pain on top of the smashed display table. Its legs had splayed out from the force of his body's impact, and glass was scattered everywhere.

Brady started down the ladder in an instant, cursing viciously under his breath. But when he had descended just halfway, the electric lights in the gallery snapped on.

"What the devil's going on here?" a voice shouted from the end of the gallery.

Brady froze in terror, seeing a bearded man in his midthirties walking toward him.

"Who the hell are you?" the man cried. He dashed to the foot of the rope ladder and looked up at Brady, then squinted at the other men poking their heads through the skylight.

"It's Dilts, one of the museum curators," whispered Kent.

Kent was too slow to pull away from the opening, and Dilts caught a glimpse of a familiar face. "Mr. Kent?"

Brady jumped the last six feet to the floor.

Dilts had turned his attention to Culver, who was moaning in pain. The destroyed table had displayed Stone Age tools, which were strewn about the floor. Brady picked up a long club carved from the bone of some prehistoric beast.

"Don't do it, Brady! Don't do it!" Cross screamed at the top of his lungs.

But Brady brought the weight of the club down on the skull of the curator with savage fury. As he beat the man about the head, Cross was reminded of a Neanderthal caveman, pummeling an animal. Finally, he stopped, satisfied his prey was dead. Throwing the club aside, he helped Culver to his feet and, with great difficulty, hauled him up the ladder. Lacey descended halfway to assist.

On the roof, Brady walked up to Cross. A mere inch of space separated their faces.

"There was no choice, swell," he said.

50

M<small>R.</small> W<small>HARTON, SO GOOD OF YOU TO COME TONIGHT.</small> M<small>AY</small> I present my daughter, Julia?"

Julia Cross stood to the right of her mother and Caroline Astor, greeting the guests at her coming-out ball in the Astors' ballroom at Thirty-Fourth Street and Fifth Avenue. Her father, George, and Granny stood immediately behind them.

In a Worth gown made of white satin, the plunging neckline embroidered with pearls interspersed with tiny diamonds, Julia was radiant. A magnificent pearl necklace graced her long, slender neck. Men's eyes widened in amazement when they saw her, and Aunt Caroline beamed with pride. Twenty eligible bachelors might well propose to her before the evening ended.

"You look lovely tonight, Miss Cross," Alfred Wharton gushed.

"Thank you, Mr. Wharton. We *must* talk about your dinosaurs tonight."

Wharton blushed, uttered something unintelligible, then moved on.

"Lieutenant Beekman, may I present my daughter, Julia?"

"Miss Cross, I got special leave to be here tonight." The handsome man in his dress uniform gave a low bow.

"I'm sorry I took you away from Geronimo and the Apaches."

"That's quite all right. He surrendered at the beginning of September."

"Well, then I'm sorry you didn't get the chance to shoot him."

Helen shot Julia a wicked look and smiled at Beekman, who bowed and moved on.

Stephen Van Cortlandt stepped up and bowed to Helen. Her face lit up at the sight of this exceptionally rich Knickerbocker.

"May I present my daughter, Julia?"

"Miss Cross, if you don't save a dance for me, *I'll* be cross," said Van Cortlandt, chuckling at his own joke.

"I didn't think it was possible. There's a woman here as beautiful as Helen Cross." Robert Cross smiled broadly, holding out his hand to Julia. He cut an impressive figure and was turning the heads of many women in the ballroom.

"And they say all Pinkertons are roughnecks," Aunt Caroline said. "You were born to wear evening dress, Robert."

"Remember, Aunt Caroline, I *am* part Livingston," Robert said, giving her a wink. "And don't you dare tell me, young lady, that there's no room on your dance card for me. If you do, I'll arrest you." He used a deep, authoritative voice that made Julia laugh.

"Maybe you can catch the thief of the Pharaoh Blue too," Aunt Caroline said with a laugh. "That's all people are talking about tonight. In the wake of the loss, I hear Egypt wants most desperately to declare war on the United States."

"Don't worry, Robert. No police work is required tonight, regardless of what Aunt Caroline says. We've chosen you to have the first dance," Helen said, giving Caroline an affectionate smile.

Robert flashed a smile at his brother too, acknowledging the great honor he'd been given.

"Good evening, Mrs. Cross."

Helen smiled at the very handsome, dashing young man in front of her and knitted her brow, trying to remember the gentleman's name.

"John Nolan!" Granny, who was standing a few feet behind, blurted out. She bulled her way between Aunt Caroline and Helen and greeted him heartily. When the others saw that the young man had Granny's seal of approval, smiles broke out all around—except for Julia. Her mouth hung open; her breathing was shallow. Seeing Nolan there—and seeing how good he looked in a white tie and cutaway coat—sent her into a mild state of shock.

"The Nolans, you know, are very close friends of the Roosevelts—and John is also a good friend of mine, I'm proud to say," Granny gushed. Caroline still had a confused look on her face. Granny spoke to her in a testy whisper. "Calm yourself, Caroline. I introduced Mr. Nolan to Julia."

Though she was still unable to recall putting his name on the invitation list, Helen extended her hand and said, "Mr. Nolan, may I present my daughter, Julia?"

"Miss Cross, I knew you were a beautiful woman, but tonight, in that gown, your beauty is increased a hundredfold," he said.

After a few seconds, the still-astonished Julia recovered herself enough to form words. "Mr. Nolan! How…good of you to come. I'm overjoyed to see you here tonight. I have a space for the fourth dance. May I?" she asked, taking up the little vellum card attached to her white-gloved wrist by a blue ribbon.

"With the greatest pleasure," Nolan said.

Julia, openly breaking the rule of filling in her dance card in the reception line, wrote down Nolan's name.

"And I'd like to introduce you to my father, Mr. John Cross, and my brother, George," she said.

Both came forward, smiled, and heartily shook the young man's hand.

As Nolan bowed, Julia saw Granny come forward and take him by the arm.

"That darling Wah Kee has sold me the most beautiful *yen tsiang*, made of the most exquisite ivory with gold fittings. Even the *ow* is pure gold! He tells me it's much easier to clean, but then I never have to clean anything. Wah Kee always does it for me. Such a gentleman."

"I'm pleased to hear it. When will you and Miss Cross be visiting my neck of the woods next?"

"Saturday morning. Julia must procure a few things for school.

With the fall term at Miss Spence's starting soon, I'll be coming down on my own."

"How wonderful. I hope you will do me the honor of letting me take you out for tea or lunch, Mrs. Rutherford."

"You can be sure of that, Mr. Nolan. Now, I want you to mingle with the guests and enjoy yourself tonight. I can see that you've already caught the eye of many young ladies," Granny said, giving him a gentle push toward the glittering assemblage before returning to the reception line with a smile.

"That Mr. Nolan is a fine-looking gentleman," Caroline whispered.

"Indeed. But then, he *is* one of us," added Granny.

Julia kept glancing about for Nolan as she received new guests. The Astors' huge ballroom could easily hold four hundred, and only about half that number had been invited, but it still made it difficult for her to see. Julia finally spotted him strolling along the perimeter of the space, admiring the paintings that hung cheek by jowl on the silk brocade walls and were stacked up to the molding that marked the base of the high, coved ceiling. As he walked, he flashed his magnetic smile at the ladies, old and young alike, who chattered among themselves about who this charming man might be.

To see him in this world was thrillingly anomalous. For the last three months, their shared universe had consisted of the Tenderloin and the Bowery, of gambling houses, opium dens, and ratting contests, of enticing depravity in all its many forms. Now there he was, amid the richest people in America, in the house of the leader of New York high society, and he didn't look a bit out of place. In fact, she thought him the handsomest fellow in the room.

The last of the guests was received, and dinner was announced. Per custom, John Cross escorted Aunt Caroline into the dining room first, followed by George and Julia, who sat at her father's left hand. Helen was the last to enter, on the arm of William Backhouse Astor II.

Caroline had spared no expense for her relative's coming-out dinner. The twelve courses were eaten on gold service at a black walnut table covered with white embroidered Irish lace over red velvet. Instead of placing high, obstructing ornaments down the length of the table, Caroline had selected a low epergne of orchids, which allowed easy conversation. Mrs. Astor's liveried servants brought out the food, à la russe, beginning with oysters on the half shell and soup à la reine accompanied by sherry.

Nolan escorted Olivia Scott-Jones, the young daughter of one of Helen's closest friends. They sat two-thirds of the way down the table from Julia. Throughout the meal, Julia kept looking over at the pair, who were talking and laughing with each other and the nearby guests. She wondered what Nolan was talking about that so engaged them. Their own conversations always centered on the sins of the Tenderloin. Was he talking to Olivia about that? The thought made her jealous—that was the world *they* shared.

As she peered down the table, Julia suddenly realized how easy it was to converse with Nolan on any topic—especially in contrast to a bore like Stephen Van Cortlandt. With her last year at Miss Spence's about to begin, it would be hard to get down to the Tenderloin as often, and this made her sad. She watched in fascination as Nolan correctly used every one of the ten pieces of silverware and five goblets at his place setting. Smoothly, he placed his finger on the rim of the champagne glass to signal to the servant that he wanted no more wine. *His manners*, Julia thought, *are impeccable.*

After a dessert of puddings, tutti-frutti ice cream, and fruit, with coffee and liqueurs on the side, the guests rose from their seats to enter the ballroom. The orchestra opened with a quadrille, and Robert led Julia in the first dance. Men in identical white tie and women in a virtual rainbow of beautiful gowns swirled about the ballroom. Julia barely paid attention to her second dance partner, Sir Geoffrey Maitland, so intent was she on watching Nolan waltz with Olivia Scott-Jones. She even stepped on Maitland's foot—and gave only the hastiest of apologies.

Nolan danced the polka and a gallop effortlessly with his next two partners. Finally it was time for the fifth dance on Julia's card.

"Mr. Nolan, I wouldn't have been more surprised if Grover Cleveland himself had attended my ball," Julia said, eyes sparkling.

Nolan laughed. Putting his white-gloved hand on the small of her back, he pulled her a shade closer.

"I knew you'd be shocked, Miss Cross, to see me out of my element."

"On the contrary, you don't seem to be out of your element at all."

"I always wanted to see what your world was like," Nolan said, looking up at the huge crystal chandelier that swung above the ballroom.

As they pranced along in a mazurka, Julia looked up into Nolan's dark blue eyes, and an odd feeling of bewilderment and exultant happiness surged through her. It was an unknown sensation, and it made her feel both confused and elated.

To her disappointment, the dance inevitably ended, and Nolan escorted her back to where Granny, her official chaperone for the evening, sat with several other dowagers in black lace gowns. After a brief rest, Julia danced with the next partner on her card, Alfred Wharton.

Normally, a gentleman could only dance with a woman to whom he'd been formally introduced or who he knew before the ball. Tonight, however, Granny had introduced Nolan to a score of young women. With his good looks and Granny's imprimatur, Nolan kept busy dancing until the German, for which he partnered with Lavinia Stewart to expertly dance the *tour de valse* around the ballroom's shiny parquet floor.

During a pause in the German, Julia sat next to Granny to rest. The heat generated by two hundred people in heavy gowns and wool evening wear made the ballroom feel like Equatorial Africa. Somehow, Julia noted, Nolan's collar stayed fresh and stiff. Staring across the ballroom at him, she decided to try something a bit untoward. In society ballrooms, men and women used a time-honored system to send covert messages without attracting the notice of a chaperone. A quick opening and folding of a woman's fan told a man she wasn't interested in him. Dropping her gloves signaled that she was in love. An experienced debutante from Miss Spence's had tutored Julia on the subject.

Eyes fixed on Nolan, she held her fan in front of her face with her right hand. Nolan, who had been watching her from across the ballroom, grasped her meaning instantly: she meant for him to follow her. Rising from her seat, Julia whispered to Granny that she needed to go to the ladies' room. Nolan met her in the drawing room off the central entry hall. Julia took hold of his hand but said nothing. Nolan smiled, bent down, and kissed her. At the touch of his lips, Julia was propelled into a magical world she could hardly bear to leave. She kept her lips pressed to his for almost half a minute, gently absorbing the smell and feel of him.

Nolan ran his hand through Julia's hair and looked into her eyes. "Your grandmother said you'd be coming down on Saturday."

"Just in time for the cockfights at Rocky's."

"We can't miss that," replied Nolan with a smile.

"But I need to ask you a favor."

"Anything."

"There's a gentleman here tonight named Van Cortlandt. I'm going to accidentally bump into him, and if you could relieve him of his wallet, I'd be most appreciative."

"You'll be my stall?" Nolan said.

"Exactly. And on Saturday, we bet the proceeds on General Sherman."

51

G ENTLEMEN, WHY DON'T WE TAKE OUR CIGARS AND BRANDY TO THE main hall?"

Pierre Lorillard V led the way out of the dining room. He was proud of the new house Bruce Price had designed for him in Tuxedo Park, New York, an up-and-coming luxury retreat in the Ramapo Mountains that his father, Lorillard IV, had just created. Cross, a weekend guest, told Lorillard how much he liked the house, but in honesty, he didn't like it at all. A hipped-roof house with an awkwardly placed conical tower, it was nowhere near as good as other cottages Price had designed. Those previous designs had simple, powerful geometries. This one was fussy and conventional, with unnecessary Adamesque decoration on the exterior. It was almost as if the young Lorillard and his wife had strong-armed Price into doing a particular type of design. In cases of a flop, Cross *never* blamed the architect.

Still, Tuxedo Park was a special place, thirteen thousand acres full of winding roads and picturesque landscaping. To great acclaim, Price, Lorillard's favorite architect, had also designed the clubhouse, stables, and many of the first cottages. A fence topped with barbed wire surrounded the development, ensuring that New York society had another exclusive summer watering hole at which they might escape the heat.

Price and Cross were good friends, and Lorillard had already thrown work Cross's way in the city. Moreover, Helen wanted to see Tuxedo Park, which had only opened in May. With all these factors weighing on him, Cross had accepted an invitation to visit. He knew or recognized a few other weekend guests, including the handsome Russian count he and Helen had seen in Newport a few weeks before.

And Cross liked Lorillard, whom he didn't find pompous or over-bearing in the way of so many scions to great fortunes. Lorillard had an endearing passion for horses, which he could discuss for hours. His family, which ran an immensely successful tobacco company, had per-haps the greatest racing stable in America. Their horses had even won the Belmont Stakes and the Epsom Derby in England.

"So where do you keep your fabulous horses, Pierre?" Cross asked.

"In New Jersey, in Rancocas," he said. "Not enough room here. But I may bring a few up."

The main hall connected directly to a veranda that stretched the width of the house's rear. The men drifted out onto it and gazed out at the setting sun.

"I think my father is prouder of Tuxedo than anything else," Lorillard said. "He carved this land out of virgin forest. It's a great feel-ing to create something that will live on after you. Architecture must be the same, eh?"

"That's true," Cross said thoughtfully. "You leave something behind for people to use."

Helen and the other wives came out onto the veranda. Although the French thought it a barbaric habit, the English and Americans split off male and female guests after dinner. The women had been chattering away in the reception room. Emily, Pierre's wife, approached Cross.

"I'm so glad you were able to bring your wife along this weekend, John. She's enchanting," Emily said. She wore a magnificent choker of diamonds and an emerald-green gown. "I think Helen is more beauti-ful than Jennie Jerome, Lord Randolph Churchill's wife."

"That's quite a compliment," Cross said, smiling at Helen.

The guests returned to the hall, where chairs had been set up for an informal piano recital. Cross found the performance quite enjoyable. The program consisted of popular music instead of the usual classical tripe. Refreshments and light food were served afterward, and the evening continued on until about 1:00 a.m., when Lorillard and his wife bade their company good night, signaling the evening was over.

The guest rooms weren't luxurious, but they were comfortable and each boasted the latest amenity in country houses: a private bathroom. The October nights were cooler, especially in the mountains, and the fireplaces were lit. In silence, Cross and Helen undressed and prepared for bed. But at about three in the morning, Cross lifted his head from his pillow to look over at Helen. She was wide-awake, staring at the pressed metal ceiling.

He touched her shoulder. She turned on her side to face him, smiled, and stroked his cheek. "Good luck, my dear," she whispered.

Cross grasped her hand and then slowly rose from the bed. He put on his robe and slippers, checked the time on his pocket watch, and made his way down the curving stair tower to the main hall. He unlocked the glass door to the veranda and waited.

About five minutes later, two figures appeared in the shadows. Cross opened the door to let them in. In walked Brady with a much shorter man.

"You know Chops Connolly, don't you, Cross?"

He nodded hello, and Chops grunted back.

"So, where is it?"

"In the main parlor," Cross whispered.

"Lead the way, Mr. Engineer," said Brady.

Last week, Bruce Price had shown Cross his drawings of all the Tuxedo houses, including Lorillard's. He'd told Price that the Kent and Van Buren designs were particular masterpieces, and in any profession, one needed to learn from a master, which delighted Price.

As he'd examined the drawings, Cross's eye had caught on the ingenious way Price had hidden Lorillard's safe in the wainscoting of the parlor rather than the usual place in the master bedroom. He quietly opened the door—and froze.

At the far end of the room, Count Aleksandrov was looking behind the paintings on the plaster walls. The men watched in silence as the Russian moved from one painting to another.

"Who the fuck are you?" Brady hissed.

The count whirled, eyes widening in shock. Then he recovered his nerve and stood erect. "I am Count Aleksandrov. I was looking for something to read," he said indignantly.

Brady smiled at Chops. "I didn't know they put books behind paintings, did you, Chops?"

"No. Far's I know, they used to put them on bookshelves."

"Mr. Cross," the count said in disbelief. "What are you doing here?"

"You two know each other, eh?" Brady said, amused. With unhurried strides, he walked up to the count and took the small leather satchel from his hand. Opening it, he found small tools and lengths of wire. "A very professional burglar's kit."

Clinging to his aristocratic bearing, the count looked straight ahead and said nothing. Cross felt almost embarrassed for him.

"I'm sorry to say that you've interfered with our plans tonight, *Count,*" Brady said.

"Ah. If you gentlemen will excuse me, I'll be getting back to my room." He began to walk away, but Brady grabbed his arm. Cross was afraid the count would start yelling and wake the house; after all, Aleksandrov could easily say he'd come downstairs and found them robbing the place. He was an aristocrat—those in New York society would believe anything he said. And how would Cross explain his presence? It would be awkward at best.

"If we could have *one* more moment of your time, Count," Brady said in a solicitous tone. In a lightning-quick movement that stunned Cross, the man looped a length of piano wire around the count's neck. He pulled the ends tight. The count's eyes bulged, his face turned blue, and a low gurgling sound came from his lips, then he slumped to the Persian carpet, his eyes staring emptily up at the wood-beamed ceiling.

"So where's the safe?" Brady asked nonchalantly, putting the piano wire back in his side pocket.

In a state of shock, Cross didn't immediately answer.

Angrily, Brady asked a second time. Without taking his eyes off the dead body, Cross pointed to the wainscoting on the right of the fireplace. "Push down on the top molding and slide the middle panel to the right," he said.

Was he going to faint? Cross felt his head spinning. This was the third man he'd seen murdered before his eyes, but that didn't make it any easier to stomach. He stumbled to the wall, putting out a hand to brace himself. Brady smirked, delighting at Cross's squeamishness.

Chops had his own bag of tools, including a doctor's stethoscope to listen to the movement of the lock's tumblers. He went to work on the safe and had it open in twenty minutes. They removed Emily Lorillard's extensive jewelry collection, which included her wedding gift, an antique gold necklace from the Spanish court of Philip II, and a large amount of cash.

Sniffing, Brady prodded the dead count with his boot.

"A great turn, the count here showing up. They'll think he stole the goods and lit out. All we have to do is make him disappear. To make sure, though, let's leave a little evidence behind."

He took the count's monogrammed cigarette case and dropped it on the rug.

"We'll need your help to get him to the fence, Mr. Engineer. He's too fuckin' big for me and Chops to carry."

52

D AMN, JULIA, YOU DON'T BET ON A BIRD IN A COCKFIGHT BECAUSE
you like the color of its feathers," moaned Charlie as they exited
the Red Rat, a gaming establishment on Ludlow Street.

Julia frowned at her brother. "It's not like it was your money lost,
little boy."

"I know," Charlie said proudly, looking over at Eddie. "My
bird won."

"Stop wasting your time teachin' her strategy, Charlie. A woman
thinks how she thinks, and ya can't do nothin' about it," Eddie said.

"Thank you, Mr. Expert on Women," Julia said, smirking.

Eddie rolled his eyes at Charlie and John Nolan, who laughed.

"And don't lecture me on betting, you little beast," Julia continued,
growing more incensed. "I'm far, far ahead of you in the ratting ring.
I've had six straight winners!"

Charlie bent his head in shame and said nothing. She was right:
he'd been on an unlucky streak. It could happen to the best of them.
That's what George had said. He'd gone with him and Eddie to the
cockfights and had also lost a lot, but it didn't stop him from gambling.
In fact, it seemed to make his brother gamble even more.

The group strolled leisurely along Ludlow, taking in the cacophony
and bustle of the streets. It was a hot, humid day for October, and the
air stank with the smell of rotted food.

Just ahead of them, a bouncer heaved a drunk into the gutter, cursing violently. They walked by as though nothing had happened.

"Where are you supposed to be this afternoon?" Julia asked.

"Science class at the Museum of Natural History. What about you?"

"The library with Jocelyn Van der Meer. Remember that, mind? Last time you got the story mixed up, and Mother was suspicious."

Charlie scowled at his sister and muttered something under his breath to Eddie.

"We have time before the dogfight. Why not pop into Hannigan's here for a sandwich?" suggested Nolan, gesturing to a small nearby restaurant. His hope of avoiding a sibling free-for-all was realized. Everyone agreed to his plan, filed into Hannigan's, and found a table.

While they waited for their food, Nolan looked surreptitiously at Julia. She was engaged in animated conversation with Charlie and Eddie about the upcoming fight and whether Mustard should be their bet. He smiled at her, and she returned the smile. Her happiness made him happy. So did her presence. Since running into Charlie at the ratting match, she'd wanted to do things with her brother—albeit occasionally. They did love to argue. But Nolan knew Julia loved the fact that Charlie had a secret life like hers.

What they were doing was forbidden, which made it fun and exciting. Julia and Charlie had been raised in a world of suffocating social rules, in which being different was the worst conceivable crime. She had explained all of this repeatedly to Nolan. All their lives, they'd been told what to do to conform: what to wear, what to eat, how to dance, and above all, with whom to associate. Now, the Cross siblings had dared to travel into a taboo world. If anyone found out about their journey, the consequences would be dire.

Is it a fair price to pay for the excitement and feeling of freedom? Nolan wondered.

Looking at Julia, he knew the answer. Every second was worth it.

53

CROSS DID HIS BEST THINKING WHEN HE WAS WALKING. EARLIER that afternoon, he'd looked at an empty lot on East Sixty-Fourth Street between Fifth and Madison Avenues. A new client had purchased it to build a house. Instead of being narrow and deep, it had a fifty-foot frontage, allowing a nice wide facade. Cross was pleased. It was a beautiful October day, and he'd decided to forgo a carriage and take the long walk back to the office.

But as he walked down Fifth Avenue past Central Park, Cross's mind shifted to the next robbery. This happened frequently, he'd found, when he was enjoying a musical at the theater or eating his breakfast. Suddenly, he'd start pondering what to rob next.

It never mattered how successful the last robbery had been; Kent wanted a new job lined up within a week so that he might begin the planning. *Preparation. Preparation. Preparation.* The words echoed ceaselessly in Cross's head.

The target still couldn't be in the city. Last week, he'd accompanied Robert on a late-night stroll, and his brother had shown him firsthand the operatives lurking off Fifth Avenue. Between the pressure of Pinkerton surveillance and the stress of dealing with the murders he'd witnessed, Cross felt worn down. Images of each man being killed flashed in his mind—Gordon being drowned, Dilts being bludgeoned to death, the count's eyes bulging out as he was strangled. Sometimes Cross felt like beating his head with his fists, so desperate was he to drive the images out.

With brute effort, Cross forced himself to consider the house design.

A stylistic change was taking place in the city. The Queen Anne, once so popular, was on the way out. In its place came the understated classicism introduced by McKim, Mead & White's house on East Thirty-Third Street, which housed two bachelor brothers named Phoenix. Built of yellow brick with terra-cotta, what it omitted from its facade made it original. Instead of picturesque ornament, it was completely flat, the detailing limited to the terra-cotta panels. Such minimalism was the direction Cross was interested in going with his houses too, he decided.

"Well, Mr. Engineer, have you decided to join us? I promise you won't be sorry," said a jolly voice. The speaker stood directly next to him. Cross whirled, startled to see the man in the derby again. Amid the pressure from Kent to plan more jobs and the flurry of preparation for Julia's coming-out ball, he'd forgotten about him.

The man stood, smiling, hands on his hips. He wore the same ill-fitting, forest-green suit. Cross noticed his unusually thick eyebrows.

"So? What do ya say?"

Though he was annoyed that the man had crept up on him, Cross held his temper in check. He'd treat the man as he would an obstreperous ten-year-old, he decided, with patience and a patronizing tone.

"It's kind of you to offer me this opportunity, but I have to refuse. I trust you'll understand?"

"Come on. Reconsider. You'll make a helluva lot more money working for us. Look what I brought you."

This time his gloved hand held what looked like a gold Tiffany cigarette case.

"Again, that's extremely kind of you, but I can't accept."

The man seemed to be at a loss for words. A frown replaced his broad grin. He placed the cigarette case in his pocket, removed his hat, and ran his hand through his hair. Looking down at the hexagonal stone pavers in the sidewalk, he seemed to be searching for something to say.

"And that's your final answer, huh?"

"Yes, I'm afraid it is," Cross said, giving him a sympathetic smile.

A middle-aged couple passed by, talking quietly among themselves. The man watched them go and then shrugged his shoulders, face still composed and mild. "I guess there's only one thing left to do," he said and pulled a revolver from his inside pocket. "Can't let the competition have an advantage over us. It's not good business."

Before the man could point the gun, Cross had vaulted the stone wall that separated the park from Fifth Avenue and was running through the woods like a wild animal. He heard the man crashing through the undergrowth behind him. Like all the men of his social class, Cross never exercised. After fifty yards of sprinting, he felt as though he might pass out. His heart was pounding so hard he thought it would burst from his chest. Sweat drenched his clothes. But he didn't dare let up the pace. At any second, he expected a bullet to pierce the base of his skull.

He tore across the East Drive to a path at the edge of the pond and headed north along its bank. People in the park stopped and stared at the chase, stupefied, as Cross and his pursuer passed by like blurs. Instead of continuing north, Cross took a hard left over the Gapstow Bridge, hoping to fool the man in the derby. But even when he crossed, he heard the footsteps pounding behind him. Running west along the footpath, he almost collided with a nanny pushing a baby carriage. He turned north on the next path and slowed to look over his shoulder. The crack of a pistol report sounded. He felt more than heard a sharp-pitched hissing by his right ear.

With a burst of newfound energy, Cross flew up the path, running like a madman. Another hissing sound shot by his shoulder. He looked ahead and found that he was at the dairy, south of the Sixty-Fifth Street Transverse Road. A Gothic-style building of stone and wood, it had a gable-roofed open shed connected to it. Cross ran into the shed and hid behind the low stone wall that supported the corner columns on the far side.

A few seconds later, the man entered the shed. When he saw no one in the long, open space, he turned and went out. Cross waited a few minutes, struggling to catch his breath, and then stood up slowly and went around to the back of the adjoining stone building.

At the corner, he craned his neck, trying to see if the man was about. No one was in sight. He started to run off—then stopped and stared at the grassed area at the side of the stone building. A dark green shape in the shadows blended in with the grass. Cross crept forward.

Twenty feet away, he saw the man lying facedown on the ground. He walked over and knelt beside him. The man's eyes were wide open, staring up into the cloudless blue sky…and a knife protruded from between his ribs. On the ground next to the body lay his derby and the revolver.

Cross looked around to see if anyone was watching. He saw no one.

◆ ◆ ◆

From a grove of trees fifty yards away, Nolan watched Cross walk away. He looked down at his shaking hands.

In his heart, he knew had done the right thing. Yes, he had betrayed his gang—his only family—but he loved Julia. He couldn't bear to see her hurt.

54

Kᴇɴᴛ ᴀɴᴅ Cʀᴏss ᴡᴇʀᴇ sᴛᴀɴᴅɪɴɢ ᴏɴ Hᴇsᴛᴇʀ Sᴛʀᴇᴇᴛ ᴡʜᴇɴ ᴛʜᴇ bullet passed through the two-foot space between them, shattering the plate-glass window of the saloon at their backs. A shard of glass ripped into a patron standing at the bar, who screamed. Startled, the horses of Kent's carriage bolted, pitching the driver onto the sidewalk. As he dove to the ground for cover, Kent saw a phaeton with two men in derbies speeding down Hester.

"Coogan," he screamed. "Get that goddamn carriage!"

Coogan, who had been keeping watch in the doorway of McGlory's, sprinted down the crowded sidewalk. Kent helped Cross stand. The architect was shaking with fear. A man not used to disrespect, let alone a murder attempt, Kent was seething with anger. It was unusual to see the calm and levelheaded criminal mastermind in such a temper.

"Who the hell do they think they are?" he screamed in the direction of the would-be assassins. "Are you all right, Mr. Cross?"

For a fraction of a second, Cross was touched by his concern. Then he realized Kent only wanted to know whether his asset had been harmed. He had paid no attention to the anguished wailing of the injured man in the saloon.

"Yes, I'm fine," he said shortly.

"Goddamn it, I'll find out who's behind this," Kent growled.

An imaginary debate had been raging in Cross's mind. He had been unsure whether to tell Kent about the rival gang's offer and about what had happened at the Central Park Dairy. Because of the mysterious circumstances surrounding the man in the green suit's death, Cross thought it possible that one of Kent's men had been assigned to him as a kind of guardian angel. In that case, there would be no reason to tell Kent about the threats, because he probably already knew. To Cross, Kent already seemed like an underworld god, all knowing and all powerful. In his company, he felt protected from further harm. No, Cross had been far more worried about the traitor than rival gang attacks. But this changed the situation.

A pistol report rang out a few blocks away. It was a common sound in the Bowery, like the howling of an alley cat. No one on the street paid it any attention.

"There's something I must tell you," Cross said cautiously.

Kent stood, expressionless.

"Two weeks ago, I was approached by one of your rivals. They asked me to leave you and join them. Of course I turned the man down. Yesterday, I refused them again, and a man tried to kill me in Central Park. But someone killed him first." Cross spoke in a contrite voice, like a little boy admitting to a misdeed.

Kent stared at him for a few seconds. Then he walked over and leaned against the brick wall of the saloon. Taking out a cigar and lighting it, he looked at the sidewalk, then back at Cross, with a perplexed expression.

"I guess I should've told you right away," Cross said, lowering his eyes.

Kent burst out laughing. The spasms of mirth seemed uncontrollable, as if he couldn't stop. "Yes, Mr. Cross," he said. "That would've been helpful. But I admire your loyalty."

"It wasn't loyalty. It was pure fear. You would've killed me for jumping ship."

"In a second."

Coogan raced up to them. "They turned south on Mott. I got close enough to get a shot off, but I missed. Got a look at the fellow, though. Think it was Big Josh Hines from Milligan's gang."

"What did the fellow who made you the offer look like?" Kent asked Cross.

"He wore a dark green suit and had these peculiar eyebrows, like caterpillars above his eyes."

"Rip Murdock," Coogan said with a grim smile. "It's Milligan."

"I hate wars. They're bad for business. But Milligan must be taught a lesson. A very hard one," Kent said.

"Should I start with Hines?" Coogan asked.

"Mr. Coogan, if you want to get rid of wasps, you don't kill them one by one. You find their nest and destroy it outright," Kent said.

"I understand. You and Mr. Cross will need someone to keep an eye on you until this business is finished. I'll see to that," Coogan said and walked away.

"Now, Mr. Cross, before we were so rudely interrupted, you were telling me about the next job."

Still shaken by the shooting, Cross wanted to go home and hide under the bedcovers, not discuss another robbery.

"Another house in Manhattan? Or Tuxedo?" Kent seemed to have forgotten that less than five minutes ago, he'd been inches from death.

Cross shook his head, unsure whether to be amazed or terrified. "Manhattan is out. There are too many Pinkertons around."

"And how do you know that?"

Cross realized his mistake as soon as the words left his mouth. He couldn't stumble with his explanation; it had to be perfect. "Cook, my old client. I ran into him at the Union League Club, and he told me. Tuxedo's tightly guarded now too."

"What about another bank?"

The last jobs in Newport and Tuxedo Park had been rich hauls. Cross had thought Kent might be pleased enough to not insist on another job so soon. But success had made him greedy.

And true to his word, Kent had given him a 7 percent share. Unsure what else to do with it, Cross had deposited the money in a separate bank account.

"I'm looking into that," Cross said, "but I've got another possibility. A far bigger take."

"I'm listening."

55

NOLAN AND JULIA HAD JUST DROPPED GRANNY OFF AT WAH KEE'S for the afternoon. Julia's grandmother had grown fond of her granddaughter's handsome friend and allowed her to step out with him unchaperoned, opportunities that came chiefly when she was enjoying herself at Wah Kee's. Opium was a miracle cure, she told her granddaughter. After ten years of daily pain, her lumbago had vanished. Her visits increased to three times a week. They always escorted Granny home, a dreamy, elated expression on her face.

Still, Julia worried—that her grandmother would buy more cats from Wah Kee. The animals were overrunning her brownstone and had already caused two servants to quit. There were dozens of them, and they had taken over the house.

But the risk was worth it. Julia loved to walk the streets of the Tenderloin and the Bowery with Nolan; their perambulations had become her consuming preoccupation. Charles Dickens, whom she greatly admired, walked for miles through London every day. She wanted to do the same thing, she told Nolan, to observe life and take in the details—the more sordid, the better.

"I can supply you with sordidness to last a lifetime," Nolan said with a mock evil leer.

But after hearing so much about Dickens—and without telling Julia—he'd purchased a secondhand copy of *Oliver Twist*, which he read and enjoyed. The description of the pickpockets rang entirely true. Fagin was his favorite character and reminded him of his mentor, Crazy Ned. Now Nolan was reading *Nicholas Nickleby*.

Instead of rat baiting or the cockfights, Nolan chose to escort Julia to a gambling den on West Thirty-Eighth Street called Cantwell's. New York City had a wide variety of gambling establishments that catered to all classes of society, and Julia was interested in all of them. She and Nolan had even been to a gambling den in Chinatown. In contrast, Cantwell's was high-class. Its four large rooms were each devoted to a specific game: roulette, faro, dice, and poker.

Nolan would never allow Julia to bet her own money, and he always put down her bet. Every gambling joint cheated, no matter how classy it seemed. In the end, the house always won. But Nolan was a friend of Cantwell's owner. He gave a nod to the croupier, and Julia's number hit again and again. She shrieked with laughter at every win, which pleased Nolan immensely. Caught up in her excitement, the other patrons at the table eagerly placed bets too—just as the house wanted. Nolan had taken Julia to other joints where he knew the dealers, and she had won at faro and dice. But Julia always quit while she was ahead, unwilling to tempt fate.

After stopping, she stayed at the wheel to watch the other gamblers. The spinning of the wheel and the way the little white ivory ball bounced crazily around mesmerized her. She offered breathless encouragement to the players and heartfelt sympathy when they lost.

From the dice room came the sound of cheering. At first, it was low in volume, but it got louder and louder. The roar was only interrupted when the player was about to roll the dice. Then came wild applause and laughter: he or she had won.

"Someone's lucky today," Julia said to Nolan.

There was a lull in the cheering. A lone voice shouted out, "Mathematicians have a special connection to the number seven. You'll see!"

Julia turned abruptly from the roulette table and rushed out of the room. Alarmed, Nolan followed. The dice room was packed like a sardine can, and Julia found herself blocked by the crowd at the doorway.

With bulldog determination, she squeezed past the dozens of wildly cheering spectators. A heavy haze of cigar smoke floated over the heads of the onlookers like a great storm cloud. Julia peeked between the bodies at the front to see her brother, George, standing at the head of the table, throwing the dice. He had a kind of crazed expression on his face, a hazy smile, as if he were in a drug-induced delirium. Julia had never seen that look on him before and barely recognized him.

"That's my brother," she said in a voice that hardly sounded like her own as Nolan stopped next to her.

Two more rolls of the dice brought two more wins. The applause grew yet more raucous. George seemed oblivious to the attention, carefully stacking his chips in neat piles, lost in his own private world.

In front of Julia, an elegant woman in a red-and-purple walking outfit leaned over to the man next to her.

"I think he's up to eight thousand," she said, as excited as if they were her own winnings.

"More like nine," the man said.

Three more passes brought three more wins. The crowd was in a frenzy. The gambling in the other rooms had ceased. The players were crowding into the room to see what the furor was about. Julia stood there, amid the noise and the chaos, and stared at her brother. Nolan watched her, baffled.

The noise had died down, the crowd anxiously awaiting the next throw.

"It has to be more than ten thousand," said the man.

George paused, looking down at his horde of chips. He picked up a few, jiggled them in his hand, and then put them back on their stack. With both hands, he began carefully taking each tall stack and placing it on the green felt of the dice table. First one, then another and another. They reminded Julia of white towers, forming the outer walls of some medieval fortification.

A stunned silence swept the room. Not a single sound was uttered.

When every chip was down, George picked up the dice in his right fist and stared down the length of the table. Julia wanted to leap forward and plead with her brother, but she remained frozen in place. The fashionable women in the crowd grabbed the arms of their escorts, squeezing them harder and harder as the tension mounted. The well-dressed men were wide-eyed. The longer George took, the more unbearable the wait became.

With a quick flick of his wrist, the dice went careening down the table, bouncing off the green felt of the barrier wall. Every person in the room held his or her breath as the white cubes came to a rest.

"Two," cried out the croupier. A loud collective moan filled the room.

The two black dots stared back at George like tiny eyes. The good cheer and bonhomie vanished in a second, and the crowd dispersed quickly, not wanting to catch George's ill luck. He stood, a lone figure at the head of the table. Another player, a man with gray muttonchop sideburns and a large belly, stepped up beside George and held the dice, ready for the next throw.

As she watched her brother, Julia felt a feeling of crushing despair descended upon her. She grabbed Nolan's hand and rushed out of the building.

56

CROSS HAD SPENT THE AFTERNOON ARGUING WITH A CLIENT OVER the cost of marble, the prospect of the next robbery hovering perpetually in the back of his mind. He felt dog tired, as if the weight of the world were pressing down on him.

Not seeing any carriages, he decided to walk to the Grand Central stop of the Third Avenue Elevated and take the train home. It was late afternoon. Crowds of people filed up the iron stairs for their evening commute. The usual ragged newsboys were hawking their papers. Alongside them, food vendors sold everything from gingerbread cakes to roasted ears of corn. An Italian in a greasy-looking derby sold sausages.

Physically and emotionally drained, Cross trudged up the stairs.

"Extra! Extra! Russian count robs the rich and is murdered!" cried a newsboy standing on the landing of the stair above.

The announcement sent a jolt through Cross. They must have found the count's body in Tuxedo. Brady had left some jewelry on his body, bait to convince the police that he'd robbed the Lorillards. Apparently, they'd bitten.

"Russian mastermind steals rare jewel! Read all about it in the *Sun!*" the boy screamed.

Amazing. The yellow press was blaming Aleksandrov for the other robberies, including the Pharaoh Blue. It was ridiculous and implausible—and perfectly fine with Cross.

He approached the newsboy, eager to get a paper—and paused, startled. Most of the newsies were filthy urchins in rags, but this child was well dressed and clean. He took another look and almost stumbled down the stairs in shock. His son, Charlie, was peddling papers!

"Extra, extra! Read all about it! Russian count robs the rich and is murdered!"

Stunned by the sight of his son, Cross regained his composure. Instead of confronting Charlie, he slipped down the opposite side of the staircase and back onto the street. Concealing himself behind one of the iron columns that supported the station above, he stared at Charlie. The boy handed out papers and took the money expertly, making change for a dollar and screaming out the lurid headline all the while. Cross couldn't decide if he was more surprised by the fact that Charlie was there or by how well the boy did the job. He had never seen Charlie do a single practical thing in his life. With servants filling their house, there was no call for it.

An unwitting smile spread across Cross's face as he watched his son work. Unaccountably, he felt a real sense of pride in his boy.

Soon Charlie was out of papers and began to count his day's earnings. A very ragged urchin approached him. From the way they smiled and laughed together, it was plain that they were friends. They ran up the next flight of stairs, and Cross followed. The boys boarded a downtown train, and Cross did the same, sitting at the very end of the car to avoid being seen. At this time of day, it was crowded. He had to stand to keep an eye on Charlie. Once he ducked down, afraid the boy was looking his way.

At Grand Street, the boys got off and made their way to the street. Following them proved more difficult than Cross had anticipated. Instead of heading to their destination in a direct line, they stopped to look in store windows or pick up junk in the gutter, to throw a rock at a rat and buy candy from a Chinese vendor. Cross had to duck into doorways and peek around corners. Squawking, an old woman chased him away with a broom.

He watched the boys approach a pushcart that sold fruit. The urchin kept the vendor busy while Charlie stole pears and peaches, stuffing them into a burlap bag he pulled out of his pants pocket. The boys continued on to a street bordering the East River. It was a dirty, ramshackle neighborhood full of abandoned buildings. Whores stood in doorways, croaking out come-ons to men walking. Flies blanketed a rotting cat in the gutter. The sidewalks were strewn with garbage.

Charlie and the urchin turned into an alleyway beside an abandoned warehouse. Cross ran across the street and craned his head around the corner, watching as the boys crawled through a window opening. He followed, finding himself in an old boiler room.

"Not a bad day, Charlie, my boy, not bad at all," the urchin was saying proudly.

"We should do some wrangling tomorrow," Charlie said.

From the shadows, Cross watched as the urchin unlocked a padlock on one of the huge boilers, climbed inside, and shut the door. Amazed, Cross hurried over to the door. Through the joints, he could see that the boys had lit candles or a lantern. He stood, listening to them talk about their plans for the morrow. Charlie would meet the urchin at nine at the pier.

So this is where Charlie learned to curse, Cross thought, amused, as expletives tumbled from his son's mouth.

In one smooth move, he swung open the boiler hatch. Two surprised boys stared back at him, faces illumined by the flickering candlelight.

"Charlie, you must introduce me to your friend—or is this your dancing instructor? And are you gentlemen free for supper tonight? I saw a charming restaurant on my way down here."

57

J UST THINK, FREDDIE. TWO THOUSAND DOLLARS CASH IN your pocket."

"You're asking me to take quite a risk, George."

"Fletcher's in on it," he lied. "We need you."

Fred Watkins, George Cross's teammate from Harvard, was a pitcher for the Boston Beaneaters of the National League. He'd had an outstanding collegiate career, and when he'd graduated, Boston had signed him immediately. He was now an average pitcher on a fifth-place team trailing Chicago by thirty games. The season was in its final two weeks, and Boston was in town to play the Giants. George had finally hit a winning streak at faro, but he still owed a packet to a fellow named Hurley, the owner of Handsome Harry's on Baxter Street. Hurley's men had caught up with George two days prior, and he'd pleaded for one last chance before they made good on their promise to kill him. With his back against the wall, he had decided to do something he'd tried and failed with Kent: fix a game.

If all went well, Watkins would throw the game, and the Giants would win this afternoon.

"You're the pitcher, Freddie. You control the game; you know that." George sat on Freddie's bed in the Windsor Hotel.

"Come on, Freddie, be a sport," Kitty said. "Help us out—and help yourself too. You don't get paid shit for being a ballplayer."

Kitty had insisted that George bring her along in an attempt to seal the deal. He'd been working on Freddie for the last two days, but the pitcher still hadn't committed. He was scheduled for the 2:00 p.m. game at the Polo Grounds, and time was running out.

"The Giants are in third place," Freddie said. "They're far better than us."

"Then we need you just in case you start winning," George pointed out.

"Think of all the things you could do with two thousand. You're a Harvard man. You can get a tip from your brother at Kidder, Peabody & Co. and invest it," Kitty said.

Freddie went over to the window and looked out at the traffic on Fifth Avenue.

"The way I'm pitching, I don't know how long the majors will keep me around." His voice sounded distant; he spoke to no one in particular. "Sure, the money would come in handy. But it's a big risk."

Kitty looked at George, frowning. It was 11:00 a.m.

After the incident on the steps outside the gambling hall, Kitty had sworn to stop helping George, but that resolution lasted less than a week. Just as George was compelled to gamble, Kitty was compelled to help him. She just couldn't stop herself. *Maybe that's what love does to a person*, she reasoned. *It makes them act in a foolish manner and do things that are bound to come to no good.* But good or no, she and George were both under a spell too powerful to resist. And if George didn't immediately come up with the money for Hurley, it wouldn't be a beating and a warning. He'd get a bullet in the head. It was their last chance.

"George, why don't you meet me at the ballpark? Freddie and I can talk things over," Kitty said. She nodded discreetly at the little table in the middle of the room. George got off the bed, placed five one-hundred-dollar bills on the table, and left.

❖ ❖ ❖

After seven innings, the score was Boston 4–0, and George was getting worried.

Sitting three rows behind him were Piker Shaw and Gyp Sullivan,

Hurley's collectors. The two men were laughing and rooting loudly for Boston; they wanted Freddie's team to win so that they could kill George after the game, before they went out for dinner.

In her own special way, Kitty thought she had convinced Freddie to cooperate. Her eyes darted repeatedly to Hurley's men. A scowl marred her pretty face.

From his time as a ballplayer, George could see that Freddie was trying to lose. But every time a Giant made contact, the ball wound up in a Boston glove. A strong wind blowing in from center field was making long fly balls, which normally would have been home runs, into long outs at the foot of the fence. Freddie practically lobbed the ball over the plate and still the Giants couldn't get a hit. When they did get men on, they promptly batted into double plays, stranding men on base. Freddie tried walking batters, but they got stranded too.

As if caught up in the spirit of the day, the Boston infielders— normally mediocre fielders—made spectacular plays to deny the Giants hits. Hanson, the third baseman, made a diving grab and snagged a ball that would have driven in two runs. George felt tension building in his temples. He massaged his head, unable to look at Kitty.

At the top of the eighth, Boston came up to bat and pounded two hits down the right field line, putting men on first and third with no outs. George's heart sank. But the reliever, Jack Singleton, bore down and struck out the side, finally giving the fans at the Polo Grounds something to cheer about. And in the bottom of the eighth, with Freddie's help, the Giants' bats came alive. Connor led off with a double to left center. Esterbrook smashed a home run over the fence in right center. The ball flew so far that it landed at the foot of the A. G. Spalding Sporting Goods sign. Keefe singled, and O'Rourke brought him home with a double. The score was 4–3. With no outs, it looked like a cinch for Freddie to get two more runs, but the next three batters popped up, grounded out, and fouled out.

Boston was up, and Morrill, their home-run hitter, drove the ball to the left field fence. George gasped, clutching at Kitty's hand, but the wind kept the ball in. Wise walked but was forced out at second in a double play. The bottom of the ninth had arrived.

Freddie had one chance left to lose the game.

Dorgan led off. Though Freddie lobbed him the ball, he popped up. Gerhardt followed with a ground out. George was down to the last out. People were heading for the exits. Shaw and Sullivan leaned forward, ready to ensure that their target wouldn't slip away with the crowd.

Freddie delivered four straight balls, miles out of the strike zone, to walk Johnson. Callahan came up to the plate and fouled off the next two pitches.

"It's time to go, Georgie," Shaw said, placing a beefy hand on his shoulder.

Callahan fouled off two more pitches, prolonging George's agony. Shaw yanked the boy from his seat, pulling him into the aisle.

"Time to go," he repeated.

On the field, Callahan swung and missed. Ten thousand people let out a collective groan. As Kitty watched helplessly, Shaw dragged George by his collar up the stairs.

But then the umpire signaled. A foul tip, dropped by the catcher. A few seconds later, the crowd started screaming wildly. George broke loose from Sullivan's grasp and ran back to the seats. His heart leaped as he saw a white orb defying the wind, sailing into dead center, and bouncing off the billboard for McCann's Celebrated Hats of the Bowery. The Giants had won on a two-run homer. Kitty threw herself into George's arms, kissing him passionately. Amid the thousands of fans yelling and jumping for joy, Shaw and Sullivan turned and stomped away, looks of disgust written large on their faces.

"I'll see you later at my place," Kitty yelled over the din. "You see, I promised Freddie a bonus if he lost."

58

IMPOSSIBLE AS IT SEEMED, NO ONE KNEW ANYTHING ABOUT THE robberies. The only word Robert heard on the street was a mad rumor about the "Engineer" who had supposedly masterminded the crimes. Usually criminals were like gossipy women, blabbing about anything and everything they'd heard. This time, there was almost total silence. In all his years as a Pinkerton, Robert had never seen such a thing. People were too scared to talk.

Following the lead of the newspapers, the public had eagerly blamed the larcenous Russian count for the robberies. Robert knew this was nonsense. The count wasn't even a real royal; he was an accomplished con artist who'd fooled the gullible rich into thinking he was of the aristocratic class. The idea that such a petty criminal had stolen the Pharaoh Blue was laughable. The man behind all this was the Engineer.

Walking west on Grand Street to the Second Avenue Elevated, he saw his nephew, George, come around the corner at Allen Street and enter a ramshackle two-story house. Robert was shocked. Seeing George in such a squalid setting was like seeing a handsome prince walking through a pigsty. Without hesitating, Robert followed George to the house. It was one of New York's vilest gambling dens, a disgusting dive where the lowest of the low went to throw away their money. *Probably a brace house*, Robert thought, casting a critical eye about him. Those unscrupulous dens offered a fixed game twenty-four hours a day.

In the next instant, and to his amazement, he saw his niece following her brother. Julia was about a block behind and had a tall, handsome young man at her side. Robert could see that they didn't want

George to notice them. After George went into the dive, they waited a minute or two and then followed.

Aside from the scum of the street, clerks from businesses and brokerage houses might visit the house during their lunchtimes. For a few seconds, Robert debated whether he should follow. In a cramped little dump of this sort, the risk of being seen by George or Julia was too great.

And he didn't need to enter to picture the interior. Robert knew all about these places. A narrow, dimly lit corridor would lead to a smoke-filled room with a faro table, its usual setup of thirteen cards in parallel rows glued down on a greasy, enameled oil cloth. At the table would be the mechanic, or dealer, with his assistant taking cards from a brass box that was always rigged. On the other side of the table stood the suckers, placing their bets on the glued-down cards.

The den had no amenities, which meant it was also a snap house, a place that rented space to individual gamblers. These men set up their own games in exchange for a 10 percent cut. A roulette game and a chuck-a-luck dice game were probably going on in back.

Robert walked across the street and stood in the doorway of a used clothing dealer's shop. He lit a cigarette and waited. Watching a building was an art; one couldn't get distracted and miss the suspect's exit. He was an expert, keeping one eye on the door of the gambling den and the other on the parade of characters passing by. The streets of New York were an endlessly fascinating kaleidoscope, packed with an incredible variety of people. On any given day, Robert would see Hebrews who looked like they'd stepped out of Russia, inscrutable Chinese men with long pigtails, and Greeks with jet-black hair and pointy noses. It was so different from Buffalo, where there were only white people who looked like him.

A beautiful, swarthy Italian girl carrying a huge basket of laundry on her head smiled as she passed. The street was a river of traffic, choked with delivery wagons, carriages, and dray carts. In this part of

Manhattan, nobody gave a damn about whether the streets were clean; manure, piss, and rotting garbage carpeted the surface.

After ten minutes, Julia and her companion rushed out of the dive. His niece looked shaken; her face was white with shock, and her hands were clenched into fists. The sight troubled Robert, but he held to his post. Her companion was familiar—perhaps from Julia's coming-out ball?—and looked as though he would protect her in such a rotten neighborhood.

An hour passed. Robert grew hungry but didn't abandon his post. He snapped his fingers at a woman peddling hot, spiced gingerbread. It would tide him over until supper.

Finally, George emerged. From the expression on his nephew's face, Robert could tell what had happened. George leaned against the brick wall of the building and lit a cigarette. After five minutes of staring down at the dirty sidewalk, he walked off.

Robert waited until George was down the block and around the corner. Then he went across the street into the dive. He walked into the faro parlor and stood at the rear, behind some men watching the game.

The dealer was talking to his assistant when Robert walked over.

"That young, well-dressed fellow in the blue suit that was just here—does he come here often?"

"What the hell does it matter to you?" the dealer snarled.

Robert grabbed the man by his collar, slammed his head down on the faro table, and held his Pinkerton shield in front of his face. "I'm sure that's an excellent bit of cheating you do with that needle squeeze on your dealing box. The police might be interested in a demonstration. Or perhaps you can answer my question instead."

"His name's George Cross," the man squeaked. "Society swell. He gambles all over the Bowery and the Five Points. He was up three thousand today, but he pissed it all away. Poor bastard never knows when to quit, so he's always in hock."

"Where does he get his money?"

"Don't know. He's got a few cons on the side. A whore gives him money sometimes. But he keeps coming back to lose."

Robert let the man off the table with a shove. "Lose?" he sneered. "You mean win."

The dealer started to laugh. "These fools *want* to lose. That's why we love 'em."

59

Brownie Snead's left hook caught Whitey Samuels square in the jaw and bounced him off the brick wall onto the hard-packed dirt of the cellar like a rubber ball. With the agility of a cancan dancer, Brownie kicked Whitey underneath the jaw. As Whitey rose to all fours, Brownie kicked him in the stomach. Still, the tough old bastard wouldn't go down.

Nolan had ten dollars on Brownie and was impatient to end the thing. But Whitey rammed his fist into Brownie's groin, sending him to the floor where he rolled about in agony.

"Ain't none of those sissy Marquess of Queensberry rules here like they got in England!" Pickle Nose Johnson yelled.

The East Side Cowboys were in the cellar of the Bucket of Blood, enjoying what they called "a free and easy," a bare knuckles brawl with no ring and no rules. They drank and ate as they watched, gathered around tables in an open space at the rear of the cellar.

Back on his feet, Whitey delivered the coup de grâce, stomping on the fallen Brownie's face three times. Finally, Brownie lay still. The gang groaned: Brownie had been the overwhelming favorite. Conversation resumed. No one attended to the downed fighter. Nolan took a sip of rye and dealt cards to the other men at his table, readying for a game of hearts.

"How ya makin' out with that society girl?" Pickle Nose asked. "Miss Julia's mighty pretty."

"She's gone back to school, but I see her in the afternoons and on weekends," Nolan said, examining his cards. He'd begun playing soon after being thrown out on the street. The cards had taught him his numbers and how to add and subtract. From an early age, he'd also learned about cheating. Nolan knew every trick—trimmed and marked cards, making two cards stick together, hold outs for concealing cards in sleeves and vests, even tiny mirrors used to read the cards of opponents. These were advantage tools and were advertised in the newspapers and sold on the Bowery.

Pickle Nose, he saw, was cheating at that very moment by palming an ace of hearts he would tuck up in his sleeve. But Nolan could cheat so well that he was able to counteract any moves against him. He'd even instructed Julia in some of the techniques, which delighted her. The game of whist was fashionable in her set, and Nolan had given her pointers on how to gain an advantage. Society played the game for money; now that she had come out, Julia was allowed to join in. Under his tutelage, she wiped out her opponents. This pleased Nolan greatly. She regularly took the proceeds and bet them on ratting contests, which she consistently won. The girl had an innate talent for picking winners, which her brother Charlie greatly resented.

Milligan came in and began making the rounds, greeting his men, telling jokes, and topping off drinks. Brownie was conscious and sitting at a table, knocking back shots to ease his aches and pains. Whitey had collected his earnings and left.

The door to the room opened again. A mousy man wearing spectacles stuck his head in. "I've got a beer delivery for Mr. Spike Milligan," he said. His voice was loud and silenced the room.

Annoyed, Milligan walked up to the man. "Goddamn it, jackass, I'm not a saloon keeper. Deliver it upstairs to the owner," he snarled.

The deliveryman, who looked like he'd been cursed and insulted often in his line of work, smiled and waved his hand in a friendly way. "No, sir. This a special order from Mr. Croker."

Milligan's face lit up. He looked at his men, who nodded and smiled in approval. Richard Croker was the Grand Sachem, or boss, of Tammany Hall. He was an Irish roughneck who'd used his fists to rise from the gutter and earn appointments as coroner and fire commissioner, positions for which he was completely unqualified. When Honest John Kelly had retired as Tammany boss two years before, Croker had been heir apparent. He held political power in New York with an iron fist. The New York City election for mayor was next month, and Croker expected the gangs to do what they did best—get out the vote for his candidate.

The deliveryman rolled a huge keg on a hand truck to the front of the room. Staring at it, Milligan seemed to glow with pride.

"Boys," he said, pointing to the keg. "This is a token of Mr. Croker's appreciation for how we've helped him in past elections. *And* it's a reminder of what we have to do next month. Mr. Croker wants Abraham Hewitt as the next mayor, not that fuckin' socialist shit Henry George or that fancy-ass Theodore Roosevelt. We have to bring out the vote for Tammany."

Nolan laughed. Milligan would get a person to vote—and then vote six more times. He was a master at getting bums, cripples, and beggars to turn up at different polling places in the various precincts. An array of costumes was provided to disguise repeat voters. In the last mayoral race, one man had voted fourteen times.

"Mr. Croker says the greatest political crime is ingratitude, and the Cowboys ain't gonna be ungrateful. Let's do our part and not let him down," Milligan called.

The gang cheered and whooped in response.

The deliveryman handed Milligan the tap for the keg and shook his hand heartily in Tammany solidarity. But outside the open door, he paused. "Mr. Kent hopes you enjoy the lager. And by the way, he's voting for Roosevelt," he shouted. Drawing a Colt, the deliveryman fired at the keg and slammed the door behind him.

There was an earsplitting explosion, and an orange-red fireball engulfed the room. The men sitting closest to the keg were blown to atoms. Pieces of bodies shot into the walls and ceiling with the veloc-ity of bullets. Shards of glass and wood penetrated skulls and torsos. The entire room filled with flames and sulfur-smelling smoke. Men screamed in agony as they burned to death. In what seemed like sec-onds, the wood beams holding the floor above creaked and began to give way. The first floor, filled to capacity with saloon patrons, came crashing down into the cellar.

Then the noise stopped, replaced by a silence punctuated only by low moans. The room was so thick with smoke and dust that a man could not see his hand in front of his face.

Nolan felt a crushing pressure on his stomach. He opened his eyes but saw only a thick, black cloud pressing down upon him.

He could only think of Julia.

60

T HE VAULT FOR THE SILVER AND LINENS WAS WELL concealed. So was the safe that held the jewelry. Who knew their exact location?"

"The servants," William Cook said. "Myself, my wife…and the architect who designed it, of course."

"Yes, the architect," Robert Cross said softly. He knew very well who that was.

"Have you recovered anything?" William Cook asked. Soon after the theft, he and his wife had replaced everything they had lost with even more expensive items, including a rare Dresden china service. It was the insult of the robbery that offended him, not the loss of money.

"Two salad forks have turned up in Philadelphia, but that's all, I'm afraid."

"It was that Russian son of a bitch, that phony bastard who stole the diamond. That's who did this! Three times, I hosted him in my house. Well, I learned my lesson. No one will ever rob me again. I've installed one of those newfangled telegraphic alarms. It's connected straight to the police precinct."

After Cook left his office, Robert sat, looking at the architectural drawings Fidelity National had lent him. He saw how close the sub-basement vault was to Broadway and the abandoned Beach tunnel. It was an extremely well planned robbery, nothing like the usual poor attempts by the none-too-bright criminals to which he was accustomed.

His colleague, Pemberton, was hunched over his desk nearby, poring over a report.

"You've worked here in the city for a while, haven't you, Pemberton?"

The white-haired man looked up and smiled.

"About a million years. Since '76."

"Remember George Leslie?"

"Couldn't forget him. Called that fellow the king of the bank robbers."

"Wasn't he some sort of engineer or architect?"

"Something like that. Came from a well-off family back in Ohio and studied engineering at the University of Cincinnati, I think. Good with building plans. Definitely the brains of the outfit."

Robert stared out the window, watching the traffic on Broadway. Then he picked up the telephone, rang up Greene, and got the name of the architect who'd built his city mansion. Flipping through the New York City directory, he jotted down addresses and telephone numbers.

◆ ◆ ◆

"Mr. Ware. So nice of you to let me come by on such short notice," Robert said.

"Anything to help you find the bastards who robbed Mr. Greene," James Ware said, showing Robert into the conference room where his architectural drawings were laid out. "I hope this is what you're looking for," he said. "It's a complete set of the house on Sixty-Fifth."

"Thank you. I understand that you came up with a very innovative design for a tenement house...won a competition, in fact."

Ware beamed at the recognition. Robert could tell he was proud of his design.

"Why yes. The whole idea was to produce a humane design, to let these poor wretches have more light and air. Perhaps even running water and indoor toilets."

"It's an important step. Those unfortunates live in the most disgusting conditions. Like animals, really," Robert said.

"Indeed. The way those landlords convert old houses into rookeries and stuff a dozen families in them is downright criminal, but the law protects them. Then they build appalling tenements. No windows except at the front and back." Ware's voice was rising with emotion. "More than five hundred people per *acre* live down there."

"Exactly what I'm saying. Animals in the zoo are treated better. By the way, Mr. Ware, where were you on the night of the robbery?" Robert said casually.

"I was in Boston that week," Ware said. "When I heard about the robbery, I was outraged."

"Such a beautiful house you designed. Did you and Mr. Greene part on good terms? Did he pay your full fee, I mean?"

"Why, thank you, Mr. Cross. And yes, he paid to the penny, even for the extra design work."

"Thank you so much for your time, Mr. Ware. I must be going now, but I should say how much I admire men like you. My brother John's an architect in the city, you know."

Ware's face lit up in recognition. "Oh, I'm a good friend of John's. Please tell him I said hello."

"I will. And thank you again."

"John's a talented man, but he always wants to learn more. That's the sign of a great architect. He's even been up here to look over my drawings," Ware said, the pride evident in his voice.

Robert stopped and turned. "Oh…recently?"

"Perhaps a month ago. Wanted to look at my tenement design because he said he was going to design one."

⁘ ⁘ ⁘

Robert walked down Madison Avenue and turned east on Twenty-Eighth Street. In a small restaurant, he ordered coffee and a ham sandwich. Taking out a notebook, he turned to the page listing his current cases. Unlike most men he knew, he enjoyed his work. Every case was a challenge that he eagerly anticipated solving. He could never leave his work behind at the office; he spent hours every evening working on his cases.

When he'd first come to work at the Pinkerton Agency, Robert had been amazed by the evil that dwelt in men and women alike. Before that, he had never known any truly bad people, people capable of committing heinous acts of violence and cruelty. Those kinds of humans soon became part of his everyday life, and instead of being revolted, he was fascinated by them. He admired their great ingenuity in committing crimes. Greed, it seemed, was the root of evil in 99 percent of his cases. The pursuit of money was never ending, like water cascading over Niagara Falls—wives poisoning husbands to inherit their fortune, children killing parents for the insurance money, clerks embezzling funds under their bosses' noses.

The cases Robert had been assigned since transferring to New York were without question the most challenging he'd ever faced. The fact that the robberies had been carried out by one gang was exciting as hell, and though the escape in the tunnel at Fidelity National still angered and depressed him, it had made him all the more zealous in hunting the criminals down.

Robert ran his finger down the list to the latest case he had been assigned: a robbery in Newport. The local police had had no luck and, under pressure from the victim, had asked the Pinkertons to take over. He finished his coffee and paid his bill. Taking Madison Avenue south, he walked to Seventeenth Street and turned right. He came to 9 West Seventeenth Street, a narrow brick building that looked like a residence. Going up the stoop to the arched entry, he knocked and announced himself. A porter led him to a small waiting room furnished with overstuffed leather chairs, where a lanky man with thinning hair and spectacles greeted him.

"I'm pleased to meet you, Mr. Cross. Mr. Goelet said that we were to offer you our every assistance. Come into my office where we can talk privately."

"Thank you, sir. I have only a few questions. Do you know which architect designed Mr. Goelet's house in Newport?"

"Oh, that would be Mr. Stanford White of McKim, Mead & White. In fact, he did this little house here too, as the Goelet family's business headquarters. It's almost like a home, wouldn't you say?"

"Indeed," Robert said, his eyes distant. "It's quite charming."

⸭ ⸭ ⸭

"Thank you for your time, Mr. White."

"Call me Stanny, Rob," the redheaded architect bellowed. "It's been a pleasure to meet you. Anything I can do to help catch those bastards, you let me know. And be sure to tell John I said hello. You must both come to my club for drinks some evening."

"I'd like that," Robert said. "And I'll be sure to tell my brother you said hello."

Solving a crime, he thought as he walked down Fifth Avenue, was like putting together one of those giant puzzles that were so popular these days. When the hundreds of pieces were first dumped out, it seemed impossible to fit them all together to form a detailed Adirondacks landscape or a Biblical scene. But slowly, piece by piece, the image became visible.

The pieces in this puzzle had started to fall into place. But instead of the accustomed feeling of elation, Robert was very troubled.

61

WHEN NOLAN OPENED HIS EYES, HE SAW A GLEAMING SKY OF pure white. The brightness was so intense his eyes began to water.

"It's about time you woke up, Rip Van Winkle," a man's voice called.

With great difficulty, Nolan lifted his head. He saw Dunn, a member of his gang, waving at him from a row of beds across a center aisle.

At that moment, he realized he was in a hospital ward, not the afterlife. The dozens of beds were filled with male patients, some covered in bandages, some not. Above him was a ceiling of pure-white plaster, with suspended electric lights bouncing illumination off it.

All Nolan could think of in that moment was how incredibly clean and bright the huge room was. Then he felt something on his face. When he lifted his arm from underneath the white sheets, a terrific pain shot up his right side. Wincing and touching his face, he discovered that there was a bandage covering his left temple and part of his forehead.

"Didn't think you'd ever wake up."

"Where the hell are we?"

"New York Hospital on Fifteenth Street."

"Christ, what happened?"

"Kent sent us a beer keg full of gunpowder and blew the shit out of the room in the Bucket of Blood. Don't ya remember?"

"I remember the keg being brought in…but after that, it's a blank."

"I bet. You've been out almost two days. They shot ya up with a gallon of morphine."

"Where are the rest of the guys?"

"*We* are the rest of the guys. Everyone else's dead, the poor bastards."

Ignoring the intense pain, Nolan raised himself up on his elbows.

"Everyone?" he asked incredulously.

"Except Swanson and a couple others who weren't there. Everyone else was wiped out: Milligan, Johnson, Pickle Nose, Brinkerhoff."

"Pickle Nose?"

"The only way they knew it was him was that big honker of his. They had to scrape bodies off the walls. Some people who were on the first floor when it collapsed bought it too."

"Pickle Nose…dead."

"I was at the far end of the room getting a deck of cards when the explosion went off. Still got thrown against the wall and broke my fuckin' leg."

Nolan began touching his torso, flinching in pain.

"I heard the doc say a couple ribs are broken, and ya got a big gash on your skull. Still, you're pretty fuckin' lucky to be alive. Good thing you was standing toward the back of the room."

Nolan collapsed back against his pillow and started sobbing. He couldn't help himself. Though they were dishonest, ignorant scum, the members of his gang were the only family he'd ever had. He'd grown up with most of the men and had come to have great affection for them. They'd relied on each other in times of trouble. Pickle Nose had been like an older brother: he'd looked out for Nolan and taught him the ways of the street. Nolan would not have survived without his help. Pug Johnson had helped him refine his pickpocketing skills. As a sign of respect, Milligan, who had treated Nolan like a son, had let him keep a large percentage of his earnings.

Nolan could barely remember his real family. What he did recall was the shouting, beatings, and near starvation doled out by his drunken father. Sometimes, he'd thought that getting kicked out into the street was the best thing that could have happened to him. All those good men who'd sheltered him were gone, never to be seen again. And it was his fault. He had brought his fate on by killing Murdock before the man could murder John Cross.

What had he done? He had acted impulsively for the love of a girl—the blood of more than a score of men stained his hands. The thought crushed Nolan. As he stared up at the ceiling, an anger deep within his chest ignited and began to burn. Gangs in New York frequently skirmished with one another, but Kent's act of revenge—murdering so many men in cold blood—was reprehensible.

"Kent's a fuckin' animal. He deserves to die," Nolan said, his voice cracking.

Dunn was distracted by movement near the door. "Here she is. Hello, my beauty," he yelled.

"Good to see you, Mr. Dunn."

The sight of Julia at the foot of his bed filled Nolan with joy. In an instant, his anger drained away. He tried to lean forward to greet her but fell back.

"This little girl's been here three times today, waiting for you to wake up."

Julia knelt by the bed, took Nolan's hand, and kissed it.

"John, I was so worried you wouldn't wake up. Oh God, it's so good to see you." She choked out the words between sobs.

Nolan ran his fingers through her hair but said nothing. For the time, her mere presence eased his pain. "What day is it?" he asked softly.

"It's noon on Tuesday."

"Shouldn't you be in school?" he asked, still stroking her hair.

Julia raised her head and smiled. "I played hooky today. When I went looking for you at the Bucket of Blood—or what's left of it—they told me what happened. But don't worry. I won't get in trouble—I already forged the excuse note, just like you taught me."

62

THERE'S A LOT OF BUILDING GOING ON IN THE CITY. BUSINESS MUST be good, John."

"Best it's ever been. There's the theater, the hospital, a few office buildings," Cross said. He wasn't a man who boasted, but as always, Robert's praise was uniquely affirming.

"I've noticed quite a few tenements getting built too. Doing any of that sort of work?"

"Sadly, no. But I'd like to try my hand at a tenement project. There's a lot of room for improvement when it comes to their design."

The two brothers were finishing dinner at Sherry's. In the last few months, Cross had never missed a dinner or a lunch with Robert. His reasons were twofold. He loved the company—and he wanted to know what the Pinkertons were up to. Were there any leads on his robberies? What about the informant who'd spoiled the bank job? It was odd that he hadn't struck again. The thought of that betrayal was a constant torment to Cross.

Adding to his dilemma, Robert's dragnet of informants throughout the city had made robbing the wealthy almost impossible and lining up robberies for Kent yet more difficult. Seeing no way out of his predicament, Cross and Helen had continued to wrack their brains for possible targets.

"You know, I saw an incredible house going up on Madison Avenue right behind Saint Pat's. U-shaped thing done in brownstone," Robert said, taking a forkful of apple pie.

"That's for Henry Villard, the president of the Northern Pacific

Railroad. He's related to Charlie McKim, a close friend of mine, who did the design. It's actually not one house but six separate dwellings arranged around an entry courtyard."

"Six? It looks like one big mansion."

"That's the genius of it. The design's based on an Italian Renaissance precedent, the Palazzo della Cancelleria in Rome, but the details have been simplified. Pilasters were eliminated, and the window surrounds were reversed…"

Cross stopped. His brother was grinning from ear to ear, a sure sign that Cross was boring the socks off him. He burst out laughing, as did Robert.

"I'm so sorry. Once I start talking about architecture, you know I can't shut my mouth," Cross said apologetically.

"You're passionate about your work. It's a wonderful thing. I'm passionate about mine too. I want to solve every case and bring every criminal to justice," Robert said, his gaze steady on Cross.

"Any progress on the robberies—Cook and the bank and all that?"

"Not much, I'm afraid. Very cunning crimes usually take time to solve. But I'll get them. I've got a damn big caseload too, along with routine duties like protecting businesses." Robert finished his coffee and stared out at the flow of traffic on Fifth Avenue. "McKim, Mead & White did Villard's place? Isn't that Stanford White's firm?" Robert asked finally.

"Why yes, he did the interior design for the houses. Stanny's a very good friend of mine. He was at Julia's coming-out ball. Tall fellow with red hair. Hands down the best architect in the city. An incredible talent."

"I think I remember him," Robert said. He paused, then added, "He must have a lot of rich clients, like the ones who have the big houses along the cliff in Newport."

"The richest of the rich. Although Aunt Caroline doesn't use him much."

"Did you go up to Newport to see the old girl this summer?"

"We went up for a week. But she was in the Berkshires."

"Did you go to the casino? I hear they have good concerts."

"Helen dragged me to one."

"I hear Tuxedo is the place to be nowadays. Lorillard's built himself a whole town up there."

"Yes, a colleague of mine, Bruce Price, designed the cottages and the clubhouse. It's quite the place."

"Didn't he do the Oceanside Hotel in Long Branch?"

Cross paused and took a sip of coffee. It gave him a few seconds to size up the situation. He shifted around in his seat and dabbed his mouth with the linen napkin while repeating in his mind the entire conversation he and his brother had had up to this moment. Each word his brother spoke threw up a red flag—tenement, White, Newport, cliff, concert, Price, Tuxedo, and Oceanside.

"Yes, Price did the hotel at Oceanside, where that big robbery took place a few weeks ago."

"Yep, the place was wiped out during a charity ball. Unbelievable," said Robert.

"Came through the metal ceiling on the top floor, they said," added Cross.

"It was ingenious. Word on the street is that a mastermind named the Engineer planned all these jobs."

A spoonful of peas in vinaigrette sauce was about to enter Cross's mouth when they slid off the utensil, bouncing against his shirt and waistcoat. "Damn," uttered Cross, who, with a flustered expression, looked across the table at his brother.

"I see your table manners haven't much improved since you were ten," said Robert with a laugh.

Trying to wipe out the tiny stains on his bright-white shirtfront, Cross replied, "Really, they call him the Engineer?"

"He's greatly admired by the underworld. Almost like a mythical hero."

Cross smiled feebly.

"Maybe Price is the Engineer. Lorillard's house was robbed, you know, and he designed it," said Robert, rapping his knuckles on the white tablecloth.

"I thought that fake Russian count did that." Cross knew Robert didn't know he was there that night. To protect their privacy, Lorillard wouldn't reveal the rest of his guest list that weekend. A society gentleman would never embarrass his guests in that manner. In their world, it just wasn't done.

Robert laughed so loud that the other patrons turned to look at him. "No, it wasn't him."

"But it can't be Price, old boy."

"And why not?"

"He's not an engineer; he's an architect. World of difference," said Cross, grinning. "One's an artist and the other's not."

Robert let out another explosive laugh.

The conversation was making Cross uncomfortable, so he decided to change the subject to something he knew Robert enjoyed talking about.

"How about dinner tomorrow night, then we'll all go to the theater?"

"Wonderful. Will George be there? I never see him anymore. How is the boy doing?"

"We forced him to come to supper last Saturday," Cross said, sighing. "He's still teaching down in the Bowery. He'll keep at it until fall term starts. He really loves those children. Urchins, every one of them."

"He seems to have turned his back on society. It must drive Helen mad. I'm sure she's picked out at least a dozen suitable wives for him," Robert said with a smile.

Cross nodded. "I've told her time and again to leave him alone, but she won't listen."

"What does he do to occupy his spare time?"

"I'm afraid it's a mystery." And it was. Cross had no idea what

George was doing with his days outside of teaching—secretly, he didn't want to know.

"Does he like the ladies, polo, horse racing…gambling?"

Cross wondered whether his brother saw him react ever so slightly to the last word, like the twitch of a cat's ear or a leaf on a branch moving in the breeze. He realized that his brother knew the truth—and was setting a trap into which he was walking blindly. It was like those tiger traps in India he had read about, in which a deep hole is covered with grass and brush that blends in with the ground cover. He had always tried to be on his guard when he was around Robert for fear of revealing something, but somehow he had grown careless. He was one step away from falling into that hole.

"He inherited Helen's looks, so I imagine he's popular with the girls. He probably hangs about with the men from Harvard. There are a lot of them in the city."

"I'd like to ring him up and ask him out to supper if he's not too busy," said Robert.

"George is very fond of you. I'm sure he'd like that."

"Ah, to be young again. I envy him," Robert said, signaling the waiter for the bill. Before John could protest, he added, "Please, let me take care of it."

As Robert walked up Fifth Avenue, his head was bent in sadness. The police and newspapers had held back the fact that the top floor of the Oceanside Hotel was robbed from above the ceiling. He knew his brother had been at the ball that night.

63

EIGHT THOUSAND? YOU OWE EIGHT THOUSAND? BUT JUST THIS morning, it was fifteen hundred." Kitty fell to her knees on the carpet of her parlor and put her hands over her face, trying to stifle her sobs.

George stood above her in silence, his head bowed.

"I can't do this, George," she moaned. "I just can't. Every day, you risk being beaten to a pulp or killed. I can't go through it anymore."

"Kitty, this is the last time. I swear. I'll never—"

"Do you know how many times you've told me that? A million!" Kitty cried, her eyes blazing with passion. "And each time I believed you with all my heart. Because I love you with all my heart. But no more, George. No more. You're killing me."

"Please..."

"Every day, we scramble for money. It never ends, and it's tearing me apart. One day, they're going to find your body in the river. I don't want to be there for that."

"You know I've tried, Kitty. You know that."

"And it's damn useless. You're powerless, George. You're like a drunk who promises with every sip that this will be his last drink. This sickness has hold of you, and I can't do anything about it." Kitty's voice had gone soft. George had never heard her sound so defeated. "I'm watching the only person I've loved in my entire life destroy himself."

"Kitty, I love you. I do. Together we can beat this. We can't give up."

Kitty stood and looked into George's face. He tried to put his arms around her, but she pushed him away. "No. It's over. I won't do this to myself, not any longer. They say if you love someone enough, you can forgive anything, endure anything, but that's not true," said Kitty. It was as if her entire being had been drained out of her body, and all that was left was a shell.

"You've said that before, darling."

"This time I mean it. It's really over. I want you to leave." Kitty spoke firmly, despite the tears welling in her eyes. "I can't see you again, George. Not ever."

George stood before her, as still as if he'd been turned to stone.

"Please go, George," Kitty said in a soft, defeated voice.

When he didn't respond, Kitty couldn't help herself. She started sobbing violently and pushed him toward the door. He tried to resist, but she kept pushing him. "Get out, damn you. Get out!"

George turned and walked out the door. Kitty slammed it behind him. The sound seemed to echo in his ears for a long time. In spite of himself, he waited in the corridor, hoping she would fling open the door and come after him.

Time passed. All he could hear was Kitty, sobbing softly on the other side of the door.

Alone, George walked slowly down the black iron staircase to the street.

64

T HE WORKMEN GRUNTED AND CURSED UNDER THEIR BREATH AS they transferred gold bars into the wagon. By itself, a single bar wasn't heavy—perhaps five pounds. But the continuous loading was exhausting. Having performed this task countless times over the years, the thought of stealing a bar no longer entered the men's minds. They might as well have been loading bricks.

After the last bar was in the wagon, the men retired to a room in the corner of the cavernous warehouse for coffee and sandwiches. The driver and armed guards would be there in twenty minutes to take the gold to the pier. At 5:00 a.m., before traffic choked the Manhattan streets, they would leave the warehouse on Eleventh Street and First Avenue.

The driver and guards arrived, locked the rear double doors, and started their journey to the pier at Front and Spruce Streets on the Lower East Side. There, the gold would be loaded on a ship bound for Belgium. Instead of an armored wagon, the investment house of Kidder, Peabody & Co. were taking the precaution of transporting gold bullion in an old converted beer wagon, pulled by four dappled gray horses. The setup was meant to avoid unwanted attention. A Pinkerton guard with a revolver sat on top behind the driver, and another guard driving a small milk delivery cart rode ahead. Rather than uniforms, the men wore work clothes.

It was a cool late October morning, and as they clip-clopped slowly through the streets, people emerged onto the sidewalks to prepare for the business day. Men brought out stands of groceries, cranked open awnings over plate glass windows, and set out barrels of goods. As they rode, the men silently scanned the streets, looking for any possible sign of trouble. They had made the trip three times a year for many years, always varying their route. Every time, the early morning scene was the same. As usual, no one paid any attention to their passage.

They crossed Houston Street and turned east on Stanton. Up ahead, before the corner of Columbia, a large masonry warehouse was under construction. Rickety-looking wooden scaffolding had been erected up to the fourth story, where brick was being laid. On the street in front of the building, construction workers in overalls were milling about, getting ready to start the day.

Just as the wagons passed in front of the building, a low creaking sound could be heard, gradually intensifying in pitch. The drivers frantically looked about for the source of the sound and—to their amazement—saw a section of the scaffolding plunging down toward them. With a terrific crash, the brick-laden wooden structure smashed onto the sidewalk, spilling into the street in front of them. The horses screamed and reared, trying to bolt. The drivers barely kept them under control.

Suddenly, and from both sides, men carrying lengths of lead pipe appeared. The construction workers joined them as they leaped onto the wagons, striking the guards viciously. The driver of the beer wagon's skull was split open like a melon, and his guard was battered until he fell off the wagon. The milk cart's driver was yanked from his seat and beaten savagely on the sidewalk. As if in a piece of well-rehearsed choreography, the assailants dragged the bodies into the warehouse. Two men jumped into the driver's seat of the beer wagon and whipped the horses forward onto the south sidewalk, around the debris. The wagon turned south, traveling at top speed, bouncing along Columbia Street and turning west on Delancey. Slowing to match the pace of traffic, it continued on to Kenmare Street and then Broome Street. At Hudson and Laight Streets, it came to the huge Saint John's Terminal, the freight station built by Commodore Vanderbilt for his New York Central Railroad.

Fifty feet tall and constructed of brick and granite, a loading platform ran the entire length of the massive structure, allowing the transfer of goods from wagons to the trains that entered the building.

The driver steered the wagon into one of the forty-foot-wide arched openings and drove up a wide wooden ramp right into an open freight car that was coupled to the many other cars of the New York Central. By yanking the reins hard to the left, the horses were forced to turn the wagon in a tight radius into the car, where the conveyance came to a halt.

As soon as the wagon was in place, Kent, Cross, Brady, and Culver ran up to the freight car and looked in. The horses were nervous and disoriented, stomping about and causing the wagon to rock back and forth.

"Get these goddamn horses off here," yelled Brady to the drivers. "Fast!"

The men jumped down and began to unharness the team, working at top speed.

"This train leaves in ten minutes," Kent said, looking at his pocket watch. "Let's check the goods. Bring a lantern; it's pitch-black in there."

The four men walked up the ramp into the car and went to the back of the wagon. With a crow bar, Brady pried open the double doors. Culver went in first with the lantern.

"Holy shit," Culver yelled.

"A big haul, eh, Mr. Culver?" Kent said.

"Look!" Culver sounded incredulous.

Standing next to a pallet stacked high with gold bars was George Cross.

65

THE MEN STOOD, LOOKING IN AMAZEMENT AT GEORGE, WHO STARED wide-eyed at his father.

"George, for God's sake, what are you doing here?" Cross said, absolutely astonished.

Kent burst out laughing. "The same thing we're doing here, Mr. Cross. Stealing the gold. *Our* gold, I should say."

George jumped out of the wagon and walked up to his father. He swallowed hard before he spoke. "Is this true?"

No words emerged from Cross's mouth. He was in shock.

"What are you doing here, Father?" George asked.

"Your father happens to be my partner, George," Kent said, smiling. The irony of the situation seemed to please him to no end.

George looked at his father, who had turned away from him. Slowly, he walked around and looked his father straight in the face. It was dark at the end of the freight car, and Culver held the lantern high, throwing spooky shadows that danced on the walls.

"But why?" George whispered.

"He was going to kill you if you didn't pay your gambling debts, son. I couldn't let that happen. So I paid off what you owed by planning robberies for him."

"And he does it extremely well," Kent said, lighting up a cigar.

George rubbed his hands over his face and walked slowly away.

"It's too bad, Georgie. Some of this gold might've paid off your current debts...which I understand are considerable," Kent said, turning to smile at Brady and Culver.

Cross looked up at his son, his expression anguished.

George nodded, resigned. "An old classmate who works at Kidder, Peabody & Co. told me about their gold bullion shipments. After the gold was loaded and the workers left, I snuck into the back and hid. The plan was to fill a satchel with bars and break out the back while the wagon was moving."

"Oh Christ, George," Cross said.

"I couldn't come to you for help. I was too damn ashamed…and anyway, you didn't have that kind of money."

"You kept on gambling after I begged you not to," Cross whispered. "Why?"

His father looked like he was shrinking, being crushed to the floor by the weight of this revelation. George wanted to shrink himself, to collapse to the size of an insect and crawl away. Kent, who was enjoying every second of the confrontation, started laughing.

"You don't understand, Father. You can't just walk away from it. I couldn't help myself, and I—"

"Don't feed me that hogwash. You knew you had to stop, and you didn't. Goddamn it, do you know the calamity you've caused? Three people are dead because of you!" Cross grabbed his son by the lapels. But he didn't shake or hit him. Tears filled his eyes, and he placed his head against George's chest and sobbed.

The wagon lurched forward as the horses were led out of the freight car.

George placed his hand on his father's shoulder. "I'm very sorry I got you involved in all this. If I'd known, I would've let this bastard kill me," George said, staring coldly at Kent, who just grinned at him.

"I'm glad I didn't, George. Without you, I never would have met your father and made all this money."

Cross scowled at Kent.

"Sorry to interrupt this tender family reunion, gentlemen, but this train is about to leave the station," Kent said.

Brady shut the wagon doors and led the way out. The men followed him down the ramp to the concrete platform. The drivers removed the ramp, and one of them shut the freight car door. Two minutes later, the wheels of the freight cars began to squeak and squeal as the train crept slowly along the track.

"Next stop will be Peekskill. Peekskill, New York," Culver said, mimicking a railroad conductor's announcement.

"A quiet little town. The perfect place to unload gold," Kent said, patting the side of the car as it moved out, "and take it to the foundry, where we can melt it down and recast it into something a little less conspicuous."

Ignoring Cross and his son, the men parted company and started to walk out to Hudson Street.

"I'll see you at McGlory's at nine," Kent said to Brady and Culver.

"Stand where you are. You're under arrest," a clear voice shouted.

Kent and his men halted, still deep within the shadows of the loading platform. Ten men stood across Hudson Street, pointing shotguns at them.

"I told you to stand where you are. And put your hands up!"

Culver, Coogan, and the driver pulled revolvers and began firing. Blasts from shotguns returned their fire. The other driver took off down the street.

In seconds, the space was so filled with white gun smoke that neither side could see the other. Cross rushed to the edge of the opening. Between gaps in the smoke, he made out his brother reloading a shotgun across the street. To his right, Culver took a blast to the chest and fell down heavily. The driver came to his aid but was hit in the head. Cross could hear Coogan firing away; the reverberation of the pistol reports inside the loading dock was deafening.

He ran back to George, who stood next to the moving train, frozen with fear.

"Follow me," Cross yelled. He grabbed his son by the sleeve and led him in the direction opposite that in which the train was moving. "We have to get on the other side," he whispered.

Gathering his strength, Cross ran along the side of the train and grabbed the brakeman's ladder. In a tremendous effort, he swung himself up between the cars, onto the coupling, and jumped off onto the other side of the platform. George did the same. Cross then pointed to a stair enclosure in the rear wall. Running as fast as they could, he and George made it up to the attic space. Exposed iron roof trusses were lined up, one after another. Cross and his son ran to the south, hopping over the bottom chords of the trusses until they came to another stair at the end of the building. A door at the bottom led directly out the rear, onto Varick Street. At the corner of West Broadway and Grand Street, soaked with sweat and breathing heavily, they hailed a hansom.

"You know your buildings," George said.

"You're damn right I do."

⋅✦⋅ ⋅✦⋅ ⋅✦⋅

Dragging Culver's limp form, Kent, Brady, and Coogan had hitched a ride on the rear platform of one of the cars as it pulled out of the terminal. At West and Morton Streets, they jumped off and ran. Two blocks away, they turned and saw that the train had stopped.

Kent and Coogan, who held Culver by the arms, laid him down gently on the dirt of a side alley. Blood was pouring from his chest. Kent worked frantically to stem the bleeding with his jacket, but it was hopeless. Culver's eyes rolled backward, showing their whites. He was gone.

Kent let out a groan, dropping his head onto Culver's chest. "The sons of bitches killed him," he said, beside himself with anger.

"Christ, that was a close call," Brady growled.

"And they're taking my gold, goddamn it," Kent yelled.

Coogan bent and met Kent's eyes. His face was grim.

"Just before the shooting began, Burgess, one of the drivers, said a Pinkerton named Robert Cross was yelling at us. Man had arrested him once in Buffalo."

Kent froze. "Cross?"

66

So, Cross's brother is a Pinkerton." Oddly, Kent seemed more amused than angry.

"A Pinkerton who killed Culver and took our gold!" Brady said.

"It was Cross who tipped them off this morning. It had to be," Kent said. "I thought he was the traitor after the bank job, but I wasn't sure. Now…"

"I told you Cross was the snitch from the very beginning, but you never believed me," Brady said. He sounded hurt.

Kent walked to the window of his apartment at the Dakota and looked out at the park. He never tired of the view, that vast expanse of green, with people and carriages coming and going. It was like living in the country without having to leave the city. When he was upset, it always had a calming effect on him.

Grimly, he tied his red silk dressing gown more tightly around his waist and sat down on the sofa. Millicent, his wife, appeared at the sliding doors of the library.

"Dinner at eight. Chicken à la Maryland, your favorite," she said.

Kent smiled and raised his hand in a gesture of approval.

"Will Mr. Brady be staying for dinner?"

"I'm afraid not, dear. He has some urgent business to attend to."

Millicent nodded, waved good-bye to Brady, and left quietly.

"Cross has played us for fools. He knew I wouldn't let him go, so he bided his time and sold us out to his brother," Kent said bitterly. "That's how he knew about the gold shipment."

"Cross has to die," Brady said. He stood before Kent, posture stiff with determination.

"Along with his entire family," Kent said, looking up at Brady to make sure he understood his orders. "That's what I promised him would happen if he betrayed us—and I never break a promise."

"It'll be my pleasure."

"It's a shame, though. We had a very lucrative run with Mr. Cross. From a business standpoint, I'll be sorry to see him go. But you know, Mr. Brady, even if he didn't tip them off, with a Pinkerton for a brother, he's still too big a risk to keep on."

"What *about* his brother?"

"I'm afraid he's become a liability as well."

⊹ ⊹ ⊹

"I wanted to thank you for your information about the gold robbery. Kidder, Peabody & Co. was most generous with their reward. It's far more than Fidelity National Bank paid for your information. And it's in gold, waiting for you in the usual location."

"I'm glad to hear that. Gold is the sovereign of sovereigns." The voice emerged from the darkness some fifty feet away.

"If you could please provide me with more details about the robbery, I'd be very grateful. Who was involved, for instance."

"I'd be glad to. Come forward, and we'll talk about it."

Robert Cross stood in the Stygian darkness of a storage pier that stretched out over the East River. He couldn't see a thing, but he knew the source of the voice was directly in front of him. Standing very still, he tried to discern whether there was anyone else on the pier. He could hear only the sound of the river, beating steadily against the pier's wooden pilings below.

Slowly, Robert walked forward, waiting for his eyes to adjust to the dark. His feet kept shuffling through puddles, bumping into piles of trash and pieces of timber. He kept his hand on the trigger of his revolver—just in case his informant turned uncooperative. About twenty feet away, he could make out the outline of a figure.

The voice spoke again. "I can give you their names and tell you where to find them—for more gold, of course."

Robert paused, straining his eyes to get a better view of the man. The fellow remained indistinguishable, a mere black outline against the greater blackness of the pier. Robert inched forward, splashing inadvertently into a puddle. He felt a sudden jolt; it rocked his entire body as if he'd been hit in the chest with a two-by-four. But he didn't fall down. He stood, stunned, as a strange sensation rushed through him.

Finally, he fell face-first into the puddle. His lifeless eyes stayed open, as wide as if he'd seen a terrifying sight.

From out of the shadows, Ned Brady appeared. He walked to an electric panel on the wall from which a long length of wire extended into the puddle and pulled the short metal lever up. Bending over Robert's body, he reached down to his neck and felt for a pulse. Nothing.

"Amazing thing, electricity," Brady said. His words echoed in the silence of the pier.

He picked up the body by the armpits and dragged it to the end of the warehouse, dropping it with a dull thud. Brady pulled up a trapdoor in the wood floor. Below the opening, the current of the East River flowed past in a muffled hush. Occasionally, a dead rat or piece of garbage passed by.

Brady was truly sorry to see the Pinkerton go. He had been a very lucrative source of extra income. Kent had constantly brushed off Brady's requests for a bigger cut on the jobs, refusing to acknowledge the value of his skills or his long service to the organization. But far more than that indignity, Brady loathed being bossed around by an upper-class swell, especially in front of the other men. Kent was rich and educated, so *of course* he always knew better. Brady hated Kent's guts, but he'd kept his volcanic temper in check and bided his time for an opportunity for revenge. And it had paid off handsomely—at least for a while.

With some difficulty, Brady lifted the body and dropped it into the opening. There was the barest sound of a splash. The Pinkerton's body was silently caught up by the rush of water, and in a second, it was gone.

67

Y OU KNOW HE MEANS TO KILL US ALL."

"Yes, George, I'm aware of that," Cross said, his voice devoid of emotion as he ran his hand through his brother's matted hair.

Robert was laid out on a marble morgue slab in the basement of police headquarters at 300 Mulberry Street. The expressionless coroner stood behind Cross and his son. One could tell that he'd silently watched the grieving relatives of the dead hundreds, if not thousands, of times before.

"I remember when I told him that I wanted to be an architect, but our father wouldn't hear of it. Father said I should go into business and become rich, so *I* could boss the architects around. Robert told me that was nonsense, that I should follow my heart and go to Paris to study like I wanted."

"He was such a good man. I wish he'd come to New York earlier." George shook his head, placing his hand on his father's shoulder. "Uncle Robert loved being part of the family."

The coroner edged closer to Cross and said in a quiet voice, "Sir, may I ask you to identify the body?"

"This is Robert Cross, my brother," Cross said heavily.

Nodding, the doctor stretched the white sheet over Robert's head. As Cross and George turned away, an attendant handed them a sack containing Robert's personal effects and his Smith and Wesson .38-caliber pocket revolver.

"What should we do, Father? Tell the Pinkertons?" George asked, nodding toward the glass doors of the room. On the other side stood half a dozen of Robert's colleagues, all of whom had angry, vengeful looks on their faces. No one murdered a Pinkerton and got away with it.

Cross turned to look at them. "No. This is a family matter now. I must take care of this myself, George."

George blocked his path, staring incredulously at his father.

"You can't take on Kent. He may seem like a gentleman, but he's an animal."

"I know that all too well," Cross said, images of the three murders he'd witnessed flashing vividly through his mind. "That's why he must be dealt with very quickly."

"But you can't do it yourself," George said. "You're no match for him and his men."

"I have no choice. I can't stand by and let him murder the rest of my family."

"Then let me help. Please, Father. I caused Uncle Robert's death—I caused all this trouble. This is my fault. You must let me help. You can't do this alone."

❖ ❖ ❖

With her face just inches from his, Helen said in a barely audible voice, "It wasn't an accident, was it, John?"

Cross walked to the parlor window. Outside, a fruit wagon trudged slowly up Madison Avenue. The driver's head was bent over, as if he'd fallen asleep at his post. His brown nag also looked as if it were sleepwalking.

Without turning to face Helen, he said, "No. Robert was murdered."

Helen took a step back, grabbing at the heavy, olive-green velvet curtains that shrouded the tall windows. She said nothing for almost a minute. Then she placed her hand on her husband's.

Cross put his arm around her waist and drew her close. He was proud of Helen for standing up so well to the news. He'd told her immediately after he returned from the morgue. From their experiences in the past few months, he knew she wouldn't collapse to the floor in a faint or fly into hysterics. Rather, and as he expected, a steely calm came over her.

Traveling home in the carriage, Cross had realized that he'd never experienced the tragic, unexpected loss of a loved one. His parents and relatives had died of natural causes after a long life, which wasn't the same thing. No one he knew well had died in the Civil War, perished of a disease, or died in an accident. He wondered whether the insulated, elite world of New York society had enveloped him and his family, their cocoon of privilege protecting them from the cruelties of the world, at the hands of which average people always seemed to suffer. The grinding poverty, disease, and filth that plagued the residents of the Lower East Side and the Bowery, just two miles away, was something one occasionally read about in the newspapers. An unemployed laborer kills himself and his family because he doesn't want them to starve to death in their squalid tenement apartment. A homesick Irish housemaid is worked to death; she can't bear life anymore and drowns herself in the lake at Central Park. Almost every week, a person was run down in the street by a runaway horse or wagon. But the victims were never of the society set. People in his world seemed immune to the random cruelties of life—until now.

He'd looked at George then, sitting next to him in the carriage. Though losing Robert ripped his insides out, secretly he was glad that it hadn't been George—or any of his children. That loss would have been too much to bear. Just the thought made him feel ill.

And it made what he had to do next all the more urgent. He couldn't lose any more of his family.

"You know what you have to do," Helen said, as if reading his mind. There was not a trace of emotion in her voice.

Cross stared at her for a few seconds, amazed at the fury in her beautiful dark eyes. It was almost as if flames were shooting out them.

"I have to think this out—and quickly."

"No. *We* have to think this out," she said.

He smiled at her. She buried her head in his chest and hugged him tightly.

"We can't fail at this, John."

⊹ ⊹ ⊹

Cross knocked lightly on Charlie's door. Entering, he saw that his son's eyes were red and swollen. The boy had been crying since he'd heard the news from his mother. Across the hall, he could hear Julia sobbing in her room. Cross sat on the bed and put his arm around Charlie, who buried his head in his father's chest.

After a few minutes, Cross spoke. "Charlie, I need you and Eddie to do a little detective work for me this afternoon."

Sniffling bravely, Charlie looked up into his father's eyes and nodded.

"I want you to follow some people and find out where they live."

68

CROSS WAITED AN HOUR AFTER THE LIGHTS WENT OUT IN THE FRONT apartment. Only then did he make his way into 181 Mott Street. It was almost 2:00 a.m. and raining. The street was deserted, save a few rats scurrying about in the gutter.

As he approached the building, he couldn't help noticing how nice its facade was. *An inescapable professional habit*, he thought wryly. There was elegant Queen Anne detailing on the brickwork, quite unlike the usual tenement design, and three glass-and-wood doors. The center one offered entry to the tenement. Cross looked across the street at George, who stood in the doorway of the Italian grocery at 178 Mott Street. George looked from side to side down the street and nodded. The coast was clear.

Once inside, Cross hefted the burlap sack he carried and walked down the center hallway to the main stair in the middle of the building. One of the new dumbbell-style tenements, the building was pinched in the center to channel light and air into the interior apartments. Cross climbed the marble steps quietly, listening for the sound of anyone descending. On the third floor, he walked to the two bathrooms located opposite the stair. Indoor plumbing and running water were another innovation in the new design. Previously, one either went to a backyard outhouse or used a chamber pot that had to be emptied into the gutter.

Cross pushed open both lavatory doors. Neither was in use. The layout was the same on every floor, he knew: two bathrooms and two one-room apartments in the front and rear. He walked silently down the hall to the front right apartment. At the entry, he put his ear to the door and listened for almost a minute, then walked back down the hall and stopped by the gaslight mounted on the wall. Standing on tiptoes, he shut off the gas jet. Pulling a large coil of narrow-diameter rubber hose from the sack, Cross fastened one end to the gas nozzle, then began to unravel the coil and carry it back to the apartment door. Kneeling, he bent the end of the stiff hose into an arc and slid about six feet of it slowly into the gap at the bottom of the door.

After inserting the hose, he walked along the hallway, pushing its length flush against the baseboard, where it wouldn't be noticed. From the sack, he pulled out long strips of rag and began stuffing them tightly in the gaps around the door. It took almost five minutes. When he finished, he turned the gas jet on as far as it could go and returned to the stair, checking the bathrooms again before he descended.

Back in the street, he met George in the doorway.

"No one's come in or out," George whispered.

Cross buttoned his jacket against the cold and leaned on the door of the grocery store. They waited in silence. Having discovered each other's secrets, a wall of shame separated father and son. They had not discussed what had happened since the confrontation at the gold wagon. It was too painful, and Robert's death had made it yet more unbearable. It seemed there was nothing to say.

After about a half hour, Cross checked his pocket watch.

"I think we can go," he said.

"Maybe we should wait a bit longer," George said worriedly.

"No, I think it will be all right," Cross said, taking his son's arm and guiding him out onto the sidewalk.

"How'd you know where the bedroom was?" George asked.

"Nick Gillesheimer did the building. He's a friend of mine, and he showed me the drawings."

They were almost to Kenmare Street when they heard an earsplitting explosion. Cross and his son spun and saw a fireball shoot out of the right front apartment windows on the third floor. A second later, a figure dove out the window, engulfed in flames, screaming its lungs out. The body landed on the sidewalk with a dull thud and lay there, burning away like a pile of kindling.

"That's a shame," Cross said, shaking his head. "I'd wanted it to look like suicide. A nice peaceful death in one's sleep."

Scores of people were running out of the buildings that surrounded 181 Mott Street. They watched the body burn in silence. Finally someone brought a blanket to douse the flames.

Fire bells began ringing off in the distance.

"Mr. Coogan must have woken up and wanted a smoke," Cross said with a smile.

69

IT WAS ALMOST 5:00 A.M. EXCEPT FOR THOSE WHO HAD TO LEAVE early for work, the city was still asleep. Only two other people waited with Cross and George on the uptown platform of the Third Avenue Elevated's Grand Street station.

Cross, who hadn't slept in more than twenty-four hours, felt wired, as with electricity, alive with unending energy. His senses seemed hypersensitive, attuned to everything around him, like a wolf sniffing the air before a hunt. In the past hour, the weather had become rainy and misty, but Cross took no notice of the raw cold.

Shrouded by a cloud of steam, the train chugged into the station, its wheels squealing to a stop on the iron rails. Cross walked alongside the train until he found an empty carriage and signaled for George to get on. They found seats on the right-hand side of the car. The track hugged the east side of the Bowery, less than twenty feet from the face of the brick buildings that housed apartments and now-shuttered stores. Most of the windows on the second, third, and fourth floors were dark.

At the intersections of Broome, Delancey, Rivington, and Stanton Streets, they passed the electric streetlights, which threw off a brilliant glow that illumined the inside of the train. When the train reached Houston Street, Cross and George got off and went down to the lower level. They crossed to the downtown side and waited about five minutes for a train, which they rode back to Grand Street. Again, they crossed back to the uptown platform, catching a train that was about to leave the station.

People had started stirring, opening up the storefronts on the street below. Lights flickered on in the apartments. Cross and his son looked out the window, but still they said nothing. The train clattered noisily along the elevated tracks, moving at about ten miles an hour. When a workman in a faded gray shirt and baggy black pants entered the car, they moved to the next carriage, which was completely empty.

The train approached Delancey Street. Cross raised the wooden window sash and stuck his head out. Satisfied, he gave his son a nod. George looked about the car and returned the nod. When the train was at the intersection of the Bowery and Rivington, Cross twisted his entire body through the window opening until his rear end was perched on the sill. Grasping the frame with his left hand, he pulled his brother's Smith and Wesson from his jacket pocket with his right. As the train reached the middle of the block, Cross extended his body as far as he could and fired off six quick shots into a lit window directly opposite. There was the sound of breaking glass and a woman screaming. The train chugged past, and Cross pulled himself into the car. He sat back down on the cushioned seat and placed the revolver in his right jacket pocket.

George calmly shut the window and looked around the carriage. They still had it to themselves. At Houston Street, they got off the train. This time, they descended to the street. It was 5:45 a.m., and many of the Bowery residents were starting their day. Cross and George passed shopkeepers setting out tables and barrels of goods and men and women hurrying to get to work on time. At Lafayette and Great Jones Streets, they hailed a hansom cab.

Still, they did not speak.

✦ ✦ ✦

As dawn broke in an apartment on the Bowery between Rivington and Stanton Streets, a woman screamed desperately, tugging with all her might at the bullet-riddled body of Ned Brady.

Kent's right-hand man slumped, lifeless, over the kitchen table. A pool of blood spread slowly toward his mug of coffee and the piece of cornmeal bread he always liked to have for breakfast.

70

H E'S NOT COMING."

"He's only ten minutes late."

"Ten minutes? Kent's never ten *seconds* late. Punctuality is an obsession for him," George said, leaning back against the trunk of an oak. The leaves on the trees in Central Park were almost gone, and the dead few that remained offered Cross and his son no protection from the cold drizzle. Even in the great coats they'd picked up from Cross's house on the way, George couldn't stop shivering.

"We should wait," Cross said impatiently.

"No!" George was almost shouting. "There's something wrong. He never misses his carriage ride in the morning, not even if it's snowing and sleeting."

Cross fingered the pistol in his coat pocket. It felt as cold as ice. He pulled his black leather gloves from his other pocket and put them on.

George looked up at the Dakota, its four massive towers looming above the park. "Wait here," he said and bolted off.

"George, for God's sake! What are you doing?" Cross shouted after him. But his son had disappeared into the underbrush.

Cautiously, Cross edged out from behind the oak and looked down the carriage path, peering through the rainy mist. In the distance, the track broke away from the Seventy-Second Street Transverse Road and curved east through the trees. He expected to see Kent's gleaming black-and-maroon phaeton gliding around the bend. But the path remained empty, shrouded in gray fog. Cross went back to the tree and positioned himself so his head was barely visible behind the trunk.

He lit a cigarette and blew clouds of smoke, watching them drift up into the sky. The cold, damp weather made them look thicker and puffier. What amazed him most in the last twelve hours was how good he felt about himself. He wasn't wracked by guilt or shame over what he'd done but rather felt a sense of pride. Ever since he'd hired a substitute in the Civil War, Cross had been dogged by the feeling that he was a coward, too scared to do his duty for his country. But he knew he wasn't a coward. He stood up and defended his family from harm without any reservation or fear. There was no hesitating. His wife and children meant everything to him, far more than designing great buildings. And he'd gotten revenge for the killing of his brother, though he couldn't shed the responsibility of getting Robert murdered. He'd have to bear that himself. There was just one more thing to do.

Five minutes later, George appeared, sprinting down the carriage path. "He's not coming," he gasped, out of breath from his run.

"How can you be sure?"

"I talked to the doorman at the Dakota. He knows me. He said that Kent is a guest at the statue unveiling today."

"So that's what all the fuss is about. I couldn't understand why there were so many carriages heading downtown so early in the day. They've come for the parade," Cross said, mind whirling.

Lost in his sorrow over Robert's death and terror over the danger confronting his family, he'd entirely forgotten the unveiling of the new Liberty statute on Bedloe's Island. For weeks, New York had been buzzing about the recently erected copper statue of a woman, holding a torch aloft, a gift to America from the people of France. No one had ever seen anything so colossal. Liberty's nose alone was five feet long.

It had taken a long time to raise the money for the statue's base and pedestal, but when Joseph Pulitzer, publisher of the *World*, sponsored a fund, thousands of nickels and dimes poured in. His friend, Richard Morris Hunt, had done the design. Thousands would march down Fifth Avenue in a parade. Then President Cleveland would go to the

"I hope he has more work for us." Eddie was smiling from ear to ear. He patted the ten-dollar bill in his pants pocket, as if to make sure it was still there.

Eddie Mooney and Charlie had found a choice viewing position by shimmying up an electric streetlight pole at Fifty-Fifth Street and Fifth Avenue. When President Cleveland had passed by in his open carriage, he'd looked up at them and waved. Eddie was sure of it.

They heard a loud clanging sound below. A New York City policeman was banging his long wooden club on the metal pole.

"Get your asses down from there, ya goddamn brats," yelled the florid-faced cop.

"Fuck off," said Charlie, kicking his foot out and knocking the cop's helmet off his head. Frustrated and unable to climb the pole after the boys, the officer grabbed his helmet and stomped away.

✠ ✠ ✠

Compared to the cacophony of Fifth Avenue, Madison Avenue was as quiet and deserted as a tomb. Cross and George walked rapidly. But at Thirtieth Street, they were shocked to see the parade had come east from Fifth to pass directly in front of Cross's house. Thousands were perched on rooftops and hanging out of windows, screaming and cheering.

"What the hell's going on?" George yelled.

After a moment's puzzlement, Cross grasped the reason for the detour.

"Fifth is unpaved from Thirtieth to Twenty-Sixth, remember? They didn't want to march through that muddy slop."

They walked down the west side of Madison Avenue to Thirtieth Street. In the distance, Cross saw the parade turning onto Twenty-Sixth Street at the top of Madison Square and heading back to Fifth Avenue.

Suddenly, he saw Julia at the rear of the crowd between Thirtieth and Twenty-Ninth Streets. George spotted her too.

"Goddamn it," Cross swore, his face going dark with rage. "I told your mother not to let the children out of the house today on any account! Why is Julia in the street? She can see the parade very well from her own parlor."

Beside his sister appeared a tall young man, a bandage covering his right cheek. He handed Julia a brown men's wallet, which the girl quickly slid into her purse.

"Isn't that the man from Julia's coming-out ball?"

"Yes, I think his name was Nolan," George said.

Nolan walked away from Julia, melding into the crowd. After a minute, he returned with another wallet. No one on the sidewalk noticed. They were facing away, busy cheering the parade as it passed by.

George and Cross looked at each other in astonishment. Then a smile came over Cross's face. "It seems our Mr. Nolan has a very interesting occupation."

As Julia and Nolan walked south on Madison Avenue, George and his father rushed across the street to their house. The front stoop was filled with cheering strangers. Helen was at the front parlor window, watching the parade. When they came into the parlor, she rushed to her husband.

"Did you..."

"He wasn't there," Cross said. "He went to that damned dedication on the island where they're unveiling the statue. I just saw Julia out in the street. Didn't I tell you to keep them inside? And where the hell is Charlie?"

"Oh God, John. I tried to mind him, but Charlie slipped out of the house early this morning. He must have gone before anyone was awake. And then that lovely Mr. Nolan came, and he was so solicitous... I didn't see the harm in letting Julia watch with him down the street."

Though he was furious, Cross kept his temper in check. "They could be dead by now, Helen."

"It'll be all right. No one will find Charlie in this throng," George said, putting his hand on his mother's shoulder. "And I'm sure Mother is right: Julia's safe with Nolan."

Cross went to the window. It was surreal to see a flood of soldiers marching straight toward his house, then turning on a dime to the left. Madison Avenue above the Square was always so sedate and quiet. The scene in front of him was jarring. He stood for almost a minute, mind whirling.

"Helen," he said. "Do you know anyone who's going to the dedication?"

"Yes, a few people. They got invitations. It's a special blue card that allows the bearer and a guest to board the steamer to the island."

Cross turned back to look at the parade.

"So you can't go unless you have one of those cards?"

"They won't let anyone on the island without one," Helen said.

Deep in thought, Cross paced back across the parlor, lit a cigarette, and inhaled deeply.

"George, go down to the street and get Julia," he said.

71

*Y*OU ROBBED ALL THOSE PLACES? *YOU* STOLE THE BLUE PHARAOH Diamond?"

"Yes," Cross said calmly.

Julia stood before her father, her mouth open in disbelief, her eyes fixed on the scarlet-and-green rug in the center of the parlor. Cross knew the words "this can't be true" were ringing through her mind.

George and Helen sat on the settee, while Nolan stood by the fireplace. The room was silent, save for the cheering of the crowds outside.

"You're a criminal?"

"Yes."

"And I've helped him. So that makes me a criminal as well," Helen said.

Julia turned to her mother, stunned. Her beauty and poise seemed so at odds with the word, with the very idea of a criminal. "But why would you do such a thing?"

"To save me," George said gravely. "To keep me from getting killed for not paying my gambling debts." He stood and took a few steps toward his sister but stopped.

"I had no choice, Julia," Cross said.

Julia looked at her brother with withering disdain. "This is all about your gambling? Our lives are in jeopardy because of you? You've destroyed our family for a pack of cards!"

Agitated, she began to pace in circles around the parlor table. Then without warning, she ran to George and began to beat her fists on his chest. Gently, Nolan pulled her away and helped settle her in an armchair. Julia was sobbing uncontrollably. Through her tears, she spat out her words into the room.

"Our prim and proper society family isn't what it seems, is it? We're all just hiding in secret worlds where we escaped to be happy, away from that harsh Knickerbocker code. A code we had to obey even if we didn't believe in it. But we all decided that we didn't want to let it govern every second of our lives. For just a little while, we wanted to be free of it. What would Aunt Caroline say about us?"

Cross chuckled drily. "She'd drop dead from a heart attack."

Revealing his life of crime to Julia was humiliating. At the same time, he was proud of her perceptiveness. She showed remarkable insight, especially for a seventeen-year-old.

"My father, mother, both my brothers—and me—we all lead double lives. We all fled the emotionally repressive world of our birth. Who could imagine such a thing?" Julia gave a wan smile, shaking her head.

George knelt in front of his sister. "You can't understand, Julia. I'm so ashamed of what I've done, but I can't help myself. I tried to repay the debt." George had tears in his eyes. "Over and over, I tried to pay it."

Julia swallowed her sobs and looked her brother squarely in the eyes. "I was at Cantwell's the day you lost ten thousand dollars. I saw you at the Yellow Dragon too, and at O'Malley's."

George looked at his sister in shock.

"You could've walked away so easily every time," Julia said, great scorn in her voice.

"That's what you don't understand. I couldn't. A sickness has hold of me."

"What absolute nonsense."

"I know it seems so, but until you've stood in my shoes, you can't understand what it's like. I'm *compelled* to do it. Like a sorcerer's spell." George went to the window and stood, silhouetted against the pane. "There's no sense trying to explain it," he said unhappily.

"You sicken me, George. It's one thing to destroy yourself. It's quite another to destroy your entire family! Because of you, we're all going to die, just like Uncle Robert. Charlie is only ten years old!"

"No one's going to die," Cross said in a commanding voice. It was more of an order than a statement. "Not if we work together."

⁌ ⁌ ⁌

"Oh my goodness, I'm so clumsy. Please forgive me."

A light but steady rain was falling, and the pier at Twenty-Third Street was clogged with black umbrellas. A short, elegantly dressed gentleman tipped his top hat to Julia and smiled.

"It's so crowded here," Julia said breathlessly.

"No problem at all, miss. What miserable weather for the unveiling."

"It's awful—so damp and cold. I should be home in front of a big fire in my parlor, drinking hot chocolate," Julia said, batting her eyelashes.

"I wish I was home right now, but I was invited and must go," the man said.

"Try to stay warm, then," Julia said, waving and skipping away. She saw the disappointment on the man's face. Clearly, he wanted nothing more than to stay and talk to a pretty girl.

Making her way through the crowd, she met up with Nolan about ten yards away. "Got it?" she asked.

Nolan pulled a blue card from his coat pocket. "You're an expert stall," he said and smiled at her proudly. Though the confrontation with her family had left Julia solemn, even sullen, the compliment brought a smile to her face.

"I've been trained by a master," she said.

He took her by the arm and ducked under her umbrella. Together, they wormed their way through the crowd. By the railing, they met Cross, Helen, and George. Looking around surreptitiously, Nolan quickly slipped Cross the blue invitation.

"Thanks, John. We're very grateful. Now we must be on our way," Cross said, patting Nolan on the shoulder.

"Good luck, Mr. Cross. Be careful dealing with Kent. Even without his men, he's dangerous." Cross saw the concern in the young man's face and was touched by it. "Are you sure you don't want me to come with you? I'd do it gladly," Nolan added.

Shaking his head, Cross shook his hand, smiling.

Beside them, Julia grabbed the sleeve of George's black greatcoat. "I'm sorry for what I said. I didn't mean it."

"No, Julia. When people get angry with one another, they say exactly what they feel. Then, later, they say they didn't mean it because they feel guilty. You meant it…and you were right," George said, hugging his sister and kissing her cheek.

Cross looked squarely into his daughter's face. He saw how worried she was. "I promise you, Julia, everything will be all right. I want to read a chapter of your book tonight. Have it ready for me, please."

A gust of cold, damp air swept up the East River. Julia shivered and gave a weak wave, eyes fixed sadly on her parents and brother.

Bulling his way through the crowd, Cross led his wife and son to the gangplank, which was admitting passengers. It led up to a steamer that had been painted bright white with red trim for the special occasion. Its two funnels billowed forth thick, black smoke. Cross handed Helen the invitation. When they got to the foot of the gangplank, where a seaman was stationed, she waved it in front of his face.

"Here's my blue card. As you can see, I've brought an extra guest, my son. I hope you don't mind." Helen gave the seaman her brightest, most charming smile.

"Ma'am, I ain't supposed to let but one guest on 'cause I—"

Helen moved closer, pouring on the charm. "It's just my son, and it's such a special day—you won't tell, will you?"

The seaman, who was no more than eighteen, broke into a shy smile and unhooked the chain barring the gangway.

As he watched the Crosses board, Nolan turned to Julia. "Your father's a brave man," he said. "Not many fathers would have the courage to do what he's about to."

Julia wrapped her arm around Nolan's waist and snuggled against him. Together, they watched the steamer cast off. The thought that she might never see her father, mother, or brother alive again lingered in Julia's mind, but with great determination, she drove it away.

٭ ٭ ٭

Fully loaded, the *Indomitable* reached the tip of the Battery. Cross and George could see thousands of cheering people lining the sea wall. But a thick mist had settled over the bay, and the Statue of Liberty Enlightening the World could not be seen. There was only a ghostly procession of navy ships, tugboats, yachts, and steamers plying the lead-colored water and continuously blowing their steam whistles.

These ships comprised the two flotillas, which were sailing down the Hudson and East rivers through the constant drizzle and mist. To the east, Cross heard a blast of artillery fire from Governor's Island, which was apparently a signal for the naval men-of-war to fire a salute. This marked the entry of President Grover Cleveland's ship into the bay. The other vessels blew their whistles even more frantically, as if to make up for the fact that they didn't have cannons to fire. The deafening noise made Cross's ears ring, and he retreated to the stateroom, which was full of people and cigar smoke. Out of the tightly packed crowd came Helen, smiling nervously. Despite their strained circumstances, she looked ravishing in her long, navy-blue coat with white rabbit-fur collar and sleeves. The matching hat, adorned with a long feather, was particularly captivating. All the men stared, and all the women were jealous.

"Senator Evarts is giving a speech first. When he finishes, Bartholdi, the sculptor, will yank a cord to pull the veil from Liberty's face," Helen said in a low voice. "Then President Cleveland will speak."

The noise made it very hard to hear. Cross signaled that they should go out on deck. By the ship's rail, Helen continued. "Kent and the other guests are already on the grandstand, waiting for the president. They're on the seaward side of the pedestal. Remember, the unveiling happens the minute Evarts finishes his speech. That's our chance."

"We must make sure we're the last to leave the ship. That will give us leave to work our way to the grandstand," Cross said to George.

Helen gasped. Cross, in a panic, looked up and down the deck.

"No. Up there," she pointed.

A V-shaped opening had formed in the heavy gray mist. Towering above them appeared the statue.

"Good God," cried George. "It's incredible."

Looking down at them was an enormous woman's head. She wore a spiked crown, and a portion of her raised arm and shoulder could be seen too. A tricolor veil hung from the crown, covering her eyes and nose and reminding Cross of veiled Arab women he'd seen in stereo-scopic views of the Holy Land. The scale of the head was overwhelming. As a boy, Cross had read about the seven wonders of the ancient world. Among them was the Colossus of Rhodes, a gargantuan statue of a god straddling a harbor. *It must have been like this*, Cross thought, mesmerized. They'd been erecting Liberty for a year; it had been finished in April, but it had been only a speck in the bay. Not until one got close up could its enormity be comprehended.

"I heard that the model was Bartholdi's mistress," said George with a sly smile.

"It has to be at least a hundred and fifty feet tall," Cross said. Hunt's pedestal, as tall as a four-story building, was beautiful in its own right, monumental without overpowering the statue. As the ship drew closer to Bedloe's Island, the presence of the copper-clad woman grew even more dramatic. All three Crosses stood, transfixed.

The *Indomitable*'s engines rumbled into reverse, and it expertly nudged up alongside the pier on the south side of the island. Cheering broke out among the excited passengers, who started filing out onto the deck. The Crosses' attention snapped back to the task at hand. The passengers spilled down the gangplank like water rushing into a trough, and Helen joined them. Cross and George hung back. About a hundred yards away, on top of the star-shaped base of the statue and hard against the pedestal, they could see a large grandstand, filled to capacity. Beside it was an elevated platform draped with the American and French flags, where the main speakers would talk. Looming above was the pedestal and the colossus.

Despite the urgency of their situation, Cross couldn't take his eyes off the statue. The tricolor veil was soaked with rain and plastered to the woman's face, allowing her features to be seen distinctly. A cord attached to the veil threaded through one of the openings of the crown, and Cross saw three men looking out.

72

CROSS AND GEORGE STAYED ON THE DOCK UNTIL THE PRESIDENT and his party were almost to the grandstand. Cross had no idea where Helen might be. For the moment, it was unimportant. Exchanging looks with George, he and his son moved as one into the crowd.

They reached the left end of the structure and, for the first time, got a good look at the crowd. To Cross's disappointment, the guests were huddled under a sea of umbrellas, making it almost impossible to recognize individual faces.

"How the hell will we find him?" George whispered.

Cross was perplexed but said, "Follow me."

He and George walked underneath the grandstand behind the speakers' platform. It was all an open-bleacher arrangement, they discovered.

"He'll be sitting in the back half," said Cross. He took off his right glove and placed his hand on the pistol in his pocket. Nodding to one another, father and son split up. Each man slowly walked under the rows of seats, looking up at the backs of the spectators.

When the president was seated, the festivities began. The Reverend Dr. Richard Storrs delivered a mercifully short prayer. He was followed by the creator of the Suez Canal, the Frenchman Ferdinand de Lesseps, who also kept his comments to a minimum. Then the main speaker, Senator Evarts, took the stand. As he droned on, George and Cross kept searching for Kent. The rows were at least a hundred feet long. Up and down they went, peering up at the exposed lower backs of the spectators. Rain dripped down from everywhere. Finally George signaled to his father, pointing to a spot above him.

Cross followed his son's gaze and saw a polished ebony cane with a distinctive serpentine gold inlay coiling up its shaft. He looked at George and nodded.

"We have a few more minutes before the speech is over," he whispered, still holding the pistol in his pocket.

Evarts was discussing the assistance rendered by France to America during the Revolution when he decided to take a pause. Two seconds later, a roar went up from the crowd. The senator turned and saw that, to his horror, the veil had been removed from Lady Liberty's face. Bartholdi, along with the builders of the statue, had thought the pause meant the long-winded speech was over. They had yanked the cord, pulling the veil off and up through the large openings in the brim of the crown. At the same time, ships in the bay blasted steam whistles and horns, and the men-of-war opened up continuous cannon fire with their big guns.

The din was even louder than before, more deafening than the eruption of an earthquake. Great columns of smoke rose from the ships, blending into the fog. The flames from their guns sent yellow and scarlet flashes into the dark gray mist.

Cross was dumbfounded by the explosion of sound. It was supposed to provide cover for his pistol shot, but he was completely caught off guard. Pulling out his weapon, he fumbled and dropped it on the wet grass. He tried to pick it up but dropped it again. When he finally gained control, he hurriedly raised the pistol to take aim at Kent's back. But the crowd had gone wild with excitement and was rising to its feet. As Cross pulled the trigger, Kent stood too. The bullet whistled through the right leg of Kent's dark gray trousers and ripped a hole in the umbrella of a man directly in front of him. Though the report was drowned out by the racket, Kent instantly realized what had happened. He looked down and, through the grandstand, saw Cross and George gaping up at him. Then he bolted to the left.

Cross gave his son a panicked look and ran in the same direction, trying to catch a glimpse of the fleeing figure. Dropping his umbrella, Kent shoved past the people in his row. At the end of the grandstand, he jumped, taking a long fall to the sodden grass.

Just twenty feet ahead, Cross saw a figure drop to the ground, roll, and take off running, his top hat falling from his head. The speed with which Kent could run surprised him. In a second, the man had disappeared around the corner of the pedestal. Cross had no idea where he was headed; the island was basically barren, and the only wooded area was hundreds of yards away.

George shot past his father, just glimpsing Kent's leg as it flashed around the northeastern corner of the pedestal. He followed and saw Kent slip in the entry on the north side. Panting, George waited for his father to catch up.

"He's gone inside," he said to Cross, who was also gasping for breath, his chest heaving like a bellows.

"There're entries on all four sides of the pedestal. He'll probably try to go out another one and make a break for the pier," Cross said.

"We have to go in and see," said George.

They entered the base, but Kent was nowhere to be seen. Three men in cutaway coats and top hats came down a stairway and walked past with quizzical looks on their faces.

"He could be down here, hiding. You look around. I'll take the stairs. Meet me on the upper level," Cross said. George ran off, and Cross began to climb. The pedestal contained one straight-run iron stair with intermediate landings. At each one, Cross had to stop and catch his breath. Finally, he came to the spiral stair in the statue itself and pulled out his pistol.

As he climbed, he observed its inner structure: it reminded Cross of a huge oil derrick supporting an intricate iron armature. The spiral stairway was dimly lit with electric bulbs that cast spooky shadows on the copper folds of the statue's toga.

He must have traversed more than a hundred steps before he

realized the climb was a waste of time. Natural light was filtering down to him from above, however, and his curiosity got the better of him. Instead of turning back, Cross continued on. The closer he got to the top, the more light flooded the stair. He was a dozen steps from the platform on the crown. It was a relief to enter a bright, wide-open space after going around and around in the cramped dark. He could rest there before going down. Perhaps he might even spot Kent, running to the pier.

When he finally reached the iron-plate platform, his eyes were immediately drawn to the big, windowless openings that lined the brim of the statue's crown. As the dark gray mist swirled in front of them, damp wind blew through the five-foot-high gaps with unexpected force. Cross ran up the last few steps of the spiral stair, rushed to one of them, and leaned out. It was an exhilarating feeling to be up so high and feel the cold breeze on his face. The bay was still enveloped in a pea soup of fog, but he could see the ceremony going on directly below him. The people looked like ants. Cross braced his arms on the sides of the opening and stretched his body out as far as it could go. The sensation was incredible.

"So good to see you again, Mr. Cross. I understand that we have business to discuss," said a voice from the shadows.

Cross was so startled that he cried out. He felt like he might faint and pitch through the opening.

Kent stepped into the light. Dressed in a black sable coat, he was twirling his cane and smiling. "I see that you've come today to dissolve our partnership. What a coincidence. I had the same idea." He drew the long, thin saber from his cane and started walking toward Cross, who staggered away from the opening. "I'll be sorry to see you go," he added. "We've had a very lucrative run."

Before Cross could reach for his pistol, Kent lunged forward and stabbed him in his left shoulder. He moved with the finesse of a Prussian swordsman. Cross watched in amazement as blood trickled onto the front of his greatcoat. He stumbled backward and fell to the platform on top of the wet tricolor that had been yanked off the statue.

"That's a very handsome coat you have on. I didn't realize it was so thick," Kent said. He raised the blade with both hands above his head, ready for the final thrust. Cross looked at him, accepting the inevitable.

As the blade commenced its downward arc, Cross bent his head, but then from the corner of his eye, he saw a pair of arms grab Kent's ankles and yank them out from under him. He fell flat on his face on top of Cross, who twisted his body to see George's head sticking out of the spiral stairway opening at the level of the platform. It almost looked like a decapitated head sitting on the floor. George clambered up the rest of the iron steps, but at the last instant, he stumbled, giving Kent time to stand up and raise the blade. As George advanced, Kent slashed him on the forehead, just above his left eyebrow. Stunned, George brought his hand to his forehead. His palm came away red.

Seeing the blood on his hand had the effect of setting a match to kerosene. George exploded with rage. He charged Kent, ramming his shoulder into his midsection as if he were tackling a football runner. Kent didn't have time to raise the blade again, and the sheer force of George's rush slammed into him, sending Kent's body out one of the tall openings that surrounded the crown. At the last second, George grabbed the side of the opening, preventing himself from falling out.

In shock, he watched as Kent plummeted through the air. Screaming, the criminal mastermind flailed his arms and legs wildly in panic until his body slammed down onto the statue's left shoulder, where the sculpted copper clasp fastened the woman's outer cloak.

Cross ran up to the adjacent opening and leaned out. Kent's lifeless body rested faceup on the shoulder of the statue. He lay with his head pointing downward, precariously perched on the raised clasp. The fall had plainly broken his back and neck. Kent's eyes stared sightlessly into the cloudy sky. The body slid a few inches downward, but the large metal fold of the cloak stopped it from falling any further.

Cold rainy wind sprayed their faces. Cross leaned farther out and saw that Kent's body was positioned directly above the ceremony. Someone, probably President Cleveland, was speaking at the podium. The steam whistles of the boats in the bay could still be heard in the distance.

Cross pulled his son back through the opening. Blood was dripping into George's eye and running down his cheek.

"We have to get down from here, George. If Kent slides off and falls on top of the guests, people are going to come running up here. They'll be asking questions we don't want to answer."

George pulled out a handkerchief and wiped his face. Looking down, he saw Kent's body slide a few more inches on the wet, slippery copper.

"Let's get the hell out of here," he said.

They began a mad dash down the spiral stair, their heavy footsteps echoing off the inside face of the copper cladding. Cross was dizzy from going around and around so many times. When he got to the bottom, he had to pause and steady himself. George grabbed him by the sleeve and led him down the stair in the pedestal. At every step, they expected to meet policemen or soldiers coming up the stairs. But there was no one.

When they finally reached ground level, Cross thought his lungs were going to explode like overfilled balloons. When George tried to drag him along, he shook him off.

"We have to get back to the pier," George yelled. He took hold of the collar of his father's coat and yanked him along. In less than a minute, they were outside the pedestal's north entry. Still, there was no one about. They made a wide circle to the south, avoiding the ongoing ceremony by walking out of sight below the base, keeping their eyes glued to the left shoulder of the statue. Cross could have sworn that the body had moved again.

When they approached the pier, they were surprised to find Helen waiting. In all the excitement, they'd forgotten about her. She beckoned to them, and they ran down the pier to meet her.

"There's a private launch leaving right now. I told them my husband took ill, and they said they'd give us a ride back to Manhattan," she said in a commanding voice.

As one, George and Cross embraced her.

"It's over, Helen. Everything will be all right," Cross whispered. He was sobbing.

Helen looked into her husband's eyes and caressed his cheek. He smiled at her.

"You were so brave, my dear," he said tenderly. He took her in his arms and hugged her. Then she turned and gave George a long, tight hug too.

The launch slowly chugged across the water, threading its way through the maze of steamers, yachts, tugboats, and navy vessels in the foggy bay. Huddled together on a bench in the little foredeck, Cross wrapped his arms around Helen and held her close, nuzzling her sweet-smelling hair. After a few minutes, he rose and approached the pilot at the wheel of the launch.

"May I use your spyglass?" he asked.

"Of course, sir. That Liberty statue is a grand sight, isn't she?" asked the pilot, a rotund and swarthy Italian.

"She is indeed," Cross said.

Through the glass, he saw that Kent's lifeless body still lay on the shoulder of the statue.

73

L OOK AT THIS WONDERFUL SUNBURST PATTERN—ALL DONE IN GOLD
thread. Doesn't it look marvelous against the dark green satin?"
Helen, walking slowly past the rows of gowns, had stopped to pull
one out for closer inspection. "There are tiny pearls entwined in the
embroidery. The House of Pingat always does such beautiful work."

Satisfied with her selection, Helen handed the gown to her husband, who rolled it up and placed it in a long canvas bag. She continued
walking and made six more selections.

Without saying a word to each other, she and Cross walked into
Henry Linden-Travers's bedroom and entered his large, paneled dressing room. Cross made the selections, taking evening wear, cutaway
coats, frock coats, waistcoats, and every pair of shoes and boots on the
shoe rack. He then gathered every silk shirt and cravat. Everything
went into another canvas bag.

Back in Mrs. Linden-Travers's bedroom, they retrieved a bag of
jewelry that must have weighed twenty pounds. Walking down the
monumental main stair, Helen smiled at her husband.

"Not a bad night," she said happily.

"Yes. I might even call it a good night," Cross said. Though weighed
down by the bags, he managed to give his wife a kiss on the cheek.

Once their travails were over, Cross and Helen had realized that
something was missing in their lives. Planning the robberies had
brought them together in a way nothing else in their twenty-three years
of marriage had ever done. And they made an excellent team. But best
of all, they had both experienced the same sense of exhilaration Kent

had described when Cross asked him why he was a criminal. It was a sense of ecstasy like no other.

Since Kent's death, whenever Cross designed a private residence or apartment building or bank, he couldn't help thinking about how he would rob it. At first, it was a parlor game, but after a time, it became a real plan that he and Helen put into action. Every other month, husband and wife planned and carried out a robbery. The anticipation was delightful. Though neither would admit it aloud, the robberies brought a renewed sense of love and commitment to their marriage. They were happy, deeply and purely happy.

On the first floor, the Crosses took a last turn around the parlor, just in case they had overlooked some item of value. When the social season ended in mid-February, the parvenus left New York for a warmer climate: Florida, California, even Italy. The Linden-Traverses were wintering in Saint Augustine. Their city mansion would be shut up for months. It was after 2:00 a.m., and the house was pitch-black. Cross and Helen used a small lantern for illumination.

In the main parlor, Helen picked up a gold cigarette case with a large ruby centered on its front and placed it in a bag. "I think we have enough for tonight, don't you?" she said.

"Mmm, maybe a bit more," Cross said, raising the lantern to look around.

After they had brought down Kent's Gents, Cross and Helen had worried that George would go back to his old ways, putting his life at risk with his debts. They sat George down for a lecture about the evils of gambling. At first, they believed his uncontrollable habit was a moral defect, as the reformers of the day claimed. Soon, though, they came to understand the nature of their son's problem. George suffered from a disease for which there was no vaccine or cure. He was unable to stop, no matter how hard he tried; the craving for gambling in any form—faro, horse racing, dice—was too powerful to fight.

But somehow, Robert's murder had changed things. Stunned by

the murder of his uncle, George hadn't gambled in a year. His mother and father were relieved but continued to hold their breath. George was walking on a tightrope. The tiniest slip would cause him to fall back into his old habits. Merely handling a deck of cards could be fatal. No matter how guilty he felt about the heartbreak he'd caused, he might not be able to fight the urge.

Still, since he had taken up his teaching position at Saint David's, George had seemed content. He had even acquiesced to his Aunt Caroline's and his mother's matchmaking efforts and had begun to socialize with some girls of his own set. All the same, Helen and Cross squirreled away some of their illicit earnings in a rainy day fund, fearful that a time when George was in danger would come again.

"Now I think we're finished," said Cross. He extinguished the lantern, and together they walked down to the basement kitchen and out to the rear courtyard.

It was a crisp, cold March night. There wasn't a cloud in the sky, only a blanket of stars shimmering above them. Cross took a deep breath, savoring the quiet. A slight breeze rustled the naked branches of the trees in the Linden-Traverses' backyard. The fresh air was invigorating; beside him, Cross saw Helen with her head tipped back, smiling.

Slowly, he opened the wrought iron gate and poked his head out, surveying East Eighty-Seventh Street. At the corner of Park Avenue, Eddie Mooney waved, the signal that it was safe to proceed. On Fifth Avenue, Charlie did the same.

From around the corner, a brougham slowly clip-clopped toward Cross. The driver, John Nolan, carefully and quietly backed it up to the gate. Behind the bench seat, a removable wall panel hid a compartment in which the goods could be stowed. Nolan smiled at Cross, who began handing him the canvas bags.

In the year that he'd spent getting to know him, Cross had grown fond of Nolan. To their mutual surprise, he didn't hold the boy's background or profession against him. In fact, with his good looks and poise, Nolan blended right into society. He'd even charmed Aunt Caroline, though she remained in utter ignorance as to his true identity. He and Julia continued to share each other's company while she was up in Poughkeepsie attending Vassar. For now, they were happy.

With the brougham loaded, Cross helped Helen up onto the seat next to Nolan, and they rattled off down Park. The few large houses amid the vacant lots in the neighborhood were dark, hazy silhouettes against a bluish-black sky. At that hour, not a soul was on the streets.

That was what all their jobs were like. Not once had anyone stopped them. If they had, they would see only a well-to-do family returning home for the night. Charlie and Eddie had melted into the darkness; soon, Charlie would find his way home. Cross had offered Eddie money to find a real room, but the boy stubbornly refused to give up his boiler.

As they rode, Cross thought about how much their lives had changed in the past eighteen months. They weren't the same people. Julia was right: their lives had been a facade, hiding a secret. He smiled at the apt architectural metaphor. There were no secrets in his family anymore.

Their double lives were known to each other, but not to the society world they still inhabited, a universe governed by unforgiving rules. But they would gladly take that risk; their clandestine life was liberating and exhilarating, and they refused to give it up. At the same time, they enjoyed the privileges of society. If it seemed hypocritical, so be it. He was proud that his family had challenged the Knickerbocker code. And Cross had no regrets about what he had done.

And he was a full-time architect again, designing some of the best buildings of his career, producing work that was truly creative and original, done in his own vision, no one else's. But every time his ego puffed up about his architecture, he'd stop himself and realize how it paled in comparison to what he'd done for his family.

At Madison Avenue and Thirtieth Street, Helen and Nolan disembarked. Cross waved to his wife as she went up the front stoop and then nodded to Nolan, who disappeared down the street. He gave the reins a snap and headed downtown.

Tonight, he would convince Bella Levine to take forty-five cents on their goods.

Reading Group Guide

1. In order to save his family, John Cross must do something he finds morally reprehensible. Would you resort to criminality to save your family from death?

2. This is a story about the double lives a family chooses to live. Which was your favorite?

3. Until 1914, Americans could ingest any drug they wanted, including dangerous drugs that are outlawed today. What did you think of Granny's preference for opium?

4. James T. Kent, a well-bred gentleman from a wealthy family, is a cold-blooded killer and gets an almost sexual satisfaction from committing crime. Was he a compelling villain?

5. New York high society had a very strict code of behavior that one had to obey or be banished. What did you think of that code? Why did that code devolve into the less-stringent rules of behavior we have today?

6. How does poverty in America today compare with that portrayed in the Gilded Age in New York City?

7. Homelessness is a great concern in our cities today. What did you think of the fact that about twenty thousand children roamed the streets of New York in the 1880s?

8.   Cross's children form friendships with people they normally would never come into contact with. What did you like about Julia and Nolan's friendship? Charlie and Eddie's? George and Kitty's?

9.   George's gambling addiction was the source of all the troubles. How did you feel about George and his illness? Were you angry with him?

10.   Cross was devastated when he learned of his son's secret. What would you as a parent have been thinking and feeling?

Read on for an excerpt from Charles Belfoure's

::::THE::::

PARIS

ARCHITECT

A NOVEL

Available now from Sourcebooks Landmark

1

J UST AS LUCIEN BERNARD ROUNDED THE CORNER AT THE RUE LA
Boétie, a man running from the opposite direction almost collided
with him. He came so close that Lucien could smell his cologne as he
raced by.

In the very second that Lucien realized he and the man wore the
same scent, L'Eau d'Aunay, he heard a loud crack. He turned around.
Just two meters away, the man lay facedown on the sidewalk, blood
streaming from the back of his bald head as though someone had
turned on a faucet inside his skull. The dark crimson fluid flowed
quickly in a narrow rivulet down his neck, over his crisp white collar,
and then onto his well-tailored navy-blue suit, changing its color to
a rich deep purple.

There had been plenty of killings in Paris in the two years since
the beginning of the German occupation in 1940, but Lucien had
never actually seen a dead body until this moment. He was oddly
mesmerized, not by the dead body, but by the new color the blood
had produced on his suit. In an art class at school, he had to paint
boring color wheel exercises. Here before him was bizarre proof that
blue and red indeed made purple.

"Stay where you are!"

A German officer holding a steel blue Luger ran up alongside him,
followed by two tall soldiers with submachine guns, which they immediately trained on Lucien.

"Don't move, you bastard, or you'll be sleeping next to your friend,"
said the officer.

Lucien couldn't have moved if he'd wanted to; he was frozen with fear.

The officer walked over to the body, then turned and strolled up to Lucien as if he were going to ask him for a light. About thirty years old, the man had a fine aquiline nose and very dark, un-Aryan brown eyes, which now stared deeply into Lucien's gray-blue ones. Lucien was unnerved. Shortly after the Germans took over, several pamphlets had been written by Frenchmen on how to deal with the occupiers. Maintain dignity and distance, do not talk to them, and above all, avoid eye contact. In the animal world, direct eye contact was a challenge and a form of aggression. But Lucien couldn't avoid breaking this rule with the German's eyes just ten centimeters from his.

"He's not my friend," Lucien said in a quiet voice.

The German's face broke out into a wide grin.

"This kike is nobody's friend anymore," said the officer, whose uniform indicated he was a major in the Waffen-SS. The two soldiers laughed.

Though Lucien was so scared that he thought he had pissed himself, he knew he had to act quickly or he could be lying dead on the ground next. Lucien managed a shallow breath to brace himself and to think. One of the strangest things about the Occupation was how incredibly pleasant and polite the Germans were when dealing with their defeated French subjects. They even gave up their seats on the Metro to the elderly.

Lucien tried the same tack.

"Is that your bullet lodged in the gentleman's skull?" he asked.

"Yes, it is. Just one shot," the major said. "But it's really not all that impressive. Jews aren't very athletic. They run so damn slow it's never much of a challenge."

The major began to go through the man's pockets, pulling out papers and a handsome alligator wallet, which he placed in the side pocket of his green-and-black tunic. He grinned up at Lucien.

"But thank you so much for admiring my marksmanship."

A wave of relief swept over Lucien—this wasn't his day to die.

"You're most welcome, Major."

The officer stood. "You may be on your way, but I suggest you visit a men's room first," he said in a solicitous voice. He gestured with his gray gloved hand at the right shoulder of Lucien's gray suit. "I'm afraid I splattered you. This filth is all over the back of your suit, which I greatly admire, by the way. Who is your tailor?"

Craning his neck to the right, Lucien could see specks of red on his shoulder. The officer produced a pen and a small brown notebook.

"Monsieur. Your tailor?"

"Millet. On the rue de Mogador." Lucien had always heard that Germans were meticulous record keepers.

The German carefully wrote this down and pocketed his notebook in his trouser pocket.

"Thank you so much. No one in the world can surpass the artistry of French tailors, not even the British. You know, the French have us beat in all the arts, I'm afraid. Even we Germans concede that Gallic culture is vastly superior to Teutonic—in everything except fighting wars, that is." The German laughed at his observation, as did the two soldiers.

Lucien followed suit and also laughed heartily.

After the laughter subsided, the major gave Lucien a curt salute. "I won't keep you any longer, monsieur."

Lucien nodded and walked away. When safely out of earshot, he muttered "German shit" under his breath and continued on at an almost leisurely pace. Running through the streets of Paris had become a death wish—as the poor devil lying facedown in the street had found out. Seeing a man murdered had frightened him, he realized, but he really wasn't upset that the man was dead. All that mattered was that *he* wasn't dead. It bothered him that he had so little compassion for his fellow man.

But no wonder—he'd been brought up in a family where compassion didn't exist.

His father, a university-trained geologist of some distinction, had had the same dog-eat-dog view of life as the most ignorant peasant. When it came to the misfortune of others, his philosophy had been tough shit, better him than me. The late Professor Jean-Baptiste Bernard hadn't seemed to realize that human beings, including his wife and children, had feelings. His love and affection had been heaped upon inanimate objects—the rocks and minerals of France and her colonies—and he demanded that his two sons love them as well. Before most children could read, Lucien and his older brother, Mathieu, had been taught the names of every sedimentary, igneous, and metamorphic rock in every one of France's nine geological provinces.

His father tested them at suppertime, setting rocks on the table for them to name. He was merciless if they made even one mistake, like the time Lucien couldn't identify bertrandite, a member of the silicate family, and his father had ordered him to put the rock in his mouth so he would never forget it. To this day, he remembered bertrandite's bitter taste.

He had hated his father, but now he wondered if he was more like his father than he wanted to admit.

As Lucien walked on in the glaring heat of the July afternoon, he looked up at the buildings clad in limestone (a sedimentary rock of the calcium carbonate family), with their beautiful rusticated bases, tall windows outlined in stone trim, and balconies with finely detailed wrought iron designs supported on carved stone consoles. Some of the massive double doors of the apartment blocks were open, and he could see children playing in the interior courtyards, just as he had done when he was a boy. He passed a street-level window from which a black-and-white cat gazed sleepily at him.

Lucien loved every building in Paris—the city of his birth, the most beautiful city in the world. In his youth, he had roamed all over Paris, exploring its monuments, grand avenues, and boulevards down to the grimiest streets and alleys in the poorest districts. He could read the history of the city in the walls of these buildings. If that Kraut bastard's aim had been off, never again would he have seen these wonderful buildings, walked these cobblestone streets, or inhaled the delicious aroma of baking bread in the boulangeries.

Farther down the rue la Boétie, he could see shopkeepers standing back from their plate-glass windows—far enough to avoid being spotted from the street but close enough to have seen the shooting. A very fat man motioned to him from the entrance of the Café d'Été. When he reached the door, the man, who seemed to be the owner, handed him a wet bar towel.

"The bathroom's in the back," he said.

Lucien thanked him and walked to the rear of the café. It was a typical dark Parisian café, narrow, a black-and-white-tiled floor with small tables along a wall, and a very poorly stocked bar on the opposite side. The Occupation had done the unthinkable in Paris: it had cut off a Frenchman's most basic necessities of life—cigarettes and wine. But the café was such an ingrained part of his existence that he still went there daily to smoke fake cigarettes made from grass and herbs and drink the watered-down swill that passed for wine. The Café d'Été patrons, who had probably seen what had happened, stopped talking and looked down at their glasses when Lucien passed, acting as if he'd been contaminated by his contact with the Germans. It reminded him of the time he'd been in a café when five German enlisted men blundered in. The place had gone totally silent, as if someone had turned off a switch on a radio. The soldiers had left immediately.

In the filthy bathroom, Lucien took off his suit jacket to begin the cleanup. A few blobs of blood the size of peas dotted the back of the jacket, and one was on the sleeve. He tried to blot out the Jew's blood, but faint stains remained. This annoyed him—he only had one good business suit. A tall, handsome man with a full head of wavy brown hair, Lucien was quite particular about his clothes. His wife, Celeste, was clever about practical matters, though. She could probably get the bloodstains out of his jacket. He stood back and looked at himself in the mirror above the sink to make sure there wasn't any blood on his face or in his hair, then suddenly looked at his watch and realized his appointment was in ten minutes. He put his jacket back on and threw the soiled towel in the sink.

Once in the street, he couldn't help looking back at the corner where the shooting had taken place. The Germans and the body were gone; only a large pool of blood marked the spot of the shooting. The Germans were unbelievably efficient people. The French would have stood around the corpse, chatting and smoking cigarettes. Full rigor mortis would have set in by the time they had carted it away. Lucien almost started trotting but slowed his pace to a brisk walk. He hated being late, but he wasn't about to be shot in the back of the skull because of his obsession with punctuality. Monsieur Manet would understand. Still, this meeting held the possibility of a job, and Lucien didn't want to make a bad first impression.

Lucien had learned early in his career that architecture was a business as well as an art, and one ought not look at a first job from a new client as a one-shot deal but rather as the first in a series of commissions. And this one had a lot of promise. The man he was to meet, Auguste Manet, owned a factory that, until the war, used to make engines for Citroën and other automobile makers. Before an initial meeting with a client, Lucien would always research his background to see if he had money, and Monsieur Manet definitely had money. Old money, from a distinguished family that went back generations. Manet had tried his hand at industry, something his class frowned upon. Wealth from business was considered dirty, not dignified. But he had multiplied the family fortune a hundredfold, cashing in on the automobile craze, specializing in engines.

Manet was in an excellent position to obtain German contracts during the Occupation. Even before the German invasion in May 1940, a mass exodus had begun, with millions fleeing the north of the country to the south, where they thought they'd be safe. Many industrialists had tried unsuccessfully to move their entire factories, including the workers, to the south. But Manet had remained calm during the panic and stayed put, with all his factories intact.

Normally, a defeated country's economy ground to a halt, but Germany was in the business of war. It needed weapons for its fight with the Russians on the Eastern Front, and suitable French businesses were awarded contracts to produce war matériel. At first, French businessmen had viewed cooperation with the Germans as treason, but faced with a choice of having their businesses appropriated by the Germans without compensation or accepting the contracts, the pragmatic French had chosen the latter. Lucien was betting that Manet was a pragmatic man and that he was producing weapons for the Luftwaffe or the Wehrmacht. And that meant new factory space, which Lucien could design for him.

Before the war, whenever Lucien was on his way to meet a client for the first time, his imagination ran wild with visions of success—especially when he knew the client was rich. He tried to rein in his imagination now, telling himself to be pessimistic. Every time he got his hopes up high these days, they were smashed to bits. Like in 1938, when he was just about to start a store on the rue de la Tour d'Auvergne and then the client went bankrupt because of a divorce. Or the big estate in Orléans whose owner was arrested for embezzlement. He told himself to be grateful for any crumb of work that he could find in wartime.

Having nearly forgotten the incident with the Jew, Lucien's mind began to formulate a generic design of a factory that would be quite suitable for any type of war production. As he turned up the avenue Marceau, he smiled as he always did whenever he thought of a new design.

2

L UCIEN CHECKED HIS WATCH AS HE OPENED THE MASSIVE WOOD door of 28 rue Galilée. It gave him a great sense of satisfaction that he was one minute early for his appointment. What other man could walk all the way across town, almost get shot by a German, clean a dead man's blood off his jacket, and make it in time? The experience reinforced his belief that one should always budget an extra fifteen minutes to get to a client appointment. His prized Cartier watch, which his parents had given him upon his graduation from college, said two p.m., which was actually the time in Germany. The Germans' first official act had been to impose the Reich's time zone on occupied France. It was really one p.m. French time. After two years of occupation, the forced time change still annoyed Lucien, even more than the swastikas and ugly Gothic-lettered signs the Germans had plastered on all the city's landmarks.

He stepped inside and was relieved to be in the dark, cool shade of the foyer. He loved these apartment blocks, created by Baron Haussmann when he tore down medieval Paris in the 1850s to re-create the city. Lucien admired the stonework and the strong horizontal lines created by the rows of windows and their metal balconies. He lived in a building on the rue du Caire that was similar to this one.

Since 1931, Lucien had abandoned all historical and classical references in his work to become a pure modernist architect, embracing the aesthetic of the Bauhaus, the style created by the German architect Walter Gropius that pioneered modern architecture and design (the one instance in which Teutonic taste definitely triumphed over the

Gallic). Still, he admired these great apartment blocks that Napoleon III had championed. His admiration had grown when he'd visited his brother in New York before the war. The apartment buildings there were junk compared to those in Paris.

He walked to the concierge's apartment, directly to the left of the entry. The glass door yawned open, and an old woman smoking a cigarette was sitting at a table covered with a garish yellow-flowered cloth. Lucien cleared his throat, and she said, without moving a muscle and still gazing into space, "He's in 3B...and the lift's out."

As Lucien climbed the ornate curving stair to the third floor, his heart began to race—not only because he was out of shape, but also because he was so anxious. Would Manet have a real project for him, or would this meeting lead to nothing? And if it was a project, would it be a chance to show his talent?

Lucien knew he had talent. He'd been told by a couple of well-known architects, whom he had worked for in Paris after graduating from school. With a few years' experience and belief in his ability, he then went out on his own. It was hard to build up a practice, doubly hard because he was a modernist, and modern architecture was just beginning to be accepted. Most clients still wanted something traditional. Nevertheless, he was able to earn a steady living. But just as an actor needed a breakout role to become a star, an architect needed a career-making project. And Lucien, now thirty-five, hadn't managed to land that one all-important project. He'd come close only once, when he'd been a finalist for a new public library but had been beaten out by Henri Devereaux, whose uncle's brother-in-law was the deputy minister of culture. Ability wasn't enough; one needed the right connections like Devereaux always seemed to have—that and luck.

He looked down at his shoes as they scraped the marble treads of the great stair. They were his client shoes, the one good pair he wore to meetings. A little worn, but they still looked shiny and fashionable, and the soles were in good shape. With leather in short supply, once a Frenchman's shoes wore out he turned to wooden soles or ones of compressed paper, which didn't fare so well in winter. Lucien was glad he still had a pair of leather-soled shoes. He hated the sound of wooden soles clattering on the streets of Paris, which reminded him of the clogs worn by peasants.

Lucien was startled when he looked up and found a pair of very expensive dark brown shoes on the third floor landing right in front of his face. Lucien's gaze traveled up the sharply creased trouser legs to a suit jacket, then to the face of Auguste Manet.

"Monsieur Bernard, what a pleasure it is to meet you."

Before Lucien reached the top step, Manet extended his hand.

Lucien pulled himself up the railing until he stood next to a lean, white-haired man in his seventies, with cheekbones that seemed to be chiseled from stone. And tall. Manet towered above Lucien. He seemed even taller than de Gaulle.

"The pleasure is my mine, monsieur."

"Monsieur Gaston was always raving about the office building you did for him, so I had to see it for myself. A beautiful job." The old man's handshake was strong and confident, something you'd expect from a man who'd made millions.

They were off to an excellent start, Lucien thought as he took an instant liking to this elderly, aristocratic businessman. Back in 1937, he'd done a building on the rue Servan for Charles Gaston, the owner of an insurance company. Four stories of limestone with a curving glass-stair tower. Lucien thought it was the best thing he'd ever designed.

"Monsieur Gaston was very kind to refer you to me. How can I help you?" Most of the time, Lucien was open to the usual small talk before getting down to business. But he was nervous and wanted to see whether a real job would come out of this.

Manet turned toward the open doors of 3B and Lucien followed. Even the back of Monsieur Manet was impressive. His posture was ramrod straight, and his suit was expensive and fit him impeccably—the German major would've wanted the name of his tailor.

"Well, Monsieur Bernard, let me tell you what I've got in mind. A guest of mine will be staying here for a while, and I wish to make some special alterations to the apartment to accommodate him," Manet said as they walked slowly through the place.

Lucien couldn't imagine what the old man would want. The vacant apartment was gorgeous, with high ceilings and tall windows, ornate wood paneling, huge columns that framed the wide entries into the main rooms, beautiful fireplaces with marble surrounds, and parquet floors. And all the bathrooms and the kitchen looked up to date with porcelain-on-steel sinks and tubs with chrome fixtures. The unit was large by Parisian standards, at least twice as large in floor area as a normal apartment.

Manet stopped and faced Lucien.

"I've been told that an architect looks at a space differently from the rest of us. The average person sees a room as it is, but instinctively the architect envisions how it could be changed for the better. Is that true?"

"Absolutely," replied Lucien with pride. "A man would view a run-down, out-of-date flat as very unappealing, but an architect, in his imagination, would renovate that space into something quite fashionable." Lucien was getting excited. Maybe the old man wanted him to redo the place from top to bottom.

"I see. Tell me, monsieur, do you like a challenge? To solve a unique problem?"

"Yes, indeed, I love to come up with a solution for any architectural problem," said Lucien, "and the more challenging, the better." He hoped he was telling Manet what he wanted to hear. If Manet asked him to fit the Arc de Triomphe in here, he'd say it was no problem. You didn't turn down work in wartime. Any fool knew that.

"That's good." Manet walked across the salon and put his hand on Lucien's shoulder in a fatherly way. "I think it's time to give you a little more background on this project, but first let us talk about your fee. I have a figure in mind—twelve thousand francs."

"Twelve hundred francs is most generous, monsieur."

"No, I said twelve thousand."

There was silence. Digits formed in Lucien's mind as if a teacher were writing them methodically on a blackboard—first a one, then a two, a comma, and three zeros. After he mentally verified the number, he said, "Monsieur, that…that is more than generous; it's ludicrous!"

"Not if your life depended on it."

Lucien thought this was such an amusing comment that he was obliged to let out his great belly laugh, the kind that annoyed his wife but always delighted his mistress. But Manet didn't laugh. His face showed no emotion at all.

"Before I give you a little more information about the project, let me ask you a personal question," Manet said.

"You have my full attention, Monsieur Manet."

"How do you feel about Jews?"

Lucien was taken aback. What the hell kind of question was that? But before giving Manet his gut response—that they were money-grubbing thieves—he took a deep breath. He didn't want to say anything that would offend Manet—and lose the job.

"They're human beings like anyone else, I suppose," he replied feebly.

Lucien had grown up in a very anti-Semitic household. The word *Jew* had always been followed by the word *bastard*. His grandfather and father had been convinced that Captain Alfred Dreyfus, a Jewish officer on the staff of the French Army headquarters back in the 1890s, was a traitor, despite evidence that a fellow officer named Esterhazy had been the one who'd sold secrets to the Germans. Lucien's grandfather had also sworn that Jews were responsible for France's humiliating defeat by the Germans in the Franco-Prussian War of 1870, although he could never provide any real proof to back up this charge. *Whether one hated them for betraying the country, for killing Christ, or screwing you over in a business deal, all other Frenchmen were anti-Semites in one way or another, weren't they?* Lucien thought. That's the way it had always been.

Lucien looked into Manet's eyes and was glad he'd kept his true feelings to himself.

He saw an earnestness that alarmed him.

"You've probably noticed that since May all Jews over the age of six are now required to wear a yellow Star of David," said Manet.

"Yes, monsieur."

Lucien was well aware that Jews had to wear a felt star. He didn't think it was such a big deal, though many Parisians were outraged. Gentiles had begun to wear the yellow stars or yellow flowers or handkerchiefs in protest. He'd even heard of a woman who'd pinned a yellow star on her dog.

"On July 16," said Manet, "almost thirteen thousand Jews were rounded up in Paris and sent to Drancy, and nine thousand were women and children."

Lucien knew about Drancy. It was an unfinished block of apartment buildings near Le Bourget Airport that an architect friend, Maurice Pappon, had worked on. A year earlier, it became the main detention camp for the Paris region, though it had no water, electric, or sanitary service. Pappon had told him that Drancy prisoners were forced onto trains to be relocated somewhere in the east.

"One hundred people killed themselves instead of being taken. Mothers with babies in their arms jumped from windows. Did you know that, monsieur?"

Lucien saw Manet's growing agitation. He needed to redirect the man's conversation to the project and the twelve thousand francs.

"It is a tragedy, monsieur. Now what kind of changes did you have in mind?"

But Manet continued as though he hadn't heard a word.

"It was bad enough that Jewish businesses were seized and bank accounts frozen, but now they're banned from restaurants, cafés, theaters, cinemas, and parks. It's not just immigrant Jews but Jews of French lineage, whose ancestors fought for France, who are being treated in this way.

"And the worst part," he continued, "is that Vichy and the French police are making most of the arrests, not the Germans."

Lucien was aware of this. The Germans used the French against the French. When a knock came at a Frenchman's door in the middle of the night, it was usually a gendarme sent by the Gestapo.

"All Parisians have suffered under the Germans, monsieur," Lucien began. "Even gentiles are arrested every day. Why, on the way here to meet you, a..." He stopped midsentence when he remembered that the dead man was a Jew. Lucien saw that Manet was staring at him, which made him uncomfortable. He looked down at the beautiful parquet floor and his client's shoes.

"Monsieur Bernard, Gaston has known you a long time. He says you are a man of great integrity and honor. A man who loves his country—and keeps his word," said Manet.

Lucien was now completely confused. What in the hell was this man talking about? Gaston really didn't know him at all, only on a professional level. They weren't friends. Gaston had no idea what kind of man Lucien truly was. He could've been a murderer or a male prostitute, and Gaston would never have known.

Manet walked over to one of the huge windows that overlooked the rue Galilée and stared out into the street for a few moments. He finally turned and faced Lucien, who was surprised by the now-grave expression on the old man's face.

"Monsieur Bernard, this *alteration* is to create a hiding place for a Jewish man who is being hunted by the Gestapo. If, by chance, they come here looking for him, I'd like him to be able to hide in a space that is undetectable, one that the Gestapo will never find. For your own safety, I won't tell you his name. But the Reich wants to arrest him to find out the whereabouts of his fortune, which is considerable."

Lucien was dumbfounded. "Are you insane? You're hiding a Jew?"

Normally, Lucien would never speak so rudely to a client, especially an enormously rich one, but Manet had crossed into forbidden territory here. Aiding Jews: the Germans called it *Judenbegunstigung*. No matter how wealthy he was, Manet could be arrested and executed for hiding Jews. It was the one crime a Frenchman couldn't buy his way out of. Wearing some dumb yellow star out of sympathy was one thing, but actually helping a Jew wanted by the Gestapo was sheer madness. What the hell had Lucien gotten himself into—or rather, what had that bastard Gaston got *him* into? Manet had some set of balls to ask him to do this for twelve thousand or even twelve million francs.

"You're asking me to commit suicide; you know that, don't you?"

"Indeed I do," said Manet. "And I'm also committing suicide."

"Then for God's sake, man, why are you doing this?" exclaimed Lucien.

Manet didn't seem put off by Lucien's question at all. He almost seemed eager to answer it. The old man smiled at Lucien.

"Let me explain something to you, Monsieur Bernard. Back in 1940, when this hell began, I realized that my first duty as a Christian was to overcome my self-centeredness, that I had to inconvenience myself when one of my human brethren was in danger—whoever he may be, or whether he was a born Frenchman or not. I've simply decided not to turn my back."

"Inconvenience myself" was a bit of an understatement under these circumstances, Lucien thought. And as for Christianity, he agreed with his father: it was a well-intentioned set of beliefs that never worked in real life.

"So, Monsieur Bernard," continued Manet, "I will pay you twelve thousand francs to design a hiding place that is invisible to the naked eye. That is your architectural challenge. I have excellent craftsmen to do the work but they're not architects; they don't have your eye and couldn't come up with as clever a solution as you could. That's why I'm asking you for your help."

"Monsieur, I absolutely refuse. This is crazy. I won't do it."

"I'm hoping you'll reconsider my proposition, Monsieur Bernard. I feel it can be a mutually beneficial arrangement. And it's just this one time."

"Never, Monsieur. I could never agree…"

"I realize that making a decision that could get you killed is not one to be made on the spot. Please, do me the favor of taking some time to think about this. But I'd like to hear from you today by six p.m., at the Café du Monde. I know you need to make a closer examination of the apartment for you to decide, so take this key and lock the door when you finish. And now, monsieur, I'll leave you to it."

Lucien nodded and tried to speak, but nothing came out.

"By the way, at nine a.m. tomorrow, I'm signing a contract to produce engines for the Heinkel Aircraft Works. My current facilities are much too small to handle such a job, so I'm planning an expansion next to my plant at Chaville. I'm looking for an architect," said Manet as he walked toward the door. "Know of one?"

3

THE ROOM STARTED SPINNING AROUND, AND LUCIEN BECAME SO disoriented that he couldn't keep his balance. He sat on the floor and thought he was going to vomit.

"Christ, what a day!" he muttered.

Normally, Lucien would do anything to get a job, no matter how despicable. Like the time he slept with the very overweight wife of the wine merchant, Gattier, so that she would persuade her husband to select Lucien to design his new store on the rue Vaneau. It had turned out beautifully—not one change had been made to his design.

This, however, was a different matter altogether. Sure, he was broke, but were twelve thousand francs and a guaranteed commission worth the risk of dying? The money wouldn't help him if he was dead. Actually, it wasn't the dying part that troubled him. It was the torture by the Gestapo that would precede the dying. Lucien had heard on good authority what the Germans did to those who wouldn't cooperate—days of barbaric treatment before death, or if the Gestapo was feeling merciful, which was a rarity, internment in a camp.

Parisians had quickly learned that not all German soldiers were the same. There were three very different types. The largest branch, the Wehrmacht, was the regular army that did most of the fighting and had some sense of decency toward the French. Next was the Waffen-SS, the special elite army unit of the Nazi Party, which fought in combat but was also used in rounding up Jews. The last and the absolute worst was the Gestapo, the secret police, who tortured, murdered, mutilated, and maimed Jews—or anyone, including fellow

Germans, for crimes against the Reich. The Gestapo's cruelty was said to be beyond imagination.

People were even scared to use the word *Gestapo*. Parisians would usually say, "*They've* arrested him." The Gestapo headquarters at 11 rue des Saussaies was just around the corner from the Palais de l'Élysée, the former residence of the French president. Everyone in Paris knew and feared this address.

No, no matter how much he needed money and craved a new project, the risk was unfathomable. Lucien had never fooled himself into believing he was the heroic type. He'd learned that in 1939, when, as an officer called up from the reserves, he'd been stationed for eight months on the Maginot Line, the string of concrete fortresses that the French government guaranteed would protect France from a German onslaught. Since no fighting had occurred in France after the fall of Poland, he'd sat on his ass reading architectural magazines his wife had sent him, designing imaginary projects. One fellow officer who was a university professor had used the time to write a history of the ancient Etruscans.

Then on May 10, 1940, the Germans had invaded, but instead of attacking the "invincible" Maginot Line, they'd swept around it, entering northern France through the Ardennes Forest. Meanwhile, Lucien had been stationed inside a bunker on the Maginot Line, never getting the chance to engage the enemy. Secretly, he'd been glad because he was terrified of fighting the Germans, who seemed like superbeings. They had crushed everyone they had invaded with incredible ease— the Poles, the Belgians, and the Dutch, plus forcing the British off the continent at Dunkirk.

After the armistice was signed on June 22, he was considered officially defeated and captured, but Lucien and other officers had had no intention of being herded into a prisoner of war camp in Germany. Uncle Albert, the brother of Lucien's mother, had spent four years in a German prison camp during the First World War and as a result spent the rest of his life unhinged, doing weird things like chasing squirrels in the park like a dog. Lucien and many other French soldiers had simply taken off their uniforms, destroyed their military papers, and then blended into civilian life with forged demobilization documents. Before the Wehrmacht had reached the garrisons of the Maginot Line at the end of June, Lucien had returned to his wife in Paris.

What he found was a ghost town. Even though Paris had been declared an open city by the British and thus safe from bombing, over a million people—out of a population of three million—fled. Lucien and his wife had decided to stay, believing that it was far less dangerous to face the Germans than the perils of the open road. It had turned out to be the right decision: with millions of other Frenchmen fleeing south, the roads became impassable and many people had gone missing or died of exposure. This mass exodus and the military's quick surrender to the Germans humiliated France in front of the world. Lucien hated the Germans with all his heart for what they did to his country. He cried the day of the surrender. But all that really mattered to him was that he and his wife were still alive.

No, Lucien wasn't a hero, and he definitely wasn't a do-gooder, one of those guys who stood up for the downtrodden. Manet had do-gooder written all over him. And to risk one's life to help a *Jew*? Lucien's father would've laughed in his face. Having grown up in Paris, Lucien had been around Jews all his life, at least indirectly. He'd heard that there were something like two hundred thousand heebs living in Paris, although he'd never met one Jew at the École Spéciale d'Architecture, where he'd studied. There were hardly any Jewish architects. Lucien had always reasoned that Jews had an innate mercantile talent, so they went into business and professions like law and medicine that would make them loads of money. Architecture, Lucien quickly learned, was not the way to go if you wanted to become rich.

But Lucien felt that Manet was right about one thing. The Jews were getting a raw deal. The Germans took away even the most basic everyday necessities—their phones had been disconnected and their bicycles confiscated. And not just the immigrant Jews from Poland, Hungary, and Russia, who lived mostly in the eastern arrondissements of Paris, but the native-born Jews too, the ones who didn't have that "Jew" look. Professional men like doctors, lawyers, and university professors suffered. And it didn't matter how famous you were. Nobel Prize winner Henri Bergson had died from pneumonia that he had contracted while waiting in a line to register himself as a Jew with the French authorities. But what was happening to the Jews was a political matter that was out of his control, even if he thought it was unfair.

For a people that were supposed to be so smart, though, Lucien thought Jews had been acting pretty dumb. Since 1933, there had been reports in French newspapers of how the Nazis treated Jews in Germany. Didn't they realize the Germans would treat them the same way here? Some had made it across the Pyrenees into Spain and Portugal, and others had gotten across the Swiss border early on. They were the smart ones; they'd realized what was in store for them and had saved themselves.

The Jews who had stayed were doomed. Since the fall of 1940, it had been impossible for them to get out of the country. Jews had even been forbidden to cross the demarcation line into unoccupied France. They had to escape the cities to avoid arrest and deportation by the Germans. There must be thousands of them hiding in the countryside, Lucien thought, whole families with kids and grandparents. The Jews who were so used to the good life now had to hide in haylofts surviving on a few grams of bread each day. Compared to a barn, Manet's hideout would be a palace.

Lucien stood up and began walking through the apartment.

Granted, it was suicide to get involved in this.

But…if it was done cleverly, maybe the Jew would never be discovered, no one would know of his involvement, and best of all, Lucien would make a huge amount of money plus get a big commission out of it. Besides, Manet was a very shrewd, successful man. He might take a calculated risk, but he wasn't reckless. The old man would've thought this all out to the last detail.

Then the image of being lashed to a chair at 11 rue des Saussaies, getting his face pummeled to a pasty red lump, came to mind. Lucien turned to walk toward the door. Still, he thought, with a little ingenuity there could be a place to hide a man in plain sight. He placed his hand on the door handle, then looked back into the empty apartment. Lucien shook his head and opened the great wooden door a few centimeters to see if anyone was about, and stepped out in the corridor.

Then again, Lucien reasoned, the commission alone would make the risk worth considering. To get such a huge project to design was an incredible opportunity that would never have come his way before the war. And God knows, he desperately needed the money; he hadn't worked since the Occupation began. His own savings were long gone, and Celeste's money wouldn't last forever. It wouldn't hurt to at least look around, he thought. He reentered the apartment and began walking through the rooms.

First, Lucien ruled out the obvious hiding places, such as behind the bookshelves—a stock cliché of American mystery movies—or in a recess at the back of a closet. As if they were the lens of a movie camera, his eyes swept over every square meter of each room, taking in every detail. At the same time, he intuitively analyzed every surface by contemplating the construction of the space behind it—as if he was thinking with X-ray vision. Though Lucien didn't know how big Manet's "guest" was, his mind placed an imaginary average-size man within each possible space to see if there was enough room. Lucien examined the beautiful wainscoting along the walls. The wide recessed panels could be removed, opening up a space big enough for a man to fit through. But was that too obvious a hiding place? Probably. There had to be a twist. What if the person had to go through the panel opening and crawl down the length of the wall to hide within another hidden compartment? If the Germans found the removable panel, there would be just an empty space behind it. Unfortunately, as Lucien inspected further, he noticed the walls behind the wainscoting weren't deep enough for a man's body.

Then Lucien noticed how unusually tall the baseboards along the floor were. Using the small tape measure he always carried with him, he confirmed they were almost forty centimeters high. Maybe they could be hinged like a flap on a mail slot, so a man could pull them up and slide on his belly into a hollowed-out space. That would've been a solution if the wall had been the right depth. Too bad, the Germans never would've looked down there.

Lucien moved on. There was a wall along a corridor that curved out in the center, creating a semicircular niche where a small bronze statue of Mercury sat on a meter-high base. A man could crouch inside the base, unless he was really tall. The statue and the wood top of the base would have to be lifted up then put back into place in order for the man to hide. That would be quite difficult to do. Even if the statue was fastened to the top from underneath and the top hinged to the base, it would be very heavy. Lucien picked up the statue and guessed it weighed around fifty kilos. Would Manet's guest have the strength to open and close the top?

Lucien walked across the room to get a better look at the niche. Lighting a cigarette, he leaned against one of the very tall wooden Doric columns that framed the opening between the salon and the dining area. He looked it up and down and saw its fluted shaft was made from one piece of exquisite chestnut. If only it sat on a tall pedestal, he thought, a person could fit inside the pedestal to hide. Then Lucien noticed how big the diameter of the column was and measured it—about fifty-six centimeters. An incredible wave of euphoria swept over him. Using his own shoulders as a guide, he calculated that the column was just wide enough to fit a normal-size man upright, even accounting for the thickness of the column wall.

Lucien was giddy with excitement. The two columns, which he knew were nonstructural and merely decorative, must be hollow. Smiling, he ran his hand over the column's shaft; a narrow hinged door could be cut in, with its vertical joints hidden by the fluting. There couldn't be any horizontal joints showing so the bottom joint would have to align with the base. The top joint had to line up with the column capital above. Though the shaft of the column was almost four meters high, a door could be made that tall if he used a piano hinge. Lucien had once designed a door with standard hinges that stood three meters high. If Manet's men were as good as advertised, this could work.

He'd done it! It was such a brilliant, elegant, and ingenious solution.

He'd fool those fucking Nazi bastards.

4

Two hours before meeting Manet and Lucien was already on his fourth glass of faux red wine. The euphoria of tricking the Germans had worn off, and the reality of being murdered by the Gestapo for getting involved in this scheme returned. A thousand things could go wrong. He knew that Parisians were betraying Jews to the Germans every day. Suppose someone tipped off the Gestapo about Manet's Jew and the column didn't work? The Jew would give up Manet, and Manet would give him up. He'd be crazy to do this.

Before he'd left the apartment on rue Galilée, Lucien had sketched out the details of the column on a scrap of paper. He turned it over now and began sketching out the building for the factory in Chaville, a suburb west of Paris. He imagined a sawtooth roof to let in light, with glass walls separated by steel mullions one meter apart. Every ten meters he added a brick wall. The entry would have a curving brick wall leading to a deeply recessed glass doorway. Maybe the whole thing could be built of poured concrete, with powerful-looking arches on the inside. He smiled as he drew the profile of the arches, each one with its own flaring buttress to resist the outward thrusts. He tried four different profiles until he settled on the one he liked best.

Lucien had visited Walter Gropius's Fagus Factory in Germany in the '30s and had been dazzled by the sleek, clean design. Since then, Lucien had always wanted to design a factory complex. Although it had come to him in a most bizarre way, this commission could be the opportunity he'd been looking for. To prove that he really had talent by designing a large, important building.

He drained the wine in his glass and stared out across the lifeless rue Kepler. The biggest shock he'd experienced when he'd returned to Paris was its surreal emptiness. The boulevard Saint-Germain, the rue de Rivoli, the Place de la Concorde—all were deserted most of the time. Before the war, even the rue Kepler would have had a steady stream of pedestrians in the evening hours. Lucien had loved to gaze out at the city while sipping his coffee or wine in a café, watching for interesting faces and especially beautiful women. But as Lucien sat by the window now, he saw very few people and it saddened him. The Boche had sucked the wonderful street life out of his beloved Paris.

Lucien never got the chance to fight the Germans. Though he hated their guts, he knew he would've been a terrible soldier in battle—he was scared of guns. Honor and service to country were ideals cherished by the French, although he'd always thought of them as a load of patriotic horse manure. But since his return to Paris, he'd had a gnawing feeling inside him that he was a coward. This was reinforced by the fact that there were so many women in Paris and so few men—most had been killed or captured during the invasion. But not Lucien. His neighbor, Madame Dehor, had a lost a son, blown to bits attempting to stop a Panzer tank. Six months after the boy's death, he could still hear her wailing uncontrollably through the thick walls of the apartment building. Secretly, Lucien was ashamed that he was so useless to his country. Sometimes, he felt guilty that he was alive.

And Lucien knew he didn't have the guts to join the Resistance. Besides, he didn't believe in their cause. It was made up of a bunch of fanatical Communists who'd commit some stupid, meaningless act of sabotage that would trigger the Germans to kill scores of hostages in retaliation.

Lucien looked at the sketch of the factory. On the whole, Manet was offering him a pretty good deal—if you removed the possibility of torture and death by the Gestapo. One secret hiding place he designed in less than an hour, in exchange for twelve thousand francs, which could buy plenty of black market goods. Plus the factory commission. He flipped the paper over to the sketch of the column, which immediately brought a smile to his face. The sense of mastery and excitement he had felt in the apartment returned. He'd experienced such intense pleasure when he'd realized that the column would work. Maybe this was something he could do to get back at the Germans. Sure, he couldn't risk his neck by shooting them, but he could risk it in his own way. And besides, given the solution he'd invented, was there really that much risk? The Gestapo would search and search the apartment and never find the hiding place. That image pleased the hell out of him.

This was suicidal. But something within Lucien compelled him to do it.

⚬ ⚬ ⚬

"You're what the Jews call a *mensch*, Monsieur Bernard," said Manet, who took a sip of wine. Lucien had made sure they had a table off by themselves.

"What the hell does that mean?" asked Lucien. It sounded kind of insulting, similar to the Jewish word *schmuck*.

"I believe it means a human being, a person who stands up and does the right thing."

"Before I do the right thing, there're a few conditions."

"Go on," said Manet.

"I'm not to know anything…I mean anything…about your goddamn Jew," said Lucien, looking around him to make sure no one was listening in on their conversation.

"I understand perfectly."

"What about the workmen who'll be doing the construction? How do I know they won't talk?"

"They are men who have worked for me for over twenty years. I can trust them and so can you."

"The tenants will wonder what's going on when they hear all the noise. Every one of them would be deported if a Jew was found in the building. If they suspected anything, they'd inform the Germans to save themselves."

"There's a risk, I agree, but the concierge has been well paid to lie if need be. All the tenants are at work during the day. Besides, your solution is ingenious because it's so simple—there won't be that much noise."

"What about the owner of the building? What if he gets wind of the work?"

"I am the owner, Monsieur Bernard."

Lucien finally relaxed and sat back in his chair. With those concerns out of the way, it was now time to get down to business.

"You mentioned a fee of twelve thousand francs, Monsieur Manet."

Manet produced a thick hardback book out of the satchel he held on his lap. He placed it on the table and pushed it toward Lucien.

"Do you like to read? This novel by the American writer Hemingway is most entertaining," he said with a great smile.

Lucien never read anything except architectural magazines. But he did go to the cinema and had seen all the American films based on great works of literature, so he could pretend he'd read the books.

"Of course, Hemingway." Gary Cooper starred in *A Farewell to Arms* in 1932. It was a damn good film.

Lucien slowly picked up the book and examined the cover, then began to fan the pages. He abruptly stopped when he saw the first franc note nestled in the hollowed-out book.

"It looks most interesting. I'll start it tonight before I go to bed."

"I know you'll enjoy it," replied Manet.

"Now, did I hear you correctly when you said you'd be needing additional factory space for your new contract?" Lucien asked, holding on to the book with both hands in his lap.

"You did indeed. Why don't you come to my office the day after tomorrow to discuss the project—say about two. I'll have all my requirements written out for you. I'm sure you'll need to go back into the apartment to take a few measurements for a drawing, so hold on to the key."

The smile suddenly vanished from Lucien's face. "But let me make one thing absolutely clear to you, monsieur. I'll never do anything like this again."

"But of course, I understand completely."

An awkward silence settled between the two men. Lucien took another sip of his wine. He wanted to get the hell out of there with his new book. Manet smiled and sipped his drink as if he were in no hurry at all.

"You asked me why I was committing suicide."

"Yes, and you told me you're a devout Christian who wants to help your fellow man," said Lucien.

"Devout? Not at all. I attend mass on Easter and Christmas and that's it. I do believe that as Christians, we have a basic duty to do what's right, but that's not quite the whole story. There's more to it."

"Really?"

"Monsieur Bernard, people think the aristocracy, with their money and privilege, have everything in life, but they're dead wrong. The children of my class lack the most important thing: a mother and a father."

"You were an orphan?"

"Not at all. I had a mother and father, but they, like others of their class, never had time for their children—attending endless social events, entertaining in the city and the country, overseeing their estates and investments. I'll bet in an average week I never spent more than an hour's time with my mother and father. They would often forget my birthday. When I was at boarding school, I didn't see them for months or even receive a letter from them. They were simply too busy for me and my brothers and sisters."

"That's a shame," said Lucien.

"No, I was raised by Madame Ducrot. She was my nanny, but she gave me as much love and affection as the best mother could. And she was a Jew."

"A Jew? How did she…"

"I have no idea how my parents picked a Jew to be our nanny. Maybe they weren't as anti-Semitic as the rest of their kind. Oh, I still got the usual Catholic instruction from priests. But she never hid the fact she was Jewish; in fact, she told us all about it—the holidays, the synagogue, the Exodus—everything."

Lucien found this fascinating.

"Several times before the war, I was a house guest of Winston Churchill's at Chartwell, his estate in England. I once asked him about a photo of an old woman on his mantel, and he told me it was Mrs. Everest, his nanny. He called her 'Woomany.' He said that when she died, he was crushed with almost unbearable sadness and grief, a thousand times worse than when his own mother died later. That's how I felt when my nanny, who was my 'real mother,' died. So you see, Monsieur Bernard, in a way, when I hide these people, I'm hiding Madame Ducrot."

A Conversation
with the Author

You're an architect by profession. Why do you like writing fiction?

Writing is far less stressful than being an architect. The architect must take a design on paper and transform it into a real building using someone else's money and scores of construction workers, comply with building codes and environmental laws, and take legal responsibility for the whole thing. It's very pleasurable to sit and take things out of one's imagination and type on the computer creating a story. It's a wonderful, liberating feeling.

What gave you the idea for the *House of Thieves*?

I came across a real-life figure named George L. Leslie who came from a wealthy Midwest family and supposedly was an architect for a while in New York. He gave up his practice and became a criminal specializing in bank robberies. From my own experience, I once unwittingly designed an addition to a house owned by a mob boss. I wondered what it would be like to be drawn into the underworld.

What was the most surprising thing you found in your research of the Gilded Age?

The horrible poverty, especially for children. Thousands were thrown out into the streets by their parents because they could not feed them. They roamed the streets like alley cats. The environmental destruction was incredible then. Rivers and public streets were literally cesspools. We complain about poverty and environmental damage, but we have it a million times better today.

Who is your favorite character in the book?

Julia. She was a rebel to begin with and wasn't to be confined by the harsh code of New York high society. Meeting Nolan, the pickpocket, opened up a wonderful new world for her that she loved. Most society girls would never dream of doing such a thing.

Acknowledgments

What I said in the acknowledgments of my first novel still holds true. If you want to get a novel published, you must have people who absolutely believe in your work and stand behind you. Again, those two special people are my literary agent, Susan Ginsburg of Writers House, and Shana Drehs, editorial director of Sourcebooks Landmark. Susan gave me a great deal of valuable guidance and advice in the writing of my second novel, plus she's always teaching me how to navigate the turbulent waters of the publishing world. Working with Shana and Anna Michels showed me again how important an editor is in this whole process. An author thinks his or her manuscript is perfect but then realizes an editor's insight can raise the book to a higher level, which is what they did.

Thanks to you all.

Charles Belfoure
Westminster, MD

About the Author

An architect by profession, Charles Belfoure has published several architectural histories, two of which have won awards from the Maryland Historical Trust. He has also received grants from the Graham Foundation and the James Marston Fitch Charitable Foundation for architectural research. A graduate of the Pratt Institute and Columbia University, he taught at Pratt as well as at Goucher College in Baltimore, Maryland. His area of specialty is historic preservation. He has been a freelance writer for the *Baltimore Sun* and the *New York Times* and is the international bestselling author of *The Paris Architect*.